MW01492985

ADVERTISING

THE

MODEL A FORD

A Collector's Guide to
Model A Ford Magazine Advertising

◆

JAMES W. THOMAS

Copyright © 2008 by James W. Thomas

Published by:

AUTOTIQUES

P.O. Box 498016
Cincinnati, Ohio 45249-8016

All rights reserved. No portion of this book may be reproduced or transmitted in any form
or by any means, electronic or mechanical, including photocopy, recording, or any information storage
and retrieval system without the permission in writing from the author except by a reviewer who may
quote brief passages in critical article reviews to be printed in a magazine, newspaper or
electronically transmitted on radio or television.

The estimated values stated in this book should only be used as a guide. They are not intended to
establish values or set prices. The author and publisher disdain any responsibility for any liability
or loss which is incurred as a result of the use or application of the contents of this book.
Likewise, while every precaution has been taken in the preparation of this book, the publisher
and author assume no responsibility for errors or omissions.

Additional copies of this book may be ordered from:

AUTOTIQUES
P.O. Box 498016
Cincinnati, Ohio 45249-8016

$39.95 plus postage and handling

E-mail: autotiques@aol.com
Web Site: www.autotiques.com

FIRST EDITION

Library of Congress Control Number: 2008901440
ISBN 978-0-9815638-2-4

Photography and Photo Editing: Ryan R. Thomas
Cover and Layout Design: Moondance Group, Inc.

Printed in The United States of America

CONTENTS

◆

		PAGE
I.	Preface	4
II.	Dedication and Acknowledgements	5
III.	The Model A Ford Ad Producers	6
IV.	Collecting Model A Ford Magazine Ads	8
V.	About This Book	11
VI.	Model A Ford Advertising	20
VII.	Model A Ford Magazine Ads by Body Style	26

A. Open Car Ads		C. Four-Door Closed Car Ads	
Roadster	27	Fordor Sedan	179
De Luxe Roadster	44	De Luxe Sedan	205
Phaeton	47	Town Sedan	213
De Luxe Phaeton	58	Three-Window Fordor Sedan	241
Convertible Cabriolet	63	Standard Sedan	249
		Town Car	253
		Station Wagon	259

B. Two-Door Closed Car Ads		D. Light Commercial Vehicle Ads	
Coupe	77	Panel Delivery	263
De Luxe Coupe	95	Special Delivery	267
Sport Coupe	105	Pick-up	268
Tudor Sedan	125	De Luxe Delivery	270
Victoria	173	Multiple Vehicles	273

E. Corporate Text Ads	277

F. Advertising Proof Ads	285

VIII.	Magazines Containing Model A Ford Ads	294
IX.	About The Author	303
X.	Selected Bibliography	304

Preface

The N. W. Ayer & Son archival files from the Model A Ford era at the Smithsonian Institute in Washington, D.C., contain interesting information about Model A Ford advertising. However, no advertising production records have been found within the Ford Motor Company or its advertising agency to provide a comprehensive listing of all Ford Model A magazine ads produced. Therefore, collectors have had no "master list" to guide their collecting efforts regarding what Model A magazine ads might be available – and in which magazines and when they appeared. Only by keeping detailed records about these ads, as they are found today, could the assembling of such a list be accomplished.

This book attempts to provide this master list. It has been compiled without benefit of being able to access existing production records of Model A magazine ads. Instead, it is the result of many years of extensive searching, researching and detailed record keeping – coupled with frequent communications with other Model A Ford advertising collectors to benefit from their collecting experiences and records. The end product is a comprehensive listing of the more than 300 different U.S. Model A magazine ads produced – along with documentation of the publish dates and magazines in which they appeared.

All known Model A Ford magazine ads for passenger cars and light commercial vehicles published in the United States are included in this book. While it is believed that all of the Model A magazine ads produced are covered, there could be new ads discovered in the future. Accordingly, the author welcomes hearing from collectors should they locate a U.S. Model A Ford magazine ad not listed in this book.

◆

This unique Model A Ford advertising illustration shows a family posing for a photograph in front of their new Ford Town Sedan. This drawing appeared as a secondary insert illustration in a two-page magazine ad featuring the Model A Cabriolet. It appeared in magazines in May 1929.

Dedication

This book is dedicated to Model A Ford advertising collectors throughout the world. May you find many Model A advertising treasures – especially that elusive one you've always been seeking – and share your finds and interests with others.

Acknowledgements

The creation of a book about Model A Ford magazine advertising has not been an easy task. It has required over three years and many hundreds of hours of searching, researching, traveling, writing and editing. It has not been accomplished without lots of encouragement, support and assistance from others.

First, I want to thank my wife, Pam, and son, Ryan, who, over the past 25 years, have been dragged through way too many car shows, swap meets, antique shows and flea markets in support of my search for Model A advertising items. Pam has also provided the support needed to help bring many diverse ideas and concepts into an organized manuscript. She also provided valued proofing assistance across several manuscript drafts. A special thanks is also owed to Ryan who spent many hours photographing all the ads included in this book. He also handled the extensive photo editing efforts necessary to bring the over 400 photographic images contained in this book to their current state.

While the vast majority of the Model A magazine ads pictured and described in this book are from my own collection, some ads have been photographed from the collections of Dr. Howard A. Minners, Bethesda, Maryland and Dr. Jordon Beller, Westmont, Illinois. Both Howard and Jordon are avid and knowledgeable Model A advertising collectors and long-time friends. I took both of them up on their generous offers to allow me full access their impressive Model A advertising collections to secure information about any magazine ads currently missing from mine.

Howard, as founder and director of the Model A Ad Collectors Club, has enthusiastically promoted and provided incentives for collecting Model A ads to many individuals. Over many years, his club newsletters have also provided collectors with a wealth of information about Model A Ford advertising. I would like to thank both Howard and Jordon for their encouragement, manuscript reviews and contributions. Both of these individuals have provided insightful and valuable suggestions regarding both the content and format of this book. Without their help this book would not have been possible.

Gratitude also goes to Eileen Valach, Office Manager at the Beller Museum in Romeoville, Illinois. Eileen spent many long hours alongside me pouring over Model A magazine ads and ad records discussing the correct identification of ads, magazines, publishing dates and page numbers. She has also spent many hours on her own confirming missing information areas in my collection and ad records. Her efforts and assistance are very much appreciated.

The Model A Ford Ad Producers

The Model A Advertising Agency

During the Model T era, it was widely known that Henry Ford was not necessarily a proponent of advertising efforts by the Ford Motor Company – which, he felt, were often unnecessary and expensive undertakings. Ford thought that by eliminating "useless advertising" the manufacturer could reduce overhead and pass the savings onto the customer.

However, during 1927, following the end of Model T Ford production and the idle factory months preceding the building of the long-awaited Model A, this attitude changed. Also modified was the long-standing policy of charging Ford dealers an assessment of three dollars per vehicle to offset advertising costs. Ford was nearing the dramatic launch of a very extensive, and expensive, advertising campaign for "The New Ford" and would fund these efforts entirely at the corporate level.

In the spring of 1927, the Ford Motor Company selected N.W. Ayer & Son as the advertising agency to manage the upcoming advertising campaign for the Model A Ford, eventually to be available at the end of that year.

N. W. AYER & SON

ADVERTISING HEADQUARTERS

PHILADELPHIA

NEW YORK   BOSTON   CHICAGO

SAN FRANCISCO

Headquartered in Philadelphia, Ayer maintained offices in New York, Boston, Chicago and San Francisco. In 1927, it was one of the oldest and most respected advertising agencies in America. As a large advertising firm, Ayer had pronounced beliefs regarding the value and power of advertising and often ran full-page magazine ads stating their views about advertising. One such ad appeared in *The Saturday Evening Post* on October 1, 1927, two months before the introduction of the Model A Ford, and provided these thoughts on advertising:

"Advertising on the printed pages of magazines and newspapers influence more than the millions of individuals who read them by day and month by month. They furnish ideas, facts and impressions that become a part of conversational store. Advertisements arouse loyalties. They make their readers into centers of beneficial influence, radiating testimony for the product and its qualities weeks and months after a particular advertisement has been bought and read."

In providing their beliefs and philosophies about advertising, Ayer also proclaimed, in a June 11, 1927 ad in the same publication, that:

"Advertising points out the merits of a product and impresses the buyer with its desirability. But advertising cannot create a single point of superiority in a product, or add a single virtue to its manufacturer." Further, that *"Advertising an unworthy product simply means that a larger number of people will presently discover its disadvantages."*

Obviously their upcoming undertaking of the advertising responsibilities for the new Model A Ford would not be hampered by the need to try to create a "point of superiority" for an "unworthy product."

The Model A Advertising Illustrator

Surely under some heavy influence from Edsel Ford, the artist selected by Ayer to draw the Model A advertising illustrations was James W. Williamson. Then 28 years old, Williamson was one of the many talented up and coming magazine illustrators of the day. Having earlier impressed Edsel with his drawings that appeared in *Vanity Fair* magazine, he was commissioned to provide the illustrations for all of the Model A Ford automobile ads. He produced drawings for both magazine and newspaper ads for Ford over the next ten years – until 1937. Peter Helck, a prominent automotive illustrator, was responsible for most of the Model A commercial vehicle and Model AA Ford truck ad illustrations.

JAMES W. WILLIAMSON

In the weeks leading up to the December 2, 1927 introduction of the Model A, Williamson labored secretly in Dearborn preparing drawings of "The New Ford." Williamson's Model A Ford illustrations, which were prepared in watercolor, colored inks, tempera and other media, were created based on his own imagination, posed photos and materials and backgrounds he derived from magazines and newspapers. Under the direction of Edsel Ford, Williamson was teamed with George Cecil, an Ayer Vice President and advertising copy chief, who wrote the ad copy text after seeing the finalized Williamson car illustration for the ad.

Williamson reported that Ford would not permit artist signatures to appear in their illustrations – indicating that Ford wasn't "advertising artists." However, there is some speculation that Williamson did manage to draw himself into at least one of his Model A ad illustrations. Peter Helck, on the other hand, seemed to get away with some quite pronounced "H" signature notations in several of his Model A commercial vehicle and Model AA truck ad illustrations.

Compared to many other car ad illustrators of this era, Williamson had a dramatically appealing style – especially in terms of his ability to capture the human side of the subjects he included in his illustrations. While many other automobile advertising illustrators drew the featured automobile quite prominently using straightforward, sometimes glamorous, backgrounds, Williamson presented everyday "slice of life" settings for the Model A. He incorporated a wide variety of adults and children (and even pets) into his drawings. His subjects fit the situation and interacted with each other – usually without "facing the camera" and definitely without distracting from the beauty of the Model A vehicle being shown. As an obvious student of human behavior, he was fond of incorporating interesting people and intriguing facial expressions befitting the theme of the ad. In many cases, he injected bits of humor not immediately apparent when first seeing his drawings. Only after viewing the illustration, gaining an understanding of the setting and then looking at the illustration again, can these initially-unnoticed human interest and humorous facets be recognized and fully appreciated.

Collecting Model A Ford Magazine Ads

It's been said that the Model A Ford is today's most popular automobile among antique car collectors. If this is so, then collecting advertising examples for this car must be the most popular hobby involving advertising for a specific automobile make.

Types of Collectors

Model A Ford magazine ad collectors are of many types. Probably most are not really collectors at all, but simply those who treasure the several magazine ads they have found over the years for their (or their grandfather's) Model A Tudor Sedan. These ads are currently framed and hanging in the den – or are out in the garage on the wall next to the Tudor. Others may occasionally be impressed with and buy a Model A Ford magazine ad as they stumble across it at a swap meet or in an antique shop. Still others take an active role in searching for these ads and keep their finds neatly arranged in albums while maintaining detailed records documenting which specific ads they have found – and which ones they would like to acquire.

Within the realm of collecting Model A Ford magazine ads are many collectors who simply like the appearance of specific ads and search only for those examples. Others have progressed to Model A Ford ad collecting as an outgrowth of owning a Model A and, in turn, are attempting to find, for example, all the 1929 Model A Fordor Sedan ads that were produced.

Others may have a collecting goal of finding an example of each basic Model A ad that was ever produced. (These collectors will find that there were over 130 different Model A passenger car and light delivery vehicle ads produced in the United States.) Others may wish to locate examples of all the individual ads produced, including all the variations that exist in the basic Model A ad formats. (These collectors will find that over 300 different Model A passenger car and light commercial vehicle ads exist.) Still others (and the author admits to being a member of this later group) constantly search for ads with the goal of acquiring a copy of each Model A Ford ad that appeared in each magazine carrying these ads. Since the same Model A ad may have appeared is as many as 20 different magazines, this expanded collecting goal increases the total number of "magazine specific" Model A ads available in the U.S. to over 900 passenger car and light commercial ads. If Model AA Ford commercial vehicle and truck ads and non-U.S. Model A and AA Ford ads are included, the above ad count levels will all be much higher.

Model A Magazine Ad Sources

Model A Ford ads, and the magazines containing these ads, remain quite available and can be readily acquired through a wide variety of sources. These sources include, but are not limited to, antique shops, flea markets, garage sales, automobile swap meets, antique and collectibles shows, ephemera and antique paper shows, old book stores, Internet auction services, and from other collectors – either by mail or personally at national or local swap meets and Model A Ford enthusiast conventions. It is common to find bins of advertising materials – much of it removed from old magazines – for sale at many of these shows and events. In other cases, individual magazines (and, sometimes, stacks of old magazines) can be found prominently displayed, or more often, in a box beneath the dealer's table.

Model A Ads in Magazines

A few magazines have an index listing the advertisers and the page numbers of their ads contained in that issue. This feature makes checking for the existence of a Model A Ford ad quite easy. However, most magazines do not offer an index and a page-by-page check of the publication will be necessary.

In searching through magazines, you'll want to limit your search activities only to the specific dates when Model A Ford ads were produced – which will, generally, be in issues published between June 1928 and July 1931. Knowing which specific magazines contained Model A ads, and the specific date ranges for each, will greatly expedite the process of paging through magazines in search of these ads.

While most Model A Ford ads were published within the above date range, there are many exceptions. It is also important to note that not all magazines carried Model A ads throughout all of the Model A production years. In some magazines, these ads appeared only in 1929, only in 1930 or only in 1930 and 1931. In others, a more limited publication run existed – such as only for the first six months of 1931. (See the "Magazines Containing Model A Ford Ads" section at the end of this book for a listing of the magazines containing Model A ads and the range of dates when these ads were published in each specific magazine.)

A special note is appropriate for those using Internet web sites or on-line auctions as sources for locating Model A Ford magazine ads. In recent years, these avenues have greatly expanded the "marriage opportunities" between distant buyers and sellers of specific collectibles – including Model A Ford magazine ads. However, when buying from these sources, be aware that reproductions of Model A ads do exist and that the condition of the ads for sale may not be described using the same criteria you would use. For example, the much-overused "in mint condition" is frequently spotted. However, there are probably very few advertising pages removed from a magazine over 75 years old that are truly in mint condition.

Ad Classification and Organization

Many Model A Ford magazine ad collectors have experienced the situation of arriving home with a recently found Model A ad only to realize that they already have two examples of this ad in their collection. Or, at the other extreme, having passed on securing an ad they thought they already had, only to later realize the ad they almost bought was, in fact, slightly different from the one they were trying to envision back home. The solution, of course, is to develop an ad classification and record-keeping system to document all of the Model A ads in your collection – and to be able to easily access these records when considering the acquisition of specific ads.

If the Model A ad has already been removed from the magazine and there is no indication as to the name of the publication, it is recommended that you note and record what is on the reverse side of the ad page. This should allow you later to identify the magazine and publish date by comparing notes with another collector. Making a note of the ad's condition will allow you later to determine if you want to upgrade from your "fair" ad copy to a recently found "excellent" copy.

Ad Classification and Organization

In a Model A Ford magazine ad collection record system, these are the classification elements you should consider noting and recording for each ad:

Model A Ad Classification Elements	
• Body style	• Publish date
• Vehicle/ad color	• Page number
• Facing left or right	• One- or two-page format
• Brief description	• Reverse side content
• Headline text	• Condition
• Magazine name	• Unique name (assigned)

Collectors use many different systems and methods for organizing their collection. Some will keep their ads grouped by Model A body style, then date, then magazine name as the grouping hierarchy. Others may initiate ad groups beginning with the magazine or publish date. Obviously, the use of a personal computer and either a database or spreadsheet software program can greatly enhance the flexibilities and classification "sorting" of your Model A ad collection records.

Preserving Your Ads

Regardless of whether you are interested in only a few specific Model A Ford magazine ads or are a serious collector interested in collecting all ad varieties that may exist, the long-term preservation of your ads should be a high priority. Temperature extremes, high humidity and light sources are all enemies of your collection. Strong light – especially sunlight or fluorescent light – will cause the inks used to print your ads to fade. Paper made from wood fibers usually contain "lignin" or "alum-rosins" which deteriorate into acid – and do so more rapidly when exposed to light. In addition, to prevent ink from running, a sizing or filler is often added in the paper production process, which can also cause an acidic reaction.

Most serious collectors will keep their Model A magazine ads in some type of archival grade, acid-free display album and store the album in a dark, low humidity area – away from extreme temperature ranges. This allows for easy access and viewing of their ads but limits the deteriorating effects time, light and the elements will impose. The long-term storage of your ads in the typical vinyl plastic envelope with a cardboard backing board commonly seen in the marketplace is not recommended. PVC (polyvinylchloride) or "vinyl" can be a real enemy of your ads because it gives off hydrochloric acid – probably not what you want sandwiched around your prized Model A Ford Town Car ad.

If "plastic" sleeves are used for long-term ad storage they should be a non-vinyl, non-PVC type plastic – such as polyester (commonly known as Mylar), polypropylene or polyethylene. In addition, the backing board or album pages in contact with your magazine ads should also be made of archival-quality "acid-free" materials.

About This Book
Model A Magazine Ads Included

Magazine Ad Coverage

This book identifies and describes over 300 different Model A Ford magazine ads appearing in magazines during the late 1920s and early 1930s. Included are more than 400 photographs and listings of over 900 separate magazine ad placements that occurred across the more than 40 different magazines used to promote "The New Ford." An attempt has been made to include all known magazine ads published for Model A Ford passenger cars and Model A Ford light commercial vehicles in the United States.

Non-U.S. Ads

There were, of course, magazine ads published for the Model A Ford in countries other than the United States. Some of these Model A Ford ads were direct replicates of the U.S. ads with a Williamson illustration and simply recast, as needed, in the language of the country in which they were published. Most of these non-U.S. ads, however, utilized completely different illustrations, advertising copy and themes. No attempt has been made to include these non-U.S. Model A magazine ads in this book. The only exceptions are the presenting of some selected examples to illustrate the use of Williamson Model A ad illustrations in non-U.S. advertising formats.

Dealer-Produced Ads

Many Model A Ford dealers and dealer groups also produced their own magazine advertising efforts – often using artwork and formats created regionally or locally on behalf of a specific Ford dealer. This book, however, covers only those magazine advertising efforts produced directly by the Ford Motor Company in their national advertising efforts. (The exception is the inclusion of several examples of selected dealer-produced ads for the Model A Ford.)

Model AA Truck and Other Ford Ads

There has been no attempt to include the many Model AA Ford large commercial vehicle and truck magazine ads also produced during the Model A years. Like the Model A passenger car and light commercial vehicle ads, these ads were also quite numerous. Ford Model AA magazine ads were produced for a large number of different commercial and truck body styles and appeared in many different magazines.

The Ford Motor Company also produced magazine advertising for other products during the Model A era. These efforts included ads for the Ford Tri-Motor airplane, Ford tractors, automobile and truck aftermarket equipment and supplies (e.g., batteries and accessories), Ford fertilizer and Ford charcoal briquette products, etc. The advertising for these products – plus the above-referenced Model AA advertising efforts – provide a wide variety of different and interesting advertising examples. However, they are all outside the scope of this book about U.S. Model A Ford passenger car and light commercial vehicle magazine ads. Perhaps the coverage of these additional Ford advertising efforts will be subjects for future books about the advertising related to "The New Ford."

Model A Body Style Ad Sections

While there are many different terms and model names used to describe the various body styles produced for the Model A Ford, this book uses only those specific body style labels actually used by the Ford Motor Company in their magazine advertisements.

Accordingly, someone indicating he owns a Model A "four-door" will not find a "four-door" magazine ad section listed in this book. Instead he will see ad listings for Model A Fordor Sedans, Three-Window Fordor Sedans, Standard Sedans, De Luxe Sedans, and Town Sedans. Likewise, while specific magazine ads were produced for the Model A Coupe, Roadster and Phaeton body styles, ads were also available for their De Luxe Coupe, De Luxe Roadster and De Luxe Phaeton counterparts and these body styles are listed separately. (Note that Ford chose to use the more formal "De Luxe" term to describe their deluxe Model A body styles.)

The Ford Motor Company did not prepare magazine ads for each of the many different Model A Ford body styles produced. For example, no U.S. magazine ad listings are found for the De Luxe Tudor (55-B De Luxe), the Business Coupe (54-A), the Convertible Sedan (400-A) and several other body styles that had somewhat limited production runs and, in turn, no individual advertising efforts in magazines. Ford also did not produce magazine ads for each advertised body style across each year it may have been produced. Accordingly, for example, no ad listings will be found for the 1928 Phaeton, the 1930 Station Wagon, the 1930 De Luxe Roadster and the 1931 Sport Coupe.

Magazine advertising was produced by Ford for the following 18 Model A body styles. Therefore, these are the specific body type classifications used to group Model A ads in this book.

Model A Body Styles Advertised in Magazines		
• Roadster	• De Luxe Coupe	• Town Sedan
• De Luxe Roadster	• Sport Coupe	• Three-Window Fordor Sedan
• Phaeton	• Tudor Sedan	• Standard Sedan
• De Luxe Phaeton	• Victoria	• Town Car
• Convertible Cabriolet	• Fordor Sedan	• Station Wagon
• Coupe	• De Luxe Sedan	• Light Commercial Vehicles

The Light Commercial Vehicle classification includes a grouped variety of commercial vehicles Ford produced using the Model A 103 ½ inch chassis – e.g., the Panel Delivery, Special Delivery, Pick-up and Deluxe Delivery. (While the Model A Station Wagon can also be considered a "light commercial" vehicle, it is covered in a separate section.)

It was common for Ford to include light commercial vehicle illustrations in the same ad with Model AA truck and larger commercial vehicle illustrations. Where both Model A light delivery vehicles and Model AA trucks or larger delivery vehicles are included in the same magazine ad, only those ads featuring predominately light commercial vehicles are included in this book.

Model A Body Style Ad Sections

Some Model A Ford passenger car ads also include more than one body style. (For example, in many of the two-page Model A magazine ads.) In these cases, the ad is classified, for inclusion in this book, according to which body style is featured most prominently in the ad. (If two or more body style illustrations appear somewhat equal in terms of size, the ad is classified according to the body style illustration featured first in the ad.)

Other Model A Ad Sections

Corporate Text Ads

A "corporate text" ad classification is also included in this book to cover those magazine ads that do not feature specific Model A body styles but were created during the Model A era to promote the Ford Motor Company and its automobile production efforts. These "text only" ads usually contain no specific vehicle information and are completely devoid of any illustrations.

Advertising Proof Ads

A section in this book is also devoted to examples of Model A Ford advertising proof ads. These ads were produced as internal ad documentation copies, while the ad was still in the developmental stage and prior to being committed to a media schedule and printed in a magazine. Therefore, these special ad pages never actually appeared in a magazine. Instead, they came from Ford Motor Company internal files or from N.W. Ayer & Sons, the Ford advertising agency that produced them.

Model A Ad Classification Criteria

The Model A Ford magazine ads listed in this book are classified and, in turn, grouped and displayed within body style groupings according to several key criteria that describe specific elements of the ad. These elements include:

Primary Illustration

Most Model A magazine ads include a primary illustration of the Model A vehicle in use. (The exceptions were the corporate "all-text" ads.) These illustrations range from complete four-color artist illustrations and line drawings by James Williamson, to black and white photographs, to simple line drawings of the car without a background. The primary illustration is used as the main classification element for dividing Model A ads into body style groups – by Coupes, De Luxe Roadsters, Fordor Sedans, etc. (Note that the primary illustration in the magazine ad often remained unchanged across a series of ads that could have had variations in the other ad elements listed on the next page.)

Model A Ad Classification Criteria

Primary Illustration

The Williamson drawings appearing in Model A Ford magazine ads were sometimes borrowed for use as illustrations in other Ford advertising efforts – in newspaper ads, dealer brochures, showroom posters, etc. Some of these illustrations also found their way into Model A advertising produced outside of the United States.

Secondary Illustration

Many Model A Ford magazine ads also include secondary illustrations of additional Ford body styles or printed text inserts listing specific features of "The New Ford." These smaller "insert illustrations" could differ across ads using the same (larger) primary illustration, resulting in the identification of several additional versions of the basic ad. These smaller Williamson insert illustrations are often simply smaller versions of the primary ad illustration used in other Model A Ford magazine ads. In other cases, however, these secondary illustrations are unique drawings and never appear as the primary illustration in a Model A Ford magazine ad.

Headline

All Model A Ford ads utilize one or more headlines, appearing either above or below the primary illustration or included as part of the ad text. While the headline usually is tied to (or summarizes) the ad theme or content of the ad text, the headline often appears to have no real association with the primary illustration used in the ad. Variations in headline wordings result in the identification of additional ad versions – even though the ads may have utilized common primary and secondary illustrations.

Ad Format

While the primary illustration and headline may remain the same, two Model A Ford magazine ads for the same body style could have been produced in slightly different ad formats – e.g., changes in headline positioning, the presence or absence of the Ford oval logo, a change to a two-page ad format, the addition or deletion of smaller insert illustrations, the switch from a full-color illustration to a black and white ad format, etc.

Ad Text

Model A Ford magazine ads include advertising copy or text extolling the virtues of "The New Ford." Some ads utilize a fairly lengthy ad text section, while in others the advertising text is quite limited. Note that two Model A ads using the same illustration, headline and format – and, therefore, appearing at first glance to be identical – could have quite different ad text content. Further, some ads that may appear to be completely identical in all elements, including ad text, may have slightly different (sometimes very minor) word variations in the text of the ad.

Model A Ad Variations

While some Model A Ford magazine ads are unique and have no content variations, others have as many as six or seven different variations based on unique combinations of the secondary illustrations, headlines, formats and text elements previously described. Accordingly, variations in these ad elements result in the magazine ad being considered as a **separate ad version** and each of these known ad versions are identified and described in this book.

In displaying Model A magazine ads in this book, a large photograph is dedicated to each of the **primary ad formats**. Beneath the primary ad photograph is a brief comment about the ad and a list of the magazines containing it – along with the publish dates and page numbers (where known).

If the primary ad format also has **ad versions**, all of these ad variations are presented (in smaller photographs) on subsequent pages – again with the magazine names, dates and page numbers listed. Individual ad photographs are used for all ad variations where there are obvious differences in the illustration, headline, format or other key ad elements. However, for ads where the only variation from the primary ad format is a minor text difference, the ad is not featured in a separate photograph but is still listed as an ad variation with a "text difference" notation.

Model A Ad Names, Labels and Codes

As a means of identifying and referencing the various Model A Ford magazine ads contained in this book, each ad has been assigned a unique name. These names, which are limited to a two or three word description of the ad, are unique to each individual ad and are based on the primary illustration or theme of the ad. The purpose of these name assignments is simply to allow a reference to a specific ad without the need for listing the Model A body style and a detailed description of the ad content. The creation of these unique ad names has been at the author's own initiation and not according to any information or classification system used by the Ford Motor Company.

Note that, while each Model A Ford ad has been assigned a unique name, there may be several different versions of that ad – according to variations existing in secondary illustrations, headlines, text, etc. – but all utilizing the same primary illustration and, therefore, ad name. These ad variations are identified by assigning alphabetical designations to each – e.g., ad "Version A," ad "Version B," ad "Version C," etc.

In addition, a separate, unique alphanumeric code is also assigned to each individual Model A ad – e.g., "Cab 3a" for the first version (Version A) of the third Cabriolet ad, "TnS 8c" for the third version (Version C) of the eighth Town Sedan ad, etc.

Most Model A magazine ads appeared as full-color advertisements. However, many were black and white – and a few were printed in two colors (i.e., in black and white but with one additional color). In this book, where a specific black and white ad is listed but is not shown, a "(B&W)" notation is included as a part of the listing.

Magazines, Dates and Page Numbers

While some Model A Ford ads appeared in only one magazine on a single date, others may have appeared in as many as 20 different magazines over the course of several months. Within each Model A body style ad grouping, primary ads and their versions are listed, by magazine, in the approximate date order in which they were published.

A list of all magazines containing Model A Ford ads, the dates they appeared and an example photograph of the magazine's front cover appears in the last section of this book.

Listing a Model A ad according to a specific page number to indicate exactly where it appeared within the magazine can present some major challenges. For those magazines that printed the magazine name and page number on all pages – including the advertising pages – the page number identification is, of course, obvious. However, some magazines printed page numbers only on the magazine text pages and, while counting the advertising pages in numbering magazine pages, skipped the printing of page numbers on the ad pages. These ads, therefore, were assigned an "invisible" page number in listing their location within the magazine. To help in these situations, some ads are listed with a plus symbol (+) following the page number. This indicates that the ad appears somewhere after that page number in the magazine – e.g., a page listing of "123+" means the ad occurs on an unnumbered page following (numbered) page 123.

Once an unnumbered ad page had been removed from the host magazine, there is often no way to know (or "calculate") the specific page number of the ad without having the benefit of seeing the original publication from which it was removed. For these reasons, some ads listed do not include a page number designation and, where a page number is listed (or "estimated"), this information should be used only as an approximation of the ad's location in the magazine.

Model A Ford ads also appeared on the covers of magazines – and, therefore, are sometimes found on heavier paper stock. While no U.S. Model A ads were placed on the front cover of a magazine, many appeared on the back of the front cover (CII) or on the inside of the back cover (CIII). In a few cases, the Model A ad appeared on the back cover (CIV) of the magazine. Some Model A magazine ads were two-page advertisements – appearing either as two separate facing pages or as a magazine centerfold (CF).

Model A Ad Rarity

Surely the most important factor related to the "difficulty in locating" or rarity of a Model A Ford ad is associated with the magazine that contained the ad. In other words, a Model A ad from a high-circulation magazine (such as *The Saturday Evening Post*) will be, everything else being equal, easier to locate than the same ad from a low-circulation magazine (such as *Liberty*).

Other factors affecting the "rarity" of specific ads are associated with the ad's desirability, popularity, and condition – and the specific collecting motivations of the individual. The many intertwined elements, beyond the **magazine** itself, that contribute to the rarity of a Model A ad include a wide variety of factors.

Model A Ad Rarity
Factors, Beyond Magazine, Affecting Ad Rarity

Body Style – An ad for a Model A Town Car ad will, generally, be seen as being much more collectable than an ad for a Model A Coupe.

Color – A black and white ad will usually be considered as less desirable than an ad appearing in full color. (However, a specific black and white ad may be more difficult to find than its full-color sister ad – thereby creating an offsetting increase in its rarity rating.)

Size – From an aesthetic viewpoint, an ad from a large format magazine will often be seen as more desirable than the same ad from a smaller sized magazine. (Likewise, a two-page ad is usually viewed as more collectable than the one-page version of the same ad.)

Appearance – An ad having a particularly attractive or interesting illustration will generally be more desired by collectors than a more plain-looking ad for the same body style. (Therefore, for example, ads featuring women's fashion elements or a holiday theme may find interest among collectors outside of the fact that it contains a Model A Ford.)

Uniqueness – An ad that is unique and appeared in only one magazine on a single date will usually be more difficult to locate than one that appeared in multiple magazines across several dates.

Geography – Collectors living in the East or West may have lower or higher probabilities of locating specific magazines that may have had large geographical circulation differences. Likewise, those living in urban versus rural locations may, for example, experience different success rates in locating farm-related magazines.

Magazine Type – An upscale magazine printed on high quality paper will contain generally more attractive ads than a magazine printed on quickly-aging pulp paper. (Confounding this, however, may be the lower survival rate – and, therefore, elevated rarity for an ad from the pulp paper publication.)

Condition – Ads with narrowly trimmed margins, tears, stains, and extreme browning or foxing will be much less desirable than the same ad in excellent condition. (Finding ads with narrow, uneven margins reflecting lack of attention in their removal from the host magazine is, unfortunately, a common occurrence.)

Collector Goals – The individual motivation of the collector is also a major factor. For the collector simply wanting a single example of an ad that happened to appear in 20 different magazines, an ad from any of the publications will suffice. However, for the collector wanting every copy of the ad ever published, locating the ad in the one obscure magazine among the 20 could be a major challenge.

Model A Ad Rarity

In summary, the assessment of the "rarity" of a specific Model A Ford magazine ad is a complex and very subjective issue – and depends quite heavily on the goals of the collector. Accordingly, an unattractive, common black and white Tudor Sedan ad in tattered condition – but coming from an obscure publication – may have a much higher "rarity rating" for the Model A magazine ad collector than the same ad found in excellent condition, in full color, in a prestigious magazine.

In this book, each of the listings of more than 900 individual Model A Ford magazine ads according to their magazine insertions employs one of the following symbols to approximate the relative "rarity" of the ad.

Model A Magazine Ad Rarity Ratings
○ Common – very easy to locate
◉ Uncommon – somewhat easy to locate
◉ Rare – somewhat difficult to locate
● Very Rare – very difficult to locate

Note that these rarity or "difficulty in locating" classifications are very subjective and based completely on the author's own experience and observations following many years of searching for Model A Ford magazine ads – with the goal of securing an example of each ad that appeared in each magazine containing the ad. Note, further, that the relative quantity of ads existing in each of these four rarity rating groups is not necessarily the same. On the contrary, the vast majority of Model A Ford ads surely fall into the "common" and "uncommon" ad classification, with a much smaller proportion in the "rare" group – and only a very limited number of ads being seen as "very rare."

Model A Ad Values

If the creation of a rating scale for the rarity of Model A Ford magazine ads is difficult, estimating the specific dollar value of a specific Model A ad is even more challenging. Currently, there are no universal price expectations or published "price guides" for Model A Ford magazine ads. However, the increasing popularity in collecting these ads and the growing availability of these ads through Internet auction sources is probably beginning to establish some general expectations here.

Model A Ad Values

As a very rough guideline (and assuming an average across all sources – e.g., the Internet, car shows, flea markets, etc.), the author's experience in observing the asking prices of Model A ads from individuals or dealers somewhat familiar with these ads is: "common" ads – $10 and lower, "uncommon" ads – $10-$20, "rare" ads – $20-$30, and "very rare" ads – $30 and higher. This last category is somewhat open-ended – with the highest price the author has ever observed paid for a Model A Ford magazine ad being $150 (through an Internet auction). On the other hand, the lowest price observed was on several Model A ads included in a large bin of miscellaneous "$1.00 each" advertising materials at an antique paper and ephemera show.

It is also important to note that the above ad value and price estimates are also based on dealing with a seller or collector who has some basic knowledge related to Model A Ford magazine advertising – and who also has a profit motive in selling an ad. In dealing with those less experienced in Model A magazine ads, much more dramatic extremes in ad rarity perceptions and, in turn, ad prices will be found. We may have all experienced a situation similar to that of the very excited individual believing that the tattered, very common Model A Ford magazine ad they found last week in their grandfather's trunk in the attic must be a one-of-a-kind treasure that should command a very high price. On the other hand, the "joy of the hunt" can be no more pronounced than when stumbling onto several obscure magazines containing desirable Model A Ford ads at the bottom of a "$3.00 per box" cardboard box at a garage sale.

The price someone is willing to pay for a Model A Ford magazine ad is, of course, based on individualized and ever-changing value assumptions. Obviously, once a collector has located and purchased a specific Model A magazine ad, a second copy of that same ad, located the next day, may have much less value to that particular collector – unless the purchase motivation is for reselling or trading the ad to another Model A Ford ad collector.

◆

This unique Model A Ford illustration shows a 1928 Phaeton arriving at the tennis club. This drawing did not appear as the primary illustration in a Model A Phaeton magazine ad. Instead, it was included as a secondary illustration in an early two-page ad also featuring the Model A Coupe. The date of the ad was July 7, 1928, within the month following the launch of Model A Ford magazine advertising in June 1928.

Model A Ford Advertising

In the Beginning

The introduction of "The New Ford" was, by all measures, one of the most awaited and dramatic product launches ever and it changed the course of automotive history. Although Henry Ford seemed to have established an earlier reputation for disliking advertising, the advertising related to the introduction and on-going promotion of the Model A was both extensive and effective.

An announcement by Edsel Ford on May 26, 1927, to 10,000 Ford dealers revealing that Ford was "starting production of a entirely new Ford car" was the first official word regarding the production of the Model A Ford. Much later, on October 11, 1927, was the indication that the first vehicle was about to roll off the assembly line. However, in between these announcements and, indeed, prior to the actual introduction of the new Ford, there was a pronounced silence – with no information available regarding what the car would be and what it would look like. Whether a carefully planned marketing ploy or simply a pronounced ignoring of the increasing curiosity of the American public, this long silence created more interest in the new Ford than could probably have been accomplished through an extensive pre-introduction advertising campaign.

While some small ads in newspapers during the latter months of 1927 proclaimed *Wait for the New Ford,"* no advertising was released until just several days prior to the December 2, 1927 Model A Ford introduction date. Finally, with interest in learning about the new Ford car at a fever pitch, the Ford Motor Company initiated a national advertising campaign to introduce the long-awaited new Ford automobile. Beginning on November 29, 1927, Ford launched a series of five full-page ads in 2,000 newspapers. The initial ads, however, provided only a general review of the characteristics of the new Ford car – with no indication of available body styles and no drawings of the car. The fourth newspaper ad, coinciding with the Model A introduction on December 2, 1927, finally revealed body style drawings and prices for "The New Ford Car."

The level of excitement and curiosity surrounding Henry's new creation was unparallel in the history of the automobile and the introduction of the Model A Ford was front-page news throughout the country. Before the end of introduction day, December 2, 1927, it was estimated that over a million people fought crowds – and, for many, sub-zero temperatures, rain and sleet – to get a look at the new Ford. In many cases, only posters depicting "The New Ford" were available for viewing, since many Ford dealers were yet to receive an actual car. The December 27, 1927 issue of *The Ford News,* a Ford Motor Company publication (and, therefore, perhaps a little biased) ran the headline that *"Ten Percent of U.S. Population Sees New Ford First Day of Show."* Others have estimated that about one-quarter of the people in the United States saw the new car within the first few days after the introduction date.

The heavy newspaper advertising campaign used to introduce "The New Ford" did not continue with the same intensity in early 1928. The extremely successful introduction of the Model A resulted in many more orders for cars than could be filled. This inability to keep production matched to demand and the longer lead time required to create and place magazine ads were surely among the reasons the newspaper-based launch campaign was not followed by advertising in magazines for over six months.

MODEL A FORD INTRODUCTION NEWSPAPER AD

THE PROVIDENCE JOURNAL, FRIDAY, DECEMBER 2, 1927

NEW FORD TUDOR SEDAN

An example of the fine coachwork of the new Ford cars. New military-type sun visor, and crown roof. Narrow pillars and new door construction give unusual vision. Both front seats fold forward, giving easy access to rear seat. Ample space between seats. Your choice of four artistic color harmonies — an unusual feature in a low-price car.

$495
(F. O. B. Detroit)

First Pictures of the New Ford Car

Get complete details ## TODAY at Ford salesrooms

FOR several years we have been working on the new Ford car. For weeks and months you have been hearing rumors about it. For the past few days you have been reading some of the details of it in the newspapers.

Whatever you do today, take at least fifteen minutes to get the full story of this new automobile.

You will realize then that it is an entirely new and different Ford car, designed and created to meet modern conditions — a car that brings you more beauty, speed, quiet, comfort, safety, economy and stamina than you ever thought possible in a low-price car.

Automobile history will be made today, for the new Ford is not only new in appearance and performance . . . it is new in mechanical design. Many features of it are exclusive Ford developments. Some are wholly new in automobile practice. Its low price is a reflection of manufacturing improvements and economies that are as epoch-making as the car itself.

Nineteen years of experience in building 15,000,000 automobiles are behind the new Ford car and have counted in its making. Resources unmatched in the motor car industry are its heritage and its birthright.

The Ford policy of owning the source of raw materials, of making virtually every part, of doing business at a small profit per car, has cut many dollars off the price you would ordinarily have to pay for a car like this.

So we say to you — learn about this new Ford car today. Compare it with any other car in the light-car field — for beauty of line — for comfort — for speed — for quick acceleration — for flexibility in traffic . . . for steadiness at all speeds . . . for power on the hills . .

for economy and low cost of up-keep . . . for its sturdy ability to stand up under countless thousands of miles of service. Then you will know why today will be remembered as one of the greatest days in the entire history of the automobile industry. . . . Then you will know why the new Ford car will be *your* car.

NOTE THESE FEATURES

Beautiful new low body lines
Choice of four colors
55 to 65 miles an hour
Remarkable acceleration
40 horse-power
Four-wheel brakes
Standard, selective gear shift
Hydraulic shock absorbers
20 to 30 miles per gallon of gasoline
Theft-proof coincidental lock
Typical Ford economy and reliability

STANDARD EQUIPMENT ON
ALL NEW FORD CARS

Starter	Dashlight
Five steel-spoke wheels	Mirror
Windshield wiper	Rear and stop light
Speedometer	Oil gauge
Gasoline gauge	Tools
Pressure grease gun lubrication	

NEW FORDOR SEDAN

A big roomy car. Wide seats. Generous leg-room front and rear. Four convenient doors. Unusually large windows. Rich upholstery and full-nickeled hardware. Dome light. Your choice of four artistic colors.

$570
(F. O. B. Detroit)

NEW FORD ROADSTER

A long, low, chummy car. As fast as it looks. Wide doors. Deep cushions. Rich upholstery. Full-nickeled hardware. Rumble seat optional. Your choice of four beautiful color harmonies.

$385
(F. O. B. Detroit)

NEW FORD COUPE

There is a bit of the European touch in the coachwork and contour of this new Ford Coupe. Handy package shelf in back of seat and unusually large waterproof luggage space in rear deck. Your choice of four beautiful colors.

$495
(F. O. B. Detroit)

NEW FORD SPORT COUPE

Combines the alert smartness of the roadster and the advantages of a closed car. Rumble seat standard. Landau irons on rear quarter. Finished in four artistic color harmonies.

$550
(F. O. B. Detroit)

NEW FORD PHAETON

Another long, low, roomy car. All four doors open forward. Curtains open and close with doors. Side curtains have unusually large windows. Your choice of four artistic colors.

$395
(F. O. B. Detroit)

FORD MOTOR COMPANY
Detroit, Michigan

© 1927, Ford Motor Co.

This full-page ad was the fourth in a series of five ads in the newspaper advertising campaign used to introduce "The New Ford." This was the first ad to show pictures and prices for the Model A Ford and appeared in 2,000 national newspapers either on or the day before the Model A introduction day – December 2, 1927.

Award Winning Advertising

The dramatic arrival and overwhelming impact of "The New Ford" in late December 1927 and early 1928 was felt well beyond the car-buying public. Advertising critics were also quite impressed with the advertising efforts used to support the introduction and on-going promotion of the Model A Ford.

The Ford advertising campaign using full-page ads in national newspapers to introduce the Model A was proclaimed as *"the most soundly coordinated advertising campaign in America's advertising history"* by the president of the Advertising Club of New York. The initial Model A advertising efforts also did not go unnoticed by the Graduate School of Business of Harvard University, which, beginning in 1924, presented annual awards for meritorious advertising. Ford received two advertising awards from Harvard.

HARVARD ADVERTISING AWARD

The first Harvard Advertising Award was in 1927 for "Advertisements Effective in Typography." Here, Harvard singled out the second ad in the series of five full-page newspaper ads for this prestigious award. The second, and more significant Harvard Advertising Award, was presented for the entire 1928 Model A newspaper and magazine advertising campaign. This award also covered the advertising efforts for the "aviation series" associated with the Ford Tri-Motor airplane produced this same year. This Harvard Advertising Award was "For the Campaign for the Ford Automobile and for the General Subject of Aviation."

In their 1930 book reviewing these Harvard Advertising Awards, the authors at Harvard indicated that *"This campaign for the Ford motor car is distinguished not only by its intrinsic worth but also by the contrast it offers to a large part of the automobile advertising that has appeared."* They also indicated that *"All advertisements in this series are remarkable for their pleasing and well-balanced layouts"* and that *"The 1928 Ford motor-car campaign marked a decidedly forward step in the advertising of automobiles."*

The prior (1927) Harvard Advertising Award campaign winner was Erma Perham Proetz of the Gardner Advertising Company for the Pet Milk campaign. The following year's winner was Barton, Durstine & Osborn, Inc., the advertising agency responsible for the 1929 General Motors Corporation advertising campaign.

It is interesting to note that these advertising awards were usually presented naming the advertising agency responsible for the advertising campaign, followed by the name of the manufacturer of the product involved. However, in the two Ford Harvard Advertising awards, N.W. Ayer & Son was not mentioned. (Perhaps the policy referenced by James Williamson about Ford not permitting illustrator signatures on their advertising drawings also extended to not allowing its advertising agency to be listed in any advertising recognition awards.)

Model A Magazine Advertising

While magazine advertising for the Model A Ford did not begin in national magazines in the United States until June 1928, several very early Model A ads were printed in a student publication from the Detroit University School in December 1927. These ads continued in this limited circulation publication into the first quarter of 1928. The first Model A ads to appear in a commercial magazine were black and white ads in Canadian farming publications. These ads first appeared in December 1927 and stretched into the early months of 1928 – still several months before the first Model A Ford magazine ad appeared in the United States.

EARLIEST MODEL A FORD MAGAZINE AD

This Model A magazine ad appeared in several Canadian farm-related magazines – including **The Grain Grower,** December 15, 1927, and **The Farmer's Guide,** January 1928 – many months before the first U.S. Model A magazine ad in June 1928.

Earliest and Latest U. S. Model A Magazine Ads

Ford launched consumer magazine advertising for the Model A in the United States in June 1928 utilizing a total of 15 magazines containing two Sport Coupe ads and one Roadster ad. In the next month (July 1928), magazine ads appeared for the Model A Tudor Sedan and the Coupe. Magazine ads did not appear for the remaining two Model A body styles announced on introduction day until October 1928 (Fordor Sedan) and April 1929 (Phaeton).

The latest Model A magazine ad to be published in the United States was a corporate text ad that did not contain an illustration of a Model A. This ad appeared in March 1932, several months after the production of the Model A passenger car had ended.

EARLIEST U.S. MAGAZINE AD

LATEST U.S. MAGAZINE AD

Ford Sport Coupe ad appearing during the first month of national Model A Ford magazine advertising in the U.S. – June 1928

Ford corporate text ad appearing as last Model A Ford ad published in the U.S. – March 1932

Model A Magazine Ad Production

Below is a review of the dates of the earliest and latest U.S. Ford Model A corporate text magazine ads and magazine ads for each Model A body style advertised by Ford. Included is the number of **basic ads** created and – including format, headline and text variations – the total number of **different ads** produced for each body style. Finally, the total number of **ad insertions** (counts of each ad's appearance in a specific magazine) are shown.

U.S. Model A Magazine Ad Production Summary					
	Date of Ads		Number of Ads		
Model A Body Style	Earliest Ad	Latest Ad	Basic Ads	Total Ads	Insertions
Sport Coupe	6/28	10/30	10	28	76
Roadster	6/28	8/30	10	22	50
Tudor Sedan	7/28	10/31	24	58	142
Coupe	7/28	5/31	10	24	77
Fordor Sedan	10/28	11/29	13	33	69
Phaeton	4/29	8/30	5	11	27
Convertible Cabriolet	4/29	7/31	7	23	69
Town Car	5/29	10/29	2	3	10
Station Wagon	6/29	6/29	1	1	5
Town Sedan	6/29	11/31	13	37	119
Corporate Text	12/29	3/32	5	7	60
De Luxe Sedan	4/30	3/31	3	7	38
Three-Window Fordor Sedan	7/30	2/31	3	10	53
De Luxe Phaeton	8/30	6/31	2	4	9
De Luxe Coupe	11/30	4/31	4	14	43
Victoria	1/31	12/31	3	9	33
Light Commercial Vehicles	1/31	2/32	17	18	25
De Luxe Roadster	4/31	6/31	1	4	16
Standard Sedan	6/31	7/31	3	3	10
Total			136	316	931

Based on the ad's primary illustration, a total of 136 basic magazine ads were created for the Model A Ford in the United States. When the (sometimes minor) variations available in many of these ads are considered, a total of 316 different Model A Ford ads were produced. These 316 ads were available for the public's viewing across a total of 931 different magazine insertions during the Model A Ford advertising years.

Model A Ford Magazine Ads By Body Style

The 316 different Model A Ford magazine ad variations produced using 136 basic advertising illustrations are reviewed by Model A body style on the following pages. Information is provided to identify each magazine that contained the ad, the date of publication, the page number (where known) and an ad rarity rating. The result is a total of 931 individual "magazine insertion" Model A Ford magazine ad listings.

Body Style Summary Information

These magazine ad listings cover the 16 different Model A passenger car body styles and five different Model A light commercial vehicles advertised by Ford. (Following the body style sections are two additional sections covering corporate text ads and advertising proof ads.) Each of the body style sections is preceded by a summary page providing a brief review of production and advertising information for that specific body style. The production information reviews the Model A body identification numbers used by Ford, the weights and prices of the vehicle and the numbers of units produced each year.

Body Identification Number. While not referenced in its advertising, Ford identified each Model A body style according to a unique body identification number. Use of these code numbers provides an accurate means of identifying specific body types by year and avoids the confusion usually associated with relying solely on a body style name in attempting to identify a specific Model A. Using the Ford body identification numbers is, for example, the only way to accurately sort and identify the 10 distinctly different four-door Model A body styles produced by Ford during 1930-1931.

Weight. The weight of the Model A Ford vehicle varied fairly dramatically by body style. Note, also, that the weight of a specific Model A body style may have changed slightly between the 1928-29 and 1930-31 model years.

Price. The dealer list price for a Model A Ford also varied rather widely by body style and changed several times over the production run for each Model A body style. In some cases, the price changed several times within the model year. As a general pattern, the price for Model A body styles introduced in late 1927 and early 1928 increased slightly in 1929 then, as a result of the pressures related to the developing economic depression, dropped slightly at the end of that year. Ford made a major announcement of price reductions for the Model A on December 1, 1929 – approximately one month following the October 29, 1929 "Black Tuesday" stock market crash. Further price reductions followed throughout 1930 and 1931. (The prices listed are FOB Detroit and have been determined from researching Ford newspaper ads to reflect, wherever possible, the prices in effect during January of the model year listed.)

Units Produced. Relatively few Model A Fords were actually produced prior to the December 2, 1927 introduction date and efforts to increase factory output to match consumer demand was a major challenge for Ford during early 1928. The production of the Model A Ford officially ceased at U.S. assembly plants during November 1931. However, a small number of Model A passenger car and light commercial vehicles were produced in 1932. (Note that, while the production information presented in the body style summaries covers U.S. output only, over 15 percent of total Model A Ford production occurred outside of the United States.)

ROADSTER

	TOTAL	1927	1928	1929	1930	1931
Ford Body Style		40-A	40-A	40-A	40-B (Std.)	40-B (Std.)
Weight (pounds)		2,050	2,050	2,050	2,200	2,155
Price (FOB Detroit)		$385	$385	$450	$435	$430
Units Produced (U.S.)	361,987	251	51,807	191,529	112,901	5,499
Number of U.S. Ads						
Primary Formats	10	–	6	2	1	1
Ad Variations	22	–	11	5	5	1
Magazine Insertions	50	–	20	8	13	9

The Roadster was one of the six Model A Ford body styles initially introduced on December 2, 1927. (Because of the later availability of the De Luxe Roadster, this body style was sometimes referred to as the "Standard Roadster" – although never so in Ford advertising.) The sporty Roadster was the lowest priced Model A, with an introduction price of $385. The available rumble seat was a $35 production option. Roadster body parts were produced by both Briggs and Budd and shipped to Ford plants for assembly.

The Model A Roadster enjoyed fairly heavy magazine advertising efforts and Roadster ads appeared in many different publications. However, unlike the case with many other Model A body styles, Ford did not place Roadster ads in farm-related publications. Across all four advertising years, Model A Roadster ads always showed the car with the top down and, in 1930, with the windshield folded forward.

The new Ford has been built to endure

THE remarkable performance of the new Ford is the direct result of the quality that has been built into every part of it.

It has beauty of line and color because beauty of line and color has come to be considered a necessity in a motor car.

Yet even more important than this outside beauty is the strength, efficiency and beauty of those parts which are on the inside—those vital mechanical parts which are the very heart of value and performance.

An example of the quality that is built into the new Ford is the use of steel forgings instead of malleable castings and steel stampings.

FORD MOTOR COMPANY
Detroit, Michigan

They are used throughout the chassis, except, of course, for the engine castings. More steel forgings, in fact, are used in the new Ford than in almost any other car regardless of price.

Added strength, quiet and reliability also come from the number of electric weldings used in the new Ford. By the use of these weldings, one-piece parts of great strength replace those formerly made up of several parts bolted, riveted or soldered together.

Some of the other features which show the strength and quality that have been built into the new Ford car are the steel bodies; the aluminum alloy pistons; the carbon chrome nickel alloy valves; the statically and dynamically balanced crankshaft which is built to withstand a twisting stress up to 60,000-inch pounds; the multiple dry-disc clutch; the Houdaille hydraulic shock absorbers; the Triplex shatter-proof glass windshield; the mechanical four-wheel brakes; the seamless, all-steel torque tube; the new one-piece, welded, steel-spoke wheels; the three-quarter floating rear axle and the all-steel rear axle housing.

So we say to you—take a little while to see and inspect this new car at the nearest Ford showrooms. Examine it carefully, part by part. Listen to its quiet, smooth-running engine. Know the thrill of driving

it. By its performance you will know there is nothing quite like it anywhere in design, quality and price.

The Roadster sells for $385; Phaeton, $395; Tudor Sedan, $495; Coupe, $495; Business Coupe, $495; Sport Coupe, with wide substantial rumble seat, $550. (F.O.B. Detroit.)

The new Ford is a great car to drive in traffic because of its quick acceleration, easy steering, short turning radius, the safety of its four-wheel brakes and the ease of shifting gears.

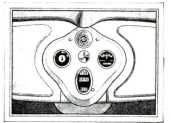

Shown above is the instrument panel on the new Ford. It is made of steel, beautifully finished in satin nickel. Instruments are in convenient, illuminated clover leaf cluster.

A couple speeds along a country road in their top-down Ford Roadster while the driver sings a merry tune. Given the tuxedo and party dress, they must be on the way home from a fancy party – where, perhaps, a little too much "hooch" was consumed.

Version A (Rdr 1a)
◉ *The American Boy,* June 1928, p. 4

This is a unique Model A ad. It appeared on only one date, in only one magazine.

BOAT RACE

Get behind the wheel and know the joy of driving this great new car

THE joy of driving the new Ford comes not alone from its speed—its safety—its comfort—its reliability—the pride you take in its beauty of line and color—but also from the pleasure it puts into motoring.

Shown here is the new Ford Sport Coupe. Rumble seat is standard equipment on this car.

Instantly you start away for your first ride you have a feeling that here is an unusually alert and capable car. That here is a car fully equal to every need and emergency. That here is a car with a new eagerness to go. A new aliveness. A new responsiveness in traffic, on hills, and on the open road.

As the days go by, you find yourself developing real friendliness for the new Ford—a growing pride that is deeper and more personal than just an acknowledgment of faithful service.

You long to be behind the wheel—to drive for the sheer joy of driving—to know again the sense of power, security and complete control that is yours when you ride in this great new car.

Watching the performance of the new Ford—studying its reliability—you begin to see that it is not just a new automobile—not just a new model—but the advanced expression of a wholly new idea in modern, economical transportation.

For now, at a low price, you can get every-

FORD MOTOR COMPANY
Detroit, Mich.

thing you want or need in a modern automobile . . . steel body . . . beautiful low lines . . . choice of colors . . . speed of 55 to 65 miles an hour . . . a four-cylinder engine which develops 40 horse-power at only 2200 revolutions a minute . . . quick acceleration . . . exceptional hill-climbing qualities . . . 20 to 30 miles per gallon of gasoline . . . protected safety gasoline tank in cowl, with the advantage of direct gravity flow . . . mechanical, self-centering, internal expanding-shoe four-wheel brakes . . . Houdaille hydraulic shock absorbers . . . typical Ford reliability, and low up-keep cost . . . Triplex shatter-proof glass windshield.

The Ford Motor Company is able to build such a really fine car at a low price only because of new manufacturing methods and production economies as unusual as the car itself. Every purchaser shares the benefits of the established Ford policy of selling at a small margin of profit—of owning the source of raw materials—of constantly giving greater value.

A couple watches the boat race from their new Ford Roadster. To get a better view, the woman has moved to perch on the top of the seat back, steadying herself using the driver's shoulder.

Version A (Rdr 2a)
◉ *The American Boy,* July 1928, p. 4

This Roadster ad is also unique and appeared only once, in July 1928.

MOUNTAIN ROAD

◆

Smooth riding ease and restful comfort
make the new Ford an especially good car for women to drive

WHEN you see the new Ford, you are impressed instantly by its low, trim, graceful lines and the beauty of its two-tone color harmonies.

As you watch it in traffic and on the open road you can note how quickly it accelerates and get some idea, too, of the speed and power of its 40-horse-power engine.

But only by driving the new Ford yourself can you fully appreciate the easy-riding comfort that is such an outstanding feature of this great new car.

One reason, of course, is the use of Houdaille hydraulic shock absorbers, formerly furnished as standard equipment on only the most expensive automobiles. Yet even these shock absorbers do not account for the complete riding comfort of the new Ford.

Equally important are the design and construction of the new transverse springs, the low center of gravity, and what engineers speak of as the low ratio of the unsprung weight to the sprung weight of the car.

All of these factors combine to soften or eliminate the force of road shocks and to make the new Ford an exceptionally comfortable and easy-riding car at all speeds.

Even rough roads may be taken at a fast pace without hard jolts or bumps or the exaggerated bouncing rebound which is the cause of most motoring fatigue.

You have a feeling of mental comfort, too, in driving the new Ford because of its reliability and the safety afforded by its steel body, four-wheel brakes and Triplex shatter-proof glass windshield. This freedom from mechanical trouble—this security—means a great deal to every woman who drives a car.

Prove this for yourself by telephoning the

Ford
FORD MOTOR COMPANY
Detroit, Michigan

nearest Ford dealer and asking him to bring the new Ford to your home for a demonstration.

Check up on comfort, on speed, on power, on acceleration, on hill climbing, on gasoline economy, on safety, on low up-keep cost, and you will know that there is nothing quite like it anywhere in design, quality and price.

The low price, in fact, is the result of new manufacturing methods and production economies as unusual as the car itself.

The new Ford comes to you equipped with four Houdaille hydraulic shock absorbers, four-wheel brakes, Triplex shatter-proof glass windshield, five steel-spoke wheels, windshield wiper, speedometer, gasoline gage, dash light, mirror, combination stop and tail light, theft-proof coincidental lock, and high pressure grease gun lubrication.

Two ladies in their new Ford Roadster negotiate a winding mountain road. The worried passenger, red scarf flying, has shifted over in the seat to put more distance between herself and the edge of the road that falls off steeply to her right.

Version A (Rdr 3a)

◉ *Country Life,* August 1928

◉ *Harper's Bazaar,* August 1928, p. 16

◉ *Vanity Fair,* August 1928, p. 84

◉ *Vogue,* August 15, 1928, p. 103+

MOUNTAIN ROAD

The second version (B) of this 1928 Roadster ad includes a very minor text change – the addition of *"four 30 x 4.5 balloon tires"* and *"electric windshield wipers on closed cars"* to the list of features of the Roadster.

Version B (Rdr 3b) [text difference]
○ *The Farmer's Wife,* August 1928, p. 19
○ *Ladies' Home Journal,* August 1928, p. 96
○ *McCall's,* August 1928, p. 54

A third *"Mountain Road"* ad version (C) features a slightly shortened headline and modified text.

Version C (Rdr 3c) ➤
○ *Good Housekeeping,* August 1928, p. 121

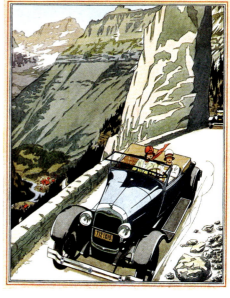

Smooth riding ease and restful comfort
make the new Ford an especially good car for women

WHEN you see the new Ford, you are impressed instantly by its low, trim, graceful lines and the beauty of its two-tone color harmonies.

As you watch it in traffic and on the open road you can note how quickly it accelerates and get some idea, too, of the speed and power of its 40-horse-power engine.

But only by driving the new Ford yourself can you fully appreciate the easy-riding comfort that is such an outstanding feature of this car.

One reason, of course, is the use of Houdaille hydraulic shock absorbers, formerly used on only the most expensive automobiles. Yet even Houdaille shock absorbers of themselves do not account for the complete riding comfort of the new Ford.

Equally important are the design and construction of the new transverse springs, the low center of gravity, and what engineers speak of as the low ratio of unsprung weight to the sprung weight of the car.

All of these factors combine to soften or eliminate the force of road shocks and to make the new Ford an exceptionally comfortable and easy-riding car at all speeds. Even rough roads may be taken at a fast pace without hard jolts or bumps or the exaggerated bouncing rebound which is the cause of most motoring fatigue.

You have a feeling of mental comfort, too, in driving the new Ford because of its reliability and the safety afforded by its steel body,

Ford Motor Co.
DETROIT, MICH.

four-wheel brakes and Triplex shatter-proof glass windshield. This freedom from mechanical trouble—this security—means a great deal to every woman who drives a car.

Prove this for yourself by asking the nearest Ford dealer to bring the new Ford to your home for a demonstration. Check up on comfort, on speed, on power, on acceleration, on economy, on safety, and you will know there is nothing like it anywhere in design, quality and price.

Every purchaser shares the benefits of the Ford policy of selling at a small margin of profit—of owning the source of raw materials—of constantly giving greater and greater value.

August 1928 Good Housekeeping

The Williamson illustration in the *"Mountain Road"* Roadster ad was also used outside of the United States. For example, it appeared, along with an insert illustration of the Model A shock absorber, in a Swedish magazine ad.

◄ Example ad from Sweden
⊙ *Husmoderns,* September 1929, p. 3

This Roadster drawing has also been spotted in Australian Ford advertising – but printed in a reversed image format in order to depict a right-hand drive Model A.

Alla vägar äro goda vägar för den nya Ford

Backtagningsförmåga och acceleration, styrka och lättframkomlighet äro de egenskaper, som göra den nya Ford så lämpad för vårt land och dess mången gång besvärliga körförhållanden.

Dessa egenskaper förklara också de nya Fordvagnarnas stora popularitet landet runt. Ty vem glädes icke åt en vagn, för vilken inga backar tyckas för branta, inga vägar oframkomliga, som säkert och oförtröttligt gör fullgod tjänst under de svåraste körförhållanden.

Ni möter icke många backar, som ej den nya Fordvagnen tar på högsta växeln. Och när Ni märker hur kvickt den accelererar —

från 8 till 40 km. på 8 sekunder – då känner Ni att den 40 hästar starka motorn har stora kraftreserver.

I en terräng som den svenska, med dess slingrande, smala vägar är det också av ovärderlig betydelse att vagnen är så behändig och lättkörd, att bromssystemet är så tillförlitligt. Fords sexbromssystem — helt inbyggt till skydd mot regn, smuts och damm — gör att vagnen även vid hög fart stannar mjukt och tyst — på några få meter.

De kraftiga, bredbladiga fjädrarna äga smidig styrka och böjlighet, och de dubbelverkande Houdaillestötdämparna förtaga vägbanans ojämnheter och göra att vagnen tar kurvorna utan krängning.

De nya Fordvagnarna äro alla utrustade med dubbelverkande, hydrauliska Houdaillestötdämpare, varför vagnarna även i tvära kurvor ligga liksom »klistrade» vid vägen.

FORD

Tudor Sedan Kr. 3.350, Fordor Sedan Kr. 3.710, Roadster Kr. 2.750, Phaeton Kr. 2.800, Standard Kupé Kr. 3.375, Special Kupé Kr. 3.550, Sport Kupé Kr. 3.575. Alla priser gälla fob Stockholm, Göteborg eller Malmö.

FORD MOTOR COMPANY A/B · STOCKHOLM

3

MISSED PUTT

◆

Look beneath the hood and study the mechanical beauty of the new Ford

When you look beneath the hood and study the engine of the new Ford, you will begin to understand how carefully this car is made, and see something, too, of the enduring quality that has been built into every part.

In the homely, yet expressive words of the man in the shop when he pays his highest tribute to a fine piece of machinery: "It is a sweet mechanical job."

There is no better illustration of the care with which the new Ford is built than the close limits of measurement maintained in manufacturing.

The diameter of the piston pin in the new Ford, for instance, is held within three ten-thousandths (.0003) of an inch. An equally close limit is followed in the diameter of the hole into which the piston pin is fitted.

In the piston assemblies, consisting of piston, connecting rod, pin and spring retainer, the four assemblies in each motor must match in weight within a limit of 3½ grams. This means that every piston assembly

must meet the weight of each of the other assemblies in the set within approximately ⅛ of an ounce.

Another example of the close limits of measurement in the new Ford is found in the crankshaft, which is both statically and dynamically balanced.

The dynamic balance, which insures equal distribution of weight in the throws of the shaft, is held within 4 grams, or approximately 1/7 of an ounce, within the 2⅛-inch radius from the center-line of the shaft. Main and connecting rod bearings on the crankshaft are held true to within three ten-thousandths (.0003) of an inch.

This same care is followed in the making of large as well as small parts. The four-wheel brake drums on the new Ford are 11 inches in diameter, yet they are held to within five one-thousandths (.005) of an inch. This is a remarkably close limit on such a wide diameter and is unusual in brake drums.

It is, of course, almost beyond imagination to conceive of measurements as close as these. They are achieved only through the use of the finest precision gages in the hands of expert workmen. These are set by Johansson master gage blocks which are accurate to one-millionth of an inch.

All of this care and this fine automobile engineering are reflected in the outstanding performance and reliability of the new Ford—in everything that goes to make it the advanced expression of a wholly new idea in modern, economical transportation.

Make it a point, therefore, to see and examine the new Ford and arrange for a demonstration. Only when you get behind the wheel can you fully appreciate its alert speed, its quick acceleration, its power, its safety and ease of control, and its truly remarkable riding comfort. There is, indeed, nothing quite like it anywhere in design, quality and price.

Ford

Ford Motor Company
Detroit, Mich.

A carefree couple in their new Ford Roadster speed by the golf course. Their noisy passing causes the (quite agitated) golfer to miss the putt he was attempting before being so abruptly distracted.

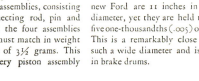

Version A (Rdr 4a)

○ *Cosmopolitan*, September 1928, p. 134
◉ *The Redbook Magazine*, September 1928, p. 98

Three different versions of the *"Missed Putt"* Roadster ad were produced.

MISSED PUTT

The angry expression on the golfer's face and the caddy's quick footwork to avoid being hit by the errant golf ball dramatize the distraction caused by the passing Ford Roadster.

The second *"Missed Putt"* ad version (B) uses a new head-line much more in line with the ad's illustration – *"All the world looks up as the new Ford Roadster flashes by."*

> **Version B (Rdr 4b)** ➤
>
> ⊙ *The American Boy,* September 1928, CII

A third ad version (C) is a two-page edition showing the Roadster partnered with a Ford Sport Coupe.

> **Version C (Rdr 4c)** ⌄
>
> ⊙ *The Literary Digest,* August 25, 1928, CF
> ⊙ *The Saturday Evening Post,* August 4, 1928, pp. 72-73

ANTIQUE SHOP

Look beneath the hood and study the mechanical beauty of the new Ford

WHEN you look beneath the hood and study the engine of the new Ford, you will begin to understand how carefully this car is made, and see something, too, of the enduring quality that has been built into every part.

In the homely, yet expressive words

The mechanical beauty of the new Ford is matched by its beauty of line, color and finish. Shown here is the roomy Tudor Sedan, in the beautiful Arabian Sand color. All Ford cars are finished in a choice of two-tone color harmonies.

of the man in the shop when he pays his highest tribute to a fine piece of machinery: "It is a sweet mechanical job."

There is no better illustration of the care with which the new Ford is built than the close limits of measurement maintained in manufacturing.

The diameter of the piston pin in the new Ford, for instance, is held within three ten-thousandths (.0003) of an inch.

In the piston assemblies, consisting of piston, connecting rod, pin and spring retainer, the four assemblies in each motor must match in weight within a limit of 3½ grams.

The dynamic balance, which insures equal distribution of weight in the throws of the crankshaft of the new Ford, is held within 4 grams, or approximately 1/7 of an ounce, within the 2⅛-inch radius from the center-line of the shaft.

Main and connecting rod bearings on the crankshaft are held true to

Ford

FORD MOTOR COMPANY
Detroit, Michigan

within three ten-thousandths (.0003) of an inch. This same care is followed in the making of large as well as small parts. The four-wheel brake drums on the new Ford are 11 inches in diameter, yet they are held to within five one-thousandths (.005) of an inch. This is a remarkably close limit on such a wide diameter and is unusual in brake drums.

It is, of course, almost beyond imagination to conceive of measurements as close as these. They are achieved only through the use of the finest precision gages in the hands of expert workmen. These are set by Johansson master gage blocks which are accurate to one-millionth of an inch.

All of this care and this fine automobile engineering are reflected in the alert speed, the quick acceleration, the safety and the remarkable riding comfort of the new Ford—in everything that goes to make it the advanced expression of a wholly new idea in modern, economical transportation.

Two ladies are spending the day antique shopping in their new top-down Ford Roadster. As they leave the antique store, they receive assistance from the shopkeeper in locating the next antique shop.

Version A (Rdr 5a)
◉ *Country Life,* September 1928, p. 27
◉ *The Sportsman,* September 1928, p. 69
◉ *Vanity Fair,* September 1928, p. 17

Version B (Rdr 5b) [text difference]
◉ *Liberty,* September 15, 1928, p. 7

November, 1928   71

The new Ford has a very simple and effective lubrication system

If you could look into the engine of the new Ford, you would be surprised at the simplicity of the lubrication system. It is a combination of pump, splash and gravity feed and is unusually effective.

Let's study it a little and see just how it works.

The oil pump draws the oil from the bottom of the oil pan through a fine mesh wire screen or filter and delivers it quickly to the valve chamber. Even when you are traveling at only thirty miles an hour, the five quarts of oil in the pan pass through the pump *twice* in every mile.

From the valve chamber the oil flows by gravity to the main bearings of the crankshaft and front camshaft bearing. Reservoirs of oil are provided for each main bearing pipe opening through a series of ingenious dams at the bottom of the valve chamber.

After filling these reservoirs, the surplus oil flows down an overflow pipe to the front of the oil pan tray. In this tray are four troughs

into which dip the scoops on the connecting rods. These scoops pick up the oil and throw it into the grooves of the swiftly moving crankpin bearings. They also send an oil spray over the cylinder walls, camshaft and timing gears. From the tray the oil flows back to the oil pan, from where it is again drawn through the oil strainer into the pump.

The only movable part in the entire Ford engine lubrication system is the oil pump. From valve chamber down, the entire flow of oil is an easy, natural flow—as simple in principle as water running downhill. There's no need of pressure.

Because the new Ford is such a good car and is built to such close and exact measurements, it should be given the care that is given every fine piece of machinery. When you consider that each piston moves up and down at the rate of 1300 times a minute, when your car is moving at only thirty miles an hour, you can see the need of complete and proper lubrication

The oiling system of the new Ford is so simple in design and effective in action that it requires practically no service attention. There is only one thing to do, but that is a very important thing . . . keep enough oil in the oil pan so that the indicator rod always registers full (F) and change the oil every 500 miles.

The lubrication of the chassis also is important. It has been made simple and easy in the new Ford by the use of the high pressure grease gun system. In order to insure best performance, the chassis should be lubricated every 500 miles.

Every 2000 miles the distributor cam should be cleaned and given a light film of vaseline. At 5000 miles, the lubricant in the differential and transmission should be drained, the housings cleaned, and new lubricant added.

Ford dealers have been specially trained to oil and grease the new Ford. They know which oil is best and they have special equipment to do the job right, and at a fair price.

Ford

Ford Motor Company
Detroit, Michigan

It's a little crowded in this Ford Roadster as a woman (behind the wheel) and two men (perched on the top of the seat) watch the horse show. Distracting their attention from the show is an approaching (ribbon-wearing) rider.

Version A (Rdr 6a)
◉ *The American Boy,* November 1928, p. 71

This drawing also appeared in a November 24, 1928 Tudor Sedan ad in *The Saturday Evening Post.*

35

DUDE RANCH

◆

Fresh and relaxed at the journey's end

ONE of the fine things about driving the new Ford is the way it takes you over the miles without fuss or fatigue.

Mentally you are at ease because you are sure of the mechanical performance of the car. No matter how long the trip, or rough or devious the roadway, you know it will bring you safely, quickly to the journey's end.

Through thickest traffic, up steepest hills, along the open road, you will drive with security and confidence because the new Ford is so alert and capable and so easy to operate and control.

The steering wheel responds readily to a light touch. Gears shift smoothly and silently. The brakes take hold quickly and firmly even on rain-swept pavements.

Unusual acceleration, speed and power are especially appreciated in emergencies. A space little longer than the car itself is all you need for parking.

These features simplify the mechanics of driving and, together with reliability, add a great deal to the mental comfort of motoring.

Physically, too, you will feel fresh and relaxed in the new Ford because it is such a roomy, easy-riding car. The restfully tilted seats are made generously wide and are deeply cushioned, with coil springs of both straight and hour-glass type. The backs are carefully

designed to conform to the curves of the body.

Perhaps the most outstanding feature of the new Ford is found in its riding comfort. Somehow it seems to just glide along, as if every road were a good road. The rough spots are there, just as they have always been, but you do not feel them. It is almost as if a giant hand had smoothed the way before you. Even bad stretches may be taken at a reasonably fast pace without hard jolts or bumps or the exaggerated bouncing which is the cause of most motoring fatigue.

One reason, of course, is the use of four

Ford

FORD MOTOR COMPANY
Detroit, Michigan

Houdaille hydraulic double-acting shock absorbers—two in the front and two in the rear. Of even greater importance, however, are the low center of gravity, the carefully planned balance of the car, and the many advantages of the transverse or crosswise springs.

These springs rest on their flexible ends with the heavy center part uppermost. Thus the very weight of the springs receives the benefit of spring action instead of hanging below as dead weight and increasing the hammer-like blows of road impacts.

Another element in decreasing unsprung weight (weight below the flexible ends of the springs) is the design and construction of the front axle and rear axle housing. Through the use of fine steel and electric welding, they are made of exceptional strength, yet kept comparatively light in weight. All of these factors combine to reduce the force of every unevenness in the road before it reaches the frame, chassis and body of the car. This means more comfort for you personally and also contributes to better performance and longer life for every mechanical part.

Attractive colors give added charm to the trim, graceful lines of the new Ford. Shown above is the new Ford Roadster in Bonnie Gray. On the left, the new Ford Coupe in Andalusite Blue.

A porter is directed in the unloading of the Ford Roadster as it arrives at the dude ranch. Guests, lounging on the porch, appear in a variety of western apparel – including riding britches, chaps and a 10-gallon hat.

Version A (Rdr 7a)

⊙ *Collier's,* May 11, 1929, CIII

○ *Cosmopolitan,* May 1929, p. 6

⊙ *Liberty,* May 4, 1929. p. 19

⊙ *The Redbook Magazine,* May 1929, p. 100

DUDE RANCH

The second (black and white) version (B) of the *"Dude Ranch"* Roadster ad uses a similar text. However, it replaces the smaller Ford Coupe insert illustration appearing in the initial ad version (A) with a Ford Sport Coupe insert illustration.

Version B (Rdr 7b) ➤
⊙ *The American Boy,* May 1929, p. 29

A third version (C) retains the same ad text and *"Fresh and relaxed at the journey's end"* headline, but changes to a Fordor Sedan insert illustration.

Fresh and relaxed at the journey's end

Fresh and relaxed at the journey's end

◄ **Version C (Rdr 7c)**
○ *The Literary Digest,* July, 20 1929, p. 51

Not all Williamson drawings appeared as the primary illustration in Model A magazine ads. Some were used only as smaller insert illustrations in ads for a different Model A body style.

For example, both of the smaller Sport Coupe (B) and Fordor Sedan (C) drawings appearing as insert illustrations in the *"Dude Ranch"* Roadster ads are unique drawings. They never appeared as the primary illustrations in magazine ads for their respective Model A body styles.

DUDE RANCH

The final version of this 1929 Ford Roadster ad is a two-page edition which includes two insert illustrations, plus a list of the *"Features of the Ford Car."*

Version D (Rdr 7d) ∨
⊙ *The Saturday Evening Post,* April 20, 1929, pp. 66-67

Women appreciate our COURTEOUS SERVICE

THE cheerfulness with which the Ford car responds to exacting demands is equalled right here in the attitude of our workmen. Your problems are made their problems — then solved with the speed and precision expected of Ford experts.

Drive in for service that saves time, money and worry. Most modern specialized equipment. Genuine Ford parts and flat-rate charges. Periodic inspection, greasing, accessories, painting, washing and polishing.

 Nolan Motor Co., Inc.
1111 18th St. N. W.
Phone, Decatur 0216-17-18

GENUINE FORD PARTS • FLAT RATES FOR REPAIRS

Ford dealers sometimes created local ads to supplement those prepared by the Ford Motor Company. As an example, a quarter-page dealer magazine ad, featuring a Model A Roadster, was prepared by the Nolan Motor Car Co., in Washington, D.C. The ad appeared in the District of Columbia Edition of the *American Motorist* magazine.

◄ **Example Ford dealer ad**
○ *American Motorist,* July 1930, p. 72

GOING GOLFING

◆

Good performance with economy

T̲HE new Ford is more than a new automobile. It is the expression of an ideal—an ideal that looks to bringing the benefits of modern transportation to all the people.

Because of this purpose, the price is low and great care has been taken to insure economy of operation and up-keep. Few features are of greater importance to millions of motorists.

Figures from many sources show that the new Ford averages 20 miles per gallon of gasoline, with thousands of Ford owners reporting greater mileage on long trips. Oil consumption is also low. There is a considerable saving on tires due to the balance of the car, ease of steering and perfected wheel design.

All tires used on new Ford cars and recommended for replacement are specially built by leading tire manufacturers according to specifications laid down by the Ford Motor Company.

Mechanical up-keep is low because of simplicity of design and the enduring quality that has been built into every part.

Definite evidence of the economy of the new Ford is shown in repeated and growing purchases by Federal and city governments, by police departments, and by large industrial companies which keep day-by-day cost records. The new Ford has been chosen only after exhaustive tests covering every feature of automobile value and performance.

FORD MOTOR COMPANY
Detroit, Michigan

A further advantage is the Ford policy of not making radical yearly changes. This serves to protect and maintain the investment of every Ford owner. Wherever possible, improvements in the new Ford are made so that present owners may take advantage of them quickly and at low cost.

The availability of Ford dealers throughout the world and close factory supervision of all service are additional reasons for the economy of the new Ford. This service begins with proper instruction when you buy the car and includes a free inspection at 500, at 1000 and at 1500 miles.

No matter where you live or where you go, you will never be very far from a Ford dealer who has been specially trained and equipped to help you get many thousands of miles of pleasant, enjoyable motoring at a minimum of trouble and expense.

Shown above, in the college scene, is the dashing Ford Roadster. On the left, the Sport Coupe. All of the new Ford cars are furnished in a choice of colors.

Two students load their golf clubs into their Ford Roadster to head off to the golf course. They receive some envious stares from their fellow classmates who, with books open (and one thrown into the air in frustration), are trying to study under a tree.

Version A (Rdr 8a)

◉ *The American Boy,* June 1929, p. 29

This ad appeared only in the June 1929 edition of one U.S. magazine.

CENTAUR DOCK

THE NEW FORD ROADSTER

Built for many thousands of miles

THE new Ford has been designed and built to give you many thousands of miles of faithful, economical service. Beneath its flashing beauty of line and color—in those vital mechanical parts which you may never see—is a high quality of material and accuracy in manufacturing. The reliability and capable performance of the car, in all weather and under all conditions, make it a particularly good choice for constant use. « « « « « It stands up under the added strain of bad roads and hard daily service in a way that has always been characteristic of the Ford. The experience of the passing months and years will increase your satisfaction in its performance and confirm your first impression that it is a "value far above the price."

Both the captain and cook from the *"Centaur"* yacht admire the new Ford Roadster parked on the dock. The woman in the Roadster must be either very short (standing on the seat) or very tall (kneeling on the seat).

Version A (Rdr 9a)
⊙ *Collier's,* June 7, 1930, CIII

Five different versions of this 1930 Model A Roadster ad were produced.

CENTAUR DOCK

The *"Centaur Dock"* ad is one of the few Ford Roadster ads to show the windshield folded down on the car.

The second version of this Roadster ad (B) is a black and white edition with a shortened text and a completely different headline – *"An admired grace of line and contour."*

Version B (Rdr 9b) ➤
⊙ *The American Boy,* June 1930, p. 31

The two-page ad edition (C) uses the same *"Built for Many Thousands of Miles"* headline and text used in an earlier ad version (A).

Version C (Rdr 9c) ⋁
⊙ *The Literary Digest,* June 28, 1930, CF

THE NEW FORD ROADSTER

An admired grace of line and contour

SEEING the new Ford as it speeds along the broad highway or parked proudly amid distinguished surroundings, you are impressed by its flowing grace of line and beautiful colors. . . . Talking to Ford owners or to experienced mechanics you hear noteworthy praise of its mechanical performance. . . . To motorists everywhere, its safety, its comfort, its reliability and its surprising ease of operation and control have put a new joy in motoring.

Built for Many Thousands of Miles

THE new Ford has been designed and built to give you many thousands of miles of faithful, economical service. Beneath its flashing beauty of line and color—in those vital mechanical parts which you may never see—is a high quality of material and accuracy in manufacturing. The reliability and capable performance of the car, in all weather and under all conditions, make it a particularly good choice for constant use. « « « «

It stands up under the added strain of bad roads and hard daily service in a way that has always been characteristic of the Ford car. The experience of the passing months and years will increase your satisfaction in its performance and confirm your first impression that it is a value far above the price. « « « «

THE NEW FORD ROADSTER

CENTAUR DOCK

The fourth and fifth versions of this 1930 Ford Roadster ad use the same (new) *"A joyous car for golden summer days"* headline and the almost identical text – but moved to appear above the Roadster illustration. However, one ad version (D) does not contain the Ford logo, while the other (E) includes it within the text of the ad.

Version D (Rdr 9d) ➤

- ◉ *Delineator,* August 1930, CIII
- ○ *The Farmer's Wife,* August 1930, p. 14
- ○ *Ladies' Home Journal,* August 1930, p. 63
- ○ *McCall's,* August 1930, p. 44
- ◉ *Pictorial Review,* August 1930, CIII
- ○ *Woman's Home Companion,* August 1930, p. 44

The Farmer's Wife, August, 1930

A joyous car for golden summer days

MANY are the delights of the Ford Roadster these golden summer days. Short the miles and pleasant because of its alert and sprightly performance. its safety and its easy-riding comfort.

And what a joy it is to travel along the way with the top down. the blue sky overhead and the fresh. cool air brushing a rosy glow upon your cheeks! Rare indeed the woman who has not hoped that some day such a car might be her very own. That dream. long cherished. may now come true. For the Ford Roadster. with all its beauty of line and mechanical excellence. is most conveniently priced. Many months of glorious motoring await your beckoning.

THE NEW FORD ROADSTER

A joyous car for golden summer days

MANY are the delights of the Ford Roadster these golden summer days. Short the miles and pleasant because of its alert and sprightly performance. its safety and its easy-riding comfort.

And what a joy it is to travel along the way with the top down. the blue sky overhead and the fresh. cool air brushing a rosy glow upon your cheeks! Rare indeed the woman who has not hoped that some day such a car might be her very own.

That dream. long cherished. may now come true. For the new Ford Roadster. with all its flashing beauty of line and unusual mechanical excellence. is most conveniently priced. Many months of glorious motoring await your beckoning.

THE NEW FORD ROADSTER

◄ Version E (Rdr 9e)

- ○ *Good Housekeeping,* August 1930, p. 157
- ◉ *Harper's Bazaar,* August 1930, p. 8+
- ◉ *True Story,* August 1930, p. 57
- ◉ *Vogue,* August 2, 1930, p. 89

This Model A Roadster ad, across its five different versions, appeared in a wide variety of publication types – including general interest magazines, upscale magazines, women's fashion magazines, and a youth-oriented magazine.

No other Model A Roadster magazine ad appeared in as many publications as did the 1930 *"Centaur Dock"* ad.

GUARD BOOTH COP

◆

Lengthening the Arm of the Law

THE substantial worth of the new Ford is reflected in its alert, capable performance and economy of operation and up-keep. Men and women everywhere have found it ideally suited to their business and social needs. Its many uses make it truly The Universal Car.

An interesting use of the Ford is by police departments for the detection and apprehension of criminals. In their ceaseless vigil, these cars are driven in all kinds of weather, virtually twenty-four hours a day.

A fleet of 12 Model A Fords in Louisville covered a total of 2,620,800 miles in twelve

months, or the equivalent of 105 times around the world. Five new Fords on police duty in Niagara Falls have been driven more than 100,000 miles each. In Miami a police Ford has gone 120,000 miles.

The average for the eighteen Fords in Omaha is 35,000 miles per car for two years of police service. The superintendent of automotive equipment says the cost of repairs has been "very low."

The police departments of New York, Chicago,

Philadelphia, Boston, Detroit, San Francisco and other large cities use hundreds of Ford cars and trucks. In New York, the total exceeds 450.

Large industrial companies operating large fleets of Ford cars and trucks report the same reliability and good service. Long, hard usage emphasizes the value of simplicity of design, high quality of materials and unusual care in manufacturing and assembling.

The first cost of the new Ford is low, and you can purchase it on convenient, economical terms through the Authorized Ford Finance Plans of the Universal Credit Company.

A policeman in a spotlight- and siren-equipped Ford Roadster pauses at a guard booth to chat with the guard on duty.

Version A (Rdr 10a)

- ◉ *The American Boy,* May 1931, CII
- ○ *The American Magazine,* May 1931, p. 111
- ◉ *Collier's,* April 11, 1931, CIII

Version A (Rdr 10a) continued

- ◉ *Liberty,* May 16, 1931, CII
- ◉ *Life,* April 3, 1931, CII
- ○ *The Literary Digest,* March 21, 1931, p. 32
- ◉ *The Redbook Magazine,* May 1931, p. 90
- ○ *The Saturday Evening Post,* March 14, 1931, p. 43
- ● *The State Trooper,* February 1931, CIV (B&W)

DE LUXE ROADSTER

	TOTAL	1930	1931
Ford Body Style		40-B (Dlx.)	40-B (Dlx.)
Weight (pounds)		2,230	2,230
Price (FOB Detroit)		$520	$475
Units Produced (U.S.)	64,315	11,318	52,997
Number of U.S. Ads			
Primary Formats	1	–	1
Ad Variations	4	–	4
Magazine Insertions	16	–	16

In hopes of offsetting the declining sales being experienced by the Model A Roadster, Ford introduced the Model A De Luxe Roadster (40-B De Luxe) in August 1930. This sporty vehicle had a side-mounted spare tire, cowl lights and a trunk rack as standard equipment. (In 1931, the fender-mounted tire and trunk rack were no longer standard equipment on this Model A body style.)

While the production of the Ford De Luxe Roadster began in 1930, magazine ads for this Model A body style were not produced until April 1931. Rather than using a variety of different ads, as was the case with the (standard) Roadster, Ford produced only one basic De Luxe Roadster ad, with several ad text variations. These ads, again unlike those for the earlier (standard) Roadster, showed the De Luxe Roadster with the top up.

SEAPLANE HOUSE

A Dashing New Ford Roadster

THE words *de luxe* are a fitting description of the beautiful new Ford De Luxe Roadster. In grace of line, color, and appointments it reflects the latest mode in a dashing sport car.

The swagger tan top has natural wood bows and can be raised or lowered easily and quickly. The wide seat is upholstered in genuine Bedouin grain leather with narrow piping. The new slanting windshield folds flat and is made of Triplex shatter-proof glass, as are the windshield wings. A comfortable rumble seat with ample room for two people is provided as standard equipment.

The new Ford De Luxe Roadster is available in a variety of special body colors, with an additional harmonizing color for the sturdy steel-spoke wheels. Many exterior metal parts are made of bright, gleaming Rustless Steel that will retain its enduring luster for the life of the car.

Two ladies have parked their new Ford De Luxe Roadster on the patio. One woman raises her arms as if they were airplane wings as she greets the couple fueling their seaplane. A boat is parked in the "garage" beneath the house.

Version A (DRd 1a)
- *Country Life*, April 1931, p. 114
- *Harper's Bazaar*, April 1931, p. 160
- *The Sportsman*, April 1931, p. 89
- *Vanity Fair*, April 1931, p. 98
- *Vogue*, April 15, 1931

SEAPLANE HOUSE

The second and third versions (B and C) of the 1931 *"Seaplane House"* ad have only slight text differences.

Version B (DRd 1b) [text difference]

○ *The Farmer's Wife,* May 1931, p. 15
○ *Good Housekeeping,* May 1931, p. 120
◉ *Holland's,* April 1931, p. 28
◉ *Liberty,* April 18, 1931, CIII
◉ *Life,* May 1, 1931, CII
○ *The Saturday Evening Post,* May 30, 1931, p. 32
◉ *True Story,* June 1931

The Canadian version of this 1931 Ford De Luxe Roadster ad includes *"The Canadian Car"* tag line.

Example ad from Canada ➤

◉ *Maclean's Magazine,* June 1, 1931

Maclean's Magazine, June 1, 1931

A Dashing Ford Roadster

The words *de luxe* are a fitting description of the beautiful Ford De Luxe Road-ter. In grace of line, colors and appointments it reflects the latest mode in a dashing sport car.

The swagger top has natural wood bows and can be raised or lowered easily and quickly. The wide seat is upholstered in genuine leather with narrow piping. The new slanting wind-shield folds flat and is made of shatterless glass, as are the windshield wings. A comfortable rumble seat is provided as standard equipment. Side fender-well is extra at small cost.

The Ford De Luxe Roadster is available in a variety of body colors, with an additional harmonizing color for the sturdy steel-spoke wheels. Many exterior metal parts are finished in bright Rustless Steel that will maintain its gleaming luster undimmed throughout the life of the car.

"THE CANADIAN CAR"

FORD MOTOR COMPANY OF CANADA, LIMITED

Version C (DRd 1c) [text difference]

◉ *Delineator,* May 1931, p. 87
○ *Ladies' Home Journal,* May 1931, p. 75
○ *Woman's Home Companion,* May 1931

The final *"Seaplane House"* ad version (D) uses a completely different, youth-oriented, format. It provides educational information on how an engine works, how an airplane flies, and how glass is made – and includes an "ecology" message signed by Henry Ford.

◄ Version D (DRd 1d)

◉ *The American Boy,* April 1931, p. 76

PHAETON

	TOTAL	1927	1928	1929	1930	1931
Ford Body Style		35-A	35-A	35-A	35-B	35-B
Weight (pounds)		2,140	2,140	2,140	2,212	2,212
Price (FOB Detroit)		$395	$395	$460	$440	$435
Units Produced (U.S.)	117,840	221	47,255	49,818	16,470	4,076
Number of U.S. Ads						
Primary Formats	5	–	–	4	1	–
Ad Variations	11	–	–	9	2	–
Magazine Insertions	27	–	–	20	7	–

The Phaeton was among the six Model A Ford body styles first announced in December 1927. The Phaeton was a four-door convertible and was introduced without outside door handles. Beginning in 1929, external door handles were added – as well as wind wings – as standard equipment. With the 1930 models and the new Model A Ford body styles, the Phaeton had wider doors, making entry easier to both the front and rear compartments. (Because of the later availability of the De Luxe Phaeton, the Phaeton was sometimes referred to as the "Standard Phaeton" – but never so in Ford advertising.)

The Model A Ford Phaeton was advertised almost exclusively in farm-related magazines, but with ads appearing only in 1929 and 1930. Ford produced a total of 11 different magazine ad versions for the Phaeton during these two years. Each of the five different basic Phaeton illustrations used in these 11 ads showed the car with its top down and the boot in place.

LEAVING HOME

◆

April, 1929   THE COUNTRY GENTLEMAN

Many factors contribute to the safety of the new Ford

SAFETY, comfort, reliability, economy, speed, acceleration, beauty—these are the features that make the new Ford such a good value. Of all, there is none more important than SAFETY.

The safety of the new Ford comes not only from its efficient brakes, but from many other factors. Among these are ease of steering and control, the Triplex shatter-proof glass windshield, and the sturdy, balanced construction of the car.

A particularly interesting feature of the Ford car is the manner in which electric welding has been carried forward to new usefulness through the creation and development of hundreds of special welding machines.

This very important and increasingly valuable tool of modern manufacturing makes it possible to use one-piece units instead of several parts riveted or bolted together, with resulting gain in strength and simplicity.

It also permits the use of steel forgings instead of castings or stampings, without increase in weight or greatly increased cost. Steel forgings are used not only in the front axle, steering gear, transmission, clutch, drive shaft and rear axle housing of the new Ford, but in the shock absorber parts, emergency brake lever, torque tube flange, and everywhere else where great strength is required. The strength of steel forgings makes for unusual safety.

Another safety factor worth noting is the manner in which the new Ford holds the road at all speeds. This is due to the low center of gravity, the carefully-planned balance or distribution of structural and mechanical weight, and the low ratio of unsprung weight to sprung weight. The co-ordinated action of the transverse springs and Houdaille hydraulic shock absorbers controls exaggerated bouncing up and down.

One of the outstanding features of the new Ford, of course, is its mechanical, internal-expanding six-brake system. This is unusually reliable and effective because the surfaces of all six brakes are fully enclosed. Thus there is no possibility of water, dirt or oil interfering with the brake action at any time or under any conditions.

Screeching and groaning are prevented by an exclusive Ford self-centering feature which brings the entire surface of the brake shoe in uniform contact with the brake drum the instant you press your foot on the brake pedal.

The value of the protection afforded by the Triplex shatter-proof glass windshield of the new Ford is shown by a recent survey indicating that 65% of injuries in automobile accidents are due to flying glass. The windshield in the new Ford is so made that it will not shatter under the hardest impact. Particularly where there are women and children, it is an important safety factor.

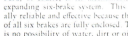

FORD MOTOR COMPANY
Detroit, Michigan

FEATURES OF THE NEW FORD CAR

Fully enclosed, silent six-brake system

Four Houdaille hydraulic double-acting shock absorbers

Triplex shatter-proof glass windshield

Vibration-absorbing engine support

Alemite chassis lubrication

Ten body types

Choice of a number of colors in each body type

Quick acceleration

55 to 65 miles an hour

Reliability and economy

As they prepare to leave home with the Phaeton's top down, Mother provides a blanket for Grandpa and Grandma brings Junior around to the car. The gardener, rolling the lawn, pauses to watch the family preparing to depart.

Version A (Phn 1a)
○ *The Country Gentleman,* April 1929, p. 95
◉ *Southern Agriculturist,* April 1, 1929, CIII (B&W)

Version B (Phn 1b) [text difference]
◉ *Capper's Farmer,* April 1929, CIII

LEAVING HOME

The second and third versions (B and C) of this Ford Phaeton magazine ad have a slightly different list of the specific *"Features of the New Ford Car"* than contained in the first ad version (A). However, the second version (B) keeps the same ad text, while the third (C) has a slightly modified text.

The Williamson drawing used in the *"Leaving Home"* ad was not limited to use only in the United States. It also appeared in several other countries – including in an English-language Ford Phaeton ad produced by Ford Motor Company Exports, Inc., Shanghai, China.

> **Example ad from China** ➤
> ◉ *The China Weekly Review,* May 25, 1929, p. 6

Note that the price of the car in the Chinese ad is listed as *"Tls.1,450 (including Bumpers & Extra Tire)."*

> **Version C (Phn 1c) [text difference]**
> ○ *Farm & Fireside,* April 1929, CII
> ○ *Successful Farming,* April 1929, p. 35

中華郵政特准掛號認爲新聞紙類

Registered at the Chinese Post Office as a newspaper for transmission with special marks privileges in China.

Personal Comfort-Better Performance

NEW FORD PHAETON
Shanghai Price Tls. 1,450 (including Bumpers & Extra Tire)

One of the fine things about driving a new Ford is the way it takes you for miles without fuss or fatigue.

Mentally you are at ease, because you are sure of the mechanical performance of the car. No matter how long the trip or rough or devious the roadway, you know it will bring you safely, quickly to the trip's end.

The steering wheel responds readily to a light touch. Gears shift smoothly and silently. Brakes take hold quickly and firmly even on rain swept pavements, while Houdaille hydraulic shock absorbers relieve the hard jolts and bumps of the rough roads. All of these factors mean more personal comfort for you, and at the same time give you a feeling of superior mechanical performance.

Ford Motor Company Exports Inc.
SHANGHAI

COLD GRANDPA!
A closer look at the family as they prepare to leave home in their Phaeton reveals why Mother is bringing a blanket to the car. Grandpa, already looking quite cold, is gathering his coat around his neck. Just imagine how cold he'll be in the back seat of the top-down Phaeton once they get out on the road!

TRAIN STATION

◆

The new Ford has a very simple and effective lubrication system

If you could look into the engine of the new Ford, you would be surprised at the simplicity of the lubrication system. It is a combination of pump, splash and gravity feed—an exclusive Ford development and unusually effective.

The oil pump draws the oil from the bottom of the oil pan through a fine mesh wire screen or filter and delivers it quickly to the valve chamber. Even when you are traveling at thirty miles an hour, the five quarts of oil in the pan pass through the pump *twice* in every mile.

From the valve chamber the oil flows by gravity to the main bearings of the crankshaft and front camshaft bearing. Reservoirs of oil are provided for each main bearing pipe opening through a series of ingenious dams at the bottom of the valve chamber.

After filling these reservoirs, the surplus oil flows down an overflow pipe to the front of the oil pan tray. In this tray are four troughs into which dip the scoops on the connecting rods. These scoops pick up the oil and throw it into the grooves of the

swiftly moving crankpin bearings. They also send an oil spray over the cylinder walls, camshaft and timing gears. From the tray the oil flows back to the oil pan, whence it is again drawn through the oil strainer into the pump.

The only movable part in the entire Ford engine lubrication system is the oil pump. From valve chamber down, the entire flow of oil is an easy, natural flow—as simple in principle as water running down-hill.

There is only one thing for you to do, but that is a very important thing . . .

All of the new Ford cars are finished in a choice of colors. Other features include four Houdaille hydraulic two-way shock absorbers, Triplex shatter-proof glass windshield, silent, fully enclosed six-brake system, theft-proof coincidental ignition lock, typical Ford reliability, economy and long life.

watch the oil. Keep enough oil in the oil pan so that the indicator rod never registers below low (L) and change the oil every 500 miles.

The lubrication of the chassis is likewise important. It has been made easy in the new Ford by the Alemite high pressure gun system. For best performance, the chassis should be lubricated every 500 miles.

Every 2000 miles the distributor cam should be cleaned and given a light film of vaseline. At 5000 miles, the lubricant in the differential and transmission should be drained, the housings flushed and new lubricant added.

Lubrication means so much to economical, satisfactory performance that it ought not to be neglected. Have your car attended to regularly. Your Ford dealer is best equipped to do this work.

Ford

FORD MOTOR COMPANY
Detroit, Michigan

The lady has just departed the train and says goodbye to her traveling companions as the train leaves the station. Her husband has secured her two suitcases to be loaded into their waiting Ford Phaeton.

Version A (Phn 2a)
⊙ *Capper's Farmer,* June 1929, p. 15
○ *Farm & Fireside,* June 1929, CIII
⊙ *Southern Agriculturist,* June 1, 1929, CIII (B&W)
○ *Successful Farming,* June 1929, CII

TRAIN STATION

A second version (B) of the 1929 Phaeton *"Train Station"* magazine ad retains the same headline but has a minor change in the text.

Version B (Phn 2b) [text difference]
○ *The Country Gentleman,* June 1929, p. 105

As with many Williamson Model A Ford ad illustrations, the *"Train Station"* drawing was also used in magazine ads outside of the United States. As an example, the illustration appeared, a month later, in a black and white Italian Model A ad.

Example ad from Italy ➤
◉ *Le Vie D'Italia,* July 1929, p. 296

BLOWING KISSES AND STARING!

A closer look at the people assembled behind the Ford Phaeton in the *"Train Station"* ad reveals the woman blowing a kiss to the two companions she has just left on the train. (One of her departing friends is returning the kiss.)

In the meantime, a man with his newspaper folded under his arm can't help but stare at the new Model A Phaeton waiting to be loaded with her luggage.

The Ford Phaeton

Features of the Ford car

Sturdy body construction ❦ ❦ Mechanical reliability ❦ ❦ Unusual number of ball and roller bearings ❦ ❦ Alemite chassis lubrication ❦ ❦ Choice of colors ❦ ❦ Four Houdaille hydraulic double-acting shock absorbers ❦ ❦ Triplex shatter-proof glass windshield ❦ ❦ Fully enclosed, silent six-brake system ❦ ❦ Quick acceleration ❦ ❦ 55 to 65 miles an hour ❦ ❦ Smoothness and security at all speeds ❦ ❦ Vibration-absorbing engine support ❦ ❦ Theft-proof ignition lock ❦ ❦ Economy and long life.

While the farm dog enjoys some attention from the visitor, a farmer (in overalls) and his friend (in a suit and tie), admire the Ford Phaeton parked beside his wheat field. Note the wind wings on the Phaeton.

Version A (Phn 3A)
○ *The Country Gentleman,* September 1929, p. 64
○ *Farm & Fireside,* September 1929, CIII
◉ *Southern Agriculturist,* September 1, 1929, CIII (B&W)
○ *Successful Farming,* September 1929, CIII

COUNTY FAIR

◆

CONSIDER THE UNSEEN VALUES
when you buy a motor car

THE FORD PHAETON

Unusual number of ball and roller bearings in the Ford car contributes to smoothness, reliability, economy and long life

IN MANNER of manufacture, as in performance, there is much that is distinctive about the Ford. Principally it concerns the unseen values which have such a great bearing on economy, reliability and long life. Fundamentally it is an expression of the Ford policy and the Ford method of building a motor car.

In designing the Ford, we decided first on the kind of car we wanted to make. Many months were then devoted to the designing of new machines and new manufacturing methods which would enable us to sell it at a price within reach of all the people. The production of such a car at such a low price is even more unusual than the car itself.

Not in exterior things only, but throughout the Ford you find the same high quality of materials and exact, careful workmanship. Prominent among its unseen values is

the extensive use of ball and roller bearings.

There are more than twenty of these in the Ford—an unusually large number. In type and kind they are carefully selected for the work they have to do and are as adequate in size as in number.

Being comparable to the jewels of a fine watch, they prevent unnecessary friction and wear, contribute to smoothness and quiet, reduce up-keep costs and add thousands of miles to the life of the car

Studying the operation of these bearings you can see their practical value to every Ford owner. Steering is made easier and safer because of the roller bearings in the steering gear and because the weight of the car is carried on roller bearings in the front wheels and front axle king pins. The uniformly good performance of the Ford rear axle is due largely to the roller bearings on the rear axle

pinion and differential. These are held to such close limits that adjustment is unnecessary.

From the engine-to-the-road, in fact, the entire drive of the Ford on all forward speeds is wholly on anti-friction ball and roller bearings.

In addition to smoother operation, this saves gasoline, gives the car more speed and power in first and second speeds, decreases noise, and increases the durability and efficiency of the transmission gears.

Similar good results are apparent also in the drive shaft, the generator—wherever ball and roller bearings are used.

There are definite reasons, therefore, for the smooth-running, alert performance of the Ford, and for its economy, reliability and long life. Throughout it has been built to endure—to serve you faithfully and well for many thousands of miles.

FORD MOTOR COMPANY
Detroit, Michigan

A mother waits with her two children in the back seat of their Model A Phaeton at the county fair. The driver chats with a friend as they watch a prize-winning cow being lead alongside the car. A Ferris wheel can be seen in the distance.

Version A (Phn 4a)
◉ *Capper's Farmer,* October 1929, p. 19
○ *The Country Gentleman,* October 1929, p. 75
○ *Farm & Fireside,* October 1929, CIII
○ *Successful Farming,* October 1929, CII

COUNTY FAIR

While this ad was published in October 1929, a feature associated with the yet-to-be-introduced 1930 Ford models is apparent in the drawing of the Phaeton – the (larger) 1930 style hubcaps.

Two additional versions (B and C) were produced for the *"County Fair"* magazine ad. Each of these versions has minor text modifications. However, the more noteworthy differences are in the drawings of the Phaetons featured in these three ad versions.

Version B (Phn 4b) ➤
◉ *Southern Agriculturist,* October 1, 1929, p. 32

CONSIDER THE UNSEEN VALUES
when you buy a motor car

THE NEW FORD PHAETON

Unusual number of ball and roller bearings in new Ford contributes to smoothness, reliability, economy and long life

In manner of manufacture, as in performance, there is much that is distinctive about the new Ford. Principally it concerns the unseen values which have such a great bearing on economy, reliability and long life. Fundamentally it is an expression of the Ford policy and the Ford method of building a motor car.

In designing the new Ford, we decided first on the kind of car we wanted to make. Many months were then devoted to the designing of new machines and new manufacturing methods which would enable us to sell it at a price within reach of all the people. The production of such a car at such a low price is even more unusual than the car itself.

Not in exterior things only, but throughout the new Ford you find the same high quality of materials and exact, careful workmanship. Prominent among its unseen values is the extensive use of ball and roller bearings.

There are more than twenty of these in the new Ford—an unusually large number. In type and kind they are carefully selected for the work they have to do and are as adequate in size as in number.

Being comparable to the jewels of a fine watch, they prevent unnecessary friction and wear, contribute to smoothness and quiet, reduce up-keep costs and add thousands of miles to the life of the car.

Studying the operation of these bearings you can see their value to every Ford owner. Steering is made easier and safer because of the roller bearings in the steering gear and because the weight of the car is carried on roller bearings on the front wheels and front axle king pins. The uniformly good performance of the Ford rear axle is due largely to the roller bearings on the rear axle pinion

and the differential. These are held in such close limits that adjustment is unnecessary.

From the engine-to-the-road, in fact, the entire drive of the new Ford on all forward speeds is wholly on anti-friction ball and roller bearings. In addition to smoother operation, this saves gasoline, gives the car more speed and power in first and second speeds, decreases noise, increases the durability and efficiency of the transmission gears.

Similar good results are apparent also in the drive shaft, the generator—wherever ball and roller bearings are used.

There are definite reasons, therefore, for the smooth-running, alert performance of the new Ford, and for its economy, reliability and long life. Throughout it has been built to endure—to serve you faithfully and well for many thousands of miles.

Ford
Ford Motor Company
Detroit, Michigan

THE AMERICAN BOY—YOUTH'S COMPANION   35

CONSIDER THE UNSEEN VALUES
when you buy a motor car

THE NEW FORD PHAETON

Unusual number of ball and roller bearings in new Ford contributes to smoothness, reliability, economy and long life

In manner of manufacture, as in performance, there is much that is distinctive about the new Ford. Principally it concerns the unseen values which have such a great bearing on economy, reliability and long life. Fundamentally it is an expression of the Ford policy and the Ford method of building a motor car.

In designing the new Ford, we decided first on the kind of car we wanted to make. Many months were then devoted to the designing of new machines and new manufacturing methods which would enable us to sell it at a price within reach of all the people. The production of such a car at such a low price is even more unusual than the car itself.

Not in exterior things only, but throughout the new Ford you find the same high quality of materials and exact, careful workmanship. Prominent among its unseen values is the extensive use of ball and roller bearings.

There are more than twenty of these in the new Ford—an unusually large number. In type and kind they are carefully selected for the work they have to do and are as adequate in size as in number.

Being comparable to the jewels of a fine watch, they prevent unnecessary friction and wear, contribute to smoothness and quiet, reduce up-keep costs and add thousands of miles to the life of the car.

Studying the operation of these bearings you can see their value to every Ford owner. Steering is made easier and safer because the roller bearings in the steering gear and because the weight of the car is carried on roller bearings on the front wheels and front axle king pins. The uniformly good performance of the Ford rear axle is due largely to the roller bearings on the rear axle pinion

and the differential. These are held to such close limits that adjustment is unnecessary.

From the engine-to-the-road, in fact, the entire drive of the Ford on all forward speeds is wholly on anti-friction ball and roller bearings. In addition to smoother operation, this saves gasoline, gives the car more speed and power in first and second speeds, decreases noise, and increases the durability and efficiency of the transmission gears.

Similar good results are apparent also in the drive shaft, the generator—wherever ball and roller bearings are used.

There are definite reasons, therefore, for the smooth-running, alert performance of the new Ford, and for its economy, reliability and long life. Throughout it has been built to endure—to serve you faithfully and well for many thousands of miles.

Ford
Ford Motor Company
Detroit, Michigan

The second ad version (B) also has the (larger) 1930 style hubcaps but the earlier 1928 "drum" style tail lamp – rather than the "tea cup" style that was available in early 1929.

The third ad version (C) also contains a component not matching the late–1929 publish date. While this ad version has correct (smaller) 1928-29 style hubcaps, it also features the earlier 1928 "drum" style tail lamp.

◄ **Version C (Phn 4c)**
◉ *The American Boy,* October 1929, p. 35

COUNTY FAIR

The artist may have received an "advance peek" at the 1930 models and (prematurely) added the 1930 style hubcaps to the Phaeton in the *"County Fair"* magazine ad. However, there appears to be no explanation for the mysterious appearance of the earlier 1928 "drum" style tail lamp in this late–1929 Model A magazine ad.

All three *"County Fair"* ad versions were published in October 1929 and, at first glance, appear to be the same. However, a closer look reveals the "mismatched" components appearing in the Phaeton drawings.

AD VERSION A

1930 (larger) style hubcaps

1929 ("tea cup") style tail lamp

AD VERSION B

1930 (larger) style hubaps

1928 ("drum") style tail lamp

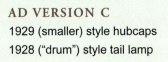

AD VERSION C

1929 (smaller) style hubcaps

1928 ("drum") style tail lamp

GOING FISHING

Built for many thousands of miles

THE new Ford has been designed and built to give you many thousands of miles of faithful, economical service. Beneath its flashing beauty of line and color—in those vital mechanical parts which you may never see—is a quality of material and craftsmanship unusual in a low-price car. Its sturdy strength, reliability and capable performance, in all weather and under all conditions, make it a particularly good choice for farm use.

It stands up under the added strain of bad roads and hard daily usage in a way that has always been characteristic of the Ford car. The experience of the passing months and years will increase your satisfaction in its performance and confirm your first impression that it is a "value far above the price."

THE NEW FORD PHAETON

Mom, Dad and Junior are leaving the farm in their new Phaeton, their picnic lunch on the back seat, and heading to the fishing hole. To the amusement of the farm hands painting the fence, they have already entangled their fishing pole lines.

Version A (Phn 5a)
- ⊙ *Capper's Farmer,* June 1930, p. 17
- ○ *The Country Gentleman,* June 1930, p. 79
- ○ *The Country Home,* June 1930, CIII
- ⊙ *Farm and Ranch,* June 1, 1930, p. 13
- ⊙ *Southern Agriculturist,* June 15, 1930, CIII (B&W)
- ○ *Successful Farming,* June 1930, CII

GOING FISHING

A second version (B) of this 1930 Phaeton ad moves the ad text to beneath the car illustration. This ad utilizes the same text – which indicates the car is *"a value far above the price"* – with only a very minor modification from that appearing in the first *"Going Fishing"* ad version (A).

Expanding on the ad's headline, the text of both ad versions proclaims that *"The new Ford has been built to give you many thousands of miles of faithful, economical service."*

The black and white *"Going Fishing"* ad version (B) appeared in only one magazine – the August 1930 edition of a magazine intended for young boys.

Version B (Phn 5b) ➤
⊙ *The American Boy,* August 1930, p. 29

Built for Many Thousands of Miles

THE NEW FORD PHAETON

THE new Ford has been designed and built to give you many thousands of miles of faithful, economical service. Beneath its flashing beauty of line and color—in those vital mechanical parts which you may never see—is a high quality of material and accuracy in manufacturing. The reliability and capable performance of the car, in all weather and under all conditions, make it a particularly good choice for long, constant use. It stands up under the added strain of bad roads and hard daily service in a way that has always been characteristic of the Ford car. The experience of the passing months will increase your satisfaction in its performance and confirm your first impression that it is a value far above the price. « « « « « « « « « «

DROPPED BRUSH!
The farm hands are so amused with the predicament of the tangled fishing lines that one of them, mouth agape, has dropped his paint brush.

It's no wonder that the farm owner is having the farm hands paint the fence around the farm. From a closer look at the full-color ad (version A), the fence color is being changed from pink to white!

DE LUXE PHAETON

	TOTAL	1930	1931
Ford Body Style		180-A	180-A
Weight (pounds)		2,285	2,285
Price (FOB Detroit)		$625	$580
Units Produced (U.S.)	6,175	3,946	2,229
Number of U.S. Ads			
Primary Formats	2	1	1
Ad Variations	4	1	3
Magazine Insertions	9	1	8

The distinctive Model A Ford De Luxe Phaeton was introduced in June 1930. Unlike the (standard) Phaeton, the De Luxe Phaeton was a two-door model with a single wide door providing access to both the front and rear seats. This low-production automobile was a very desirable Model A body style. It featured high sides, low seats and a very sporty appearance – while easily accommodating four passengers. While only one interior trim scheme was used, the De Luxe Phaeton was available in a wide variety of exterior color combinations.

Ford produced only one magazine ad for the Model A De Luxe Phaeton in 1930 – and limited its exposure to only one magazine on a single date. In 1931, a second ad with three different variations was released. As with the earlier (standard) Phaeton advertising efforts, the magazines selected to contain De Luxe Phaeton ads were, primarily, farm-related publications. However, none of the backgrounds illustrated in the De Luxe Phaeton ads actually depicted rural settings.

WINDSHIELD DOWN DOG

◆

The New Ford De Luxe Phaeton

THIS car, newly added to the Ford line, has achieved distinguished favor because of its low, fleet lines, beautiful colors, and attractive sport treatment. The spirit of youth is reflected in its sprightly appearance and alert performance. To an unusual degree, it combines style and utility.   «   «   «   «   «   «   «   «   «   «   «   «   «

   Among its pleasing features are an adjustable front seat, folding windshield and windshield wings of Triplex shatter-proof glass and a side fender well for the spare tire. Upholstery and trimming are in keeping with the latest mode. The rear quarter is slightly depressed below the belt to receive the top when down, thus preserving the straight flowing lines of the car.

Two couples speed on their way to the polo match in their new De Luxe Phaeton. With the windshield folded down, their dog is enjoying the breeze but the man in the rear seat needs to keep a tight grip on his hat.

Version A (DPh 1a)
◉ *Collier's*, August 30, 1930, CIII

This rare ad is difficult to find in good condition because it appeared only once – on the third cover of a single magazine.

59

SHOPPING DOWNTOWN

◆

Why You Can Drive the New Ford So Many Thousands of Miles

THE NEW FORD has made an unusual record for reliability and long life. In police service it has been driven 100,000 and 120,000 miles under the severest driving conditions. Leading industrial companies operating large fleets of Fords report "satisfactory economical service" after many months and years of constant use. The value of good materials, simplicity of design and accuracy in manufacturing is especially apparent after the first 25,000 miles.

Throughout the chassis, you find many reasons for the good performance of the Ford. None is more important than the crankshaft.

The crankshaft is frequently called the heart of the automobile because of the part it plays in transmitting the power developed by the pistons to the flywheel and driveshaft. It must be properly balanced to insure smooth operation. It must be accurate in size to insure proper clearance in the bearings. It must be true in alignment and weight to reduce friction and give long continuous service without adjustment.

The crankshaft of the Ford has great strength because it is made of carbon manganese steel, specially developed by Ford metallurgists. It will resist a twisting stress of 2½ tons at a leverage of twelve inches from its axis.

In the many steps in its manufacture, the Ford crankshaft is machined to measurements as fine as one-half of a thousandth part

THE NEW FORD DE LUXE PHAETON

of an inch. In all, Ford crankshafts receive more than 150 checks for accuracy.

The greatest care is taken to make sure that the Ford crankshaft will be in perfect balance in all positions and at all speeds. The machines for the dynamic balance tests are set upon foundations of gum rubber and are so delicately adjusted that the very air that surrounds them is first cleansed and then held at 68 degrees by thermostatic control.

Though weighing many pounds, the Ford crankshaft is so carefully balanced that it will remain motionless when placed upon two perfectly leveled parallel bars, yet will turn if so small a weight as a ten-cent piece is placed on any connecting-rod bearing.

This same care is followed as standard practice in the manufacture of the Ford flywheel,

pistons, connecting-rods, valves, camshaft and other mechanical parts.

You can see, therefore, why the Ford delivers reliable, economical service for so many thousands of miles. It gives good performance on the road because good performance has been built into it at the factory.

You can purchase a Ford on convenient, economical terms through the Authorized Ford Finance Plans of the Universal Credit Company.

The Ford crankshaft is made of special carbon manganese steel and balanced statically and dynamically. Ford crankshafts receive more than 150 checks for accuracy.

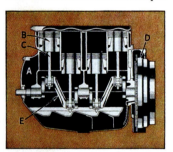

This illustration shows the Ford cylinder bloc (A), piston (B), connecting-rod (C), flywheel (D), and crankshaft (E). The care with which these parts are made is an important factor in the smoothness, reliability, economy and long life of the new Ford.

With their new Ford De Luxe Phaeton parked downtown, the husband loads packages from today's shopping activities. Meanwhile, two men take a close look at the Model A Ford parked next to the De Luxe Phaeton.

Version A (DPh 2a)

⊙ *Capper's Farmer,* May 1931, p. 17
○ *The Country Gentleman,* May 1931, p. 72
○ *The Country Home,* May 1931, CIII
○ *The Farm Journal,* May 1931, p. 19
○ *The Saturday Evening Post,* April 25, 1931, p. 41
○ *Successful Farming,* May 1931, CIII

SHOPPING DOWNTOWN

A second, black and white, version (B) of the 1931 *"Downtown Shopping"* ad contains some modifications in the De Luxe Phaeton illustration and a very slight text difference.

At first glance, the two illustrations appear to be the same. However, the second version (B) is missing the bottom half of the pole supporting the banner as well as the truck and men beneath the banner. Also missing is the Model A and men to the left of the car, the chair to the right of the car, and the cat in the foreground. Finally, "AAA" no longer appears on the small sign attached to the pole.

Version B (DPh 2b) ➤

◉ *Southern Agriculturist,* May 1, 1931, p. 23

Why You Can Drive the Ford So Many Thousands of Miles

THE FORD has made an unusual record for reliability and long life. In police service it has been driven 100,000 and 120,000 miles under the severest driving conditions. Leading industrial companies operating large fleets of Fords report "satisfactory economical service" after many months and years of constant use. The value of good materials, simplicity of design and accuracy in manufacturing is especially apparent after the first 25,000 miles.

Throughout the chassis, you find many reasons for the good performance of the Ford. None is more important than the crankshaft.

The crankshaft is frequently called the heart of the automobile because of the part it plays in transmitting the power developed in the cylinders to the flywheel and driveshaft.

It must be properly balanced to insure smooth operation. It must be accurate in size to insure proper clearance in the bearings. It must be true in alignment and weight to reduce friction and give long continuous service without adjustment.

The crankshaft of the Ford has great strength because it is made of carbon manganese steel, specially developed for this use by Ford metallurgists. It will resist a twisting stress of 2½ tons at a leverage of twelve inches from its axis.

In the many steps in its manufacture, the Ford crankshaft is machined to measurements as fine as one-half of a thousandth part of an inch. In all, Ford crankshafts receive more than one hundred and fifty checks for accuracy.

The greatest care is taken to make sure that the Ford crankshaft will be in perfect balance in all positions and at all speeds. The machines for the dynamic balance tests are set upon foundations of gum rubber and are very delicately adjusted.

Though weighing many pounds, the Ford crankshaft is so carefully balanced that it will remain motionless when placed upon two perfectly leveled parallel bars, yet will turn if so small a weight as a ten-cent piece is placed on any connecting-rod bearing.

This same care is followed as standard practice in the manufacture of the Ford flywheel, pistons, connecting-rods, valves, camshaft and other mechanical parts.

You can see, therefore, why the Ford delivers reliable, economical service for so many thousands of miles. It gives good performance on the road because good performance has been built into it at the factory.

You can purchase a Ford on convenient, economical terms, through the Authorized Ford Finance Plans of the Universal Credit Company.

This illustration shows the Ford cylinder block (A) piston (B), connecting-rod (C), flywheel (D), and crankshaft (E). The care with which these parts are made is an important factor in the smoothness, reliability, economy and long life of the new Ford.

The Ford crankshaft is made of special carbon manganese steel and balanced statically and dynamically. Ford crankshafts receive more than 150 checks for accuracy.

THE FORD DE LUXE PHAETON

FORD MOTOR COMPANY

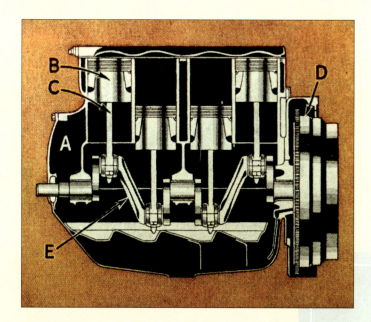

Almost the entire text of this 1931 De Luxe Phaeton magazine ad is devoted to discussing the Model A Ford's crankshaft. The text indicates that:

"The crankshaft is frequently called the heart of the automobile because of the part it plays in transmitting the power developed by the pistons to the flywheel and driveshaft."

AN INSIDE LOOK.

In touting the reliability and long life of the new Ford, each of the first two versions of the *"Shopping Downtown"* ad contain insert drawings showing a cutaway view of the Ford Model A engine and the Ford crankshaft.

SHOPPING DOWNTOWN

The third version (C) of this Ford De Luxe Phaeton magazine ad uses a completely different format.

Typical of the many unique Model A ads appearing in *The American Boy* magazine, this ad incorporates the same drawing of the Model A used in other ad versions, but includes it in a smaller size so that multiple topics aimed at young boys can also be included. In doing so, it attempts to educate its readers across a wide variety of topics related to The Ford Motor Company.

Version C (DPh 2c) ➤

⦿ *The American Boy,* June 1931, CIV

This unique ad contains four different insert illustrations – including ones showing the Model A Ford assembly line, Ford ball and roller bearings and the Ford "999" Racing Car – plus an inspirational statement signed by Henry Ford.

The text includes several miscellaneous Ford promotional mentions about a rural mail carrier in Iowa who drove his Ford over 73,000 miles a year and Ford winning prizes in a car race held in Poland. Finally, that two policemen in Indiana probably owe their lives to the Triplex shatter-proof glass in the new Ford because two bullets fired by bandits were found imbedded in their windshield.

YOU'RE INVITED.
The *"Downtown Shopping"* ad includes an insert illustration of the Ford assembly line. The text asks the reader *"Will you be in Detroit this summer?"* and encourages a visit to the Ford assembly plant.

THE AMERICAN BOY—YOUTH'S COMPANION

INTERESTING THINGS FOR YOU TO KNOW

Will you be in Detroit this Summer?

There is Much to Do

Many Balls and Rollers

The Famous "999" Racing Car

CONVERTIBLE CABRIOLET

	TOTAL	1929	1930	1931
Ford Body Style		68-A	68-B	68-B 68-C
Weight (pounds)		2,339	2,273	2,273
Price (FOB Detroit)		$670	$645	$595
Units Produced (U.S.)	54,090	16,421	25,868	11,801
Number of U.S. Ads				
Primary Formats	7	4	1	2
Ad Variations	23	12	6	5
Magazine Insertions	69	33	18	18

The Convertible Cabriolet was a deluxe Model A Ford body style introduced in early 1929. This vehicle, with a body supplied by Briggs, was somewhat more expensive than most other Model A's. It combined the sporty appeal of the Roadster with the wind-up window convenience of the Coupe – with a price tag higher than each.

While commonly known as simply the "Cabriolet," Ford always referred to this Model A body style as the "Convertible Cabriolet" in its advertising.

Ford created a total of 23 different magazine ad variations for the Cabriolet and, compared to most other Model A body styles, used relatively more upscale magazines to promote this vehicle. In these ads, the Cabriolet was usually shown in an upscale setting with the top down and an accessory boot covering the top. The last ad produced for this body style introduced the new 68-C Cabriolet in July 1931, following the debut of the slant-windshield Model A's.

FOX HUNT

◆

The New Ford Convertible Cabriolet

THE new Ford Convertible Cabriolet is a splendid choice for the family needing more than one car.

It is trim and smart, yet in good taste always because of its quiet simplicity of line and modish colors. It is reliable, long-lived and economical to drive because of the enduring quality that has been built into every part.

Safety, comfort, quick acceleration, smoothness, speed and power—all these it has in full measure with the additional advantage of being easy to operate and control under all conditions. To the woman driver, this is an increasingly important factor.

The convertible feature makes the new Ford Cabriolet particularly adaptable for business, for shopping, and for social engagements in all kinds of weather. Quickly, and with surprising ease, you can transform it from an open to a closed car. The top is of tan whipcord, rubber interlined, light in weight, yet absolutely waterproof. The door windows have nickel frames and fit snugly into the top. The rumble seat gives space for two more passengers

Other new Ford body types are the Town Car (chauffeur-driven), the Town Sedan, and the Station Wagon. These supplement the Fordor Sedan, Tudor Sedan, Coupe, Sport Coupe, Business Coupe, Phaeton and Roadster.

All, with the exception of the Station Wagon, are furnished in a choice of colors. All have four Houdaille hydraulic two-way shock absorbers, Triplex shatter-proof glass windshield, and a fully enclosed six-brake system.

FORD MOTOR COMPANY
Detroit, Michigan

A top-down, windows-up Cabriolet passes a fenced estate during a fox hunt as one of the hunters graciously tips his cap. The text presents an upscale review of a car that is *"trim and smart, yet in good taste."*

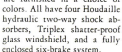

Version A (Cab 1a)

◉ *Country Life,* April 1929, p. 25
○ *Good Housekeeping,* May 1929, p. 125
◉ *Harper's Bazaar,* April 1929, p. 156
◉ *The Sportsman,* April 1929, p. 82
◉ *Vanity Fair,* April 1929, p. 112+
◉ *Vogue,* April 13, 1929, p. 25

FOX HUNT

Four different versions of the 1929 *"Fox Hunt"* Cabriolet magazine ad were produced.

While the second version (B) has only minor text changes, the third (C) includes an insert illustration of a Town Sedan, a completely different text and a new headline – *"Good Performance with Economy."*

> **Version C (Cab 1c)** ➤
> ○ *Cosmopolitan,* July 1929, CIII
> ◉ *The Redbook Magazine,* July 1929, p. 102

The fourth version (D) features another headline change and a more simplified ad text.

> **Version B (Cab1b) [text difference]**
> ○ *Ladies' Home Journal,* May 1929, p. 92
> ○ *McCall's,* May 1929, p. 102

As the only black and white edition of this Cabriolet ad, the fourth version (D) appeared only in *The American Boy.* It contains a relatively larger illustration, a new headline – *"Features of the Ford car"* – and a text listing specific characteristics of the new Ford.

> ◀ **Version D (Cab 1d)**
> ◉ *The American Boy,* September 1929, p. 31

DOCK NO. 2

JULY 1929

A Trim and Sturdy Craft

THE joy of driving the new Ford comes not alone from its speed—its safety—its comfort—its reliability—the pride you take in its beauty of line and color—but also from the pleasure it puts into motoring.

Instantly you start away for your first ride you have a feeling that here is an unusually alert and capable car. That here is a car fully equal to every need and emergency. That here is a car with a new eagerness to go. A new aliveness. A new responsiveness in traffic, on hills, and on the open road.

As the days go by, you will find yourself developing something of a real friendliness for the new Ford—a growing pride that is deeper and more personal than just an acknowledgment of faithful service.

You long to be behind the wheel—to drive for sheer joy of driving—to know again the sense of power, security and complete control that is yours when you ride in this trim and sturdy car.

It is this appreciation of fine performance that has given the

new Ford an honored place in the two-car garage and made it, indeed, the favored car for many occasions.

Especially will you like the Convertible Cabriolet, recently introduced. It sells for slightly more than most Ford cars and has many distinctive features. Being convertible, it combines the smart style and freedom of the roadster with the snug comfort of the coupe and is thus a splendid all-year, all-weather car. Its ease of control makes it a particularly good choice for the woman driver.

FORD MOTOR COMPANY
Detroit, Michigan

Having parked their new Ford Cabriolet, this couple is admiring their sailboat being painted at *"MYC Dock No. 2."* While touting the speed, safety, comfort and reliability of the new Cabriolet, this ad indicates it *"sells for slightly more than most Ford cars."*

Version A (Cab 2a)

◉ *Country Life*, July 1929, CIII

◉ *Harper's Bazaar*, July 1929

◉ *The Sportsman*, July 1929, p. 75

◉ *Vanity Fair*, July 1929, p. 96

◉ *Vogue*, July 20, 1929, p. 97

DOCK NO. 2

A second version (B) of this 1929 Cabriolet magazine ad uses a *"Good Performance with Economy"* headline and adds an insert illustration of a Model A Town Sedan and a Henry Ford signed statement on Ford service.

Version B (Cab 2b) ➤

⊙ *Liberty,* June 29, 1929

While a third ad version (C) has only a slight text change, the fourth (D) is a two-page edition with a different Town Sedan insert illustration.

Version C (Cab 2c) [text difference]

⊙ *Collier's,* July 6, 1929, CIII

Version D (Cab 2d) ⋁

⊙ *The Literary Digest,* May 4, 1929, CF
⊙ *The Saturday Evening Post,* May 18, 1929, pp. 94-95

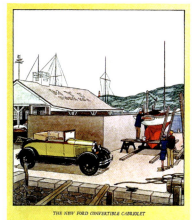

June 29, 1929   Liberty

GOOD PERFORMANCE WITH ECONOMY

"It has always been our belief that a sale does not complete the transaction between us and the buyer, but establishes a new obligation on us to see that his car gives him service. We are as much interested in his economical operation of the car as he is in our economical manufacture of it.

"For that reason we have installed a system of controlled service to take care of all Ford car needs in an economical and improved manner. We wish all users of Ford cars to know what they are entitled to in this respect, so that they may readily avail themselves of this service."

Henry Ford

THE NEW FORD CONVERTIBLE CABRIOLET

THE new Ford is more than a new automobile. It is the expression of an ideal—an ideal that looks to bringing the benefits of modern transportation to all the people.

Because of this purpose, the price is low and great care has been taken to insure economy of operation and up-keep. Few features are of greater importance to millions of motorists.

Figures from many sources show that the new Ford averages 20 miles per gallon of gasoline, with thousands of Ford owners reporting greater mileage on long trips. Oil consumption is also low. There is a considerable saving on tires due to special Ford design, the balance of the car, ease of steering and perfected wheel design.

Mechanical up-keep is low because of simplicity of design and the enduring quality that has been built into every part.

Definite evidence of the economy of the new Ford is shown in repeated and growing purchases by Federal and city governments, by police departments, and by large industrial companies which keep day-by-day cost records.

The new Ford has been chosen only after exhaustive tests covering every feature of automobile value and performance—from the time of purchase throughout the life of the car. Here the Ford policy of not making yearly changes serves to protect and maintain the investment of every Ford owner. Wherever possible, improvements in the new Ford are made so that present owners may take advantage of them quickly and at low cost.

The availability of Ford dealers throughout the world and close

Ford Motor Company, Detroit, Michigan

factory supervision of all service are additional reasons for the economy of the new Ford. This service begins with proper instruction when you buy the car and includes a free inspection and checking-up of important parts at 500, at 1000 and at 1500 miles.

No matter where you live or where you go, you will never be very far from a Ford dealer who has been specially trained and equipped to help you get many thousands of miles of pleasant, enjoyable motoring at a minimum of trouble and expense.

The newest Ford car—the Town Sedan. Distinguished by its roomy comfort, beautiful colors and rich finish. Rear and rear quarter windows have silk curtains. Driver's seat is adjustable. Folding center arm and side arm rests add to comfort of rear seat. Three side windows, large rear window, and narrow pillars give unusual vision.

GOOD PERFORMANCE WITH ECONOMY

THE new Ford is more than a new automobile. It is the expression of an ideal—an ideal that looks to bringing the benefits of modern transportation to all the people.

Because of this purpose, the price is low and great care has been taken to insure economy of operation and up-keep. Few features are of greater importance to millions of motorists.

Figures from many sources show that the new Ford averages 20 miles per gallon of gasoline, with thousands of Ford owners reporting greater mileage on long trips. Oil consumption is also low. There is a considerable saving on tires due to the balance of the car, ease of steering and perfected wheel design.

All tires used on new Ford cars and recommended for replacement are specially built by leading tire manufacturers according to specifications laid down by the Ford Motor Company.

Mechanical up-keep is low because of simplicity of design and the enduring quality that has been built into every part.

Definite evidence of the economy of the new Ford is shown in repeated and growing purchases by Federal and city governments, by police departments, and by large industrial companies which keep day-by-day cost records. The new Ford has been chosen only after exhaustive tests covering every feature of automobile value and performance.

A further advantage is the Ford policy of not making radical yearly changes. This serves to protect and maintain the investment of every Ford owner. Wherever possible, improvements in the new Ford are made so that present owners may take advantage of them quickly and at low cost.

The availability of Ford dealers throughout the world and close factory supervision of all service are additional reasons for the economy of the new Ford. This service begins with proper instruction when you buy the car and includes a free inspection or checking-up of important parts at 500, at 1000 and at 1500 miles.

No matter where you live or where you go, you will never be very far from a Ford dealer who has been specially trained and equipped to help you get many thousands of miles of pleasant, enjoyable motoring at a minimum of trouble and expense.

"Good performance with economy" is the reason for the unusual value that is brought to you in the new Ford.

Shown here is one of the newest Ford cars—the Convertible Cabriolet. Combines the comfort of a closed car in winter and the airy freedom of a roadster in summer. A splendid all-year, all-weather car for every member of the family.

Another new Ford car is the Town Sedan. Distinguished by its roomy comfort and rich finish. Interior hardware is of satin finish nickel. Rear window and rear quarter windows have silk curtains. Driver's seat is adjustable. Folding center arm and side arm rests add to comfort of rear seat. Rear compartment also has dome light and flexible robe rail. Three side windows, large rear window, and narrow pillars give unusual vision.

SERVICE

"It has always been our belief that a sale does not complete the transaction between us and the buyer, but establishes a new obligation on us to see that his car gives him service. We are as much interested in his economical operation of the car as he is in our economical manufacture of it.

"For that reason we have installed a system of controlled service to take care of all Ford car needs in an economical and improved manner. We wish all users of Ford cars to know what they are entitled to in this respect, so that they may readily avail themselves of this service."

Henry Ford

LEAVING CLUB

◆

THE NEW FORD CONVERTIBLE CABRIOLET

Features of the new Ford car

Sturdy body construction ⋄⋗ *Ease of control* ⋄⋗ *Four Houdaille hydraulic double-acting shock absorbers* ⋄⋗ *Triplex shatter-proof glass windshield* ⋄⋗ *Fully enclosed, silent six-brake system* ⋄⋗ *Quick acceleration* ⋄⋗ *55 to 65 miles an hour* ⋄⋗ *Smoothness and security at all speeds* ⋄⋗ *Vibration-absorbing engine support* ⋄⋗ *Choice of colors* ⋄⋗ *Tilting beam headlamps* ⋄⋗ *Theft-proof ignition lock* ⋄⋗ *Reliability* ⋄⋗ *Economy* ⋄⋗ *Long life*

It's getting dark and time for the couple in their new Cabriolet, with two friends in the rumble seat, to leave the Club. As they pull away, the club manager waves and wishes them a "good evening."

Version A (Cab 3a)
◉ *Country Life,* August 1929, p. 83
◉ *Harper's Bazaar,* August 1929
◉ *The Sportsman,* August 1929, p. 73
◉ *Vanity Fair,* August 1929, p. 16
◉ *Vogue,* August 12, 1929, p. 111+

LEAVING CLUB

A second version (B) of this 1929 Cabriolet magazine ad drops the *"new"* designation in the headline but leaves all other ad components unchanged. (Note that, across virtually all Model Ford A ads, the term "The New Ford" was usually used instead of referring to the "Model A Ford.")

Version B (Cab 3b) ➤
⊙ *Collier's,* August 3, 1929, CIII
○ *The Saturday Evening Post,* July 13, 1929, p. 73

The third ad version (C) retains the review of the Cabriolet benefits contained in the text – but with the minor text addition of *"Balance"* to the list of the *"Features of The Ford Car."*

Version C (Cab 3c) [text difference]
⊙ *Liberty,* August, 24 1929, p. 19
○ *The Literary Digest,* August 17, 1929, p. 34

The New Ford Convertible Cabriolet

Features of the Ford car

Sturdy body construction ⋆⋆ Ease of control ⋆⋆ Four Houdaille hydraulic double-acting shock absorbers ⋆⋆ Triplex shatter-proof glass windshield ⋆⋆ Fully enclosed, silent six-brake system ⋆⋆ Quick acceleration ⋆⋆ 55 to 65 miles an hour ⋆⋆ Smoothness and security at all speeds ⋆⋆ Vibration-absorbing engine support ⋆⋆ Choice of colors ⋆⋆ Tilting beam headlamps ⋆⋆ Theft-proof ignition lock ⋆⋆ Reliability ⋆⋆ Economy ⋆⋆ Long life

LIPSTICK TO GO?
A closer look at the couple in the rumble seat of the Cabriolet reveals that the man is holding the lady's compact and mirror so she can do a little makeup repair as the car leaves the Club.

Given the "speed drawings" of the car's wheels, the car is already in motion. Therefore, the rumble seat couple must have a lot of confidence in the smooth ride provided by the Cabriolet!

RAINY DAY GOLF

◆

LADIES' HOME JOURNAL   September, 1929

The Ford Convertible Cabriolet

Features of the Ford car

Ease of control ❖ ❖ Trim, smart lines ❖ ❖ Choice of beautiful colors ❖ ❖ Sturdy steel body construction ❖ ❖ Four Houdaille hydraulic double-acting shock absorbers ❖ ❖ Fully enclosed, silent six-brake system ❖ ❖ Triplex shatter-proof glass windshield ❖ ❖ Quick acceleration ❖ ❖ 55 to 65 miles an hour ❖ ❖ Smoothness, balance and security at all speeds ❖ ❖ Vibration-absorbing engine support ❖ ❖ Tilting beam headlamps ❖ ❖ Reliability ❖ ❖ Economy ❖ ❖ Long life

Two women in their new Cabriolet slow down to watch as their friend studies her putt on the rain-soaked golf green. The rainy day setting provides the opportunity for one of the few Cabriolet drawings showing the car with the top up.

Version A (Cab 4a)
○ *The Farmer's Wife,* September 1929
○ *Good Housekeeping,* September 1929, p. 19
○ *Ladies' Home Journal,* September 1929, p. 84
○ *McCall's,* September 1929

TENT DANCE

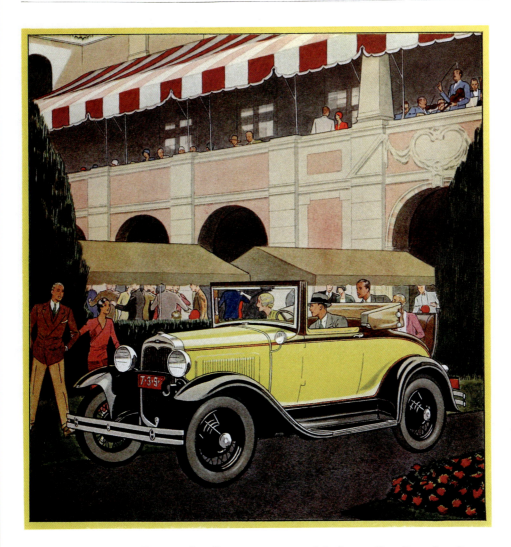

COUNTRY LIFE

The New Ford Convertible Cabriolet

PROUDLY you will drive the new Ford Cabriolet because of its distinctive grace of line and alert, capable performance. It has the further advantage of being a most practical car. « « « « « « « «

On clear, brisk days, the blue sky overhead, you can enjoy the airy freedom of a roadster. When dark clouds come, it takes but a few moments to raise the top and command the snug comfort of a coupe. It is thus a splendid car for all the year, for every changing mood of mind or weather. « « « « « « « «

Ease of control, comfort, the safety of fully enclosed four-wheel brakes and a Triplex shatter-proof glass windshield, reliability, economy and long life are among the other outstanding features of the new Ford Cabriolet. « « «

Two couples are greeted as they arrive at the party in their new Ford Cabriolet. This is a festive occasion as people dance under the tents and an orchestra plays from the balcony.

Version A (Cab 5a)
○ *Cosmopolitan,* May 1930, p. 117
◉ *Country Life,* April 1930, p. 90
◉ *Delineator,* June 1930, p. 69
(continued)

71

TENT DANCE

◄ Version A (Cab 5a) [continued]
○ *Good Housekeeping,* June 1930, p. 137
○ *Ladies' Home Journal,* June 1930, p. 67
○ *McCall's,* June 1930, p. 124+
◉ *Pictorial Review,* June 1930, p. 46
◉ *The Sportsman,* April 1930, p. 81
◉ *Vogue,* April 12, 1930, p. 34
○ *Woman's Home Companion,* June 1930, p. 70

Version B (Cab 5b) [text difference]
● *Junior League Magazine,* April 1930, p. 3 (B&W)

Version C (Cab 5c) ∇
○ *The American Magazine,* May 1930, p. 105
◉ *The Redbook Magazine,* May 1930, p. 100

While a minor ad text variation exists in the second *"Tent Dance"* ad version (B), this 1930 Cabriolet ad was also produced with a *"Quality that endures"* headline and a completely different text (version C).

The fourth version (D) of this 1930 Cabriolet ad has minor ad text differences.

THE NEW FORD CONVERTIBLE CABRIOLET

Quality that endures

THE extra value built into the new Ford car is reflected in its alert, capable performance, reliability and long life.　"　"　"　"
Beneath its flashing beauty of line and color, there is a mechanical excellence unusual in a low-priced car. Many measurements are accurate to the thousandth of an inch. Every part has been carefully designed and made to give you many thousands of miles of faithful, uninterrupted service.
In safety, comfort, speed, power, economy — in all that goes to make a good automobile — it is a value far above the price. The quality of the new Ford is a quality that endures.　"　"　"　"

Version D (Cab 5d) [text difference]
◉ *The American Boy,* April 1930, p. 31 (B&W)
◉ *Collier's,* April, 12, 1930, CIII

The fifth *"Tent Dance"* Cabriolet ad version (E) employs a completely new text and a different headline – *"Beauty of line and mechanical excellence."*

◄ Version E (Cab 5e)
◉ *True Story,* June 1930, p. 59

THE NEW FORD CONVERTIBLE CABRIOLET

Beauty of line and mechanical excellence

BEAUTY has been built into the graceful flowing lines of the new Ford and there is an appealing charm in its fresh and varied harmony of color. Yet more distinctive even than this beauty of line and color is its alert and sprightly performance.
As days go by you will find that it becomes more and more your favorite car to drive — so responsive, so easy to handle, so safe and comfortable that it puts a new joy in motoring. The city dweller — the farmer — the industrial worker — the owner of the spacious two-car garage in the suburbs — to all of these it brings a new measure of reliable, economical service.
Craftsmanship has been put into mass production. Today, more than ever, the new Ford is "a value far above the price."

TENT DANCE

The two-page edition (F) of this 1930 Cabriolet ad includes a smaller insert illustration of the car with its top up.

Version F (Cab 5f) ⋁
⊙ *The Literary Digest,* May 31, 1930, CF
⊙ *The Saturday Evening Post,* May 17, 1930, pp. 80-81

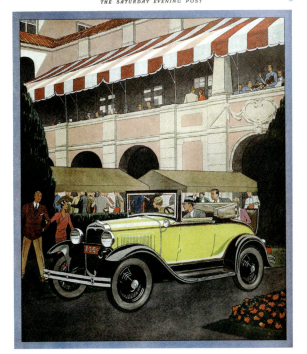

The Williamson drawing used in the Cabriolet *"Tent Dance"* ad also appeared one month later in a Cabriolet ad published in a Dutch magazine.

This black and white ad uses a somewhat modified illustration and a different license plate number on the Cabriolet. (Note the text proclaiming the car comes *met dicky seat!*)

◄ **Example ad from Holland**
⊙ *Sport in Beeld,* June 1930, p. 30

LITTLE THEATER

MAY 1931

RICHLY COSTUMED FOR A LEADING ROLE

UPON the roadways of the world, the Ford plays an important part in the widening activities of busy men and women. Its distinctive beauty of line and color is apparent at a glance. Through many months of constant use you will develop a sincere pride in its alert and faithful performance.

The high quality of the Ford is revealed also in every detail of interior finish and appointment—in those all-important little things which discerning eyes are quick to note and remember.

The richness of the upholstery and the carefully tailored trimming—the excellent taste in hardware—the ease with which the windows go up and down in the substantial doors—the deep, well-sprung cushions in the restful seats—the pleasing harmony of color . . . all of these bespeak the care and craftsmanship that have gone into the building of the Ford car. There are thirteen different body types for your selection. The illustration above shows the beautiful Ford Convertible Cabriolet.

Having parked her Ford Cabriolet in front of the *"Little Theater,"* the aspiring actress has unwrapped her costume and is attempting a **"trial fitting."** The play in which she will be performing is being put on by the local *"Junior League."*

Version A (Cab 6a)

◉ *The Sportsman,* May 1931, p. 83

This specific version of the *"Little Theater"* ad appeared in only one magazine.

LITTLE THEATER

The ad text is just slightly lengthier in the second version (B) of the *"Little Theater"* Cabriolet ad. This ad version appeared in many different magazines.

Version B (Cab 6b) ➤

○ *Cosmopolitan,* May 1931
◉ *Delineator,* June 1931, p. 49
◉ *Holland's,* May 1931, p. 38
○ *Ladies' Home Journal,* June 1931, p. 72
○ *The Literary Digest,* April 18, 1931, CII
○ *McCall's,* May 1931, p. 59
◉ *Pictorial Review,* May 1931. p. 4
◉ *The Saturday Evening Post,* April 11, 1931, p. 77
◉ *True Story,* May 1931
○ *Woman's Home Companion,* June 1931, p. 77
○ *Woman's World,* May 1931, p. 21

The last (black and white) *"Little Theater"* ad version (C) contains an additional text change and appeared only in the *Junior League Magazine* – befitting the sponsor of the play listed in the ad's illustration.

Version C (Cab 6c) [text difference]
● *Junior League Magazine,* May 1931, p. 3 (B&W)

RICHLY COSTUMED FOR A LEADING ROLE

Upon the roadways of the world, the new Ford plays an important part in the widening activities of the modern woman. Its distinctive beauty of line and color is apparent at a glance. Through many months of constant use you will develop a sincere pride in its reliability and faithful performance.

The high quality of the new Ford is revealed also in every detail of its interior finish — in those all-important little things a woman's discerning eye is quick to note and remember.

The richness of the upholstery and the carefully tailored trimming — the excellent taste in appointments — the ease with which the windows go up and down in the substantial doors — the deep, well-sprung cushions in the restful seats — the pleasing harmony of color . . . all of these bespeak the care and craftsmanship that have gone into the building of the Ford car.

In addition to the Convertible Cabriolet, illustrated above, there are twelve other Ford body types for your selection, in a changing variety of attractive colors. The low first cost of the new Ford means a distinct saving and you may purchase on convenient, economical terms through the Authorized Ford Finance Plans of the Universal Credit Company.

Refuse substitutes; buy the advertised brand every time!

IS THIS A MODEL A TOWN CAR?

Perhaps in an attempt to increase the prestige of the setting used to position the Cabriolet, the artist has placed a Town Car on the hill in the distant background of the *"Little Theater"* ad. While the small size of the illustration prohibits a positive identification, the car's overall appearance (and color) indicates this could be a Model A Ford Town Car – except for its having a rear spare tire.

WEDDING PROCESSION

◆

Country Life

THE NEW FORD CONVERTIBLE CABRIOLET

In Every Gay Procession . . .

FLYING along smooth ribbons of road . . . cresting steep hills under summer skies . . . slipping quietly out of traffic tangles . . . in every gay procession, you will find joy in driving the new Ford Convertible Cabriolet. Graceful of line . . . with a smart low roof, and slanting windshield. Lightly controlled, and sure in performance.

When the sun is high, you can put back the top . . . and feel the roadster-joy of the wind against your face. Or top-up, enjoy the snug protection of a coupe in bad weather.

There are other conveniences. An adjustable seat . . . easy to bring forward for a woman at the wheel. A windshield made of safety glass, set on an angle that thwarts glaring headlights! A new sliding seam on the rear curtain . . . so it opens easily, fastens tight. And a roomy rumble-seat, grand for stowing away extra cargo . . . friends, relatives, or baggage.

It's upholstered in rich Bedford Cord, that wears and wears and wears. It's finished in a choice of colors, to match the gay season. Practical, economical, yet smart as tomorrow . . . it's the Convertible Cabriolet . . . presented by Ford.

A couple speeds after the *"Just Married"* couple's car in their new slant-windshield Model A Cabriolet. As the two cars pass by in a cloud of dust, the startled policeman can only stare at the new Ford Cabriolet.

Version A (Cab 7a)
◉ *Country Life,* July 1931, p. 86
◉ *Vanity Fair,* July 1931, p. 73
◉ *Vogue,* July 1, 1931, p. 76+

Version B (Cab 7b) [text difference]
● *Junior League Magazine,* July 1931, p. 3 (B&W)
◉ *Life,* July 24, 1931, CII

COUPE

	TOTAL	1927	1928	1929	1930	1931
Ford Body Style		45-A	45-A	45-A	45-B (Std.)	45-B (Std.)
Weight (pounds)		2,200	2,200	2,200	2,257	2,257
Price (FOB Detroit)		$495	$495	$550	$500	$490
Units Produced (U.S.)	556,220	611	70,784	178,982	226,027	79,816
Number of U.S. Ads						
Primary Formats	10	–	1	5	3	1
Ad Variations	24	–	3	10	7	4
Magazine Insertions	77	–	7	26	38	6

The Coupe was among the first six Model A body styles announced by Ford in December 1927. Because several Model A body types used "coupe" as part of their names, this body style was sometimes referred to as the Standard Coupe. However, the "standard" designation was very rarely used by Ford – and then only when making direct comparisons to the Special Coupe, Business Coupe, De Luxe Coupe or Sport Coupe models.

Between July 1928 and July 1929, Ford produced a "leatherback" coupe version, called the Special Coupe (49-A), and temporarily suspended production of the (standard) Coupe (45-A). The Business Coupe (54-A) was first available in May 1928. This car featured a Sport Coupe type artificial leather top without the landau bars and, in the 1929 models, oval side windows. The 1930 and 1931 De Luxe Coupe used the same body type number as the Coupe (45-B).

While no magazine ads were produced for the Model A Special Coupe and Business Coupe, Ford produced a total of 24 different ad versions for the (standard) Coupe during 1928-1931.

CHURCH ARCHWAY

◆

GET behind the wheel and know the joy of driving this great new car

THE joy of driving the new Ford comes not alone from its speed—its safety—its comfort—its reliability—the pride you take in its beauty of line and color—but also from the pleasure it puts into motoring.

Instantly you start away for your first ride you have a feeling that here is an unusually alert and capable car. That here is a car that is fully equal to every need and emergency. That here is a car with a new eagerness to go. A new aliveness. A new responsiveness in traffic, on hills, and on the open road.

As the days go by, you find yourself developing a real friendliness for

Looking forward from the roomy front seat of the new Ford, you are impressed by its sweeping lines and appearance of rugged strength. Windshield is of Triplex shatter-proof glass—an important safety feature.

the new Ford—a growing pride that is deeper and more personal than just an acknowledgment of faithful service.

You long to be behind the wheel—to drive for the sheer joy of driving—to know again the sense of power, security and complete control that is yours when you ride in this great new car.

Watching the performance of the new Ford—studying its reliability—you begin to see that it is not just a new automobile—not just a new model—but the advanced expression of a wholly new idea in modern, economical transportation.

For now, at a low price, you can get everything you want or need in a modern automobile . . . steel bodies . . . beautiful low lines . . . choice of colors . . . speed of 55 to 65 miles an hour . . . a four-cylinder engine which develops 40 horse-power at only 2200 revolutions a minute . . . quick acceleration . . . exceptional hill-climbing qualities . . . 20 to 30

miles per gallon of gasoline, depending on your speed . . . protected safety gasoline tank in cowl, with the advantage of direct gravity flow . . . mechanical, self-centering, internal expanding-shoe four-wheel brakes which are positive in action, yet may be applied with the slightest pressure of the foot . . . separate emergency or parking brake independent of four-wheel brakes . . . Houdaille hydraulic shock absorbers . . . new easy-riding transverse springs of exclusive Ford design . . . typical Ford reliability and low up-keep cost . . . Triplex shatter-proof glass windshield.

The Ford Motor Company is able to build such a really fine car at a low price only because of new manufacturing methods and production economies as unusual as the car itself.

The Ford Roadster sells for $385; Phaeton for $395; Tudor Sedan for $495; Coupe for $495; Business Coupe for $495; Sport Coupe, with wide, substantial rumble seat, for $550. (All prices are F.O.B. Detroit.)

Ford

FORD MOTOR COMPANY
Detroit, Mich.

Services are over and the Ford Coupe prepares to leave from under the church's massive archway. The text lists prices for the new Ford cars. This ad includes an insert illustration providing a view from inside the Model A Ford.

Version A (Cpe 1a)

○ *Cosmopolitan*, July 1928, p. 117

⊙ *The Redbook Magazine,* July 1928, p. 119

This is the earliest magazine ad for the Model A Ford Coupe.

CHURCH ARCHWAY

The second version (B) of this Model A Coupe ad uses a similar text, but does not include the prices of the new Ford cars. It also adds a second insert illustration of a Ford Phaeton – a unique drawing never used as the primary illustration in a Model A Phaeton magazine ad.

Version B (Cpe 1b) ➤

◉ *Country Life,* July 1928, CIII
◉ *Liberty,* July 21, 1928, p. 18
◉ *The Sportsman,* July 1928, p. 69

The two-page ad edition (C) retains these two inserts, utilizes an expanded text and adds a third insert – a list of the *"Features of the New Ford Car."*

Version C (Cpe 1c) ⋁

◉ *The Literary Digest,* July 28, 1928, CF
◉ *The Saturday Evening Post,* July 7, 1928, pp. 64-65

JULY 1928   69

GET behind the wheel and know the joy of driving this great new car

FORD MOTOR COMPANY
Detroit, Michigan

RIVIERA THEATER

◆

The new Ford has a very simple and effective lubrication system

If you could look into the engine of the new Ford, you would be surprised at the simplicity of the lubrication system. It is a combination of pump, splash and gravity feed—an exclusive Ford development.

The oil pump draws the oil from the bottom of the oil pan through a fine mesh wire screen or filter and delivers it to the valve chamber. Even when you are traveling at thirty miles an hour, the five quarts of oil in the pan pass through the pump *twice* in every mile.

There's an air of rugged strength in the low, trim lines of the new Ford. Other features are 55 to 65 miles an hour, quick acceleration, smoothness at all speeds, fully-enclosed, silent six brake system, Houdaille shock absorbers, Triplex shatter-proof windshield, economy and long life.

From the valve chamber the oil flows by gravity to the main bearings of the crankshaft and the front camshaft bearing. Reservoirs of oil are provided for each main bearing pipe opening through a series of ingenious dams placed at the bottom of the valve chamber.

After filling these reservoirs, the surplus oil flows down an overflow pipe to the front of the oil pan tray. In this tray are four troughs into which dip the scoops on the connecting rods. These scoops pick up the oil and throw it into the grooves of the swiftly moving crankpin bearings. They also send an oil spray over the cylinder walls, camshaft and timing gears. From the tray the oil flows back to the oil pan, whence it is again drawn through the oil strainer into the pump.

The oiling system of the new Ford is so simple in design and effective in action that it requires practically no service attention. Like every other Ford part, it has been built to give you many thousands of miles of use at a minimum of trouble and expense.

There is only one thing to do, but that is a very important thing . . . *watch the oil!*

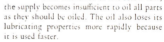
FORD MOTOR COMPANY
Detroit, Michigan

Keep enough oil in the oil pan so that the indicator rod never registers below low (L) and change the oil every 500 miles. If the oil level is allowed to fall below low, the supply becomes insufficient to oil all parts as they should be oiled. The oil also loses its lubricating properties more rapidly because it is used faster.

The lubrication of the chassis is also important. It has been made simple and easy in the new Ford through the high pressure grease gun system. To insure best performance, the chassis should be lubricated every 500 miles.

Every 1000 miles the distributor cam should be cleaned and given a light film of vaseline. At 5000 miles, the lubricant in the differential and transmission should be drained, the housings flushed with kerosene and new lubricant added.

The oiling and greasing of an automobile is so important and means so much to economical, satisfactory performance that it ought not to be neglected or carelessly done. Ford dealers everywhere have been specially trained to oil and grease the new Ford. They know the best oil to use for each part during each season and they have special equipment to do a good and thorough job at a fair price.

It's a cold winter day as the new Ford Coupe negotiates downtown traffic, its windshield wipers working against the snow. The *"Riviera Theater"* is in the background. The smaller insert illustration of a Tudor Sedan also features a winter setting.

Version A (Cpe 2a)

⊙ *Collier's,* January 19, 1929, CIII

Version B (Cpe 2b) [text difference]

○ *Cosmopolitan,* January 1929, CIII

⊙ *Liberty,* January 12, 1929, p. 11

⊙ *The Redbook Magazine,* January 1929, p. 90

RIVIERA THEATER

The second and third versions (B and C) of this 1929 Coupe ad have only very minor text changes. The fourth and fifth versions (D and E) are two-page editions, each with different insert illustrations.

Version C (Cpe 2c) [text difference]
◉ *Country Life,* January 1929, p. 11
◉ *The Sportsman,* January 1929, p. 77
◉ *Vanity Fair,* January 1929, p. 16+

Version D (Cpe 2d) ➤
◉ *The Saturday Evening Post,* January 19, 1929, pp. 60-61

◄ **Version E (Cpe 2e)**
◉ *The Literary Digest,* February 9, 1929, CF

Simplicity of electrical and ignition systems a feature of the new Ford

EVERY time you step into your automobile and start your engine, you put an electric light and power plant to work. With but a turn of the ignition key and the pressure of a foot, you set many parts in motion.

The electrical and ignition systems of the new Ford are particularly reliable in action because they are simple in design. Many features are exclusive Ford developments.

The dynamo-type generator is an example of this trouble-saving simplicity and its influence on continuously good performance.

Practically the only thing to do is to have the charging rate adjusted as the seasons change or for special driving conditions. Even oiling is necessary only once in every 2,000 miles and there is no possibility of oil getting into the commutator. Ford engineering has eliminated the need of a bearing on the commutator end.

Closely allied to the electrical system is the ignition system. It, too, is of new mechanical design in the new Ford. There is but one high tension cable and that connects the coil with the distributor. Even cables from the distributor to the spark plugs have been eliminated. Special care has also been taken to make the distributor water-proof, thus preventing short circuits from rain, snow, etc.

The electrical and ignition systems of the new Ford are so simple in design and so carefully made that they will give you surprisingly little trouble. Yet that doesn't mean they should be neglected. Certain little attentions are needed from time to time.

Water in the storage battery should be maintained at the correct level and the connections kept clean. The generator charging rate should be adjusted as indicated. Spark plugs should be cleaned or replaced at regular intervals. Distributor points should also be kept clean and

Ford MOTOR COMPANY
Detroit, Michigan

the distributor cam given a light film of vaseline every 1000 miles. These are just little things, but they mean a great deal to your car. You can have them looked after at very small cost by the Ford dealer when the car is oiled and greased.

A thorough checking-up at regular intervals will lengthen the life of your car and give you many thousands of miles of care-free, economical motoring.

The new Fordor Sedan, in Rose Beige. All of the new Ford cars are finished in a choice of beautiful colors— an unusual feature in a low-price car.

> ### FEATURES OF THE NEW FORD
> *Beautiful low lines*
> *Choice of colors*
> *Remarkable acceleration*
> *Smoothness at all speeds*
> *55 to 65 miles an hour*
> *Fully enclosed, silent six-brake system*
> *New transverse springs*
> *Houdaille hydraulic shock absorbers*
> *Triplex shatter-proof windshield*
> *Economy of operation*
> *Reliability and long life*

A man has parked his new Ford Coupe at the train station. The sign on the station indicates that Los Angeles is 71 miles away. In the distant left background, a man is waving from his buckboard.

Version A (Cpe 3a)
◉ *Collier's,* March 16, 1929, CIII
◉ *Country Life,* March 1929, p. 27
◉ *The Sportsman,* March 1929, p. 77
◉ *Vanity Fair,* March 1929, p. 25

CALIFORNIA STATION

A second version (B) of this 1929 Ford Coupe magazine ad retains the same headline and a slightly different ad text – but drops the smaller insert illustration of the Fordor Sedan.

Perhaps because of the space saved without the second insert illustration, this ad version appeared only in smaller sized magazines.

The text of the *"California Station"* Model A Coupe ads concentrates on the electrical and ignition systems of the new Ford.

Version B (Cpe 3b) ➤

○ *Cosmopolitan,* March 1929, p. 115

◉ *Liberty,* March 9, 1929, p. 17

◉ *The Redbook Magazine,* March 1929, p. 94

Simplicity of electrical and ignition systems is a feature of the new Ford

EVERY time you step into your automobile and start your engine, you put an electric light and power plant to work. With but a turn of the ignition key and the pressure of a foot, you set many parts in motion.

The electrical and ignition systems of the new Ford are particularly reliable in action because they are simple in design. Many features are exclusive Ford developments.

Take the generator, for example. It is of the dynamo or power-house type and has been built to prevent most forms of trouble. Practically the only thing you need do is to have the charging rate adjusted as the seasons change. Even oiling is necessary only once a year and there is no possibility of oil getting into the commutator. Ford engineering has eliminated the need of a bearing on the commutator end.

Closely allied to the electrical system is the ignition system. It, too, is of new mechanical design in the new Ford. There is but one high tension cable and that connects the coil on the dash with the distributor. Even cables from the distributor to the spark-plugs have also been eliminated. Special care has also been taken to make the distributor water-proof, thus preventing short circuits from rain, snow, etc.

FEATURES
OF THE NEW FORD

Beautiful low lines
Choice of colors
Remarkable acceleration
Smoothness at all speeds
55 to 65 miles an hour
Fully enclosed six-brake system
Houdaille shock absorbers
Triplex shatter-proof windshield
Economy of operation
Reliability and long life

FORD MOTOR COMPANY
Detroit, Michigan

Throughout, the electrical and ignition systems of the new Ford are so simple in design and so carefully made that they will give you surprisingly little trouble. Yet that doesn't mean they should be neglected. Certain little attentions are needed from time to time.

Water in the storage battery should be maintained at the correct level and connections kept clean. The generator charging rate should be adjusted as indicated. Spark-plugs should be cleaned at regular intervals. Distributor points should also be kept clean and the distributor cam given a light film of vaseline every 1000 miles.

These are just little things, but they mean a great deal to your car. You can have them looked after at very small cost by the Ford dealer when you take the car in for oiling and greasing.

A thorough checking-up at regular intervals will lengthen the life of your car and give you many thousands of miles of carefree, economical motoring.

TRAIN DOG RELEASE.

A closer look at the activities at the train station reveals the man with the Ford Coupe has arrived to pick up his dog, which has enjoyed a train ride and has just been liberated from its traveling cage. As the dog exits the cage, the man – hat removed and a hand on his hip – is telling his friends about this travel-weary pet.

While the second version of the *"California Station"* ad (B) has a slightly cropped illustration, a man in a cowboy hat, rolling a cigarette, can be seen ("off camera" at the right) in the un-cropped Williamson drawing (version A).

EXAMINING BUMPER

You will like the new Ford Coupe not only because of its beautiful lines and colors, but also because it is such a comfortable, easy-riding car. All of the new Fords are equipped with four Houdaille hydraulic shock absorbers — two front and two rear. Formerly these shock absorbers were used only on the most expensive cars.

Simplicity of electrical and ignition systems a feature of the new Ford

EVERY time you step into your automobile and start your engine, you put an electric light and power plant to work. With but a turn of the ignition key and the pressure of a foot, you set many parts in motion.

The electrical and ignition systems of the new Ford are particularly reliable in action because they are simple in design. Many features are exclusive Ford developments.

The dynamo-type generator is an example of this trouble-saving simplicity and its influence on continuously good performance.

Practically the only thing you need do is to have the charging rate adjusted as the seasons change. Even oiling is necessary only once a year and there is no possibility of oil getting into the commutator. Ford engineering has eliminated the need of a bearing on the commutator end.

Closely allied to the electrical system is the ignition system. It, too, is of new mechanical design in the new Ford. There is but one high tension cable and that connects the coil on the dash with the distributor. Even cables from the distributor to the spark plugs have been eliminated. Special care has also been taken to make the distributor water-proof, thus preventing short circuits from rain, etc.

FORD MOTOR COMPANY
Detroit, Michigan

The electrical and ignition systems of the new Ford are so simple in design and so carefully made that they will give you little trouble. Yet that doesn't mean they should be neglected. Certain little attentions are needed from time to time. Water in the storage battery should be maintained at the correct level and the connections kept clean. The generator charging rate should be adjusted as indicated. Spark plugs should be cleaned at regular intervals. Distributor points should also be kept clean and the distributor cam given a light film of vaseline every 2000 miles.

These are just little things, but they mean a great deal to your car. You can have them looked after at very small cost by the Ford dealer when you see him about oiling and greasing.

A thorough checking-up at regular intervals will lengthen the life of your car and give you many thousands of miles of carefree, economical motoring.

The beauty of the graceful, flowing lines of the new Ford Sport Coupe is further emphasized by the rich, attractive colors. All of the new Fords are finished in a variety of two-tone color harmonies.

This 1929 magazine ad shows several boys inspecting the new Ford Coupe and includes a smaller insert image of a Sport Coupe. This is the only U.S. Model A passenger car magazine ad using a car photograph instead of a drawing.

Version A (Cpe 4a)
⊙ *The American Boy,* March 1929, p. 29

This is a unique Model A ad. It appeared only once, in March 1929.

110   *THE SATURDAY EVENING POST*   September 7, 1929

Consider the unseen values when you buy a motor car

THE FORD COUPE

Unusual number of ball and roller bearings in the Ford contributes to smoothness, reliability, economy and long life

IN MANNER of manufacture, as in performance, there is much that is distinctive about the Ford. Principally it concerns the unseen values which have such a great bearing on economy, reliability and long life. Fundamentally it is an expression of the Ford policy and the Ford method of building a motor car.

In designing the Ford, we decided first on the kind of car we wanted to make. Many months were then devoted to the designing of new machines and new manufacturing methods which would enable us to sell it at a price within reach of all the people. The production of such a car at such a low price is even more unusual than the car itself.

Not in exterior things only, but throughout the Ford you find the same high quality of materials and exact, careful workmanship. Prominent among its unseen values is the extensive use of ball and roller bearings.

There are more than twenty of these in the Ford—an unusually large number. In type and kind they are carefully selected for the work they have to do and are as adequate in size as in number.

Being comparable to the jewels of a fine watch, they prevent unnecessary friction and wear, contribute to smoothness and quiet, reduce up-keep costs and add thousands of miles to the life of the car.

Studying the operation of these bearings you can see their practical value to every Ford owner. Steering is made easier and safer because of the roller bearings in the steering gear and because the weight of the car is carried on roller bearings in the front wheels and front axle king pins. The uniformly good performance of the Ford rear axle is due largely to the roller bearings on the rear axle

pinion and differential. These are held to such close limits that adjustment is unnecessary.

From the engine-to-the-road, in fact, the entire drive of the Ford on all forward speeds is wholly on anti-friction ball and roller bearings. In addition to smoother operation, this saves gasoline, gives the car more speed and power in first and second speeds, decreases noise, and increases the durability and efficiency of the transmission gears.

Similar good results are apparent also in the drive shaft, the generator—wherever ball and roller bearings are used.

There are definite reasons, therefore, for the smooth-running, alert performance of the Ford, and for its economy, reliability and long life. Throughout it has been built to endure—to serve you faithfully and well for many thousands of miles.

FORD MOTOR COMPANY
Detroit, Michigan

As Albert provides some last-minute counsel, two women depart the *"Albert Mathews Decorator"* shop in their new Ford Coupe. In line with the decorating theme of the ad, the Coupe is shown framed by the shop curtains – in complimenting colors.

Version A (Cpe 5a)

⊙ *Collier's,* October, 26, 1929, CIII

○ *Cosmopolitan,* November 1929, p. 117

⊙ *Liberty,* November 16, 1929, p. 15

○ *The Saturday Evening Post,* September 7, 1929, p. 110

⊙ *The Redbook Magazine,* November 1929

The Farmer's Wife, October, 1929

A splendid car for the busy mother

The Ford is a splendid choice for the busy mother not only because of its comfort and reliability, but because it is such an easy car to operate and control under all conditions.

Somehow, it seems as if everything has been planned and arranged for the particular convenience of the woman motorist.

Starting is easy because of the efficient, dependable self-starter. Gears shift smoothly, silently, without effort. On the open road or in traffic, you have a feeling of security and confidence because of the safety of the silent, fully enclosed six-brake system, the substantial balance of the car, and the additional protection of a Triplex shatter-proof glass windshield

Quick acceleration, alert speed, and the ability to park in a small space without confusion, are other features you will especially appreciate in city driving.

A further advantage to the woman motorist is the country-wide availability of Ford dealers and the manner in which they are trained and equipped to give you prompt, courteous, intelligent service at all times. The interest of the Ford dealer is the interest of a friend—to relieve you of every detail in the care of the car and help you get many thousands of miles of pleasant, economical motoring.

THE FORD COUPE

FORD MOTOR COMPANY
Detroit, Michigan

It's the first day of school and mother has just left off her daughter at *"Misses Stuart's Academy for Young Ladies."* As Mom waves goodbye and the headmistress comforts the girl, her future classmates watch from behind the bushes.

Version A (Cpe 6a)
- ○ *The Farmer's Wife,* October 1929, p. 19
- ○ *Good Housekeeping,* October 1929, p. 122
- ○ *Ladies' Home Journal,* October 1929, p. 106
- ○ *McCall's,* October 1929, p. 83

INTERRUPTED PUTT

◆

THE NEW FORD COUPE

An Admired Grace of Line and Contour

SEEING the new Ford as it speeds along the broad highway or parked proudly beside the cool green of the Country Club, you are impressed by its flowing grace of line and contour. . . . There is about it, in appearance and in performance, a substantial excellence which sets it apart and gives it character and position unusual in a low-priced car. . . . To women especially, its safety, its comfort, its reliability and its surprising ease of operation and control have put a new joy in motoring.

Two women in their new Ford Coupe drive by the golf course at the country club. As their caddies watch, three women golfers in the process of lining up their putts interrupt their game to admire the new Ford car.

Version A (Cpe 7a)
○ *The American Magazine,* April 1930, p. 114
◉ *Liberty,* April 5, 1930, p. 15
◉ *The Redbook Magazine,* April 1930, CII
◉ *True Story,* May 1930, p. 59

INTERRUPTED PUTT

A second version (B) of the *"Interrupted Putt"* 1930 Coupe ad finds the headline and text moved to above the illustration of the car.

Version B (Cpe 7b) ➤

○ *Cosmopolitan,* April 1930, p. 116
◉ *Country Life,* March 1930, p. 81
◉ *Delineator,* April 1930, p. 61
○ *The Farmer's Wife,* April 1930, p. 35
○ *Good Housekeeping,* April 1930
◉ *Harper's Bazaar,* April 1930, p. 16+
○ *Ladies' Home Journal,* April 1930, p. 91
○ *McCall's,* April 1930, p. 112+
◉ *Pictorial Review,* April 1930, p. 39
◉ *The Sportsman,* March 1930, p. 81

(continued)

Version B (Cpe 7b) (continued) ⋁

◉ *Vanity Fair,* April 1930, p. 75
◉ *Vogue,* March 15, 1930, p. 129
○ *Woman's Home Companion,* April 1930, p. 56

Note that this Model A Coupe advertising drawing changes to a reversed, mirror image illustration when appearing in an Argentine magazine. This allows the car to appear with a right-hand steering wheel, as is the case with cars in Argentina.

◁ **Example ad from Argentina**

◉ *Caras y Caretas,* June 1930

OUTSIDE TEA PARTY

◆

October, 1930   3

THE NEW FORD COUPE

Safely to the journey's end. LONG TRIPS are pleasant in the new Ford because of its easy-riding comfort. The restful, well-upholstered seats invite you to sit back and relax and enjoy the panorama of the passing miles. Steadily, evenly, you travel along because of the specially designed springs and four Houdaille double-acting hydraulic shock absorbers. They cushion the car against hard jolts and bumps and smooth your path along every highway. « « « « « « « « «

Equally important to the enjoyment of motoring is your confidence in the mechanical reliability of the Ford. No matter where you go—near or far—day or night—you know it will bring you safely, quickly, comfortably to the journey's end. « « « « « « « « « «

Please mention the Junior League Magazine when answering advertisements.

With a new Ford Coupe parked in the driveway, a tea party begins on the patio at the home. Protected from the sun under the awning, two of the women – and the maid serving them – gaze at the new Model A Ford.

Version A (Cpe 8a)
● *Junior League Magazine,* October 1930, p. 3

This very rare black and white Model A ad is unique. It appeared only once, in October 1930.

CHRISTMAS GIFT VISIT

A Treasured *Gift* at Christmas Time

DREAMS will come true in many homes this Christmas. For there, among the holiday gifts, will be a gleaming new Ford. From Dad to Mother. Or from Mother and Dad to Son or Daughter.

Not a gift for the day only, but one that will be treasured through the year. A practical, useful gift that will bring countless happy hours and shorten the miles to friends and distant places.

Illustrated above is the new Ford Coupe. There are many other body types to select from, in a variety of colors. A choice of Mohair or Bedford Cord is offered in the Town Sedan, De Luxe Sedan, and De Luxe Coupe.

A mother and daughter stop to drop off Christmas gifts at a friend's home. As the maid answers the door, the daughter hides a present behind her back. Given the number of gifts remaining in the Ford Coupe, more deliveries will be made on this holiday excursion.

Version A (Cpe 9a)

⊙ *Country Life,* December 1930, p. 86

⊙ *Harper's Bazaar,* December 1930, p. 112+

⊙ *The Sportsman,* December 1930, p. 73

⊙ *Vanity Fair,* December 1930, p. 32

⊙ *Vogue,* December 22, 1930, p. 73

CHRISTMAS GIFT VISIT

Two additional versions (B and C) of the 1930 *"Christmas Gift Visit"* Coupe magazine ad have only very minor ad text differences.

Version B (Cpe 9b) [text difference]
- ◉ *Collier's,* December 20, 1930, CIII
- ◉ *Delineator,* December 1930, p. 53
- ○ *The Farmer's Wife,* December 1930, p. 14
- ○ *Ladies' Home Journal,* December 1930, p. 42
- ○ *McCall's,* December 1930, p. 44
- ◉ *Pictorial Review,* December 1930, CIII
- ○ *Woman's Home Companion,* December 1930, CIV

Version C (Cpe 9c) [text difference]
- ○ *The American Magazine,* December 1930, p. 105
- ○ *Cosmopolitan,* December 1930, p. 115
- ○ *Good Housekeeping,* December 1930, p. 135
- ● *Junior League Magazine,* December 1930, p. 3 (B&W)
- ◉ *Liberty,* December 13, 1930, p. 19
- ◉ *The Redbook Magazine,* December 1930, p. 84
- ◉ *True Story,* December 1930, p. 59

Version D (Cpe 9d) ∀
- ◉ *The Literary Digest,* December 13, 1930, CF

The fourth version (D) of this 1930 Coupe ad is a two-page edition that includes an insert illustration showing the Johansson Gage Blocks used by Ford to maintain accuracy in the manufacturing dimensions.

THE LITERARY DIGEST FOR DECEMBER 13, 1930

CRAFTSMANSHIP
in volume production

The Ford crankshaft is made of carbon manganese steel and is ground, machined and polished to measurements as fine as five ten-thousdths of an inch. Ford crankshafts receive more than 150 gage tests for accuracy.

The main and connecting rod bearings are polished to mirror-like smoothness within a tolerance of one one-thousandth of an inch. End clearances between the connecting rod bearing faces and those of the crank-shaft are held to the unusually close limit of five one-thousandths of an inch.

Great care is taken to insure the proper static and dynamic balance of the crank-shaft. The machines used for the dynamic balance tests are set upon foundations of gum rubber and are so delicately adjusted that the very air which surrounds them is first cleansed and then held at 68° by thermostatic control.

Though weighing many pounds, the Ford crankshaft is so carefully balanced that it will remain motionless in any position when placed upon two perfectly levelled parallel bars, yet will turn if but two grams weight is placed on any connecting rod bearing.

In addition to the many check-ups and inspections in manufacture, every Ford crank-shaft is set in the motor block and given a run-in test approximating actual service. Only then does it receive the final O. K.

This accuracy in manufacturing, combined with simplicity of design and the high quality of materials, has a definite bearing on the good performance of the Ford and its economy of operation and up-keep. Throughout, it has been made to give you many months and years of satisfactory motoring.

ONE OF THE outstanding features of the new Ford is the precise care with which each part is made and assembled. Many measurements are accurate to within one one-thousandth of an inch. Some to three ten-thousandths of an inch.

This craftsmanship in volume production is particularly apparent in the pistons, valves and crank-shaft — the most important moving parts of an automobile engine.

To insure perfect fit in the cylinders, the aluminum pistons of the new Ford are held true to within one one-thousandth of an inch of the specified diameter of 3⅞ inches. In weight they are not permitted to vary more than two grams (1/14 of an ounce). The wrist-pin holes are diamond bored within a variation of three ten-thousandths of an inch.

The Ford valves are made of chrome silicon alloy, selected because of its durability and resistance to the oxidizing effect of hot gases. The valve stems are held exact in diameter to within one one-thousandth of an inch along their entire length. There is never a variation of more than two one-thousandths of an inch from the seat to the mushroom end.

Each half of the hole in the guide through which the valve stem passes is made to limits of five ten-thousandths of an inch. This insures accurate centering of the valve and minimizes the possibility of gas leakage and loss of compression. It also reduces carbon deposits which cause sticking.

A TREASURED CHRISTMAS GIFT

Dreams will come true in many homes this Christmas. For there, among the holiday gifts, will be a gleaming new Ford. From Dad to Mother. Or from Mother and Dad to Son or Daughter. Not a gift for the day only, but one that will be used and treasured throughout the year. A practical, lasting gift that will bring countless happy hours and shorten the miles to friends and distant places.

PHARMACIST POINTING

◆

15

NEW FORD COUPE

A striking example of value far above the price. Among its many features are . . . beautiful lines, colors and upholstery, ease of control, quick acceleration, 55 to 65 miles an hour, Triplex shatter-proof glass windshield, silent, fully enclosed four-wheel brakes, four Houdaille double-acting hydraulic shock absorbers, aluminum pistons, chrome silicon alloy valves, Rustless Steel and more than twenty ball and roller bearings. The first cost of the Ford is low and you can purchase it on economical terms through the Authorized Ford Finance Plans of the Universal Credit Company.

CRAFTSMANSHIP
in volume production

ONE of the outstanding features of the new Ford is the precise care with which each part is made and assembled. Many measurements are accurate to within one one-thousandth of an inch. Some to three ten-thousandths of an inch.

This craftsmanship in volume production is particularly apparent in the pistons, valves and crankshaft—three of the most important moving parts of an automobile engine.

To insure perfect fit in the cylinders, the aluminum pistons of the new Ford are held true to within one one-thousandth of an inch of the specified diameter of 3⅞ inches. In weight they are not permitted to vary more than two grams (1/14 of an ounce). The wrist-pin holes are diamond bored within a variation of three ten-thousandths of an inch.

The Ford valves are made of chrome silicon alloy, selected because of its durability and resistance to the oxidizing effect of hot gases. The valve stems are held exact in diameter to within one one-thousandth of an inch along their entire length. There is never a variation of more than two one-thousandths of an inch from the seat to the mushroom end.

Each half of the hole in the guide through which the valve stem passes is made to limits of five ten-thousandths of an inch. This insures accurate centering of the valve and minimizes the possibility of gas leakage and loss of compression. It also reduces carbon deposits which cause sticking.

The Ford crankshaft is made of carbon manganese steel and is machined and polished to measurements as fine as five ten-thousandths of an inch. Ford crankshafts receive more than 150 gage tests for accuracy.

The main and connecting rod bearings are polished to mirror-like smoothness within a tolerance of one one-thousandth of an inch. End clearances between the connecting rod bearing faces and those of the crankshaft are held to the close limit of five one-thousandths of an inch.

Great care is taken to insure the proper static and dynamic balance of the crankshafts. The machines used for the dynamic balance tests are set upon foundations of gum rubber and are so delicately adjusted that the very air which surrounds them is first cleansed and then held at 68° by thermostatic control.

This accuracy in manufacturing, combined with simplicity of design and the high quality of materials, has a definite bearing on the good performance and economy of the new Ford. Throughout, it has been made to give you many months and years of satisfactory motoring.

Ford

As the drug salesman prepares to leave the drug store in his new Ford Coupe, the pharmacist points to his Ford De Luxe Delivery car parked around the corner. The insert illustration shows the Ford Johansson Gage Blocks.

Version A (Cpe 10a)

⊙ *Southern Agriculturist*, January 15, 1931, p. 15

This is the only 1931 Model A Coupe ad illustration produced.

PHARMACIST POINTING

Two additional black and white versions of this 1931 Coupe ad appeared in *The State Trooper* magazine. One (B) uses the same illustration, but no insert. Another (C) utilizes a different headline and contains two inserts – about the Ford Triplex shatter-proof windshield.

Version B (Cpe 10b) ➤
● *The State Trooper,* January 1931, CIV

While each of the three one-page versions of the *"Pharmacist Pointing"* ad was produced in black and white, the two-page version (D) appeared in color.

CRAFTSMANSHIP
in volume production

NEW FORD COUPE

No Flying Glass Here

Thirteen Million Square Feet of Glass

The Ford Coupe—one of many body types. You may purchase the Ford on convenient, economical terms through the Authorized Ford Finance Plans of the Universal Credit Company

For Greater Safety on Every Highway

ALL FORD CARS ARE EQUIPPED WITH SHATTER-PROOF GLASS WINDSHIELDS

Following the initial (January 1931) appearance in *The State Trooper,* a modified version of this Coupe ad appeared in both the April and May 1931 issues of this magazine.

◄ **Version C (Cpe 10c)**
● *The State Trooper,* April and May, 1931, both CIV

The State Trooper was a very specialized magazine and contained many unique black and white Model A Ford ads. This difficult to find magazine is the only U.S. publication where a specific Model A ad was repeat-printed in sequential issues.

PHARMACIST POINTING

The fourth version (D) of this 1931 Coupe ad appears in color in a two-page format and includes a smaller insert illustration of the Ford Pick-up.

Version D (Cpe 10d) ⩔

⊙ *The Literary Digest,* September 20, 1930, CF

⊙ *The Saturday Evening Post,* September 6, 1930, pp. 84-85

The New Ford Serves Many Businesses

Experience of large fleet owners reveals the unusual reliability and economy of the new Ford

A SIGNIFICANT TRIBUTE to the value of the new Ford is found in its increasing use by Federal, state and city governments and by large industrial companies which keep careful day-by-day cost records. In most instances, the Ford has been chosen only after exhaustive tests of every factor that contributes to good performance—speed, power, safety, comfort, low cost of operation and up-keep, reliability and long life.

Prominent among the companies using the Ford are the American Can Company, Associated Companies of the Bell System, Armour and Company, The Borden Company, Continental Baking Corporation, Fairbanks, Morse & Company, Inc., Firestone Tire and Rubber Company, General Electric Company, General Foods Sales Company, Inc., Goodyear Tire and Rubber Company, H. J. Heinz Company, Kellogg Company, Knickerbocker Ice Company, Morton Salt Company, Otis Elevator Company, Pillsbury Flour Mills Company, The Procter & Gamble Company, Swift & Company, Units of Union Carbide and Carbon Corporation, Western Union Telegraph Company, and the Westinghouse Electric and Manufacturing Company.

Each of these companies uses a large number of Ford cars and trucks, and one uses more than eight thousand.

Modern business moves at a fast pace and it needs the Ford. Daily, in countless ways and places, it helps to speed the production and delivery of the world's goods and extend the useful service of men and companies.

Constant, steady operation over many thousands of miles emphasizes the advantages of the sound design of the Ford car, its high quality of materials, and accuracy in manufacturing.

An example of the value built into the Ford is the use of more than twenty ball and roller bearings. They are hidden within the car and you may never see them. Yet they play an important part in satisfactory, economical performance. Their function is similar to the jewels of a fine watch.

Throughout the Ford chassis, a ball or roller bearing is used wherever it is needed to reduce friction and wear and give smooth, reliable mechanical operation. At many points, as on the transmission counter-shaft, clutch release, fan and pump shaft, and front drive shaft, these ball and roller bearings are used where less costly types of bearings might be considered adequate.

Additional instances of the high quality built into the Ford are the extensive use of steel forgings, fully enclosed four-wheel brakes, Rustless Steel, four Houdaille double-acting hydraulic shock absorbers, aluminum pistons, chrome silicon alloy valves, torque-tube drive, three-quarter floating rear axle, and the Triplex shatter-proof glass wind-shield.

The Ford policy has always been to use the best possible material for each part and then, through large production, provide it for the public at low cost.

FORD MOTOR COMPANY

THE NEW FORD, WITH PICK-UP BODY AND CLOSED CAB

THE NEW FORD COUPE

The headline and text in the two-page ad edition deal exclusively with commercial applications of the Model A Ford – in line with the illustration of the pharmacist pointing to the De Luxe Delivery Car with his drug store name painted on the side.

LET'S BE PRECISE.
The initial black and white version of this 1931 Coupe ad (A) includes an insert illustration showing the Johansson Gage Blocks used by Ford to ensure consistent measurement accuracy in the Model A manufacturing process.

DE LUXE COUPE

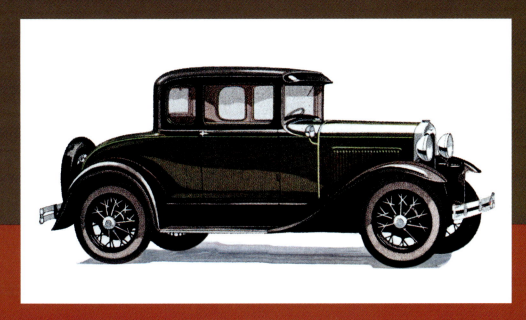

	TOTAL	1930	1931
Ford Body Style		45-B (Dlx.)	45-B (Dlx.)
Weight (pounds)		2,265	2,265
Price (FOB Detroit)		$550	$525
Units Produced (U.S.)	52,004	28,937	23,067
Number of U.S. Ads			
Primary Formats	4	1	3
Ad Variations	14	1	13
Magazine Insertions	43	6	37

The Model A De Luxe Coupe was first announced in February 1930. This body style shared the Ford 45-B body identification number with the (standard) Coupe. Both a dome light and cowl lights – and, in June 1931, a roll-down rear window – were standard equipment on this deluxe model. Note that the relatively low total production for the De Luxe Coupe, at slightly over 50,000 units, was less than one-tenth that of the (standard) Coupe, at over 550,000 units.

A total of 14 different magazine ad variations were created to promote the Model A De Luxe Coupe. The single ad introducing the De Luxe Coupe in 1930 appeared in only upscale magazines. However, the 1931 magazine ads appeared in a wide variety of publications – including general interest, women's fashion, upscale, youth-oriented and farm-related publications. While the 1930 magazine ad featured a De Luxe Coupe with a maroon body color, all of the 1931 ads contained De Luxe Coupes with black bodies.

TEA CUPS AND FLOWERS

The New Ford De Luxe Coupe

The new Ford De Luxe Coupe is a particularly good choice at this season of the year. Within its fully enclosed body you will travel in snug comfort through the winds and snows of winter, soon to come. The added strain that cold weather puts on a motor car will emphasize the mechanical reliability of the Ford and its good performance under all conditions. You will take pride, also, in the graceful lines of the new Ford De Luxe Coupe and the rich quality of its upholstery. In this body type, you may choose either tan Bedford cord or brown mohair. A variety of body colors is offered, in keeping with the latest mode.

Viewed from the porch of the house – over two tea cups, a bouquet and a new Ford Deluxe Coupe – the day's activities at the horse barn are coming to life. As the women chat, the men prepare the horse and wagon for a morning ride.

Version A (DCp 1a)
◉ *Country Life,* November 1930, p. 84
◉ *Harper's Bazaar,* November 1930, p. 144
● *Junior League Magazine,* November 1930, p. 3 (B&W)
◉ *The Sportsman,* November 1930, p. 75
◉ *Vanity Fair,* November 1930, p. 90
◉ *Vogue,* November 24, 1930, p. 18

ACADEMY DISMISSAL

◆

THE NEW FORD DE LUXE COUPE

The new Ford is an economical car to own and drive

THE new Ford is a splendid car to own and drive because of its attractive lines and colors, safety, comfort, speed, reliability and long life.

There are, in addition, three other features of importance to every far-seeing automobile owner ... low first cost, low cost of operation, and low yearly depreciation.

During the life of the car, the day-by-day economy of the Ford will amount to considerably more than the saving on the first cost. You save when you buy the Ford and you save every mile you drive.

Hearst's International–Cosmopolitan for March 1931

Evidence of the economy of the new Ford is shown in its selection by large industrial companies which keep accurate cost records. Many of these operate fleets of fifty, one hundred, and two hundred Ford cars and trucks. One company has eight thousand. The experience of these careful buyers is a dependable guide for you to follow in the purchase of a motor car.

The reasons for the good performance and economy of the new Ford are simplicity of design, high quality of materials,

and care in manufacturing and assembling. Many vital parts are made to limits of one one-thousandth of an inch. Some to three ten-thousandths of an inch.

The more you see of the performance of the new Ford, the more certain you become of this fact. . . . It brings you everything you want or need in a motor car at an unusually low price. You may purchase it on convenient, economical terms through the Authorized Ford Finance Plans of the Universal Credit Company.

Ford

It's the end of the school day and uniformed boys stream out of the pink-shuttered *"Ladd Ridleys Academy."* A mother has parked her new Ford De Luxe Coupe in front of the school as she picks up her children.

Version A (DCp 2a)

○ *The American Magazine,* March 1931, CIII

○ *Cosmopolitan,* March 1931, p. 100

⊙ *The Redbook Magazine,* March 1931, CII

ACADEMY DISMISSAL

Six additional versions of the 1931 De Luxe Coupe *"Academy Dismissal"* magazine ad were prepared.

The second ad version (B) retains the same ad text, but re-positions the headline to above the De Luxe Coupe illustration and adds a second headline below the illustration.

> **Version B (DCp 2b)** ➤
>
> ⊙ *The American Boy,* February 1931, CIV

The third ad version (C) changes to *"A Beautiful Car for the Busy Mother"* headline – which seems more befitting of the "busy mom" depicted in the ad's illustration.

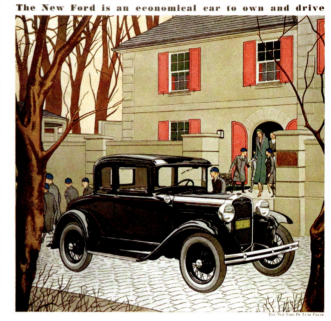

The New Ford is an economical car to own and drive

THE NEW FORD DE LUXE COUPE

LOW FIRST COST, LOW COST OF OPERATION AND UP-KEEP, AND LOW YEARLY DEPRECIATION MEAN A DISTINCT SAVING TO EVERY PURCHASER

The new Ford is a splendid car to own and drive because of its attractive lines and colors, safety, comfort, speed, reliability and long life.

There are, in addition, three other features of importance to every far-seeing automobile owner . . . low first cost, low cost of operation and up-keep, and low yearly depreciation.

During the life of the car, the day-by-day economy of owning a Ford will amount to considerably more than the saving on the first cost. You save when you purchase the new Ford and you save every mile you drive.

Evidence of the economy of the new Ford is shown in its selection by large industrial companies which keep accurate cost records. Many of these operate fleets of fifty, one hundred and two hundred Ford cars and trucks. One company has eight thousand. The experience of these careful buyers is a dependable guide for you to follow in the purchase of a motor car. The reasons for the good performance and economy of the new Ford are simplicity of design, high quality of materials and care in manufacturing and assembling. Many vital parts are made to limits of one one-thousandth of an inch. Some to three ten-thousandths of an inch.

The more you see of the new Ford—the more you talk to Ford owners—the more certain you become of this fact. . . . It brings you everything you want or need in a motor car at an unusually low price. You may purchase it on convenient, economical terms through the Authorized Ford Finance Plans of the Universal Credit Company.

THE NEW FORD DE LUXE COUPE

A Beautiful Car for the Busy Mother

BEAUTY of line and color, ease of control, and dependable mechanical performance make the new Ford De Luxe Coupe a splendid car for the busy modern mother. Another noteworthy feature is the richness of its interior finish and appointments.

For upholstery you may choose soft, luxurious mohair with a deep, substantial pile, or fashionable brown Bedford cord. Both have been selected for long wear as well as attractive appearance.

Other appreciated details of the new Ford De Luxe Coupe are the adjustable seat, dome light, mahogany finish mouldings on the doors and windows, distinctive hardware, cowl lights and bright gleaming Rustless Steel for many exterior metal parts.

> ◀ **Version C (DCp 2c)**
>
> ⊙ *Country Life,* March 1931, CIII
> ⊙ *Delineator,* February 1931, p. 66
> ○ *The Farmer's Wife,* February 1931, p. 43
> ○ *Good Housekeeping,* February 1931
> ⊙ *Harper's Bazaar,* February 1931, p. 128
> ⊙ *Holland's,* February 1931, p. 37
> ○ *Ladies' Home Journal,* February 1931, p. 63
> ○ *McCall's,* February 1931, p. 64
> ⊙ *Pictorial Review,* February 1931, p. 33
> ⊙ *True Story,* February 1931, p. 55
> ⊙ *Vanity Fair,* March 1931, p. 25
> ⊙ *Vogue,* March 1, 1931, p. 17
> ○ *Woman's Home Companion,* February 1931, p. 93
> ○ *Woman's World,* February 1931, p. 25

ACADEMY DISMISSAL

The fourth *"Academy Dismissal"* ad version (D) introduces a new *"The Ford is the Universal Car"* headline. (The "universal car" was a frequent theme used in earlier Model T Ford advertising efforts.)

> **Version D (DCp 2d)**
> ◉ *Life,* February 6, 1931, CII
> ○ *The Literary Digest,* February 21, 1931, CII

Two additional versions of this De Luxe Coupe ad (E and F) utilize this same (new) headline but contain some minor text and headline positioning changes.

THE NEW FORD DE LUXE COUPE

The Ford is the Universal Car

IN CITY, town and country, the new Ford is helping to shorten the miles and extend the limits of opportunity for millions of people.

It brings the open fields closer to the city and removes the isolation of rural districts. Daily it carries great numbers of men to work and home again, takes children safely to school and lightens the duties of women everywhere. Thousands of salesmen use it to cover larger territories and render better service to their customers and the companies for which they work.

Where heavy storms break down the wires, the Ford fights its way through mud and snow and enables linemen to make quick repairs, so that the business of the nation may go on. While you sleep, the new Ford delivers the necessities of life to countless homes, and speeds a physician on a hurried call.

Policemen use it for greater protection to widening areas.

Wherever there is movement of men and materials, you will find the Ford is an accepted part of the program of the day because of its low first cost, good performance and economy of operation and up-keep. You may purchase it on convenient, economical terms through the Authorized Ford Finance Plans of the Universal Credit Company.

> **Version E (DCp 2e)** [text difference]
> ○ *The Saturday Evening Post,* February 14, 1931, p. 39

> **Version F (DCp 2f)** [text difference]
> ◉ *The Sportsman,* March 1931, p. 77

The final (seventh) version (G) of the *"Academy Dismissal"* ad features a new headline indicating the Model A is *"Well-suited to a Woman's Needs."* This ad version appeared only once, in black and white.

> ◀ **Version G (DCp 2g)**
> ● *Junior League Magazine,* March 1931, p. 3

March, 1931   3

Well-suited to a Woman's Needs

THE new Ford is a particularly good choice for the woman motorist because it is such an easy car to drive. Gears shift smoothly and silently. The steering wheel responds to a light touch. The fully enclosed four-wheel brakes take hold quickly and effectively. A space little longer than the car itself is all you need for parking.

Other factors contributing to your feeling of security and confidence in the new Ford are its quick acceleration and alert speed, sturdy body construction, shatter-proof glass windshield and mechanical reliability. In every least little detail it is built to endure — to give you many thousands of miles of economical care-free motoring.

THE NEW FORD DE LUXE COUPE

LEAVING POST OFFICE

◆

THE COUNTRY GENTLEMAN   March, 1931

The New Ford is an economical car to own and drive

THE NEW FORD DE LUXE COUPE

**LOW FIRST COST, LOW COST OF OPERATION AND UP-KEEP, AND LOW
YEARLY DEPRECIATION MEAN A DISTINCT SAVING TO EVERY PURCHASER**

THE new Ford is a splendid car to own and drive because of its attractive lines and colors, safety, comfort, speed, reliability and long life.

There are, in addition, three other features of importance to every far-seeing automobile owner . . . low first cost, low cost of operation and up-keep, and low yearly depreciation.

During the life of the car, the day-by-day economy of owning a Ford will amount to considerably more than the saving on the first cost. You save when you purchase the new Ford and you save every mile you drive.

Evidence of the economy of the new Ford is shown in its selection by large industrial companies which keep accurate cost records. Many of these operate fleets of fifty, one hundred and two hundred Ford cars and trucks. One company has eight thousand. The experience of these careful buyers is a dependable guide for you to follow in the purchase of a motor car. The reasons for the good performance and

economy of the new Ford are simplicity of design, high quality of materials and care in manufacturing and assembling. Many vital parts are made to limits of one one-thousandth of an inch. Some to three ten-thousandths of an inch.

The more you see of the new Ford—the more you talk to Ford owners—the more certain you become of this fact. . . . It brings you everything you want or need in a motor car at an unusually low price. You may purchase it on convenient, economical terms through the Authorized Ford Finance Plans of the Universal Credit Company.

A mother has parked her new Ford De Luxe Coupe to shop and has sent her son to pick up the mail. Junior, packages under his arm, is a little concerned as he reads the letter he has just picked up at the post office.

Version A (DCp 3a)

- ⊙ *Capper's Farmer,* March 1931, CIII
- ○ *The Country Gentleman,* March 1931, p. 62
- ⊙ *Holland's,* March 1931, p. 37
- ⊙ *Southern Agriculturist,* February 1, 1931, p. 17 (B&W)

LEAVING POST OFFICE

A total of four different variations were created for the 1931 *"Leaving Post Office"* magazine ad.

The second version (B) of this De Luxe Coupe ad moves the main headline to below the illustration and does not include the secondary headline used in the initial ad version (A).

Version B (DCp 3b) ➤

○ *The Country Home,* March 1931, CIII

○ *The Farm Journal,* March 1931, p. 17

○ *Successful Farming,* March 1931, CIII

THE NEW FORD DE LUXE COUPE

The new Ford is an economical car to own and drive

THE new Ford is a splendid car to own and drive because of its attractive lines and colors, safety, comfort, speed, reliability and long life.

There are, in addition, three other features of importance to every far-seeing automobile owner ... low first cost, low cost of operation, and low yearly depreciation. During the life of the car, the day-by-day economy of the Ford will amount to considerably more than the saving on the first cost. You save when you buy the Ford and you save every mile you drive.

Evidence of the economy of the new Ford is shown in its selection by large industrial companies which keep accurate cost records. Many of these operate fleets of fifty, one hundred, and two hundred Ford cars and trucks. One company has eight thousand. The experience of these careful buyers is a dependable guide for you to follow in the purchase of a motor car.

The reasons for the good performance and economy of the new Ford are simplicity of design, high quality of materials,

and care in manufacturing and assembling. Many vital parts are made to limits of one one-thousandth of an inch. Some to three ten-thousandths of an inch.

The more you see of the performance of the new Ford, the more certain you become of this fact. ... It brings you everything you want or need in a motor car at an unusually low price. You may purchase it on convenient, economical terms through the Authorized Ford Finance Plans of the Universal Credit Company.

Ford

THE AMERICAN BOY—YOUTH'S COMPANION

THE NEW FORD DE LUXE COUPE

The Ford is the Universal Car

IN CITY, town and country, the new Ford is helping to shorten the miles and extend the limits of opportunity for millions of people.

It brings the open fields closer to the city and removes the isolation of rural districts. Daily it carries great numbers of men to work and home again, takes children safely to school and lightens the duties of women everywhere. Thousands of salesmen use it to cover larger territories and thereby render better service to their customers and

the companies for which they work. Where heavy storms break down the wires, the Ford fights its way through mud and snow and enables linemen to make quick repairs, so that the business of the nation may go on. While you sleep, the Ford delivers the necessities of life to countless homes, and speeds a physician on a hurried call. Along dark-

ened highways, policemen use its alert speed and reliability for greater protection to widening areas.

Wherever there is movement of men and materials, you will find the new Ford is an accepted part of the program of the day because of its low first cost, good performance and economy of operation. You may purchase it on convenient, economical terms through the Authorized Ford Finance Plans of the Universal Credit Company.

The third *"Leaving Post Office"* ad version (C) returns to the *"The Ford is the Universal Car"* headline used in previous De Luxe Coupe ads. This ad version appeared only once in one magazine.

◀ **Version C (DCp 3c)**

⊙ *The American Boy,* March 1931, CIII

Note that, while each of these ads shows a windshield wiper motor on the Model A De Luxe Coupe, none include the wiper blade.

LEAVING POST OFFICE

The final version (D) of the *"Leaving Post Office"* ad is a black and white edition that changes to a *"Beauty that Appeals to Women's Eyes"* headline.

> **Version D (DCp 3d)** ➤
> ● *Junior League Magazine,* April 1931, p. 3

As with the earlier ad versions, this ad also does not show a wiper blade on the windshield wiper motor. These last two versions of this De Luxe Coupe ad were the only versions not to appear in a farm-related magazine.

Not all magazine ads featuring a Model A Ford were prepared by the Ford Motor Company.

Some manufacturers of automotive products and after-market components also attempted to capitalize on the popularity of the Model A to promote their products.

In this example from early 1932, the General Tire and Rubber Company features a Model A De Luxe Coupe (with a 1931 Ohio license plate) in one of their magazine ads. The tire ad is for *"Streamlined Jumbo"* tires that ride on only 12 pounds of air and are touted as *"The greatest safety factor ever developed for the automobile."*

> ◄ **Example non-Ford Sponsored Model A ad**
> ○ *The Saturday Evening Post,* January 9, 1932, p. 99

WEDDING GOWN SHOP

◆

B E A U T Y   T H A T   A P P E A L S   T O   W O M E N ' S   E Y E S

MEN speak knowingly of ball and roller bearings, of valves and pistons, of the many points of mechanical excellence that make the new Ford such a good car to drive.

But to a woman's appraising eye, trained to line and color, there are no features of greater importance than its distinctive beauty of appearance and the richness of its appointments.

The new Ford De Luxe Coupe, illustrated above, is a striking example of this high

quality. The comfortable, roomy seat is deeply cushioned and upholstered in luxurious mohair or fashionable Bedford cord, according to your preference. Hardware reflects the quiet good taste and character that you expect in a Ford car.

In addition to the deep, rich black, you may choose from a variety of body colors.

Most bright metal parts are made of Rustless Steel that will maintain its gleaming luster undimmed throughout the life of the car. Every detail reflects unceasing care and craftsmanship in manufacture.

With all of its beauty of line and color and alert, capable performance, the new Ford sells at a low price. You may purchase it on convenient, economical terms through the Authorized Ford Finance Plans of the Universal Credit Company.

While her new Ford De Luxe Coupe waits at the curb, the bride-to-be gets a fitting at the *"Wedding Gowns and Trousseau"* shop. The woman, in her wedding gown, turns to wave as two fur-clad ladies approach the door of the shop.

Version A (DCp 4a)
○ *The Farmer's Wife,* April 1931, CIII
○ *Woman's World,* April 1931, CIII

This is the last magazine ad produced for the Model A Ford De Luxe Coupe.

WEDDING GOWN SHOP

A second version (B) of this 1931 De Luxe Coupe ad is a two-page edition and includes insert illustrations of Ford ball and roller bearings.

Version B (DCp 4b) ⌄

⊙ *The Literary Digest,* April 4, 1931, pp. 26-27

⊙ *The Saturday Evening Post,* March 28, 1931. pp. 76-77

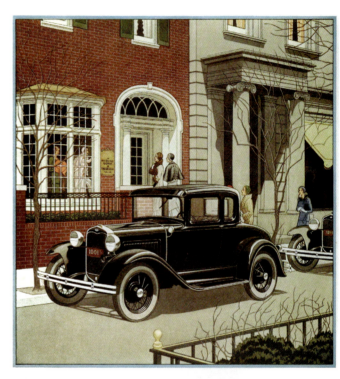

THE SATURDAY EVENING POST — March 28, 1931

The Unseen Value That Makes

Large number of ball and roller bearings reduces friction and wear and gives greater reliability and economy

You step into the new Ford, press your foot on the starter and away you go. Smoothly, evenly, it carries you along your way for many thousands of miles each year. You have no fear of mechanical trouble and you accept its good performance as a matter of course. You have confidence that it will serve you faithfully and well under all conditions.

Though you may never lift the hood of your car, it is interesting to know some of the reasons for the reliability of the Ford and its economy of operation and up-keep. The extensive use of ball and roller bearings is an example of the quality that has been built into it.

These ball and roller bearings are used at more than twenty different places in the chassis of the new Ford. By allowing moving parts to run smoothly and freely, they

This simple illustration shows how the ball bearings in the new Ford minimize friction by reducing the contact surface between moving parts.

Roller bearings are used in the new Ford wherever a wide bearing surface is needed. The contact is along the entire line marked A and B.

THERE ARE MORE THAN TWENTY BALL AND ROLLER BEARINGS IN THE NEW FORD

reduce friction and wear to a minimum. To you as a car owner, this means smooth, quiet mechanical operation, more speed and power, increased gasoline mileage, greater durability and longer life.

The function of the ball and roller bearings of the new Ford is similar to that of the jewels in a watch. Since they are placed at every point in the chassis where they are needed to prevent friction, the new Ford may be called a full-jeweled car, in the same sense that a fine watch is full-jeweled.

As important as the large number of ball and roller bearings in the new Ford is their adequate size, and the manner in which each type has been selected for the work it has to do.

Ball bearings are used where their ball-shaped construction will give the greatest smoothness and efficiency. Roller bearings are used wherever a larger bearing surface is needed to carry a heavier load. The deciding factor is what is best for the car and for Ford owners.

Steering is made easier and safer in the new Ford because of the roller bearings in the front wheels, at the spindle bolts and in the steering mechanism. There are ball bearings on the clutch and ball and roller bearings in the transmission. A roller bearing on the drive shaft at the universal joint provides perfect alignment of those vital parts and prevents loss of power. Adjustments on the rear axle pinion and differential are made unnecessary by the close limits to which those roller bearings are held. The ball bearing on the generator armature gives greater reliability to that important part of the electrical system.

The value of the large number of ball and roller bearings in the new Ford is especially apparent after the first 25,000 miles. By reducing friction and wear, they also reduce the need of replacement parts.

In many other parts of the new Ford you will find this same high quality of materials and fine craftsmanship in manufacture. The performance of the car under the severest driving conditions reflects the quality that has been built into it. The first cost of the new Ford is low and you can purchase it on economical terms through the Authorized Ford Finance Plans of the Universal Credit Company.

(Ford)

FORD MOTOR COMPANY

Here are types of ball and roller bearings used in the new Ford. Bearings of the ball and roller type are placed at more than twenty points in the chassis to reduce friction and wear. Each bearing assembly contains a number of separate balls or rollers as shown in the illustration above.

THE SATURDAY EVENING POST — 77

The New Ford a Fine Car

BEAUTY OF LINE, COLOR AND UPHOLSTERY *In addition to mechanical excellence, the new Ford is distinguished by beauty of line and color and the richness of its appointments. In the new Ford De Luxe Coupe, illustrated above, you may choose upholstery of luxurious mohair or Bedford cord. Many exterior parts are made of bright, gleaming Rustless Steel. A choice of attractive colors is offered in all new Ford cars. The Triplex shatter-proof glass windshield gives added safety.*

In many Model A ads, the headline and text of the ad seems to have no relationship to the illustration. A good example of this miss-matching is apparent in the *"Wedding Gown Shop"* ad. Here, the "female, upcoming wedding" theme of the illustration does not fit the ad content – which concentrates completely on Ford ball and roller bearings.

NO FRICTION HERE!

This insert illustration points out that these bearings reduce the friction between moving parts in the new Ford.

SPORT COUPE

	TOTAL	1927	1928	1929	1930	1931
Ford Body Style		50-A	50-A	50-A	50-B	50-B
Weight (pounds)		2,265	2,265	2,265	2,283	2,283
Price (FOB Detroit)		$550	$550	$550	$530	$500
Units Produced (U.S.)	302,990	732	79,099	134,292	69,167	19,700
Number of U.S. Ads						
Primary Formats	10	–	3	4	3	–
Ad Variations	28	–	7	8	13	–
Magazine Insertions	76	–	19	16	41	–

The stylish Model A Ford Sport Coupe was first introduced as one of the six body styles announced by Ford in December 1927. This Model A body style provided the interior appointments of the closed car while appearing, on the outside, as a roadster with a fold-down top. Contributing to the suggestion of the Sport Coupe being a convertible were fixed, non-folding, landau irons positioned behind the side windows. With this appearance, the Sport Coupe is often confused, at first glance, with the Cabriolet – until the Coupe-style sun visor is noticed.

Magazine advertising for the Model A Sport Coupe centered around 10 basic ad illustrations – with many of these primary ads having numerous variations in headline, text and other ad elements. The magazines containing Sport Coupe ads covered a wide variety of publications – including women's fashion, upscale, general interest, youth-oriented and farm-related magazines.

DOWNTOWN RAIN

June, 1928   LADIES' HOME JOURNAL

Your first glance will tell you that the new Ford is an exceptionally good-looking car.

You will like its low, fleet lines—the exquisite two-tone color harmonies—the sweep of the full-crown fenders—the richness of its upholstery and appointments—the undeniable air of style and speed and strength about it all.

Then, as you stand away and study the complete car, you will begin to realize that the beauty of the new Ford is not of the every-day conventional sort, but a new kind of motor car beauty —a refreshing new note that is as outstanding as the performance of the car itself.

Pride of ownership will be yours when you ride in the new Ford because of its unusual beauty of line and color. Yet your greatest thrill will come when you sit behind the wheel and know the joy of driving this great new car yourself.

It is so alert—so capable—so comfortable—

Shown above is the instrument panel of the new Ford. It is done in satin-finish nickel and is just one example of the quiet simplicity and air of richness that distinguish the new Ford cars.

A Beautiful Car
for the Modern Mother and her Daughter

so responsive and reliable under all conditions. The new Ford will do 55 to 65 miles an hour, and that means you will have speed enough for every need and emergency. It is an especially good car for women to handle in traffic because of its easy steering, short turning radius, remarkable acceleration, multiple dry-disc clutch, and standard selective gear shift with ball and roller bearings. You change gears swiftly and silently in the new Ford with but the pressure of a finger.

Four-wheel brakes and a Triplex shatter-proof glass windshield bring new confidence in driving and give you the safety demanded by modern motoring conditions. New riding comfort is brought to you by the low center of gravity, the minimum unsprung weight, the new transverse springs with

Town car style is combined with speed, safety, comfort, reliability, economy and ease of driving in this smart, low Ford Sport Coupe. Wide, substantial rumble seat is standard equipment.

Houdaille shock absorbers, and the ample room provided for all passengers.

Above all you will find the new Ford a great car to drive because of its reliability. You know it has been built to give you thousands upon thousands of miles of faithful, uninterrupted service. This freedom from trouble—this mental comfort—means a great deal to every woman who drives a car.

The new Ford is also an economical car to drive because it runs 20 to 30 miles per gallon of gasoline, depending on your speed. Cost of up-keep also is low.

Take a little while today to inspect every detail of the new Ford car and ask the nearest Ford dealer to call at your home and take you for a ride in it—in thickest traffic, on open roads, on steepest hills. You will know then that it is a joy for women to drive.

Prices are low because of Ford manufacturing methods and production economies that are as unusual as the car itself.

The Roadster sells for $385; the Phaeton for $395; the Tudor Sedan for $495; the Coupe for $495, and the Sport Coupe, with wide, substantial rumble seat, for $550. (All prices are F.O.B. Detroit.)

Ford

FORD MOTOR COMPANY
Detroit, Michigan

© 1928

The doorman from the *"Silversmiths"* shop holds a large umbrella as a mother and daughter return to their Ford Sport Coupe. This early ad lists prices for the five available Ford body styles. (Note the open-end front bumper and bumper-mounted license plate.)

Version A (SpC 1a)
○ *The Farmer's Wife,* June 1928, CIII
○ *Good Housekeeping,* June 1928, p. 157
◉ *Harper's Bazaar,* June 1928, p. 129
○ *Ladies' Home Journal,* June 1928, p. 124
○ *McCall's,* June 1928, p. 33
◉ *Vogue,* June 15, 1928, p. 105

The new Ford has been built to endure

THE remarkable performance of the new Ford is the direct result of the quality that has been built into every part of it.

It has beauty of line and color because beauty of line and color has come to be considered a necessity in an automobile today.

Yet even more important than this outside beauty is the strength, efficiency and beauty of those parts which are on the inside—those vital mechanical parts which are the very heart of motor car value and performance.

An example of the quality that is built into the new Ford is the use of steel forgings instead of malleable castings and steel stampings. They are used throughout the chassis, except, of course, for the engine castings.

More steel forgings, in fact, are used in the new Ford than are used in almost any other car regardless of price.

Added strength, quiet and reliability also come from the number of electric weldings used in the new Ford. By the use of these weldings, one-piece parts of great strength replace those formerly made up of several parts bolted, riveted or soldered together. Some of the other features which show the strength and quality that have been built into the new Ford car are the steel bodies; the aluminum alloy pistons; the carbon chrome nickel alloy valves; the statically and dynamically balanced crankshaft which is built to withstand a twisting stress up to 60,000-inch pounds; the multiple dry-disc clutch; the standard gear shift with bronze, ball and roller bearings; the low center of gravity and minimum unsprung weight which combine with the Houdaille hydraulic shock absorbers and the new transverse springs to make the new Ford such an easy-riding car; the Triplex shatter-proof glass windshield; the new steering gear which prevents road shocks from being transmitted to the hands of the driver and is unusually strong because the column and the housing of the steering gear mechanism are welded into a single all-steel unit; the mechanical four-wheel brakes; the seamless, all-steel torque tube; the new one-piece, welded,

FORD MOTOR COMPANY
Detroit, Mich.

steel-spoke wheels; and the all-steel rear axle housing.

There are definite reasons, therefore, why the new Ford is more than a new automobile—more than just a new model. It is the advanced expression of a wholly new idea in modern, economical transportation.

So we say to you—take a little while to see and inspect this new car at the nearest Ford showrooms. Examine it carefully, part by part. Listen to its quiet, smooth-running engine. Know the thrill of driving it. By its performance you will know there is nothing quite like it in design, quality and price.

The Roadster sells for $385; the Phaeton for $395; the Tudor Sedan for $495; the Coupe for $495; the Business Coupe for $495; the Sport Coupe, with rumble seat, for $550. (All prices are F.O.B. Detroit.)

The new Ford is a great car in traffic because of its quick acceleration, easy steering, short turning radius, standard gear shift on ball and roller bearings, and the safety of its four-wheel brakes.

Shown below is the instrument panel on the new Ford. It is made of steel, beautifully finished in satin nickel. Instruments are in convenient closer leaf cluster, illuminated by light in center.

As the lady prepares to leave in her new Ford Sport Coupe, two men (one restraining a large dog) and the gardener look on. Note the Ford instrument panel and the (right-facing) Phaeton shown in the insert illustrations.

Version A (SpC 2a)
- ◉ *Country Life,* June 1928, p. 27
- ◉ *The Sportsman,* June 1928, p. 60
- ◉ *Vanity Fair,* June 1928, p. 20+

DOG CONTROL

The second version (B) of this 1928 Ford Sport Coupe ad retains the two insert illustrations but contains a very minor ad text change.

> ### Version B (SpC 2b) [text difference]
> ⊙ *Liberty,* June 23, 1928, p. 20

The third *"Dog Control"* ad version (C) features a left-facing Phaeton in the inset illustration. (The Phaeton in the two earlier ad versions was facing to the right.)

> ### Version C (SpC 2c) ➤
> ○ *Cosmopolitan,* June 1928. p. 117
> ⊙ *The Redbook Magazine,* June 1928, p. 102

Hearst's International–Cosmopolitan for June, 1928

The new Ford has been built to endure

THE remarkable performance of the new Ford is the direct result of the quality that has been built into every part.

It has beauty of line and color because beauty of line and color has come to be considered a necessity in a motor car today.

Yet even more important than this outside beauty is the strength, efficiency and beauty of those parts which are on the inside—those vital mechanical parts which are the very heart of value and performance. It is well to look to this mechanical beauty when you buy an automobile.

An example of the quality that is

The new Ford is a great car to drive in traffic because of its quick acceleration, easy steering, short turning radius, and the safety of its four-wheel brakes. Gears shift easily and silently because of the multiple dry-disc clutch and standard selective gear shift transmission.

built into the new Ford is the use of steel forgings instead of malleable castings and steel stampings. They are used throughout the chassis, except, of course, for the engine castings.

More steel forgings, in fact, are used in the new Ford than in almost any other car regardless of price.

Added strength, quiet and reliability also come from the number of electric weldings used in the new Ford. By the use of these weldings, one-piece parts of great strength replace those formerly made up of several parts which were bolted, riveted or soldered together.

Some of the other features which show the strength and quality that have been built into the new Ford car are the steel bodies; the aluminum alloy pistons; the carbon chrome nickel alloy valves; the statically and dynamically balanced crankshaft which is built to withstand a twisting stress up to 60,000-inch pounds; the multiple dry-disc clutch and the standard selective gear shift transmission; the low center of gravity and minimum unsprung weight which combine with the Houdaille hydraulic shock absorbers and the new transverse springs to make the new Ford such an easy-riding car; the Triplex shatter-proof glass windshield; the new steering gear which prevents road shocks from being transmitted

FORD MOTOR CO.
Detroit, Mich.

to the hands of the driver and is unusually strong because the column and the housing of the steering gear mechanism are welded into a single all-steel unit; the mechanical four-wheel brakes; the seamless, all-steel torque tube; the new one-piece, welded, steel-spoke wheels; the three-quarter floating rear axle; and the all-steel rear axle housing.

There are definite reasons, therefore, why the new Ford is more than a new automobile—more than just a new model. It is the advanced expression of a wholly new idea in modern, economical transportation.

The Roadster sells for $385; the Phaeton for $395; the Coupe for $495; the Tudor Sedan for $495; and the Sport Coupe, with wide, substantial rumble seat, for $550. (All prices are F. O. B. Detroit.)

Shown below is the instrument panel on the new Ford. It is made of steel, beautifully finished in satin nickel. Instruments are in convenient clover leaf cluster, illuminated by light in center.

RESTRAINING FIDO.

A closer look at the details drawn into this Model A Sport Coupe ad reveals why the man to the left of the car is forced to restrain his large dog.

As the lady prepares to leave in her Sport Coupe her small dog has pulled its leash from her hand and has run beneath the front bumper of the car. From there it has caught the attention of the larger dog, which is obviously somewhat agitated by its presence.

DOG CONTROL

The fourth version (D) of the Sport Coupe *"Dog Control"* ad is a two-page edition containing four different insert illustrations – including a (right-facing) Phaeton and a Model A Fordor Sedan. (Neither of these two Model A Ford insert drawings appear as the primary illustration in any Phaeton or Fordor Sedan ad.)

The text of this ad indicates that:

"More steel forgings, in fact, are used in the new Ford than in almost any other car regardless of price. Added strength, quiet and reliability also come from the number of electrical weldings used in the new Ford."

Each of the four *"Dog Control"* Sport Coupe ad versions contains a close-up view of the Model A Ford instrument panel.

Version D (SpC 2d) ▽
- ⊙ *The Literary Digest*, June 30, 1928, CF
- ⊙ *The Saturday Evening Post*, June 9, 1928, pp. 66-67

---

86   THE SATURDAY EVENING POST   June 9, 1928   THE SATURDAY EVENING POST   87

The new Ford has been built to endure

Long life and economy of new model as important as its beauty, speed, safety and quiet comfort

THE remarkable performance of the new Ford is the direct result of the quality that has been built into every part of it.

It has beauty of line and color because beauty of line and color have come to be considered a necessity in a motor car today.

Yet even more important than this outside beauty are the strength, efficiency and beauty of those parts which are on the inside—those vital mechanical parts which are the very heart of value and performance. It is well to look to this mechanical beauty when you buy an automobile.

Instantly you examine the body construction of the new Ford, its engine, its transmission, its oiling, cooling and ignition systems, you will understand some of the reasons for its speed, safety, comfort, quiet, reliability and economy of operation and up-keep.

Steel forgings instead of castings and stampings

An example of the quality that is built into the new Ford is the use of steel forgings instead of malleable castings and steel stampings. They are used throughout the chassis, except, of course, for the engine castings.

More steel forgings, in fact, are used in the new Ford than in almost any other car regardless of price.

Just what this means to every motorist is shown in the strength of the forged-steel spring perches alone. They will withstand 15,000 pounds pressure before indicating a permanent change in their structure. This is thirty times the strain put on each spring perch under normal running conditions.

Added strength, quiet and reliability also come from the number of electric weldings used in the new

Ford. By the use of these weldings, one-piece parts of great strength replace those formerly made up of several parts bolted, riveted or soldered together.

The perfecting of electric welding machines to do this work was the result of ten years of constant experimenting in shop and laboratory.

Some of the other features which show the strength and quality that have been built into the new Ford car are the steel bodies, the carbon chrome nickel alloy valves, the five-bearing camshaft, the heavy crankshaft which is statically and dynamically balanced and built to withstand a twisting stress up to 60,000-inch pounds; the new pump, splash and gravity oil system; the

multiple dry-disc clutch; the standard gear shift with ball and roller bearings; the new battery, coil and distributor ignition; the low center of gravity and minimum unsprung weight which combine with the Houdaille hydraulic shock absorbers and the new transverse springs to make the new Ford such an easy-riding car; the Triplex shatter-proof glass windshield; the new steering gear which prevents road shocks from being transmitted to the hands of the driver and is unusually strong because the column and the housing of the steering gear mechanism are welded into a single all-steel unit; the mechanical four-wheel brakes, the seamless, all-steel torque tube; the new one-piece, welded, steel-spoke wheels; the aluminum alloy pistons which were selected because of their light weight and heat-conducting

qualities; the three-quarter floating rear axle, and the all-steel rear axle housing.

There are definite reasons, therefore, why the new Ford is more than a new automobile—more than just a new model. It is the advanced expression of a new idea in modern, economical transportation.

FEATURES OF THE NEW FORD CAR

Steel bodies
Beautiful low lines
Choice of colors
55 to 65 miles an hour   40 horse-power
Remarkable acceleration
Four-wheel brakes
New transverse springs
Houdaille hydraulic shock absorbers
20 to 30 miles per gallon of gasoline
Triplex shatter-proof glass windshield
Reliability and low up-keep cost

So we say to you—take a little while to see and inspect this new car at the nearest Ford showrooms. Examine it carefully, part by part. Listen to its quiet, smooth-running engine. Know the thrill of driving it. By its performance you will know there is nothing quite like it in design, quality and price.

New manufacturing methods make the low price possible

The low price of the new Ford is made possible only by manufacturing methods and production economics as unusual as the car itself.

The Roadster sells for $385; Phaeton, $395; Tudor Sedan, $495; Coupe, $495; Business Coupe, $495; Sport Coupe, with rumble seat, $550. (All prices are F.O.B. Detroit.)

These prices include five steel-spoke wheels, four 30 x 4.50 balloon tires, windshield wiper, speedometer, gasoline gage on instrument panel, dash light, mirror, combination stop and tail light, theft-proof coincidental ignition lock, high-pressure grease gun lubrication, and Triplex shatter-proof glass windshield.

FORD MOTOR COMPANY
Detroit, Michigan

KISSING AND FLIRTING

◆

McCALL'S MAGAZINE SEPTEMBER 1928

Greater Even Than Its Beauty is the Reliability of the New Ford

THE NEW FORD SPORT COUPE IN THE POPULAR ARABIAN SAND COLOR

WOMEN's eyes are quick to note and appreciate the trim, graceful lines of the new Ford, its exquisite two-tone color harmonies, the rich simplicity and quiet good taste reflected in every least little detail of finish and appointment.

Yet greater even than this beauty is the mechanical reliability of the car.

As the days and months and years go by, and your speedometer tells of thousands upon thousands of miles of faithful, uninterrupted service, you will realize that this very reliability is perhaps the most important reason why the new Ford is such a good car for a woman to drive.

You will find new joy in motoring because you will have a new feeling of confidence and security. No matter how long the trip, or rough or devious the roadway, you

Here you can see the roominess of the new Ford Tudor Sedan. Built to accommodate five people in real comfort. Note, too, the restful tilt of the well-upholstered seats.

know that your Ford will take you safely, comfortably and speedily to the journey's end.

For the new Ford has been built to endure. Its beauty is not confined to externals only, but goes deep down into every part of the car.

The price is low because of established Ford methods of manufacture and production which are as unusual as the car itself. Every purchaser shares the benefits of the Ford policy of selling at a small margin of profit—of owning the source of raw materials—of constantly giving greater and greater value.

You see the quality of the car reflected in the mechanical, internal expanding-shoe four-wheel brakes; the new transverse springs and Houdaille

FORD MOTOR COMPANY
Detroit, Michigan

hydraulic shock absorbers; the Triplex shatter-proof glass windshield; the standard selective sliding gear shift; the $^3/_4$ irreversible steering gear; the 40-horse-power engine; the all-steel rear axle housing—in every detail that contributes to ease of control, safety, speed, comfort, economy and long life.

Take a little while today to see the new Ford and arrange for a demonstration. Drive it yourself through thickest traffic. On roughest roads. On steepest hills. You will know then that here is everything you want or need in a modern automobile.

Not only are the prices of the new Ford surprisingly low but these prices include five steel-spoke wheels, four 30 x 4.50 balloon tires, electric windshield wiper on closed cars, speedometer, ammeter, gasoline gage on instrument panel, dash light, mirror, combination stop and tail light, theft-proof coincidental ignition lock, and high pressure grease gun lubrication.

As two (arm-in-arm) ladies prepare to leave in their new Ford Sport Coupe, one receives a kiss from the gentleman at the door. Meanwhile, the hired hand takes a minute from his car polishing duties to flirt with the maid as he comments on the new Ford car.

Version A (SpC 3a)

○ *The Farmer's Wife,* September 1928, p. 17

◉ *Harper's Bazaar,* September 1928, p. 157

○ *Ladies' Home Journal,* September 1928, p. 124

○ *McCall's,* September 1928, p. 33

Version B (SpC 3b) [text difference]

○ *Good Housekeeping,* September 1928, p. 110

ICE SKATERS

LADIES' HOME JOURNAL   February, 1929

Built to serve you faithfully and well for many thousands of miles

THE new Ford is a remarkably fine car for one that costs so little. It is simple in design, constructed of the finest materials, and built with unusual accuracy.

These are the reasons it performs so wonderfully. These are also the reasons its service requirements are so few and the up-keep cost so low.

An example of the simplicity of Ford manufacturing methods is shown in the engine lubrication system. It is reliable and effective

Long, low and fleet are the lines and strikingly beautiful the colors of this new Fordor Sedan. Distinguished, too, by a richness of finish and appointment unusual in a low-price car. Five people can ride in comfort in the new Fordor Sedan because of the wide seats and generous room in both front and rear compartments.

in action, yet so carefully designed and made that it requires practically no service attention. There is, in fact, only one thing for you to do but that is a very important thing . . . *watch the oil!* Keep enough oil in the oil pan so that the indicator rod never registers below low (L) and change the oil regularly every 500 miles.

If the oil level is allowed to fall below low, the supply becomes insufficient to oil all parts as they should be oiled. The oil also loses its lubrication properties more rapidly because it is used faster.

In addition to having the engine oil changed, you will also find that it pays to have the chassis lubricated every 500 miles. This has been made easy in the new Ford through the use of the high pressure grease gun system.

The oiling and greasing of an automobile is so important and means so much to economical, satisfactory performance that it ought not to be neglected or delegated to inexperienced hands.

When you consider that each piston moves up and down 1300 times a minute

Ford Motor Company
Detroit, Michigan

when you are traveling at only thirty miles an hour, you can see the need of complete and proper lubrication. And the piston is only one of many moving parts in the engine!

Ford dealers are the most competent to handle the lubrication requirements of the new Ford. They know what oil and grease are best for each season of the year and they have the equipment to do a prompt and thorough job at a fair price.

All the features of the new Ford are brought to you in this Tudor Sedan. Beautiful lines and choice of colors . . . 55 to 65 miles an hour . . . fully enclosed, silent six-brake system . . . four Houdaille hydraulic shock absorbers . . . Triplex shatter-proof glass windshield . . . reliability and low cost of up-keep.

It's a cold winter day as a couple arrives at the frozen lake to join in the ice skating fun. Their new Ford Sport Coupe receives an admiring glance from a nearby lady, ice skates in hand.

Version A (SpC 4a)

○ *The Farmer's Wife,* February 1929, p. 19

○ *Good Housekeeping,* February 1929, p. 143

○ *Ladies' Home Journal,* February 1929, p. 82

○ *McCall's,* February 1929, p. 9

ICE SKATERS

While a second *"Ice Skaters"* ad version (B) contains only a minor ad text change, it retains the insert illustrations of a Fordor Sedan and a Tudor Sedan.

Version B (SpC 4b) [text difference]

◉ *Harper's Bazaar,* February 1929, p. 129

◉ *Vanity Fair,* February 1929, p. 26

◉ *Vogue,* February 16, 1929, p. 322

A third version (C) is in black and white and has a completely different headline and text. It contains a single insert illustration of a Tudor Sedan.

The fourth version (D) of this 1929 Sport Coupe ad is a two-page edition with a new headline and text – and three insert illustrations.

Version D (SpC 4d) ∨

◉ *The Literary Digest,* December 15, 1928, CF

◉ *The Saturday Evening Post,* December 8, 1928, pp. 68-69

Version C (SpC 4c) ∨

◉ *The American Boy,* December 1929, p. 29

Boys who like mechanical things will appreciate the simplicity of the new Ford

Remarkable Simplicity of Design
is revealed in the
many exclusive mechanical features of the New Ford

FORD MOTOR COMPANY
Detroit, Michigan

WATCHING AIRPLANE

Fuel system of the new Ford has been designed for reliability and long service

THE practical value of Ford simplicity of design is especially apparent in the fuel system. The whole purpose is to give you many thousands of miles of use without trouble of any kind.

The very location of the gasoline tank is an example of this careful planning. It has been built integral with the cowl to permit the use of a direct gravity feed without any intermediate step—the simplest and most effective way of supplying gasoline to the carburetor without variations in pressure.

Because of the central location of the gasoline tank in the new Ford, there is no need of a long fuel line with its multiplied possibilities of trouble. The Ford fuel line, as a matter of fact, is only eighteen inches long and is easily accessible all the way.

The tank itself is made of heavy pressed steel, and is terne plated to prevent rust or corrosion. An additional factor of strength is the fact that it is composed of only two pieces, instead of the usual three or four, and is electrically welded—not soldered.

The carburetor in the new Ford also has many interesting features. It is unusually reliable in action because there are no moving

parts in any way affecting the mixture. All adjustments are fixed except the needle valve and idler, so there is practically nothing to get out of order. "Keep-it-clean" and "don't tinker" are the two big things to remember in the care of the Ford carburetor.

The choke on the dash of the new Ford acts not only as a primer but likewise provides a convenient way for you to regulate the gasoline mixture and thereby increase gasoline mileage.

For quick starting, the choke button should be turned one full turn

This new Ford is distinguished by the trim, graceful simplicity of its lines and the beauty of its colors. Without being extreme, it has struck a new note in automobile designing. Shown above is the new Ford Sport Coupe. On the left is the new Fordor Sedan.

counter-clockwise and then pulled outward, to be released the instant the engine starts. As the engine warms up, the choke should be turned clockwise until it is approximately ¼ turn open.

Throughout, the fuel system of the new Ford is so simple in design and so carefully made that it requires very little attention.

There are really only three things to do, at intervals of 1000 to 2000 miles. (1) Clean the sediment bulb. (2) Remove the carburetor screen and wash it in gasoline. (3) Take out the drain plug at the bottom of the carburetor and drain the carburetor.

Make it a point to have your Ford dealer look after these little details for you when you take the car to him for oiling and greasing.

A periodic checking-up costs little, but it has a great deal to do with long life and continuously good performance.

Ford

FORD MOTOR COMPANY
Detroit, Michigan

It's dusk as a new Ford Sport Coupe speeds along a country road with its lights on. All attention is suddenly drawn upward to a Ford Tri-Motor airplane as it approaches a navigational beacon.

Version A (SpC 5a)
◉ *The American Boy,* April 1929, p. 31

This ad is one of several unique Model A ads appearing in *The American Boy.*

DEALER PRIMPING

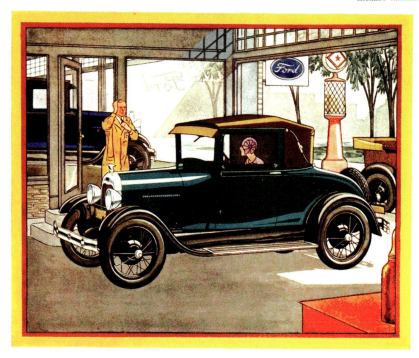

McCALL'S MAGAZINE JULY 1929

Prompt, Courteous, Economical Service for
the Woman Motorist

The assurance of good dealer service is as much a feature of the new Ford as its beauty of line and color, safety, comfort, reliability, economy and ease of control. It is of special importance to the woman driver who wants to be sure of the mechanical performance of the car at all times, yet does not wish to bother with mechanical details.

We are particularly interested in this matter because we believe it is our duty not only to make a good automobile, but to help the purchaser get the greatest possible use from it at a minimum of trouble and expense. Because of this, the entire Ford dealer organization has been trained and equipped to service the new Ford.

When you receive your new Ford, the dealer will explain the simple little things that should be attended to at regular intervals to insure the best performance. He will also tell you about the Free Inspection Service to which every purchaser of the new Ford is entitled at 500, 1000 and 1500 miles.

This inspection includes a check-up of the battery, generator charging rate, distributor,

carburetor adjustment, lights, brakes, shock absorbers, tire inflation and steering gear. The engine oil is also changed and the chassis lubricated through the high pressure grease gun system. A check-up of wheel alignment and spring shackles is made during the final inspection.

No charge whatever is made for labor or materials incidental to this service except where repairs are necessary because of accident,

neglect, or misuse. The labor of changing the engine oil and lubricating the chassis is also free, although a charge is made for new oil.

While this inspection is free only at 500, 1000, and 1500 miles, it should not be stopped then, but continued throughout the life of your car. A nominal charge is made after the first 1500 miles.

Every time, in fact, that you take your Ford to the dealer for oiling and greasing, it will be a good plan to have him check over important points that have a bearing on continuously good performance and tell you exactly what the car needs. You will find him prompt in his work, fair in his charges, and sincerely eager to do a good job at all times.

His constant effort is to relieve you of every detail in the care of your car and to help you get thousands upon thousands of miles of motoring without a care—without even lifting the hood.

That is the purpose for which the new Ford was designed and built. That is the true meaning of *Ford Service.*

Ford
FORD MOTOR COMPANY
Detroit, Michigan

As the woman pulls her new Sport Coupe into the Ford dealership, the dealer prepares to greet her – but first takes a second to smooth his hair and adjust his tie. (This is the only Model A magazine ad to show the quail radiator cap accessory.)

Version A (SpC 6a)
○ *The Farmer's Wife,* July 1929, p. 19
○ *Ladies' Home Journal,* July 1929, p. 77
○ *McCall's,* July 1929, p. 62

Version B (SpC 6b) [text difference]
○ *Good Housekeeping,* July 1929, p. 126

POLO FIELD

VALUE *far above the* PRICE

THE FORD SPORT COUPE

In REVIEWING the many advantages of the new Ford, it is particularly interesting to note the relation between value and price.

The low first cost of the new Ford is a point to keep in mind at all times because it means a considerable saving to you in the purchase of the car.

Equally important, however, is the reason for this low price and the manner in which it has been achieved without sacrifice of quality or performance. On the basis of actual, comparative worth, the new Ford represents a value far above the price you pay.

That price is made possible only through manufacturing methods and production economies that are as unusual as the car itself.

Every purchaser shares the benefits of the Ford policy of owning the source of most raw materials—of making thousands of cars a day—of selling at a small margin of profit—and of constantly giving greater and greater value.

Were the new Ford made in any other way, under any other policy, it would unquestionably cost you much more than the present price.

The use of the Triplex shatter-proof glass for the windshield is a definite indication of this quality. So are the four Houdaille double-acting hydraulic shock absorbers. The silent, fully enclosed six-brake

system. The aluminum pistons. The chrome silicon alloy valves. The all-steel rear axle shaft housing. The simplicity and efficiency of the lubrication, cooling, ignition and fuel systems. The unusually large number of ball and roller bearings. The extensive use of fine steel forgings instead of castings or stampings. The many other mechanical and structural features that count so much in reliability, economy and long life.

All of these are important considerations to every man or woman who is contemplating the purchase of a motor car. All are important reasons why the new Ford delivers a value far above the price.

FORD MOTOR COMPANY
Detroit, Michigan

Mr. Jackson pulls his new Ford Sport Coupe into his assigned parking space at the polo field as a chauffeur waits in the Town Car to the right. This is one of the few Model A ads where the featured person looks directly "at the camera."

Version A (SpC 7a)
⊙ *The Saturday Evening Post*, August 10, 1929, p. 41

This is a unique Model A ad for the 1929 Sport Coupe. It appeared only once, in only one magazine.

TENNIS CLUB

◆

The Farmer's Wife, May, 1930

A charming companion for a busy day

THE NEW FORD SPORT COUPE

THE NEW FORD offers many advantages to the woman who uses an automobile constantly for quick trips to the Country Club, for shopping, the theater, for the many social and business activities of a busy day. Rarely is there to be found such an ideal combination of charm and utility. « «
In addition to its beauty of line and color, the new Ford brings you an unusual degree of mechanical excellence and good performance. You will drive with a new feeling of confidence because of its safety and ease of operation and control. « « « « « « « « «

A woman, tennis racquet in hand, exits her new Ford Sport Coupe after arriving at the tennis club. As the waiter serves her friends on the balcony, they interrupt their lunch to stand and greet her.

Version A (SpC 8a)
⊙ *Delineator,* May 1930, p. 61
○ *The Farmer's Wife,* May 1930, p. 18
○ *Ladies' Home Journal,* May 1930, p. 103
○ *McCall's,* May 1930, p. 94
⊙ *Pictorial Review,* May 1930
○ *Woman's Home Companion,* May 1930, p. 49

TENNIS CLUB

With a minor text change, a second version (B) of this 1930 Sport Coupe ad was produced and appeared only in the most upscale magazines of the era.

Version B (SpC 8b) [text difference]
◉ *Country Life,* June 1930, p. 81
◉ *Harper's Bazaar,* June 1930
◉ *The Sportsman,* June 1930, p. 90
◉ *Vanity Fair,* June 1930, p. 20+
◉ *Vogue,* June 7, 1930, p. 112

A third *"Tennis Club"* ad version (C) has the headline moved to beneath the Sport Coupe illustration.

Version C (SpC 8c) ▽
○ *Good Housekeeping,* May 1930, p. 174

Many Model A Ford ads (or the illustrations used in these ads) were adapted to appear in Ford advertising placed outside of the United States.

As an example, the Sport Coupe *"Tennis Club"* ad, using a typical Williamson illustration, appeared in several Canadian magazines – both in English and in French.

◀ **Example French Canadian ad**
◉ *Le Samedi,* May 1930

FEEDING BEAR

◆

THE NEW FORD SPORT COUPE

After the First Twenty-five Thousand Miles

THE value of sound design, good materials, and careful construction is especially apparent in the new Ford after the first twenty-five thousand miles. Long continuous service emphasizes its mechanical reliability and economy of operation and up-keep. The passing months and years bring a growing pride in its appearance and increasing respect for the substantial worth that has been built into it. From every standpoint, you know you have made a far-seeing, satisfactory purchase.

Throughout the car you will find many reasons for its alert, capable performance and many instances of

value far above the price you pay. Prominent among these are the four Houdaille double-acting hydraulic shock absorbers, Triplex shatter-proof glass windshield, internal-expanding four-wheel brakes with all working parts fully enclosed, five steel-spoke wheels, aluminum pistons, chrome silicon alloy valves, chrome alloy transmission gears and shafts, torque-tube drive, three-quarter floating rear axle, with all-steel axle housing, extensive use of steel forgings and electric welding, more than twenty ball and roller bearings, and bright, enduring Rustless Steel for many exterior parts.

Ford

A man has stopped his new Sport Coupe to feed a bear cub. Several additional bears approach as the woman films the unfolding events from the car. (This ad shows the car with a windshield wiper blade and a rumble seat step plate.)

Version A (Spc 9a)
◉ *Country Life,* August 1930, p. 86
◉ *The Sportsman,* August 1930, p. 79
◉ *Vogue,* September 1, 1930, p. 82

A total of seven different versions of this Sport Coupe ad were produced.

FEEDING BEAR

The two-page edition (B) of this 1930 Ford Sport Coupe ad uses a modified ad text and includes a smaller insert drawing of a Tudor Sedan.

Version B (SpC 9b)

⊙ *The Literary Digest,* August 23, 1930, CF
⊙ *The Saturday Evening Post,* August 9, 1930, pp. 50-51

**Sport Coupe with wiper blade
and step plate
(ad versions A, B and G)**

**Sport Coupe without wiper
blade and step plate
(ad versions C, D, E and F)**

FEEDING BEAR

The third version (C) of the *"Feeding Bear"* ad uses the same *"After the First Twenty-five Thousand Miles "* headline and, at first glance, the identical Sport Coupe illustration.

However, a closer look reveals some minor differences in the illustration. For some reason, in this and in subsequent *"Feeding Bear"* ad versions, the Sport Coupe is drawn without its windshield wiper blade and its rumble seat step plate.

Version C (SpC 9c) ➤

⊙ *Collier's,* August 2, 1930, CIII

◯ *The Country Gentleman,* September 1930, p. 50

THE NEW FORD SPORT COUPE

After the First Twenty-five Thousand Miles THE value of sound design, good materials, and careful construction is especially apparent in the new Ford after the first twenty-five thousand miles. Long, continuous service emphasizes its mechanical reliability, and economy of operation and up-keep. Throughout the car you will find many reasons for its alert, capable performance and many instances of value far above the price you pay.

Prominent among these are the four Houdaille double-acting hydraulic shock absorbers, Triplex shatter-proof glass windshield, fully enclosed four-wheel brakes, five steel-spoke wheels, aluminum pistons, chrome silicon alloy valves, chrome alloy transmission gears and shafts, torque-tube drive, three-quarter floating rear axle, more than twenty ball and roller bearings, and bright, enduring Rustless Steel for many exterior parts. Unusual accuracy in manufacturing is another feature of the Ford car.

After the First Twenty-five Thousand Miles

THE value of sound design, good materials, and careful construction is especially apparent in the new Ford after the first twenty-five thousand miles. Long, continuous service emphasizes its mechanical reliability, and economy of operation and up-keep. Throughout the car you will find many reasons for its alert, capable performance and many instances of value far above the price.

Prominent among these are the four Houdaille double-acting hydraulic shock absorbers, Triplex shatter-proof glass windshield, fully enclosed four-wheel brakes, five steel-spoke wheels, aluminum pistons, chrome silicon alloy valves, chrome alloy transmission gears and shafts, torque-tube drive, three-quarter floating rear axle, more than twenty ball and roller bearings, and bright, enduring Rustless Steel for many exterior parts. Unusual accuracy in manufacturing and assembling is another important feature of the Ford car.

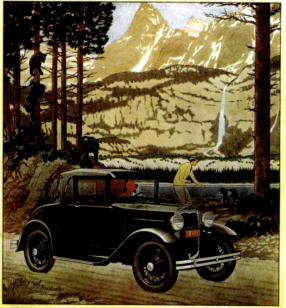

THE NEW FORD SPORT COUPE

A possible explanation for the missing wiper blade and step plate could be that they were simply omitted in the initial ad drawing and later added to an updated drawing as the mistake was discovered. However, this explanation can not be confirmed by the wide mix of magazine publish dates for the ad versions with and without these elements.

The fourth ad version (D) uses the same drawing and text – but with the headline and text moved to above the Sport Coupe illustration.

◄ **Version D (SpC 9d)**

◯ *Country Home,* September 1930, CIII

◯ *Successful Farming,* September 1930, CIII

FEEDING BEAR

The fifth *"Feeding Bear"* ad version (E) employs a completely new text and changes to a *"Built for many thousands of miles"* headline.

In pointing out the durability of the new Ford, the ad text indicates that *"Beneath the flashing beauty of line and color – in those vital mechanical parts which you may never see – is a high quality of material and accuracy in manufacturing."*

Version E (SpC 9e) ➤

○ *The American Magazine,* August 1930, p. 105

○ *Cosmopolitan,* August 1930, CIII

◉ *Liberty,* August 23, 1930

◉ *The Redbook Magazine,* August 1930, CII

Built for many thousands of miles

THE new Ford has been designed and built to give you many thousands of miles of faithful, economical service. Beneath its flashing beauty of line and color—in those vital mechanical parts which you may never see — is a high quality of material and accuracy in manufacturing.

The reliability and capable performance of the car, in all weather and under all conditions, make it a particularly good choice for long, constant use.

It stands up under the added strain of bad roads and hard daily service in a way that has always been characteristic of the Ford car. The experience of the passing months will increase your satisfaction in its performance and confirm your first impression that it is a value far above the price.

THE NEW FORD SPORT COUPE

THE NEW FORD SPORT COUPE

A distinctive beauty of line and color

THE BEAUTY of the new Ford, so apparent in line and color, extends also to the upholstery and appointments. You note it as you open the doors and see the attractive interiors. You find it also in those important little details of trim and finish which a woman's practiced eye is quick to catch. « « « « There is about the car a distinctive style or tone which reflects the substantial quality that has been built into it. In external things, as in mechanical construction, the new Ford has been built to endure. « « « « « «

A black and white edition of the *"Feeding Bear"* Sport Coupe magazine ad was also produced. This ad version (F) features a completely different headline and text. This version appeared only once, in a single magazine.

Note the unusual ad format that includes a line drawn as a border around the entire Sport Coupe ad.

◀ **Version F (SpC 9f)**

● *Junior League Magazine,* July 1930, p. 3

FEEDING BEAR

The seventh *"Feeding Bear"* ad version (G) is also in black and white but features an illustration with many minor changes. These include a different license plate on the Sport Coupe, a lower top on the car, a slightly smaller bear cub, the man's hand positioned a little higher, the bottom of his sweater rising up in the back and numerous forest vegetation changes.

Also adding to the list of changed components in this "mutant" ad version is the return of the windshield wiper motor, wiper blade and rumble seat step plate.

Version G (SpC 9g) ➤

⊙ *The American Boy,* September 1930, p. 31

⊙ *Southern Agriculturist,* September 1, 1930, p. 4

● *The State Trooper,* September and October, 1930, both p. 4

**Drawing in ad
Versions A through F**

**Drawing in ad
Version G**

PONY BOY

◆

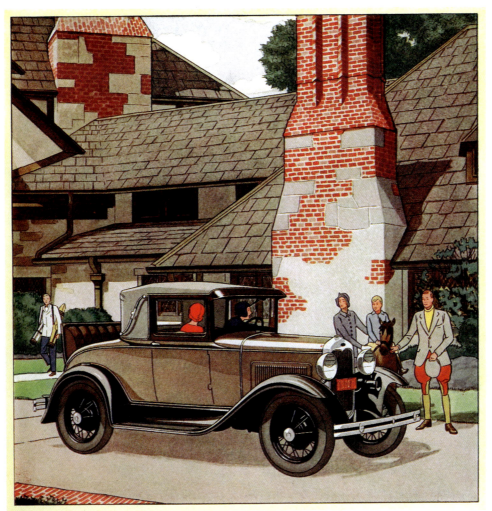

A distinctive beauty of line and color

THE BEAUTY of the new Ford, so apparent in line and color, extends also to the upholstery and appointments. You note it as you open the doors and see the attractive interiors. You find it also in those important little details of trim and finish which a woman's practiced eye is quick to catch.   «   «   «   «

There is about the car a distinctive style or tone which reflects the substantial quality that has been built into it. In external things, as in mechanical construction, the new Ford has been built to endure.   «   «

THE NEW FORD SPORT COUPE

Two women have parked their new Ford Sport Coupe, with its rumble seat open. As the passenger watches the porter bringing two sets of golf clubs to their car, the driver talks with the parents who are steadying their young boy on his pony.

Version A (SpC 10a)

○ *The American Magazine,* September 1930, p. 105

○ *Cosmopolitan,* September 1930, p. 131

◉ *Country Life,* September 1930, p. 109

○ *Good Housekeeping,* October 1930

(continued)

PONY BOY

Version A (SpC 10a) [continued]

⊙ *Harper's Bazaar,* September 1930, p. 141

⊙ *Liberty,* September 20, 1930, p. 39

⊙ *The Redbook Magazine,* September 1930 p. 111

⊙ *True Story,* October 1930

⊙ *Vanity Fair,* September 1930, p. 92+

⊙ *Vogue,* September 29, 1930, p. 88

The second version (B) of this 1930 Sport Coupe ad utilizes a different headline and text – and adds the Ford logo.

The third version (C) is a two-page edition presenting a third headline and ad text modifications.

Version C (SpC 10c) ⱽ

⊙ *The Saturday Evening Post,* October 4, 1930, pp. 38-39

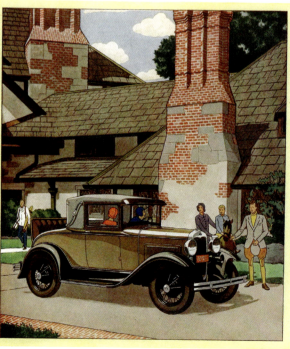

TUDOR SEDAN

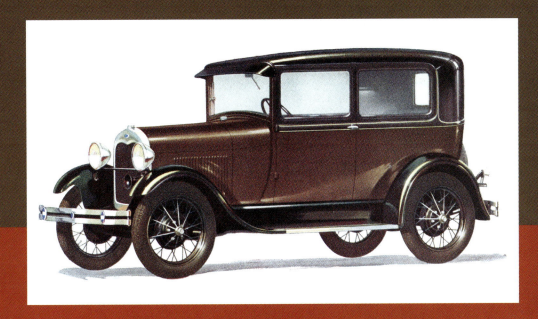

	TOTAL	1927	1928	1929	1930	1931
Ford Body Style		55-A	55-A	55-A	55-B	55-B (Std.) 55-B (Dlx.)
Weight (pounds)		2,340	2,340	2,340	2,375	2,375
Price (FOB Detroit)		$495	$495	$525	$500	$490
Units Produced (U.S.)	1,258,978	1,798	208,562	523,922	376,271	148,425
Number of U.S. Ads						
Primary Formats	24	–	6	7	6	5
Ad Variations	58	–	19	16	14	9
Magazine Insertions	142	–	37	40	41	24

The Model A Ford Tudor Sedan was one of the original six body styles introduced by Ford in December 1927. The Tudor Sedan proved to be quite popular and was the best selling Model A body style. Over 1.2 million Tudor Sedan units were produced.

This Model A body style was advertised quite heavily using a wide variety of magazines – including women's fashion, upscale, general interest, youth-oriented and farm-related publications. More magazine ads were devoted to the Tudor Sedan (over 50 different ad variations and over 140 total magazine insertions) than to any other Model A Ford body style.

Ford introduced the Model A De Luxe Tudor Sedan (55-B De Luxe) in June 1931 and priced this vehicle at $525. However, no magazines ads were produced for this 1931 Model A Ford body style.

WHITE COLUMNS

◆

Women like the new Ford because it is *so safe—*
so sure—so easy to handle

THE joy of driving the new Ford comes not alone from its speed—its safety—its comfort—the pride you take in its beauty of line and color—but also from the pleasure it puts into motoring.

Instantly you start away for your first ride, you have a feeling that here is an unusually alert and capable car. That here is a car fully equal to every need and emergency. That here is a car with a new eagerness to go. A new aliveness. A new responsiveness in traffic, on hills, and on the open road.

As the days go by, you will find yourself developing a real friendliness for the new Ford—a growing pride that is deeper and more personal than just an acknowledgment of faithful service.

You long to be behind the wheel—to drive for the sheer joy of driving—to know again the sense of power, security and complete control that is yours when you ride in this great new car.

For here, at a low price, is everything you want or need in a modern automobile . . . beautiful low lines and choice of colors . . . strength and safety because of the steel body, Triplex shatter-proof safety glass windshield, and four-wheel brakes . . . ample power and speed for every hill and emergency because of the 40-horsepower engine . . . quick acceleration . . . exceptional comfort because of the new transverse springs, Houdaille shock

FORD MOTOR COMPANY
Detroit, Mich.

absorbers, and the generous room provided for all passengers . . . ease of control . . . the economy of 20 to 30 miles per gallon of gasoline . . . reliability and low up-keep cost.

Telephone the nearest Ford dealer and ask him to bring the new Ford to your home for a demonstration. Drive it yourself—through thickest traffic, on steepest hills, over roughest roads. By its performance you will know that there is nothing quite like it anywhere in design, quality and price.

The Roadster sells for $385; Phaeton, $395; Tudor Sedan, $495; Coupe, $495; Business Coupe, $495; Sport Coupe, $550; Fordor Sedan, $625. (F.O.B. Detroit.)

Two women in their new Ford Tudor Sedan arrive at a house with tall white columns to pick up their friend. As a reminder of the days in the not-all-too-distant past, a post for tethering a horse is in place at the front of the house.

Version A (TdS 1a)
○ *Ladies' Home Journal,* July 1928, p. 88
○ *McCall's,* July 1928, p. 53

Note that open bumpers are shown in this first magazine ad for the Tudor Sedan.

WHITE COLUMNS

Four additional versions of this 1928 Tudor Sedan ad all use the same illustration, headline and basic ad text. However, minor text differences exist across each of the five *"White Columns"* ad versions.

Version B (TdS 1b) [text difference]

◉ *Vanity Fair,* July 1928, p. 96

◉ *Vogue,* July 15, 1928, p. 105

Version C (TdS 1c) [text difference]

○ *Good Housekeeping,* July 1928, p. 104

Version D (TdS 1d) [text difference]

○ *The Farmer's Wife,,* July 1928, CIII

Version E (TdS 1e) [text difference]

◉ *Harper's Bazaar,* July 1928, p. 113

LADIES' GOLF DAY.
A closer look at the *"White Columns"* ad illustration reveals one man grabbing the car door while the other carries the woman's golf clubs to the waiting Tudor Sedan.

Las Mujeres Prefieren el Nuevo Ford *por la Seguridad que Ofrece, por su Estabilidad, y por la Facilidad con que se Dirige*

As an example of the use of a Williamson drawing in a non-U.S. Model A ad, the *"White Columns"* ad also appeared in a magazine published in Havana, Cuba in late 1929.

◀ Example ad from Cuba

◉ *Social,* November 1929, p. 82

PICNIC DOG

Everything you want or need in a modern automobile

EVERYTHING you want or need in a modern automobile is brought to you at a low price in the new Ford . . . beauty of line and color—speed of 55 to 65 miles an hour—four-wheel brakes to balance this speed and to provide the safety demanded by present-day motoring conditions—flashing pick-up and ease of control that put a new joy in motoring— power for any hill because of a remarkably efficient engine which develops 40-brake-horse-power at only 2200 revolutions a minute— Houdaille hydraulic shock absorbers and wide, roomy seats for restful comfort—the economy of 20 to 30 miles on a gallon of gasoline —reliability and low cost of up-keep.

The sturdy strength and sweeping lines of the new Ford are shown in this view from the driver's seat. The windshields of all the new Ford cars are made of Triplex shatter-proof glass—an important safety feature.

Check over these features and you will find that not one essential thing that you require of a motor car is omitted from this list.

Yet the completeness of the new Ford goes farther even than this. It extends to every least little detail of finish and appointment and to the equipment which is standard on the car. This includes speedometer, gasoline gage on instrument panel, electric windshield wiper on closed cars, five steel-spoke wheels, four 30 x 4.50 balloon tires, dash light, mirror, combination stop and tail light, oil indicator rod, theft-proof coincidental ignition lock, high pressure grease gun lubrication, and Triplex shatter-proof glass windshield.

Five years ago—three years ago—one year ago—it would have been impossible to produce such a really fine car at such a low price. It is possible today only because of the development of new machines, new manufacturing methods and new production economies that are as remarkable as the car itself.

The Ford Motor Company did not set out to make a new car at a certain figure. It decided on the kind of car

it wanted to make and then found ways to build it at the lowest possible price.

Every purchaser shares the benefits of the established Ford policy of selling millions of cars at a small margin of profit—of owning or controlling the source of raw materials—of constantly giving greater and greater value without greatly increased cost.

As Henry Ford himself has said: "We make our own steel—we make our own glass—we mine our own coal. But we do not charge a profit on any of these items or from these operations. Our only profit is on the automobile we sell."

When you know the joy of driving the new Ford—when you see its outstanding performance and reliability under all conditions—you will know that it is not just a new automobile— not just a new model—but the advanced expression of a new idea in modern, economical transportation.

Throughout, the new Ford is an example of fine automobile engineering. Many features are exclusive Ford developments. Some are wholly new in automobile practice. In every least little detail it has been built to endure—to serve you faithfully and well for many months and years.

FORD MOTOR COMPANY
Detroit, Michigan

As they begin their picnic, the family dog, one foot already on a plate, lunges for the held-high, but teetering, drumstick. This draws the attention of the men who are trying to use the rear bumper of the Ford Tudor Sedan as a bottle opener.

Version A (TdS 2a)

○ *Cosmopolitan,* August 1928, CII

◉ *The Redbook Magazine,* August 1928, p. 102

◉ *The Sportsman,* August 1928, p. 65

PICNIC DOG

While a second version (B) of this 1928 Tudor Sedan ad features only a minor text change, the third version (C) utilizes a completely different headline and text.

Version B (TdS 2b) [text difference]
⊙ *Liberty*, August 18, 1928, p. 18

Version C (TdS 2c) ➤
⊙ *The American Boy*, August 1928, CIV

CHICKEN TO GO!
Will Spot be successful in his attempt to join in the picnic fun?

SHOULD WE TRY AGAIN?
As evidenced by the broken top on the bottle sitting on the ground, the first attempt at using the "bumper bottle opener" was somewhat unsuccessful. (Given that this ad was published in 1928, during Prohibition, it is assumed that these bottles surely contain only grape juice!)

NANNY INCLUDED

There is something quite remarkable about the easy-riding comfort of the new Ford

WHEN you see the new Ford, you are impressed instantly by its low, trim, graceful lines and the beauty of its two-tone color harmonies.

As you watch it in traffic and on the open road you can note how quickly it accelerates and get some idea, too, of the speed and power of its 40-horse-power engine.

But only by driving the new Ford yourself can you fully appreciate the easy-riding comfort that is such an outstanding feature of this great new car.

One reason, of course, is the use of four Houdaille hydraulic shock absorbers, formerly furnished as standard equipment on only the most expensive automobiles. Yet even these shock absorbers of themselves do not account for the complete riding comfort of the new Ford.

Equally important are the design and construction of the new transverse springs, the low center of gravity, and the low ratio of unsprung weight to the sprung weight of the car.

All of these factors combine to soften or eliminate the force of road shocks and to make the new Ford an exceptionally comfortable and easy-riding car at all speeds. Even rough roads may be taken at a fast pace

FORD MOTOR COMPANY
Detroit, Michigan

without hard jolts or bumps or the exaggerated bouncing rebound which is the cause of most motoring fatigue.

You have a feeling of mental comfort, too, in driving the new Ford because of its reliability and the safety afforded by its Triplex shatter-proof glass windshield and its six-brake system. (The four-wheel brakes and separate emergency brakes are of the mechanical, internal expanding-type and are all fully enclosed.)

This freedom from mechanical trouble—this safety and security—mean a great deal to everyone who drives a car.

Prove this for yourself by asking the nearest Ford dealer to bring the new Ford to your home for a demonstration. Check up on comfort, on speed, on power, on acceleration, on hill climbing, on economy, on safety. You will know then that here at a low price is everything you want or need in a modern automobile.

Here you can see the roominess of the new Ford Tudor Sedan. Built to accommodate five people in real comfort. Both front seats fold forward, giving easy access front and rear.

A new Ford Tudor Sedan travels along a narrow road beside a large, walled house. Inside the car, the nanny minds the two kids in the back seat. This ad also contains an insert illustration showing the roominess of the new Ford.

Version A (TdS 3a)
○ *Cosmopolitan,* October 1928, p. 100
◉ *The Redbook Magazine,* October 1928, p. 94

The one-page version of this ad appeared in only two magazines.

NANNY INCLUDED

The two-page edition (B) of this 1928 Tudor Sedan ad uses a different headline and includes insert illustrations of the Model A Ford engine and a Ford Roadster.

Version B (TdS 3b) ∇

⊙ *The Literary Digest,* September 22, 1928, CF

⊙ *The Saturday Evening Post,* September 1, 1928, pp. 72-73

Look beneath the hood and study the mechanical beauty of the new Ford

WHEN you look beneath the hood and study the engine of the new Ford, you will begin to understand how carefully this car is made, and see something, too, of the enduring quality that has been built into every part.

Even if you know but little about the inside of an automobile and do not want to bother with mechanical details, you will sense the value of this care and this quality and realize that it means a great deal to you in the performance of the car.

As an engineer or technical man, you will marvel at the simplicity of design of the new Ford and spend long hours in studying the many improvements embodied in its construction. In the homely, yet expressive words of the man in the shop when he pays his highest tribute to a fine piece of machinery: "It is a sweet mechanical job."

There is no better illustration of the care with which the new Ford is built than the close limits of measurement maintained in manufacturing.

In the new Ford, for instance, the diameter of the piston pin is held within three ten-thousandths (.0003) of an inch. An equally close limit is followed in the diameter of the hole into which the piston pin is fitted.

The weight of the aluminum alloy pistons is set at 17¼ ounces. No piston is permitted to come under this weight and it must not exceed this weight by more than 2 grams.

In the piston assemblies, consisting of piston, connecting rod, pin and spring retainer, the four assemblies in each motor must match in weight within a limit of 3½ grams. This means that every piston assembly must meet the weight of each of the other assemblies in the set within approximately ¼ of an ounce.

Another example of the close limits of measurement in the new Ford is found in the crankshaft, which is both statically and dynamically balanced.

The dynamic balance, which insures equal distribution of weight in the throws of the shaft, is held within 4 grams or approximately ½ of an ounce, within the 2¼-inch radius from the center-line of the shaft. Main and connecting rod bearings on the crankshaft are held true to within three ten-thousandths (.0003) of an inch.

This same care is followed in the making of large as well as small parts. The four-wheel brake drums on the new Ford are 11 inches in diameter, yet they are held to within five one-thousandths (.005) of an inch. This is a remarkably close limit on such a wide diameter and is unusual in brake drums.

It is, of course, almost beyond imagination to conceive of measurements as close as these. They are achieved only through the use of the finest precision gages in the hands of expert workmen. All of these gages are set by Johansson master gage blocks which are accurate to one-millionth of an inch.

All of this care and this fine automobile engineering are reflected in the outstanding performance of the new Ford in everything that goes to make it the advanced expression of a wholly new idea in modern, economical transportation.

Make it a point, therefore, to see and examine the new Ford and arrange for a demonstration. Only when you get behind the wheel can you fully appreciate its alert speed, its quick acceleration, its safety and its truly remarkable riding comfort.

The price of the new Ford is low because of Ford manufacturing methods. It includes the following standard equipment—four Houdaille hydraulic shock absorbers, four-wheel brakes and separate emergency or parking brakes (all six brakes of the mechanical, internal-expanding type and fully enclosed), five steel-spoke wheels, four 30 x 4.50 balloon tires, electric windshield wiper on closed cars, speedometer, gasoline gage on instrument panel, dash light, mirror, combination stop and tail light, theft-proof coincidental ignition lock, high pressure grease gun lubrication, and Triplex shatter-proof glass windshield.

FEATURES OF THE NEW FORD CAR

Beautiful low lines

Choice of colors

55 to 65 miles an hour

40 horse-power

Remarkable acceleration

Fully-enclosed six-brake system

New transverse springs

Houdaille hydraulic shock absorbers

20 to 30 miles per gallon of gasoline

Triplex shatter-proof glass windshield

Reliability and low up-keep cost

The engine in the new Ford is unusually simple and efficient. It is unique in design and performance and develops 40-brake horse-power at only 2200 revolutions a minute. This means you can do 55 to 65 miles an hour in the new Ford and yet you do not have a motor with a high revolution speed.

The mechanical beauty of the new Ford is matched by its beauty of line, color and finish. Shown here is the roomy Tudor Sedan, in the Arabian Sand color. All Ford cars are finished in a choice of two-tone color harmonies.

You'll get a real thrill in driving the new Ford Roadster because of its alert speed and easy-riding comfort. All of the new Ford cars come to you equipped with four Houdaille hydraulic shock absorbers—two front and two rear.

FORD MOTOR COMPANY
Detroit, Michigan

In line with the *"Look beneath the hood and study the mechanical beauty of the new Ford"* headline used in this ad, this is the only magazine ad that shows a close-up view of the Model A Ford engine.

PATIO PARTY

There is something quite remarkable about the easy-riding comfort of the new Ford

WHEN you see the new Ford you are impressed instantly by its low, trim, graceful lines and the beauty of its two-tone color harmonies.

As you watch it in traffic, on hills, and on the open road you can note how quickly it accelerates and get some idea, too, of the speed and power of its 40-horse-power engine.

But only by driving the new Ford

The Ford Business Coupe—a splendid car for constant use in all kinds of weather. The body has been specially designed to meet the needs of business executives, salesmen and physicians.

yourself can you fully appreciate the easy-riding comfort which is such an outstanding feature of this great new car.

One reason, of course, is the fact that the new Ford is equipped with four Houdaille hydraulic shock absorbers—two front and two rear. Yet even these shock absorbers do not account for the complete riding comfort of the new Ford.

Equally important is the low center of gravity and the low ratio of unsprung weight to sprung weight, due principally to the design and construction of the new transverse springs.

The riding quality of any car, as you may know, depends to a great extent upon the ratio of the weight carried above the flexible ends of the springs (the sprung weight) to the weight carried below the flexible ends of the springs (the unsprung weight).

Unsprung weight is, in effect, a hammer with which every unevenness encountered by the wheels deals a

FORD MOTOR COMPANY
Detroit, Michigan

blow against the sprung weight. The flexible ends of the springs must absorb these blows if the car is to ride comfortably.

It follows that the lower the proportion of unsprung weight, the less violent the blows delivered against the frame, body and motor of the car.

Here you can see the advantage of the transverse type of spring used in the new Ford. In this design, the springs rest on their flexible ends with the heavy center part uppermost.

The weight of the springs, therefore, becomes part of the sprung weight instead of the unsprung weight and the force of road shocks is thereby reduced. Rebound of the springs to such impacts is controlled by the specially designed Houdaille hydraulic shock absorbers.

These shock absorbers give the springs a free range of action on smooth highways. Yet there is instant shock absorbing effect as soon as the car encounters any bump or rut in the road.

It's a sunny afternoon at the beach house as guests gather on the patio for a party. As drinks are served, two men gaze past the palm tree to the ocean beyond. An insert illustration for the Ford Business Coupe also appears in this ad.

Version A (TdS 4a)
◉ *Country Life,* October 1928, p. 27
◉ *The Sportsman,* October 1928, p. 74

Three different versions of this Tudor Sedan ad appeared in late 1928.

PATIO PARTY

The two-page edition (B) of this 1928 Tudor Sedan magazine ad includes five insert illustrations.

Version B (TdS 4b) ∨

⊙ *The Literary Digest,* October 20, 1928, CF

⊙ *The Saturday Evening Post,* September 29, 1928, pp. 72-73

The third *"Patio Party"* ad version (C) employs a different headline and a text similar to, although somewhat lengthier than, that contained in the first one-page ad version (A).

The small Ford Business Coupe insert illustration that appears in both of the first two versions of this Tudor Sedan ad is not present in the third ad version (C).

Version C (TdS 4c) ➤

⊙ *The American Boy,* October 1928, p. 67

LOCK DRUG CO.

NOVEMBER 1928

The safety of the fully-enclosed *Six-Brake System* is an outstanding feature of the New Ford

ONE of the first things you will notice when you drive the new Ford is the quick, silent, effective action of its six-brake system.

This system gives you the highest degree of safety and reliability because the four-wheel brakes and the separate emergency or parking brakes are all of the mechanical, internal expanding type, with braking surfaces fully enclosed for protection against mud, water, sand and grease.

The many advantages of this type of braking system have long been recognized. They are brought to you in the new Ford through a series of mechanical improvements embodying much that is new in design and manufacture.

There is perhaps no single feature of the new Ford which represents such a decided step forward in automobile engineering as the unique yet simple way by which a special drum has been constructed to permit the use of two separate sets of internal brakes on the rear wheels.

The brake construction

This illustration shows the convenient location of the wedge or screw that adjusts the brake shoes on the new Ford. The wedge or screw is so notched that all brakes can be set alike simply by listening to the "clicks." All adjustments should be made when brakes are cold.

on the front wheels also is unusual. Here the brakes are fully enclosed without the necessity of a leather boot or sliding joint to protect the linkage between the brake rods and the mechanism on the brake plate. Such simplicity of design helps to insure reliability and long life.

A further improvement in braking performance is effected by the self-centering feature of the four-wheel brakes—an exclusive Ford feature. This brings the entire surface of the shoe in contact with the drum the instant you press your foot on the brake pedal.

An example of the close limits of measurement used in manufacturing the new Ford is found in the brake drums.

These drums measure eleven inches in diameter, yet they are held to within five one-thousandths (.005) of an inch—a remarkably fine limit on such a wide diameter. The plates on which the braking mechanism is mounted are of

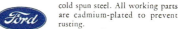

FORD MOTOR COMPANY
Detroit, Michigan

cold spun steel. All working parts are cadmium-plated to prevent rusting.

There are definite reasons, therefore, for the safety and reliability of the new Ford brakes—for their quick ease of operation—for the smooth yet commanding way they take hold at a slight pressure on the brake pedal or hand lever. This comforting assurance that your brakes are fully equal to every need or emergency means a great deal to your peace of mind and adds immeasurably to the joy of motoring.

Another feature of the brakes on the new Ford is the ease of adjustment. It can be done quickly and without trouble.

The four-wheel brakes are adjusted by turning a regulating wedge or screw conveniently located on the outside of each brake plate. This screw is so notched that all four brakes can be set alike simply by listening to the "clicks."

The emergency or parking brakes require little attention. However, should they need adjustment, consult your Instruction Book for a clear explanation.

If you do not care to do the work yourself, see a Ford dealer, who will give you prompt, courteous and economical service.

The clock on the *"Locke Drug Co."* building indicates it's a little past five o'clock and rush hour is in full force. The Ford Tudor Sedan fights the downtown traffic as it takes five tired "car poolers" home for the day.

Version A (TdS 5a)
- *Country Life,* November 1928, p. 97
- *The Sportsman,* November 1928, p. 69
- *Vanity Fair,* November 1928, p. 48

LOCK DRUG CO.

The two-page ad edition (B) of this Tudor Sedan ad includes Fordor and Roadster insert illustrations—plus an illustration of the Ford wheel showing the brake adjusting wedge.

Version B (TdS 5b) ⋁

⊙ *The Literary Digest,* November 17, 1928, CF

⊙ *The Saturday Evening Post,* November 24, 1928, pp. 90-91

The third *"Lock Drug Co."* ad version (C) has only a minor text change.

Version C (TdS 5c) [text difference]

⊙ *Liberty,* November 10, 1928, p. 5

While the print quality is poor, the Williamson drawing used in the *"Lock Drug Co."* Tudor Sedan ad also appeared in a Chilean Model A magazine ad.

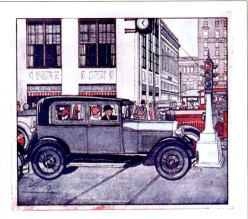

◄ **Example ad from Chile**

⊙ *Zig Zag,* January 26, 1929, CIII

LOCK DRUG CO.

Two additional versions of this Tudor Sedan ad were produced at the end of 1928 (D) and in early 1929 (E).

These ad versions utilize the same primary illustration, but have different headlines and insert illustrations. The fifth version (E) replaces the Model A brake insert illustration used in all four earlier versions with a drawing of a Ford Roadster.

> **Version D (TdS 5d)** ➤
>
> ○ *Cosmopolitan,* December 1928, p. 100
> ◉ *The Redbook Magazine,* December 1928, p. 92

Remarkable Simplicity of Design Is Revealed in the New Ford

"MAKE it better—make it simpler" has always been the keynote of Ford engineering and manufacturing methods. This policy has been carried forward to its highest, fullest expression in the new Ford.

You see evidence of a carefully planned simplicity of design the instant you lift the hood. It becomes increasingly apparent as you study each detail of the many mechanical improvements embodied in the construction of the car.

A striking example of the practical value of Ford engineering and manufacturing methods is found in the six-brake system. This system is unusually reliable and effective because both the four-wheel brakes and the separate emergency or parking brakes are of the mechanical, internal expanding type with

all braking surfaces fully enclosed for protection against water, sand, dirt and grease.

For many years this has been recognized as the ideal combination. It is now brought to you on the new Ford because an easy, simple way has been found to accommodate two sets of full internal brakes in a specially designed two-in-one brake drum on the rear wheels.

Another exclusive Ford development is shown in the construction of the housing which encloses the steering gear mechanism. This is made of three steel forgings, electrically welded together. Through electric welding the housing is then joined to the steering column, thus making a single one-piece steel unit of

It is surprisingly easy to adjust the four-wheel brakes on the new Ford. All adjustments are made from the outside by means of a notched regulating screw or wedge, without removing any parts.

great strength. Many other parts of the new Ford are also electrically welded, thus giving greater strength than if several parts were used and riveted or bolted together.

The ignition system of the new Ford also reflects much that is new in mechanical design. A unique feature is the elimination of high-tension cables from the distributor to the spark-plugs, these connections being made by means of thin bronze springs. There is but one high-tension cable and this connects the coil with the distributor.

The distributor head is water-proof and has been specially designed to prevent short circuits from rain, snow, etc.

The whole idea back of the new Ford is to bring the benefits of modern, economical transportation to all the people, and to help every motorist get the greatest use from his car over the longest period of time at a minimum of trouble and expense.

FORD MOTOR COMPANY
Detroit, Michigan

As is the case with many other Model A ads contained in *The American Boy,* this *"Lock Drug Co."* ad version (E) appears in black and white.

> **◀ Version E (TdS 5e)**
>
> ◉ *The American Boy,* January 1929, p. 29

While many of the ads appearing in this publication use the same primary illustration found in ads in other magazines, they often have quite different headlines, secondary insert illustrations and text formats.

You have a feeling of safety and security when you drive the new Ford

ONE of the first things you will notice when you drive the new Ford is the quick, effective, silent action of its six-brake system.

This system gives you the highest degree of safety and reliability because the four-wheel service brakes and the separate emergency or parking brakes are all of the mechanical, internal expanding type, with braking surfaces fully enclosed for protection against mud, water, sand and grease.

The many advantages of this type of braking system have long been recognized. They are brought to you in the new Ford through a series of mechanical improvements embodying much that is new in design and manufacture.

A particularly unique feature is the simple way in which a special drum has been constructed to permit the use of two separate sets of full internal brakes on the rear wheels.

The brake construction on the front wheels also is unusual. Here the brakes are fully enclosed without the need of a leather boot or sliding joint to protect the linkage between the brake rods and the mechanism on the brake plate.

A further improvement in braking performance is effected by the self-centering feature of the four-wheel brakes—an exclusive Ford feature. This construction brings the entire surface of the shoe in contact with the drum

the instant you press your foot on the brake pedal.

An example of the close limits of measurement used in manufacturing the new Ford is found in the brake drums. These drums measure eleven inches in diameter, yet they are held to within five one-thousandths (.005) of an inch—a remarkably fine limit on such a wide diameter. The plates on which the braking mechanism is mounted are of cold spun steel.

There are definite reasons, therefore, for the safety and reliability of the new Ford brakes—their quick ease of operation—for the smooth yet commanding way they take hold at a slight pressure on the brake pedal or hand lever.

Another feature of the brakes on the new Ford is the ease of making adjustments without special tools and without removing a single part.

The four-wheel brakes are adjusted by turning a wedge or screw located on the outside of each brake plate. This screw is so notched that all four brakes can be set alike simply by listening to the "clicks."

Throughout the new Ford you will find this same trouble-saving simplicity of design. It is one reason why the up-keep cost of the new Ford is so low.

FORD MOTOR COMPANY
Detroit, Michigan

Make it a point to see your Ford dealer and talk over with him the simple little things that should be attended to for continuously good performance.

He works under close factory supervision and he has been specially trained and equipped to help you get the greatest possible use from your car over the longest period of time at a minimum of trouble and expense.

Alert and powerful is the new Ford Roadster—a car that puts a new joy in motoring. Finished in a choice of beautiful colors. Top can be raised or lowered quickly by one person. Equipped with rumble seat at slight additional cost.

LONG FUR COAT

◆

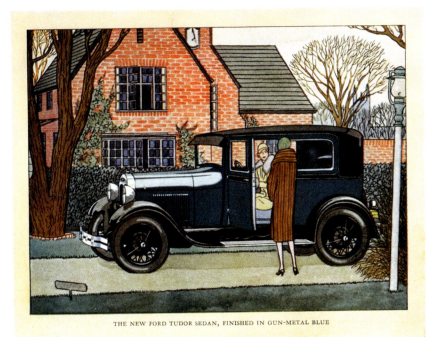

THE NEW FORD TUDOR SEDAN, FINISHED IN GUN-METAL BLUE

Even in the little things you can see the quality that has been built into the new Ford

MEN talk enthusiastically of the speed and power of the 40-horse-power engine of the new Ford—of the simplicity of its ignition and oiling systems—the advantages of its three-quarter floating rear axle—the safety of its six mechanical, internal expanding brakes—the easy-riding comfort of its transverse springs and Houdaille hydraulic shock absorbers —of the many other mechanical improvements embodied in the construction of the car.

All of these mechanical features are worthy of note because they have such a direct bearing on alert, satisfying, economical and reliable performance.

To a woman's quick eye, however, there are many other points which show the quality that has been built into the new Ford—important little details of finish and

An interior view of the new Ford Tudor Sedan, showing the generous space provided in the rear compartment. Five people can ride in real comfort in this car.

appointment that few men ever notice or fully appreciate.

A man will glance casually at the upholstery of the new Ford and say that it is "good-looking." A woman, examining it closely and comparing it with the over-stuffed suite in the library of her home, will know that it has been made for long wear as well as appearance.

Men will admire the colors of the new Ford, but only a woman, from her fuller knowledge of clothes and style, will realize that they are colors which will not tire.

It means something, too, to a woman to know that the pyroxylin lacquer finish of the new Ford is not affected by the heat of summer or the cold of winter, is not easily marred or scratched, improves with polishing

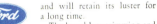

FORD MOTOR COMPANY
Detroit, Michigan

and will retain its luster for a long time.

The broad lace trimming and the gathered door pockets in the Tudor Sedan; the arm rests, oval bow-light, flexible robe rail, and embossed paneling around the doors of the Fordor Sedan; the roomy comfort of the rumble seat in the Sport Coupe; the Triplex shatter-proof glass windshield; the instrument panel finished in satin nickel; the use of both straight and hour-glass coil springs for the seat cushions; the ease with which windows can be raised or lowered; the ease of steering and shifting gears; the very manner in which the doors open and close—all these are indicative of the care that has been taken in the making of the new Ford.

Its beauty of mechanical design is matched by its beauty of line, color and appointment. Even in the very little things you can see evidence of a quality of material and workmanship unusual in a low-price car.

The Ford Tudor Sedan is ready to depart as two women chat. While both women are dressed in furs on this cold December day, several windows at the house are wide open.

○ *The Farmer's Wife*, December 1928, CIII
○ *Good Housekeeping*, December 1928, p. 94

Version A (TdS 6a)

◉ *Harper's Bazaar*, December 1928, p. 136
○ *Ladies' Home Journal*, December 1928, p. 88
○ *McCall's*, December 1928, p. 9
◉ *Vanity Fair*, December 1928, p. 25
◉ *Vogue*, December 22, 1928, CII

January, 1929   THE COUNTRY GENTLEMAN

A YEAR OF PROGRESS

Since December 2, 1927, nearly 800,000 new Ford cars have been built. Production has been gradually increased from a few hundred a day to more than 6500 a day. We expect to make 2,000,000 automobiles in 1929.

These are impressive figures. But they are only that. The big thing is that the new Ford has more than lived up to all expectations.

Our policy has always been to make the best automobile it is possible to make at a low price. We have been doing it for twenty years. The public expects us to keep on doing it. That obligation includes good design as well as good materials.

The new Ford is built on sound principles. There is nothing of an experiment about it. Our whole effort has been toward simplicity —to give you outstanding service with as little machinery as possible.

Take the motor. It has made a remarkable record because it combines every essential of good performance—power, acceleration, smoothness, speed, reliability, economy and

"The new Ford car embodies the best results of our experience in making 15,000,000 automobiles. We consider it our most important contribution to the progress and prosperity of the country, and to the daily welfare of millions of people."

Henry Ford

long life. Had any other type of motor been better, we would have chosen that.

From every part of the world come reports of its reliability. Many of the new Fords have been driven 50,000 miles in the past year. Some more than 100,000 miles. There is no telling how far they will go. The average life of the Model T was seven years. We believe this new car will do even better. It is also

FORD MOTOR COMPANY
Detroit, Michigan

economical to operate and the cost of up-keep is low.

The engine is the heart of the motor car, of course. Yet there are other features almost as important. For instance, the fully enclosed six-brake system of the new Ford. Its remarkable smoothness, comfort and stability at all speeds. Its easy riding qualities. The beauty of its lines and colors.

In a word, the quality of the new Ford goes clear through. Nothing has been done for show.

The new Ford was a good car when it was first introduced. It is a better car today. Constantly we are finding better ways of doing things. As soon as we are sure of them we put them into the car. This eliminates loss to owners occasioned by yearly models.

Our mission is to make the best automobile that can be made to sell at a low price. In ever-increasing measure, the new Ford is the expression of that ideal.

A couple standing in the snow admires the new Ford Tudor Sedan. This ad reveals that Ford will make two million cars in 1929 and provides a Henry Ford-signed statement about Ford's *"contributions to the progress and prosperity of the country."*

Version A (TdS 7a)
○ *The Country Gentleman,* January 1929, p. 103
○ *Farm & Fireside,* January 1929, p. 4 (B&W)
◉ *Southern Agriculturist,* January 1, 1929, CII (B&W)
○ *Successful Farming,* January 1929, CII

PONDERING HOOD

The issue date for this Tudor Sedan ad was January 1929. This was appropriate timing for the *"A Year of Progress"* headline and the text theme used one year following the December 1927 introduction of the Model A Ford.

The drawing in a very rare second version (B) of this Model A ad is identical except for the red ribbon tied to the radiator cap of the Tudor Sedan. This unique ad appeared in only one magazine on one date.

Version B (TdS 7b) ➤

● *Capper's Farmer,* January 1929, CII

A third version of this drawing adds a wreath with a red ribbon in the window of the house. This drawing, which provides a more panoramic view, appeared as a secondary insert illustration in a December 8, 1928 magazine ad featuring a Sport Coupe and a Fordor Sedan. This expanded drawing shows a young man seeming to be saying *How about me?* as his sister thanks their grandfather for her Christmas gift of a new Ford Tudor Sedan.

KIDS ON SLED

THE NEW TUDOR SEDAN

Winter days are happy days
for the woman who drives the new Ford

THERE are so many things to do—so many places to go—when you drive a new Ford.

Snow may be falling thick and fast outside, yet it need not delay your day. Snug and dry in the new Ford, you can take the children safely to school—do your marketing and your shopping—wear your prettiest dress and shoes to the matinee—be off with the family for a good old-fashioned party on the ice or snow—

share the healthfulness of keen, crisp days in the out-of-doors.

The new Ford is an especially good all-weather car for the woman driver because it is so reliable and dependable—so alert—and so easy-to-handle under all conditions.

Somehow, everything seems just right. Your feet reach the pedals without effort. Seats are wide, roomy and comfortable. Starting is easy, even in cold weather.

Gears shift silently and smoothly. The steering wheel responds instantly to your touch. And you do have more confidence in driving when you note how quickly and firmly the brakes take hold, even on slippery pavements.

Right at this season it is good to know that the six brakes on the new Ford are internal brakes. That is, all braking surfaces are fully enclosed for protection against snow, ice, water and mud. This insures efficient brake action the whole year through.

The new Ford is not just a new car, but the expression of an idea—an idea of service. It has been planned and built to bring the benefits of modern, economical transportation to all the people.

To give men the means by which they can do more work and better

FORD MOTOR COMPANY
Detroit, Michigan

work and thereby increase their earning capacity. To help women in the equally important business of running a home. To put more achievement and happiness into human lives and to make this a better world in which to live.

Because of this larger purpose, the price of the new Ford is low. In furtherance of it, the entire Ford dealer organization has been specially trained to take care of your car. We believe it is our duty not only to make a good automobile, but to help every motorist get the greatest possible use for the longest period of time at a minimum of trouble and expense.

Shown here is the new Ford Coupe—a particularly snug and cozy car for winter driving. The quick ease of steering and of shifting gears is a joy to the woman driver.

The graceful lines of the new Fordor Sedan are shown in this illustration. Upholstery is soft and luxurious, yet long-wearing. All appointments are fully nickeled. All Ford cars are finished in a choice of beautiful two-tone color harmonies.

A new snow has fallen and a mother readies her daughter to join the sled- and ski-equipped play group. In addition to the Ford Tudor Sedan, this ad includes insert illustrations of a Ford Coupe and Fordor Sedan – also shown in snow settings.

Version A (TdS 8a)

○ *The Farmer's Wife,* January 1929, CIII
◉ *Harper's Bazaar,* January 1929, p. 33
○ *Ladies' Home Journal,* January 1929, p. 66
○ *McCall's,* January 1929, p. 59
◉ *Vogue,* January 19, 1929, p. 34

KIDS ON SLED

The second version (B) of this 1929 Tudor Sedan magazine ad contains only minor text changes. However, the third version (C) incorporates a new headline and text – concentrating on the *"remarkable"* Model A Ford engine.

Version B (TdS 8b) [text difference]

○ *Good Housekeeping*, January 1929, p. 121

Version C (TdS 8c) ➤

⊙ *Capper's Farmer*, February 1929, p. 43
○ *The Country Gentleman*, February 1929, p. 110
○ *Farm & Fireside*, February 1929, p. 39
⊙ *Southern Agriculturist*, February 1, 1929, CII (B&W)
○ *Successful Farming*, February 1929, CIII

"Svijet"

The new Ford has a remarkable engine

THE engine of the new Ford represents a new development in modern automobile engineering. It is unique in design and performance because it gives you unusual acceleration, smoothness, speed and power without sacrifice of reliability and economy. Ford engineering has found the way to include every essential feature of good performance without the necessity of a high speed motor.

The design of the cylinder head is just one factor in this performance.

FEATURES OF
THE NEW FORD CAR

Beautiful low lines
Choice of colors
Remarkable acceleration
Smoothness at all speeds
55 to 65 miles an hour
Fully enclosed, silent 4-wheel brake system
New transverse springs
Houdaille shock absorbers
Triplex shatter-proof windshield
Economy of operation
Reliability and long life

Others are the specially designed carburetor, the new hot-spot manifold, the carefully planned large valve diameter, the carbon chrome nickel alloy valves, the aluminum pistons, the statically and dynamically balanced crankshaft and flywheel, and the simplicity of the electrical, ignition, cooling, lubrication and fuel systems.

Of special importance is the manner in which engine vibration is absorbed before it reaches the chassis of the car, thereby preventing unpleasant vibration periods.

This is done in the new Ford through the introduction of a flexible front end support that is both simple and practical – a truly remarkable improvement in engine mounting developed after many months of testing and experimenting.

Quality of materials and careful workmanship also have a great deal to do with the continuously good performance of the new Ford. The diameter of the piston pin, for instance, is held within three ten-thousandths of an inch. An equally close limit is followed in the hole into which the piston pin is fitted.

The weight of the aluminum alloy pistons is set at 17.25 ounces. No piston is permitted to come under

Ford
Ford Motor Company
Detroit, Michigan

this weight nor exceed it by more than 2 grams. In the piston assemblies, consisting of piston, connecting rod, pin and spring retainers, the four assemblies in each motor must match in weight within a limit of 3 1/2 grams. This means that every piston assembly must meet the weight of each of the other assemblies in the set within approximately 1/8 of an ounce.

The dynamic balance, which insures equal distribution of weight in the throws of the crankshaft, is held within 4 grams, or approximately 1/7 of an ounce, within the 2.1/8-inch radius from the center-line of the shaft. Main and connecting rod bearings on the crankshaft are held true to within three ten-thousandths (.0003) of an inch.

Deep-seated, therefore, is the quality of the new Ford. You can see but a part of it with your eyes. Beneath the hood are countless invisible values summed up, they count for more than any one spectacular feature.

Our policy has always been to see that you get the very best materials – the most careful workmanship – the soundest design that can be built into a low-priced automobile. Today, more than ever, the new Ford is the fulfillment of that ideal.

"Svijet"

Najkorisniji posao na automobilskom tržištu

Ako ste prije htjeli da nabavite luksusna kola, sa kapacitetom većim od 100 kilometara na sat, idealnim perima, snabdievena sa svim savršenstvima moderne tehnike i najrafiniranije elegancije, što je upravo svojstvenost luksusnih kola, pomislite koju cijenu ste do nedavno morali platiti, da biste osvarili ovu svoju želju? 80.000 do 120.000 dinara ili još više! Baš cijena novih Ford kola u odnosu s onim što ona nude i s obzirom na njihovu kakvoću, sa kojom se druga kola ne mogu usporediti, karakteristično

je obilježje nove tvorevine Henry Forda i sasvim opravdava osobinu "potpuna promjena dosadašnjeg mjerila za automobilističke vrijednosti".

Pregledajte dakle ova nova Ford-kola, ispitajte ih u pojedinostima, isprobajte ih, upravljajte sami njima, Vi ćete se osvjedočiti, da Vam se nije nikad pružila tako zgodna prilika, da učinite tako dobar i jeftin posao.

U vožnji su velika kola, u potrošnji mala, vrijede – u svakom slučaju – više što stoje.

Bezželjni, posvema zatvoreni mehanički sistem na čest kočnica sa unutarnim ekspanzinim. Nožnom polugom pošutuju se kočnice na četiri kotača, a ručnom polugom dvije od potmenutih kočnica stražnih kotača, koje su potpuno neovisne od ostalih.

Protiv loma potpuno sigurni stakleni vjetrobran iz tripleks stakla. Čelici dvostruko djeluju "Houdaille» ublaživača udara (Stossdämpfer).

CIJENE

Faeton	. . . .	Din 48.800
Roadster	. . . .	48.000
Coupé	. . . .	57.800
Tudor-Sedan	. . . .	56.100
Fordor-Sedan	. . . .	63.200
Sport-Coupé	. . . .	57.800
Poslovni Coupé	. . . .	56.000

Cijene se razumijevaju za kola, ocarinjena uključivo ublaživača stresa, sa gumama i rezervnim točkom. Pridržava se pravo - mijene cijene bez prethodnog saopćenja.

Ford
Ford

Neobvezatno i besplatno predvodjenje kod svakog Fordovog preprodavača

FORD

FORD MOTOR COMPANY, TRIESTE

645

While used as a smaller image, the U.S. *"Kids on Sled"* Williamson drawing also appeared in a black and white Tudor Sedan ad in a 1929 magazine from Jugoslavia.

This ad lists prices for the Model A Ford – with one of the lower priced body styles being the *"Faeton"* costing *"Din 48,800."*

◄ **Example ad from Jugoslavia**

● *Svijet*, December 24, 1929, p. 645

CIRCUS BOUND

◆

July, 1929   29

The new Ford Tudor Sedan

ECONOMICAL TRANSPORTATION

for All The People

TWENTY-ONE years ago, when the Model T was first made, and again in December, 1927, when the new Ford was introduced, the policy of the Ford Motor Company was announced in these words—

"We will build a motor car for the great multitude. It will be large enough for the family, but small enough for the individual to run and care for. It will be constructed of the best materials, by the best men to be hired, after the simplest designs that modern engineering can devise. But it will be so low in price that no man making a good salary will be unable to own one."

Nearly seventeen million Ford automobiles have been made since this announcement was first printed. The passing years have brought many changes—in appearance—in performance—in manner of manufacture. But there is one thing that has never changed—the fundamental idea behind the Ford car.

The Ford Motor Company was formed, and exists today, not merely to make automobiles —but to provide economical transportation for all the people. Far more important than the car itself is the part it plays in the lives, the happiness, and the prosperity of millions of people.

Before the Ford was introduced, the automobile was considered more or less as an expensive toy, for only the wealthy to drive. There

was no conception of its uses and possibilities as we know them today. It was accepted in much the same manner that the airplane was accepted five years ago. Great emphasis was placed upon its racing speed and very little upon its practical utility.

With the coming of the Ford, however, it became possible for men in all walks of life to enjoy the benefits of transportation that formerly had been limited to a fortunate few.

A great change came over the country and with it a new prosperity. By freeing the movements of men, the Ford also freed their thoughts and created new opportunities. The barriers of time and distance were broken down. Good roads followed close behind the automobile and the isolation of country districts disappeared. The nation grew as people learned to use this newly developed horsepower and fit it to their needs.

Into the hands of men of moderate means—to the workers in factories—to the toilers on the farm—was given a means to increase their income and

enjoy the leisure which that increased income should bring. The working day became shorter because men could do in eight hours the tasks that previously had taken ten or twelve —and do them better. Always it should be remembered that we do not have automobiles because we are prosperous. We are prosperous because we have them.

Today, with all its improvements—with all its new beauty of line and color—with all the betterments and changes that have been made during the past twenty-one years—the Ford is still "a motor car for the great multitude."

It is not just a new automobile—not just so many mechanical parts carefully put together to run on wheels—but Progress—Achievement—a part of the very life and fabric of the nation.

Business of every kind moves forward at a faster pace because of it. To countless homes it brings the rewards of widening opportunity, happiness, and priceless hours of relaxation in the open air.

All of this not merely because of its safety, its comfort, its reliability, its speed, its acceleration, its ease of control, but because of a fundamental purpose that is greater than all of these.

Because, in larger degree than ever, it provides economical transportation for all the people.

FORD MOTOR COMPANY
Detroit, Michigan

A Ford Tudor Sedan speeds along the country road as a boy runs to catch up. Those in the Tudor Sedan, driver included, turn to look at the racing boy while his friend in the car points to a sign identifying the circus as their destination.

Version A (TdS 9a)
◉ *The American Boy,* July 1929, p. 29

This is a unique Model A ad. It appeared only once, in black and white, in a single magazine.

CIRCUS BOUND

As with many Model A magazine ads depicting a family in the car, this 1929 Tudor Sedan ad shows the mother riding in the back seat while a child occupies the front passenger seat.

This ad captures the scene of a young boy running in an attempt to catch up with a passing Ford Tudor Sedan. Inside the car, the driver and the three passengers have all turned to look at the boy as they speed away.

In front of the car, on the left side of the road, a poster on the side of a barn indicates that the circus is in town. (The date on the poster is *"July 7"* – matching the July publish date of the ad.) As the boy in the Tudor Sedan looks back at his friend, he points to the circus sign in excited anticipation of their upcoming destination.

The American Boy magazine contained many unique Model A Ford ads. Some of these ads were simply different versions of a Model A color ad set in a different format – and often surrounded by text and smaller insert illustrations specifically written for the intended male youth audience of this publication. Others, such as the *"Circus Bound"* Tudor Sedan ad, were unique black and white Model A ads that only appeared in this magazine.

In the *"Circus Bound"* Tudor Sedan ad, the unique Williamson illustration appears to be unrelated to the *"Economical Transportation for All The People"* headline. However, the ad text does match the headline and provides a rather philosophical review of the intentions of the Ford Motor Company in *"providing a motor car for the great multitude."*

The text of this ad indicates that:

"Before the Ford was introduced, the automobile was considered more or less an expensive toy, for only the wealthy to drive. There was no conception of its uses and possibilities as we know them today. It was accepted in much the same manner that the airplane was accepted five years ago. Great emphasis was placed on its racing speed and very little upon its practical utility. With the coming of the Ford, however, it became possible for men in all walks of life to enjoy the benefits of transportation that formerly had been limited to a fortunate few."

WAIT FOR ME!
Obviously jealous of his circus-bound friend, the trailing boy appears somewhat upset as he realizes he is being left out.

143

CORN BORER CHECK

◆

The new Ford Tudor Sedan

ECONOMICAL TRANSPORTATION
for All
The People

TWENTY-ONE years ago, when the Model T was first made, and again in December, 1927, when the new Ford was introduced, the policy of the Ford Motor Company was announced in these words—

"We will build a motor car for the great multitude. It will be large enough for the family, but small enough for the individual to run and care for. It will be constructed of the best materials, by the best men to be hired, after the simplest designs that modern engineering can devise. But it will be so low in price that no man making a good salary will be unable to own one."

More than seventeen million Ford automobiles have been made since this announcement was first printed. The passing years have brought many changes—in appearance—in performance—in manner of manufacture. But there is one thing that has never changed—the fundamental idea behind the Ford car.

The Ford Motor Company was formed, and exists today, not merely to make automobiles, but to provide economical transportation for all the people. Far more important than the car itself is the part it plays in the lives, the happiness, and the prosperity of millions of people.

Before the Ford was introduced, the automobile was considered more or less as an expensive toy, for only the wealthy to drive. There

was no conception of its uses and possibilities as we know them today. It was accepted in much the same manner that the airplane was accepted five years ago. Great emphasis was placed upon its racing speed and very little upon its practical utility.

With the coming of the Ford, however, it became possible for men in all walks of life to enjoy the benefits of transportation that formerly had been limited to a fortunate few.

A great change came over the country and with it a new prosperity. By freeing the movements of men, the Ford also freed their thoughts and created new opportunities. The barriers of time and distance were broken down. Good roads followed close behind the automobile and the isolation of country districts disappeared. The nation grew as people learned to use this newly developed horse-power and fit it to their needs.

Into the hands of men of moderate means—to the workers in factories—to the toilers on the farm—was given a means to increase their income and

enjoy the leisure which that increased income should bring. The working day became shorter because men could do in eight hours the tasks that previously had taken ten or twelve—and do them better. Always it should be remembered that we do not have automobiles because we are prosperous. We are prosperous because we have them.

Today, with all its improvements—with all its new beauty of line and color—with all the betterments and changes that have been made during the past twenty-one years—the Ford is still "a motor car for the great multitude."

It is not just a new automobile—not just so many mechanical parts carefully put together to run on wheels—but Progress—Achievement—a part of the very life and fabric of the nation.

Business of every kind moves forward at a faster pace because of it. To countless homes it brings the rewards of widening opportunity, happiness, and priceless hours of relaxation in the open air.

All of this not merely because of its safety, its comfort, its reliability, its speed, its acceleration, its ease of control, but because of a fundamental purpose that is greater than all of these.

Because, in larger degree than ever, it provides economical transportation for all the people.

FORD MOTOR COMPANY
Detroit, Michigan

An armed guard gives the "okay" to a new Ford Tudor Sedan containing five people as they stop at a check-point for the *"European Corn Borer Quarantine."* The text reviews Ford's commitment to building a car *"for all the people."*

Version A (Tdr 10a)

○ *The Country Gentleman,* August 1929, p. 83
◉ *Southern Agriculturist,* August 1, 1929, p. 24 (B&W)

This 1929 Tudor Sedan ad appears with three different text variations.

CORN BORER CHECK

Two additional versions of this 1929 Tudor Sedan ad use the same basic illustration, headline and ad text. However, minor text differences exist for the second and third versions (B and C).

Version B (TdS 10b) [text difference]
○ *Farm & Fireside*, August 1929, p. CII
○ *Successful Farming*, August 1929, CIII

Version C (TdS 10c) [text difference]
⊙ *Capper's Farmer*, September 1929, CIII

All versions of this Tudor Sedan ad appeared only in farm-related publications in August and September 1929.

The (long) text in this Model A ad reaffirms the Ford Motor Company policy announced when the Model T was first made and again when the Model A was introduced:

"We will build a motor car for the great multitude. It will be large enough for the family, but small enough for the individual to run and care for. It will be constructed of the best materials, by the best men to be hired, after the simplest designs that modern engineering can devise. But it will be so low in price that no man making a good salary will be unable to own one."

In keeping with the theme of the headline, the ad text continues with:

"The Ford Motor Company was formed, and exists today, not only to make automobiles, but to provide economical transportation for all the people. Far more important than the car itself is the part it plays in the lives, the happiness, and the prosperity of millions of people."

OUCH!
It must be getting dark as one of the guards is tending to the road flares placed down the middle of the road at the check-point. However, his attention is drawn to the new Ford Tudor Sedan and not to watching his fingers as he attempts to light the wick of the first flare.

OVER THE BRIDGE

♦

ECONOMICAL TRANSPORTATION
for All The People

Twenty-one years ago, when the Model T was first made, and again in December, 1927, when the new Ford was introduced, the policy of the Ford Motor Company was announced in these words—

"We will build a motor car for the great multitude. It will be large enough for the family, but small enough for the individual to run and care for. It will be constructed of the best materials, after the simplest designs that modern engineering can devise. But it will be so low in price that no man making a good salary will be unable to own one."

More than seventeen million Ford automobiles have been made since this announcement was first printed. The passing years have brought many changes—in appearance—in performance—in manner of manufacture. But there is one thing that has never changed—the fundamental idea behind the Ford car.

The Ford Motor Company was formed, and exists today, not merely to make automobiles, but to provide economical transportation for all the people. Far more important than the car itself is the part it plays in the lives, happiness, and the prosperity of millions of people.

Before the Ford was introduced, the automobile was considered as an expensive toy. There was no conception of its uses and possibilities as we know them today. It was accepted in much the same manner that the airplane was accepted five years ago. Great emphasis was placed upon its racing speed—little upon its practical utility.

With the coming of the Ford, it became possible for men in all walks of life to enjoy the benefits of transportation that formerly had been limited to a fortunate few.

A great change came over

THE NEW FORD TUDOR SEDAN

the country and with it a new prosperity. By freeing the movements of men, the Ford also freed their thoughts and created new opportunities. The barriers of time and distance were broken down. Good roads followed close behind the automobile and the isolation of country districts disappeared. The nation grew as people learned to use this newly developed horse-power and fit it to their needs.

Into the hands of men of moderate means—to the workers in factories—to the toilers on the farm—was given a means to increase their income and enjoy the leisure which that increased income should bring. The working day became shorter because men could do in eight hours

Ford

FORD MOTOR COMPANY
Detroit, Michigan

the tasks that previously had taken ten or twelve—and do them better.

Today, with all its improvements—with all its new beauty of line and color—with all the changes that have been made during the past twenty-one years—the Ford is still "a motor car for the great multitude."

Business of every kind moves forward at a faster pace because of it. To countless homes it brings the rewards of widening opportunity, happiness, and priceless hours of relaxation.

All of this not merely because of its safety, its comfort, its speed, its reliability, but because of a fundamental purpose that is greater than all of these. Because, in larger degree than ever, it provides economical transportation for all the people.

Hearst's International–Cosmopolitan for September 1929

As their new Ford Tudor Sedan drives off the narrow one-lane bridge, a man in the back seat with a pipe leans forward to talk to the driver. In the background, across the lake, a park and swimming area appear at the edge of the water.

Version A (TdS 11a)

⊙ *Collier's,* August 31, 1929, CIII
○ *Cosmopolitan,* September 1929, p. 115
⊙ *Liberty,* September 21, 1929, p. 17
⊙ *The Redbook Magazine,* September 1929, p. 98
⊙ *Southern Agriculturist,* July 1, 1929, (B&W)

OVER THE BRIDGE

The first *"Over the Bridge"* ad version (A) uses the same headline as in the Tudor Sedan *"Corn Borer Check"* ad appearing one month earlier.

Two additional versions of this Tudor Sedan ad were produced with a different headline – *"Value far above the Price."* While both versions utilize this same new headline, it appears both below (version B) and above (version C) the Tudor Sedan illustration.

Version B (TdS 11b) ➤

○ *The Literary Digest,* September 14, 1929, p. 43

The Literary Digest for September 14, 1929

THE FORD TUDOR SEDAN

VALUE *far above* the PRICE

IN REVIEWING the many advantages of the Ford, it is particularly interesting to note the relation between value and price.

The low first cost of the Ford is a point to keep in mind at all times because it means a considerable saving to you in the purchase of the car.

Equally important, however, is the reason for this low price and the manner in which it has been achieved without sacrifice of quality or performance. On the basis of actual, comparative worth, the Ford represents a value far above the price you pay.

This is made possible only through manufacturing methods and production economies that are as unusual as the car itself.

Every purchaser shares the benefits of the Ford policy of owning the source of most raw materials—of making thousands of cars a day—and of selling at a small margin of profit. Were the Ford made in any other way, under any other policy, it would unquestionably cost you much more than the present price.

The use of the Triplex shatterproof glass for the windshield is a definite indication of this quality. So are the four Houdaille hydraulic double-acting shock absorbers. The silent, fully

enclosed six-brake system. The aluminum pistons. The chrome silicon alloy valves. The simplicity and efficiency of the lubrication, cooling, ignition and fuel systems. The unusually large number of ball and roller bearings. The extensive use of fine steel forgings instead of castings or stampings. The many other mechanical features that count so much in reliability, economy and long life.

All of these are important considerations to every man or woman who is contemplating the purchase of a motor car. All are important reasons why the Ford delivers a value far above the price.

FORD MOTOR COMPANY Detroit, Michigan

August, 1929   29

VALUE *far above* the PRICE

THE NEW FORD TUDOR SEDAN

IN REVIEWING the many advantages of the new Ford, it is particularly interesting to note the relation between value and price.

The low first cost of the new Ford is a point to keep in mind at all times because it means a considerable saving to you in the purchase of the car.

Equally important, however, is the reason for this low price and the manner in which it has been achieved without sacrifice of quality or performance. On the basis of actual, comparative worth, the new Ford represents a value far above the price you pay.

This is made possible only through

manufacturing methods and production economies that are as unusual as the car itself.

Every purchaser shares the benefits of the Ford policy of owning the source of most raw materials—of making thousands of cars a day—and of selling at a small margin of profit.

Were the new Ford made in any other way, under any other policy, it would unquestionably cost you much more.

The use of the Triplex shatterproof glass for the windshield is a definite indication of this quality. So are the four Houdaille hydraulic shock absorbers. The

silent, fully enclosed six-brake system. The aluminum pistons. The chrome silicon alloy valves. The simplicity and efficiency of the lubrication, cooling, ignition and fuel systems. The large number of ball and roller bearings. The extensive use of fine steel forgings instead of castings or stampings. The many other mechanical features that count so much in reliability, economy and long life.

All of these are important considerations to everyone who is contemplating the purchase of a motor car. All are important reasons why the new Ford delivers a value far above the price.

FORD MOTOR COMPANY Detroit, Michigan

◄ **Version C (TdS 11c)**

◉ *The American Boy,* August 1929, p. 29

While most Model A ads appearing in **The American Boy** have texts that differ from those appearing in other magazines, the text in this black and white ad (C) remains virtually unchanged from that used in one of the color ad versions (B). However, the headline is moved to appear above the illustration in this final edition of the Tudor Sedan *"Over the Bridge"* magazine ad.

TRI-MOTOR LANDING

◆

VALUE *far above the* PRICE

IN REVIEWING the many advantages of the Ford, it is particularly interesting to note the relation between value and price.

The low first cost of the Ford is a point to keep in mind at all times because it means a considerable saving to you in the purchase of the car.

Equally important, however, is the reason for this low price and the manner in which it has been achieved without sacrifice of quality or performance. On the basis of actual, comparative worth, the Ford represents a value far above the price you pay.

This is made possible only through manufacturing methods and production economies that are as unusual as the car itself. Every purchaser shares the benefits of the Ford policy of owning the source of most raw materials—of making many thousands of cars a day—and of selling at a small margin of profit.

Ford

FORD MOTOR COMPANY
Detroit, Michigan

THE FORD TUDOR SEDAN

Were the Ford made in any other way, under any other policy, it would unquestionably cost you much more than its present price.

The use of the Triplex shatter-proof glass for the windshield is a definite indication of this quality. So are the four Houdaille hydraulic shock absorbers. The silent, fully enclosed six-brake system. The aluminum pistons. The chrome silicon alloy valves. The simplicity of the lubrica-

tion, cooling, ignition and fuel systems. The large number of ball and roller bearings. The extensive use of fine steel forgings instead of castings or stampings. The many other mechanical features that count so much in reliability, economy and long life.

All of these are important considerations to every man or woman who is contemplating the purchase of a motor car. All are important reasons why the Ford delivers a value far above the price.

Hearst's International–Cosmopolitan for October 1929

The startled lady in the new Ford Tudor Sedan looks up to see a Ford Tri-Motor airplane only about 30 feet overhead. The airplane is in the process of landing as it follows a red arrow "sky sign" pointing to the runway.

Version A (TdS 12a)
◉ *Collier's*, September 28, 1929, CIII
○ *Cosmopolitan*, October 1929, p. 115
◉ *Liberty*, October 19, 1929, p. 18+
◉ *The Redbook Magazine*, October 1929, p. 94

TRI-MOTOR LANDING

The *"Tri-Motor Landing"* ad is one of the few Tudor Sedan ad drawings that does not point out the roominess of the car by showing passengers in the back seat of the car.

Each of the two additional versions of this 1929 Tudor Sedan ad use different headlines and different texts. One (B) stresses the *"unseen values"* in the new Ford car, the other (C) concentrates on the *"unusual riding comfort"* of the new Ford.

> **Version B (TdS 12b)** ➤
> ○ *The Literary Digest,* October 12, 1929, p. 44

> ◄ **Version C (TdS 12c)**
> ○ *The Saturday Evening Post,* October 5, 1929, p. 43

The length of the ad text in the larger magazine format (*The Saturday Evening Post,* version C) is somewhat shorter than that contained in the smaller ad format (*The Literary Digest,* version B). This permits the latter ad to have a slightly larger text size for easier reading and a relatively large blank space above the headline – similar to that found in the first *"Tri-Motor Landing"* ad version (A).

LAST CHANCE

◆

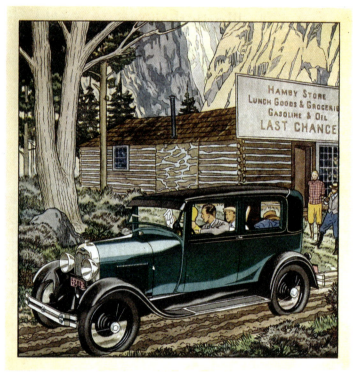

THE FORD IS AN UNUSUALLY STRONG AND STURDY CAR

The Ford Tudor Sedan, shown here, brings you all the features of the Ford cars—ease of control, quick acceleration, 55 to 65 miles an hour, smoothness, balance and security at all speeds, four Houdaille double-acting hydraulic shock absorbers, silent, fully enclosed six-brake system, Triplex shatter-proof glass windshield, Alemite chassis lubrication, economy, reliability, long life.

THE FORD is an unusually strong and sturdy car because of the enduring quality that has been built into every part. Of special interest and importance to every motorist is the extensive use of fine steel.

The story of Ford steel dates back to 1905, when the Ford Motor Company developed the use of a new alloy which raised the tensile strength of steel threefold. That was the beginning of the Ford idea of using specific steels for specific parts—an idea which has perhaps its highest expression in the new car.

Today, more than forty different kinds of steel are used in the Ford—each particular kind being selected and perfected to fit the particular needs of each part. Seven kinds of steel are used in the transmission alone because research and experience have proved that seven kinds of steel will give greater efficiency and reliability than one or two.

There is no limit to selection—no thought that any certain steel must be made to do for many parts to save expense. The Ford policy has always been to use the best possible material for each part, and then, through large production, to give it to the public at low cost.

The Ford open-hearth furnaces have a yearly capacity of 600,000 tons. The quality and uniformity of this steel are held to even closer limits than those used in industry generally.

As important as the steel itself is the Ford method of heat-treating by automatic control so that the same piece of steel, though in one unit, may have different degrees of hardness at different points.

A further development of this one-piece principle has been made possible by perfecting the art of electric welding. This permits the use of an unusual number of steel forgings instead of malleable iron or stampings, without increased weight, yet with a considerable gain in strength and simplicity.

Such high quality of material has a direct bearing on the performance of the Ford car. Throughout, it has been designed and built to give you many thousands of miles of faithful, uninterrupted service at a very low cost per mile.

A family continues on the unpaved road into the wilderness in their new Ford Tudor Sedan. They have just departed the *"Hamby Store"* – which was their *"last chance"* for supplies before continuing on with their backwoods adventure.

Version A (TdS 13a)
- ⦿ *Capper's Farmer,* November 1929. p. 19
- ○ *The Country Gentleman,* November 1929, p. 116
- ⦿ *Farm & Fireside,* November 1929, CII
- ⦿ *Southern Agriculturist,* November 1, 1929, CIII (B&W)
- ○ *Successful Farming,* November 1929, CII

LAST CHANCE

This 1929 Tudor Sedan ad appeared only in farm-related publications.

The "driving off into the wilderness" illustration is befitting the *"The Ford is an Unusually Strong and Sturdy Car"* headline used in the ad. The ad text elaborates on the Ford idea of using different types of steel for specific parts on the Ford car – and indicates that:

"The story of Ford steel dates back to 1905, when the Ford Motor Company developed the use of a new alloy which raised the tensile strength of steel three-fold."

The text reveals that:

"Today, more than forty different kinds of steel are used in the Ford."

The challenging experience to be faced by the family as they drive into the wilderness is accentuated by the *"last chance"* message painted in large capital letters on the sign – and by the apparent darker nature of the colors appearing in front of, as compared to behind, the departing Tudor Sedan.

THEY SAID TO TURN LEFT AT THE BIG ROCK.
As Junior looks on from the back seat, Mom has the map out. It appears that she will serve as the navigator for their upcoming adventure.

'RECON WE'LL EVER SEE EM AGAIN?
The rather grim nature of the setting is further dramatized by the concerned looks of the two men standing in front of the log-built store. While they have sold the family some supplies they will need for their adventure and offered them some advice and directions, they appear a little concerned as they watch the Tudor Sedan pull away from the general store.

ADMIRING TUDOR

Pride of Possession

THE NEW FORD TUDOR SEDAN

YOU will take a real pride in the smart style and fresh new beauty of the Ford just as you will find an ever-growing satisfaction in its alert, capable performance. From the new deep radiator to the tip of the curving rear fender, there is an unbroken sweep of line — a flowing grace of contour and harmony of color heretofore thought possible only in an expensive automobile. Craftsmanship has been put into mass production.

As the women say "hello," a man pauses to admire the new Ford Tudor Sedan he has parked in the driveway. The new Ford has also caught the attention of the man holding his newspaper. In this "winter" ad version, both ladies wear furs – given the cold February weather.

Version A (TdS 14a)
○ *Collier's,* February 15, 1930, CIII
◉ *Farm and Ranch,* February 1, 1930, p. 13
○ *Liberty,* February 8, 1930, p. 38+

Note the "eyebrow" front fenders and 1928-29 style front bumper on this early 1930 Tudor.

ADMIRING TUDOR

The first (A), second (B) and third (C) editions of this 1930 Tudor Sedan ad represent the "winter" ad version – with both women still clad in their furs.

The second version (B) is a black and white edition.

Version B (TdS 14b) ➤
⊙ *Southern Agriculturist,* May 15, 1930

Note that, unlike the earlier (February) version of this 1930 Tudor Sedan ad (A), the later (March and May) renditions are drawn with 1930-31 style front bumpers.

The two-page edition of this ad (C) retains the same basic illustration, but employs a new headline.

Version C (TdS 14c) ⋁
⊙ *The Literary Digest,* March 8, 1930, pp. 34-35
⊙ *The Saturday Evening Post,* March 22, 1930, pp. 76-77

ADMIRING TUDOR

Two additional versions (D and E) of this Tudor Sedan ad using the same headline were produced. However, in what could be called the "spring" edition of the *"Admiring Tudor"* ad, the furs and heavy coat worn by the women in the earlier February and March ad versions (A and B) have now disappeared.

Version D (TdS 14d) ➤

○ *The Country Home,* May 1930, CIII

◉ *Farm and Ranch,* May 3, 1930, p. 13

○ *Successful Farming,* May 1930, CIII

Note that *Farm and Ranch* published both the "winter" (February) and "spring" (May) ad versions.

Version E (TdS 14e) [text difference]

○ *The Country Gentleman,* May 1930, p. 56

THE NEW FORD TUDOR SEDAN

EXTRA VALUE WITHOUT EXTRA COST

THE constant effort of the Ford Motor Company is to find ways to give you greater and greater value without increase in price — frequently at lowered price. This applies not only to the manufacture of the car, but to other important factors that concern its usefulness to millions of people. It is obvious that savings in production would be of little value if they were sacrificed later in high selling costs.

Because the Ford is made economically, distributed economically, serviced economically — and because it runs economically — it is a value far above the price you pay. Among its outstanding features are the Triplex shatter-proof glass windshield, Rustless Steel, five steel-spoke wheels, four Houdaille double-acting hydraulic shock absorbers, large number of ball and roller bearings, the extensive use of fine steel forgings instead of castings or stampings, and unusual accuracy in manufacturing.

"Winter Ad" Illustration
(women with furs)
Ad versions A, B and C

"Spring Ad" Illustration
(women without furs)
Ad versions D and E

ADMIRING TUDOR

The Williamson drawing used in the *"Admiring Tudor"* ad is also found in magazine ads produced outside of the U.S. These include ads from Italy, Sweden, Argentina, Canada, and others.

Example ad from Italy ➤
◉ *L'Illustrazione Italiana,* August 1930, p. 74

As with some Williamson drawings, the *"Admiring Tudor"* illustration was also employed in Model A advertising efforts beyond magazine ads. As an example, this drawing also appeared on the cover of both an English- and Spanish-language Model A sales folder.

Example Spanish-language Model A Ford sales folder from Ecuador ▽

Eleganza di linee e bellezza di colori

Le carrozzerie della nuova Ford perfezionata si sono imposte all'ammirazione per la eleganza delle linee e la bellezza dei colori. Una loro caratteristica è data dall'impiego dell'acciaio inossidabile per tutte le parti esterne: cornice del radiatore, guarnizione del cofano, fanali anteriori e posteriori, copripolvere dei mozzi, tappi del radiatore e del serbatoio della benzina, ecc. Questo acciaio inossidabile non si corrode e non si scaglia, e manterrà inalterato il proprio splendore per tutto il tempo che durerà la vostra vettura. L'impiego di questo acciaio inossidabile nelle nuove carrozzerie, è un'altra prova della politica di Ford di dare "un valore superiore al prezzo". Provate la nuova Ford perfezionata. Vi renderete conto della sua costruzione vigorosa e del comfort che è in grado di offrirvi.

FORD ITALIANA SOCIETA ANONIMA · TRIESTE

Nueva Belleza para el Nuevo Ford

RAILROAD SNOW

◆

March, 1930

THE COUNTRY GENTLEMAN

Adding New Beauty to Outstanding Performance

THE NEW FORD TUDOR SEDAN

The Model A Ford was a good car when it was first introduced. It has constantly been made a better car. For it has never been the policy of the Ford Motor Company to stand still.

Changes are not made for the mere sake of changing or to meet a fleeting fancy. Yet hardly a week passes, but that some improvement is made—some new way is found to increase the value and service of the car. As soon as these improvements are fully tested in actual practice they are passed on to the public.

The new Ford bodies are a reflection of this policy of constant improvement. In flowing grace of line, in harmony of design and color, they set a new high standard for a low-priced car. New beauty and new refinements of finish have been placed within the means of every one.

In this connection, it is interesting to note and remember that these beautiful new bodies are but one of many features that make the new Ford a value far above the price.

Others are the fully enclosed, silent six-brake system, four Houdaille double-acting hydraulic shock absorbers, specially designed transverse springs, Triplex shatter-proof glass windshield, five steel-spoke wheels, unusually large number of ball and roller bearings, the extensive use of fine steel forgings instead of castings or stampings, aluminum pistons, chrome silicon alloy valves, chrome alloy transmission gears and shaft, torque tube drive, three-quarter floating rear axle, and bright Rustless Steel of enduring luster for the radiator shell, hub caps,

head lamps, cowl finish strip and other exposed metal parts.

In the making of this car, craftsmanship has been put into mass production. Millions of parts are made, each one so accurate and so exactly like the other that all fit perfectly to the thousandth of an inch when brought together for assembly into complete units. This care is reflected in the safety, comfort, speed, power, economy, reliability and long life of the Ford.

Seeing the smart style and substantial sturdiness of these new body lines, you will realize that another forward step has been taken. Riding in the car, you will know that today, more than ever, the new Ford brings you a "value far above the price."

FORD MOTOR COMPANY
Detroit, Michigan

The husband has parked his new Ford Tudor Sedan in the snow by the railroad tracks and is talking with a man while his wife chats with another through the window of the car. In the meantime, the kids are waiting in the back seat.

Version A (TdS 15a)
○ *The Country Gentleman*, March 1930, p. 137

This 1930 Tudor Sedan ad version appeared in only one magazine.

RAILROAD SNOW

The building behind the Tudor Sedan in this drawing must be a bank or contain something quite important – given the heavy bars across the window.

Two additional variations (B and C) in the *"Railroad Snow"* Tudor Sedan ad utilize the same *"Adding New Beauty to Outstanding Performance"* headline but have slight changes in the ad text.

Version B (TdS 15b) [text difference]
⊙ *Capper's Farmer,* March 1930, CIII
⊙ *Southern Agriculturist,* March 15, 1930, CIII (B&W)

Version C (TdS 15c) [text difference]
○ *Country Home,* March 1930, p. 61
○ *Successful Farming,* March 1930, CIII

Note that the 1930 *"Railroad Snow"* Tudor Sedan ad appeared only in farm-related publications.

The text in this Tudor Sedan ad extols the beauty and refinements that have been made in the New Ford Car:

"The Model A Ford was a good car when it was first introduced. It has constantly been made a better car. For it has never been the policy of the Ford Motor Company to stand still."

"Changes are not made for the mere sake of changing or to meet a fleeting fancy. Yet hardly a week passes, but that some improvement is made – some new way is found to increase the value and service of the car. As soon as those improvements are fully tested in actual practice they are passed on to the public."

"The new Ford bodies are a reflection of this policy of constant improvement. In flowing grace of line, in harmony of design and color, they set a new standard for a low-priced car. New beauty and new refinements of finish have been placed within the means of every one."

COMBAT KIDS!
A closer look at the drawing used in this Tudor Sedan ad reveals some extracurricular activity occurring in the back seat of the Tudor Sedan. Here, one of the young boys has pulled the cap down over the eyes of his brother – who, in turn, seems rather eager to defend himself.

TAKING A BREAK
TUDOR SEDAN

THE NEW FORD TUDOR SEDAN

Outstanding Features of the New Ford

New streamline bodies. • • Choice of colors. • • Adjustable front seats in most bodies. • • Triplex shatter-proof glass windshield. • • Four Houdaille double-acting hydraulic shock absorbers. • • Bright, enduring Rustless Steel for many exterior metal parts. • • Fully enclosed four-wheel brakes. • • Five steel-spoke wheels. • • Aluminum pistons. • • Chrome silicon alloy valves. • • Torque-tube drive. • • Three-quarter floating rear axle. • • More than twenty ball and roller bearings. • • Extensive use of fine steel forgings. • • 55 to 65 miles an hour. • • Quick acceleration. • • Ease of control. • • Low first cost. • • Low cost of operation and up-keep. • • Reliability and long life. • • Good dealer service.

The farmer is taking a break and has interrupted his plowing to gaze at the Ford Tudor Sedan that has stopped next to his field. As the farmer leans on the fence, the Tudor Sedan's driver slides over to the passenger's seat to chat with him.

Version A (TdS 16a)
◉ *Southern Agriculturist,* July 15, 1930, CIII

This unique Tudor Sedan ad appeared only in black and white and only in one magazine.

TAKING A BREAK

Tudor Sedan and De Luxe Sedan Ads

The basic illustration used for the *"Taking a Break"* ad for the Ford Tudor Sedan is also utilized, slightly modified, in an ad for the Ford De Luxe Sedan.

Without changing other aspects of the illustration, modifications were made to the Tudor Sedan drawing – by adding rear door handles, slightly changing the appearance of the windows (and view through the windows) and adding cowl lights – to produce a De Luxe Sedan.

The resulting Tudor Sedan and De Luxe Sedan ads use the same headline but have slightly different ad texts.

It is not known which of the two Model A drawings was prepared first and then modified to produce the second ad. Perhaps this modification was made to the basic Williamson illustration by another artist in order to meet the last minute need to have a second illustration available for the other car.

Both the Tudor Sedan and the De Luxe Sedan *"Taking a Break"* magazine ads were published in July 1930. While the Tudor Sedan ad appeared in only one magazine, the De Luxe Sedan ad appeared in five different publications.

"Taking a Break"
Tudor Sedan
Ad Illustration
July 1930

"Taking a Break"
De Luxe Sedan
Ad Illustration
July 1930

This is the only Model A Ford magazine ad where one basic vehicle drawing was modified to depict two different Model A body styles.

CAMPSITE

After the first twenty-five thousand miles

THE value of sound design, good materials, and careful construction is especially apparent in the new Ford after the first 25,000 miles. Long continuous service emphasizes its mechanical reliability and economy of operation and up-keep. The passing months and years bring a growing pride in its appearance and an increasing respect for the substantial worth that has been built into it. From every standpoint, you know you have made a far-seeing, satisfactory purchase. « « « « « « «

Throughout the car you will find many reasons for its alert, capable performance and many instances of value far above the price you pay. Prominent among these are the four Houdaille double-acting hydraulic shock absorbers, Triplex shatter-proof glass windshield, fully enclosed four-wheel brakes, five steel-spoke wheels, aluminum pistons, chrome silicon alloy valves, chrome alloy transmission gears and shafts, torque-tube drive, three-quarter floating rear axle, extensive use of steel forgings, more than twenty ball and roller bearings, and bright, enduring Rustless Steel for many exterior parts. « « « « « « « «

THE NEW FORD TUDOR SEDAN

The day is almost over and the family has parked their Ford Tudor Sedan at their overnight campsite. As the travelers prepare to settle in, the new Tudor Sedan has attracted the attention of a campsite guest.

Version A (TdS 17a)
● *Capper's Farmer,* September 1930, CIII
● *Farm and Ranch,* September 6, 1930, p. 13

This Tudor Sedan ad is one of the rarest Model A Ford magazine ads.

CAMPSITE

This Model A Tudor Sedan ad appeared only in two farm-related magazines – in September of 1930.

The headline of *"Campsite"* ad supports the illustration showing the Model A in a traveling mode and proclaims the qualities apparent in the new Ford *"After the first twenty-five thousand miles."*

The campers set up behind the Ford Tudor Sedan must be heavy travelers, as evidenced by the many souvenir pennants hanging from their (non-Ford) car.

WE'VE BEEN THERE!
Based on the pennants, their neighbor's recent travel destinations have included *"Lake Louise"* and *"Yellowstone."*

PUMP, PLAN AND COOK!
It appears that the family's routine in setting up their campsite is well-orchestrated.

Dad's inflating the air mattress with the car's tire pump has been interrupted while he shows off their new Ford Tudor Sedan to their campsite guest. The tire pump, still connected to the air mattress in the foreground of the ad, awaits his return.

Meanwhile, Mom is checking the map while it is still light enough to review the next day's travel plans and Junior, dressed in his kickers, tends to the pot of soup at the camp stove.

RANGER VISIT.
The green tie and uniformed attire of their guest reveals that he may be the local Park Ranger who is welcoming them to the park's camping area.

BROOK SCHOOL

◆

THE NEW FORD TUDOR SEDAN

Safely to the journey's end. LONG trips are pleasant in the new Ford because of its easy-riding comfort. The restful, well-upholstered seats invite you to sit back and relax and enjoy the panorama of the passing miles. Steadily, evenly, you travel along because of the specially designed springs and four Houdaille hydraulic shock absorbers. They cushion the car against hard jolts and bumps and smooth your path along every highway. « « Equally important to the enjoyment of motoring is your confidence in the mechanical reliability of the Ford. No matter where you go—near or far—day or night—you know it will bring you safely, quickly, comfortably to the journey's end.

A couple parks their new Tudor Sedan in front of the *"Brook School"* to drop off their daughter. While Mother talks with the head mistress, Father looks up – his attention drawn to the young ladies peeking out of the upstairs windows.

Version A (TdS 18a)
- *Country Life,* October 1930, p. 102
- *Harper's Bazaar,* October 1930, p. 169
- *The Sportsman,* October 1930, p. 84
- *Vanity Fair,* October 1930, p. 96+
- *Vogue,* October 27, 1930, p. 25

BROOK SCHOOL

The first version of the *"Brook School"* Tudor Sedan ad (A) appeared only in the most upscale magazines of the day. However, the second version (B) was contained in many different types of magazines. This Tudor Sedan ad appeared in a total of 16 different U.S. magazines in October 1930.

This second ad version (B) incorporates only a very minor ad text change – the addition of *"double-acting"* in describing the Ford *"Houdaille hydraulic shock absorbers."*

MacLean's Magazine, September 1, 1930

THE NEW FORD TUDOR SEDAN

Safely to the journey's end. Long trips are pleasant in the new Ford because of its easy-riding comfort. The restful, well-upholstered seats invite you to sit back and relax and enjoy the panorama of the passing miles. Steadily, evenly, you travel along because of the specially designed springs and four Houdaille double-acting hydraulic shock absorbers. They cushion the car against hard jolts and bumps and smooth your path along every highway. «   «   » Equally important to the enjoyment of motoring is your confidence in the mechanical reliability of the Ford. No matter where you go—near or far—day or night—you know it will bring you safely, quickly, comfortably to the journey's end.

FORD MOTOR COMPANY Ford OF CANADA, LIMITED
"The Canadian Car"

Version B (TdS 18b) [text difference]

○ *The American Magazine,* October 1930, p. 107
◉ *Capper's Farmer,* October 1930, CIII
◉ *Collier's,* September 27, 1930, CIII
○ *Cosmopolitan,* October 1930
◉ *Delineator,* October 1930, p. 77
○ *The Farmer's Wife,* October 1930, p. 17
○ *Ladies' Home Journal,* October 1930, p. 60
○ *McCall's,* October 1930
◉ *Pictorial Review,* October 1930, CIII
◉ *The Redbook Magazine,* October 1930, CII
○ *Woman's Home Companion,* October 1930, p. 59

Many of the Model A Ford ads with illustrations drawn by Williamson for the U.S. market also appeared in Canadian magazines and were sometimes prepared in both English and French language editions.

◁ Example ad from Canada
◉ *Maclean's,* September 1, 1930, p. 43

While the ad texts sometimes differed, the formats of Canadian Model A Ford ads with Williamson illustrations were usually identical to their U.S. counterparts. The exceptions were the additions of the *"The Ford Motor Company of Canada, Limited"* identification phrase and the *"The Canadian Car"* tag line added beneath the Ford oval logo.

163

CHRISTMAS TREE SELECTION

THE COUNTRY GENTLEMAN   December, 1930

THE NEW FORD TUDOR SEDAN

You save in many ways when you buy a Ford

LOW FIRST COST is just one advantage of buying a Ford. Of even greater importance is the saving in the cost of operation and up-keep. As the months and years go by, this saving will total many dollars.

The economy of the Ford is due to its simplicity of design, high quality of materials, and accuracy in manufacturing and assembling. Every part has been made to endure—to serve you faithfully and well for many thousands of miles.

Ford owners everywhere will tell you of the economy and reliability of the new Ford. A salesman who travels long distances daily by automobile writes:

"I purchased a Model A Ford Coupe on May 8, 1928, and at this writing have run it 75,888 miles. After I had driven 44,400 miles, I spent $45 in repairs, and at 61,000 miles had an additional amount of work done costing $25. I have never had the brakes relined. My tire mileage has averaged better than 18,000 miles."

Another Ford owner tells of traveling 24,000 miles in a year, in all kinds of weather, and says "the only parts expense was 75c for a shock-absorber link and 50c for a new rubber for the windshield wiper."

A total of 39,721 miles is reported by a Ford owner on 1685 gallons of gasoline. Another Ford owner, describing a 13,000-mile trip across the continent and back by way of Calgary and Banff, writes: "We were amazed at the performance of the Ford. We drove

constantly at fifty miles an hour and averaged better than twenty miles per gallon of gasoline.

"Not counting the day at Grand Canyon, we drove home to New York from Los Angeles in just eight days. The car was extremely economical to operate, comfortable and speedy."

Large industrial companies which keep accurate cost records are buying more and more Ford cars every year because of their proved economy of operation and up-keep. Many of these have fleets of fifty, one hundred and two hundred Ford cars and trucks. One large corporation operates more than eight thousand. The experience of these careful buyers is a dependable guide for you to follow in the purchase of an automobile.

During their visit to the farm, this family has selected and cut their Christmas tree. Dad, ax still in his hand, mops his brow. As they prepare to leave for home, Mom loads packages into the back seat of their Tudor Sedan.

Version A (TdS 19a)

○ *The American Boy,* December 1930, p. 33 (B&W)

◉ *Capper's Farmer,* December 1930, CII

○ *The Country Gentleman,* December 1930, p. 36

◉ *Farm and Ranch,* December 6, 1930, p. 13

◉ *Southern Agriculturist,* December 1, 1930, p. 4 (B&W)

CHRISTMAS TREE SELECTION

Given the Christmas holiday theme of the 1929 Tudor Sedan *"Christmas Tree Selection"* ad, it appeared (in two different versions) only in December farm-related magazine issues.

The second ad version (B) has a slight change in the advertising text. In this version, one sentence was removed from the glowing testimonial provided by a satisfied Ford owner. Perhaps this shortening of the ad text was done to allow a better fit with the smaller page size of the two magazines containing the second ad version (B).

Version B (TdS 19b) [text difference]
O *The Country Home,* December 1930, CIII
O *Successful Farming,* December 1930, CIII

The text in this Tudor Sedan ad employs several owner testimonials for the new Model A Ford:

"I purchased a Model A Ford Coupe on May 8, 1929, and at this writing have run it 75,888 miles. After I had driven 44,000 miles, I spent $45 in repairs, and at 61,000 miles had an additional amount of work done costing $25."

"A total of 39,721 miles is reported by a Ford owner on 1685 gallons of gasoline. Another Ford owner, describing a trip across the continent, writes: 'We were amazed at the performance of the Ford. We drove constantly at fifty miles an hour and averaged twenty miles per gallon of gasoline. Not counting the day at Grand Canyon, we drove home to New York from Los Angeles in just eight days.'"

ESCAPING TURKEY!
A closer look at this ad helps explain the details drawn at the front of and just below the Model A Tudor Sedan.

Having escaped the Thanksgiving holiday dinner table, the alarmed turkey appears now to be taking no chances. Here, one glance at the man with the ax in his hand, and knowing Christmas dinner is approaching, causes the turkey to make a quick exit.

MIDTOWN TRUST CO.

◆

Well-Suited to a Woman's Needs

THE new Ford is a particularly good choice for the woman motorist because it is such an easy car to drive. Gears shift smoothly and silently. The steering wheel responds to a light touch. The fully enclosed four-wheel brakes take hold quickly and effectively. A space little longer than the car itself is all you need for parking.

Other factors contributing to your feeling of security and confidence in the new Ford are its quick acceleration and alert speed, substantial steel body construction, shatter-proof glass windshield and mechanical reliability. In every least little detail it is built to endure—to give you many thousands of miles of economical, care-free motoring.

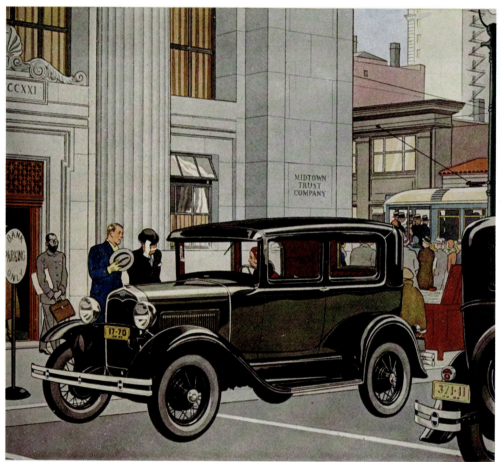

The new Ford Tudor Sedan is a splendid family car at a low price. You may purchase it on convenient terms through the Authorized Ford Finance Plans of the Universal Credit Company

An attendant holds their files and briefcase as two businessmen greet the woman pulling up in her new Tudor Sedan. The woman, an important customer, parks at the *"Bank Parking Only"* spot in front of the *"Midtown Trust Company."*

Version A (TdS 20a)
○ *The Farmer's Wife,* March 1931, p. 17
○ *McCall's,* April 1931, p. 69
○ *Woman's World,* March 1931, p. 37

This first ad for the 1931 Tudor Sedan was produced in five different versions.

MIDTOWN TRUST CO.

A second variation (B) in this Tudor Sedan ad utilizes the same ad text but features a different headline: *"Safely Through the Down-town Traffic."*

Version B (TdS 20b) ➢

⊙ *Delineator,* April 1931

○ *Good Housekeeping,* April 1931, p. 49

○ *Ladies' Home Journal,* April 1931, p. 65

⊙ *Pictorial Review,* April 1931, p. 96

⊙ *True Story,* April 1931, p. 69

○ *Woman's Home Companion,* April 1931, p. 69

The third version (C) has a different, economy oriented, headline and an expanded ad text.

Safely Through the Down-town Traffic

THE new Ford is a particularly good choice for the woman motorist because it is such an easy car to drive. Gears shift smoothly and silently. The steering wheel responds to a light touch. The fully enclosed four-wheel brakes take hold quickly and effectively. A space little longer than the car itself is all you need for parking.

Other factors contributing to your feeling of security and confidence in the new Ford are its quick acceleration and alert speed, substantial steel body construction, shatter-proof glass windshield and mechanical reliability. In every least little detail it is built to endure—to give you many thousands of miles of economical, care-free motoring.

The new Ford Tudor Sedan is a splendid family car at a low price. You may purchase it on convenient terms through the Authorized Ford Finance Plans of the Universal Credit Company

Liberty   March 21, 1931

The new Ford is an economical car to own and drive

THE new Ford is a splendid car to own and drive because of its attractive lines and colors, safety, comfort, speed, reliability and long life.

There are, in addition, three other features of importance to every far-seeing automobile owner ... low first cost, low cost of operation, and low yearly depreciation. During the life of the car, the day-by-day economy of the Ford will amount to considerably more than the saving on the first cost. You save when you buy the Ford and you save every mile you drive.

Evidence of the economy of the new Ford is shown in its selection by large industrial companies which keep accurate cost records. Many of these operate fleets of fifty, one hundred, and two hundred Ford cars and trucks. One company has eight thousand. The experience of these careful buyers is a dependable guide for you to follow in the purchase of a motor car.

The reasons for the good performance and economy of the new Ford are simplicity of design, high quality of materials,

and care in manufacturing and assembling. Many vital parts are made to limits of one one-thousandth of an inch. Some to three ten-thousandths of an inch.

The more you see of the performance of the new Ford, the more certain you become of this fact. . . . It brings you everything you want or need in a motor car at an unusually low price. You may purchase it on convenient, economical terms through the Authorized Ford Finance Plans of the Universal Credit Company.

THE NEW FORD TUDOR SEDAN

◁ **Version C (TdS 20c)**

⊙ *Liberty,* March 21, 1931, CII

⊙ *Life,* February 27, 1931, CIV

○ *The Literary Digest,* March 7, 1931, p. 28

The text in the third ad version (C) points out the inherent value of the new Ford car – although through a somewhat cryptic economic message:

"During the life of the car, the day-to-day economy of the Ford will amount to considerably more than the savings on the first cost."

MIDTOWN TRUST CO.

Two additional versions of this 1931 Tudor Sedan ad were produced. The fourth version (D) keeps the same *"The new Ford is an economical car to own and drive"* headline, but adds a second headline and moves the text to beneath the illustration.

Version D (TdS 20d) ➤

⊙ *Collier's, March 14,* 1931, CIII

○ *The Saturday Evening Post,* February 28, 1931, p. 48

The fifth ad version (E) is a black and white edition and utilizes a completely different text and headline – *"You save in many ways when you buy a Ford."*

◀ **Version E (TdS 20e)**

● *The State Trooper,* December 1930, p. 2

This last *"Midtown Trust Co."* ad version (E) includes several Ford owner testimonials about the performance and economy of the new Ford. (The text for this ad version is identical to that used in an earlier Tudor Sedan *"Escaping Turkey"* ad version.)

Complementing the glowing owner testimonials about the new Ford, the ad text also indicates:

"The economy of the Ford is due to its simplicity of design, high quality of materials, and accuracy in manufacturing."

ROCKING HORSE RANCH

NEW FORD TUDOR SEDAN

The Unseen Value That Makes the New Ford a Fine Car

You step into the new Ford, press your foot on the starter and away you go. Smoothly, evenly, it carries you along for many thousands of miles each year. You have no fear of mechanical trouble and you accept its good performance as a matter of course. You have confidence that it will serve you faithfully and well under all conditions.

Though you may never raise the hood of the car, it is interesting to know some of the reasons for the reliability of the Ford and its economy of operation and up-keep. The extensive use of ball and roller bearings is an example of value far above the price.

These ball and roller bearings — and there are more than twenty of them in the new Ford — allow moving parts to run smoothly and freely, thus reducing friction and wear to a minimum. To you as a car owner, this means smooth, quiet mechanical operation, more speed and power, increased gasoline mileage, greater durability and longer life.

The function of the ball and roller bearings of the new Ford is similar to that of the jewels in a watch. Since they are placed at every point in the chassis where they are needed to prevent friction, the new Ford may be called a full-jeweled car, in the same sense that a fine watch is full-jeweled.

As important as the number of ball and roller bearings in the new Ford is their adequate size, and the manner in which each type has been selected for the work it has to do.

Ball bearings are used where their ball-shaped construction will give the greatest smoothness and efficiency. Roller bearings are used wherever a larger bearing surface is needed to carry a heavier load.

Steering is made easier and safer in the new Ford because of the roller bearings in the front wheels, at the spindle bolts and in the steering mechanism. There are ball bearings on the clutch and ball and roller bearings in the transmission. A roller bearing on the drive shaft at the universal joint provides perfect alignment of those vital parts and prevents loss of power. Adjustments on the rear axle pinion and differential are made unnecessary by the close limits to which those roller bearings are held. The ball bearing on the generator armature gives greater reliability to that important part of the electrical system.

The value of the large number of ball and roller bearings in the new Ford is especially apparent after the first year. By reducing friction and wear, they also reduce the cost of up-keep and the need of replacement parts.

In many other parts of the new Ford you find this same high quality of materials and fine craftsmanship in manufacture. The performance of the car under the severest driving conditions reflects the value built into it.

The first cost of the new Ford is low and you can purchase it on economical terms through the Authorized Ford Finance Plans of the Universal Credit Company.

PRINTED IN U. S. A.   THE INLAND PRESS, DETROIT

The ranch hand has met three guests at the train station and is bringing them to the *"Rocking Horse"* ranch in a new Ford Tudor Sedan. As the passing rider tips his hat, all attention is drawn to the cowboy and his pack mule.

Version A (TdS 21a)
● *The State Trooper,* March 1931, CIV

This is a unique ad. It appeared in only one magazine, in March 1931.

SCHOOL'S OUT

◆

April, 1931 THE COUNTRY GENTLEMAN

New Ford Tudor Sedan

The Unseen Value That Makes the New Ford a Fine Car

You step into the new Ford, press your foot on the starter and away you go. Smoothly, evenly, it carries you along your way, for many thousands of miles each year. You have no fear of mechanical trouble and you accept its good performance as a matter of course. You have confidence that it will serve you faithfully and well under all conditions.

Though you may never raise the hood of your car, it is interesting to know some of the reasons for the reliability of the Ford and its economy of operation and up-keep. The extensive use of ball and roller bearings is an example of value far above the price.

These ball and roller bearings—and there are more than twenty of them in the new Ford—allow moving parts to run smoothly and freely, thus reducing friction and wear to a minimum. To you as a car owner, this means smooth, quiet mechanical operation, more speed and power, increased gasoline mileage, greater durability and longer life.

The function of the ball and roller bearings of the new Ford is similar to that of the jewels in a watch. Since they are placed at every point in the chassis where they are needed to prevent friction, the new Ford may be called a full-jeweled car, in the same sense that a fine watch is full-jeweled.

As important as the number of ball and roller bearings in the new Ford is their adequate size, and the manner in which each type has been selected for the work it has to do.

Ball bearings are used where their ball-shaped construction will give the greatest smoothness and efficiency. Roller bearings are used wherever a larger bearing surface is needed to carry a heavier load.

Steering is made easier and safer in the new Ford because of the roller bearings in the front wheels, at the spindle bolts and in the steering mechanism. There are ball bearings on the clutch and ball and roller bearings in the transmission. A roller bearing on the

drive shaft at the universal joint provides perfect alignment of those vital parts and prevents loss of power. Adjustments on the rear axle pinion and differential are made unnecessary by the close limits to which those roller bearings are held. The ball bearing on the generator gives greater reliability to that important part of the electrical system.

The value of the large number of ball and roller bearings in the new Ford is especially apparent after the first year. By reducing friction and wear, they also reduce cost of up-keep and the need of replacement parts.

In many other parts of the new Ford you find this same high quality of materials and fine craftsmanship in manufacture. The performance of the car under the severest driving conditions reflects the value that has been built into it. The first cost of the new Ford is low and you can purchase it on convenient, economical terms through the Authorized Ford Finance Plans of the Universal Credit Company.

Ford

The one-room school house is letting out for the day and Mom has just picked up four kids in her new Ford Tudor Sedan. As the teacher waves from the window, kids run to a car parked, with its door open, at the front of the school.

Version A (TdS 22a)
- ◉ *Capper's Farmer,* March 1931
- ○ *The Country Gentleman,* April 1931, p. 83
- ○ *The Country Home,* April 1931, CII
- ○ *The Farm Journal,* April 1931, p. 15
- ◉ *Southern Agriculturist,* March 1, 1931, p. 3 (B&W)
- ○ *Successful Farming,* April 1931, CIII

TRAFFIC COP

17

For Greater Safety on Every Highway

ALL FORD CARS ARE EQUIPPED WITH SHATTER-PROOF GLASS WINDSHIELDS

FOR greater safety in driving, every Ford car is equipped with a Triplex shatter-proof glass windshield. By reducing the dangers of flying glass it has saved many lives and prevented countless injuries in automobile accidents.

The value of this important safety factor has been known for years, but its use has been limited by expense. It is brought to you on the Ford as standard equipment only because of the efficiency and economy of Ford methods. Much pioneering work has been done in finding ways to manufacture in large volume at low cost.

It is interesting to know how the Triplex shatter-proof glass windshield of the Ford is made and why it gives so much extra protection. The process of manufacture requires many separate operations, yet it can be explained in a few simple words.

Two pieces of plate glass, carefully ground and polished, are covered on one side with a thin coating of gelatine. This coating is baked, sprayed with celluloid, and treated with a solvent.

Then, between the two pieces of glass, like the middle of a sandwich, is inserted a layer of special celluloid. This also has been treated with a solvent.

THE FORD TUDOR SEDAN. *One of the many Ford body types. You can purchase a Ford on economical terms through the Authorized Ford Finance Plans of the Universal Credit Company.*

Thirteen Million Square Feet of Glass

The Ford Motor Company was the pioneer in making glass by a continuous machine process. Its manufacturing economies and unusual facilities make it possible to give you a Triplex shatter-proof glass windshield on the Ford without extra cost. The Rouge plant alone has a capacity of 13,000,000 square feet of glass annually. This calls for 27,300,000 pounds of silica sand, 8,580,000 pounds of soda ash, 7,930,000 pounds of limestone, 1,820,000 pounds of salt cake, 6,136,000 pounds of cullet, 78,000 pounds of charcoal, and 156,000 pounds of arsenic, 118,440,000 pounds of sand, 7,873,000 pounds of stucco, 2,715,000 pounds of garnet, and 724,000 pounds of rouge.

When heat and pressure are applied to the glass sandwich, this solvent helps to dissolve the surfaces in contact and they are actually fused together. It is almost like a welding process. The result is a single sheet of beautiful, clear, laminated glass. The final operation is sealing the edges as protection against air and moisture.

This laminated windshield will withstand a 50% harder impact before breaking than plate glass of equal thickness, and is more flexible under impact. When struck an unusually hard blow, it will crack, but the danger from flying glass is minimized because the pieces adhere to the layer of celluloid.

The greatest care is taken to insure uniform high quality. Plate glass is used for clear vision. One sheet in 150 is taken for test. For the impact test, a heavy steel ball is dropped sixteen feet to the center of a large sheet.

Other samples are subjected to ultra-violet rays and infra-red rays which give, in a few hours, an exposure equal to several years of normal driving. This is done to check the effect of the sun's rays and heat on the

crystal clearness of the glass in actual use. Many improvements have been made in the past three years so that today, Triplex shatter-proof glass is recognized as one of the greatest contributions to safety since four-wheel brakes. High speed and crowded traffic emphasize the need of the protection it affords. It is just another instance of the extra value that has been built into every part of the Ford.

No Flying Glass Here

A woman and three children were in this Ford when a passing car upturned a horseshoe in the road and sent it crashing into the windshield. No one was hurt because there was no flying glass.

As a woman in her new Ford Tudor Sedan approaches the traffic signal, the traffic cop points and yells at the driver of the approaching (sans cowl lights) Ford Cabriolet – drawing the attention of everyone, including the pedestrian behind the car.

Version A (TdS 23a)
⊙ *Southern Agriculturist*, April 1, 1931, p. 17

While the ad illustration depicts a city traffic setting, this unique ad appeared only in this farm-related magazine.

171

FRAMED TUDOR

◆

EDITOR SAYS

73,000 miles is only
a start

SOME time ago we published an account of a Ford that had been driven 73,000 miles in less than a year by three mail carriers in Iowa.

The article created much comment and brought many letters telling of the unusual reliability, economy and long life of the Ford. Here is an interesting letter from the editor of a newspaper in Kansas.

"In one of your recent advertisements in weekly newspapers you tell of a Ford that has been driven 73,000 miles in less than a year.

"That's no mileage at all for a Ford. There is a Ford in this community that was driven 120,000 miles before it was traded in.

"The car was bought in August, 1928, and driven until November, 1930, by its owner. He is a carrier of the *Wichita Daily Eagle,* making a route of 150 miles daily with a morning and evening paper.

"Operating and up-keep costs were exceptionally low. After the car was traded in for a new Ford I am informed that it was overhauled and is now giving good service to its new owner."

Letters like this are indicative of the substantial worth of the Ford and the high quality built into every part.

A fleet of 42 Model A Fords in Louisville covered a total of 2,620,800 miles in twelve months, or the equivalent of 105 times around the world. Five new Fords on police duty in Niagara Falls have been driven more than 100,000 miles each. In Miami a police Ford has gone 120,000 miles.

The average for eighteen Fords in Omaha is 35,000 miles per car for two years of police service.

In every detail of construction the Ford is made to endure — to serve you faithfully and well for many thousands of miles. The price is low because of large production and unusual Ford manufacturing facilities.

THE BEAUTIFUL FORD TUDOR SEDAN

PRINTED IN U. S. A.

This unique black and white ad displays the new Ford Tudor Sedan in a frame with no background illustration. The ad text explains an earlier-published account of a Ford being driven 120,000 miles before it was traded in.

Version A (TdS 24a)
● *The State Trooper,* October 1931

This is one of the latest Model A passenger car ads. It appeared only once, in an October 1931 magazine.

VICTORIA

	TOTAL	1930	1931
Ford Body Style		190-A	190-A
Weight (pounds)		2,372	2,372
Price (FOB Detroit)		$625	$580
Units Produced (U.S.)	40,212	6,306	33,906
Number of U.S. Ads			
Primary Formats	3	–	3
Ad Variations	9	–	9
Magazine Insertions	33	–	33

One of the later Model A Ford body styles produced was the distinctive Victoria. (This body style was sometimes referred to as the Victoria Coupe.) First introduced in November 1930, the Victoria had the two-panel radiator shell and slant-windshield features associated with the new 1931 models. Its lower roof profile, curving bustle back and spare wheel set at a new angle made this new vehicle a welcomed addition to the Model A line of deluxe body styles. Victoria bodies were produced by both Murray (steel back) and Briggs (leather back).

Only three basic magazine ads (with nine variations) were prepared for the Model A Victoria. While the Victoria was available in two different top treatments – a steel roof and an artificial leather covered roof – all of the color magazine ad variations show the Victoria "leatherback" body style. On the other hand, the single black and white Victoria magazine ad features the steel top. Model A Ford Victoria magazine ads appeared only in 1931.

CHAUFFEUR AT CLUB

The New Ford Victoria

A NEW FORD BODY TYPE OF DISTINCTIVE BEAUTY

THE newest, latest addition to the wide variety of Ford body types is the distinguished four-passenger Victoria. It marks a new degree of beauty and of value in a low-price car.

The striking lines of the Ford Victoria are especially apparent in the graceful sweep of the straighter, lower top, the slanting windshield and the curving bustle back, with the spare wheel set at a conforming angle. There is a suggestion of continental design also in the shape and size of the side windows and the intimate interior arrangement. The comfortable, deeply cushioned seats are upholstered in luxurious mohair or fashionable Bedford cord, optional with the purchaser. Appointments and hardware reflect the mode and manner of a custom-built automobile.

With all its new beauty and outstanding mechanical performance, the Ford Victoria sells at a low price. You may purchase it on economical terms through the Authorized Ford Finance Plans of the Universal Credit Company.

An evening at the hunt club is coming to an end as a chauffeur-driven Ford Victoria pulls up to pick up the young mother and her daughter.

○ *The American Magazine,* April 1931, p. 115
○ *Cosmopolitan,* April 1931, p. 99

Version A (Vic 1a)
○ *Good Housekeeping,* March 1931, p. 131
◉ *Liberty,* January 24, 1931, p. 19
◉ *Life,* January 2, 1931, CIV
◉ *The Redbook Magazine,* April 1931, CIII
◉ *True Story,* March 1931

CHAUFFEUR AT CLUB

This 1931 magazine ad, the first for the new Ford Victoria, touts the *"striking lines"* of this new body style.

The second and third versions (B and C) of the *"Chauffeur at Club"* ad utilize the same illustration and headline but contain very minor ad text changes.

Version B (Vic 1b) [text difference]
○ *The Literary Digest,* January 3, 1931, p. 19

Version C (Vic 1c) [text difference]
◉ *Collier's,* February 14, 1931, CIII
◉ *Delineator,* March 1931, p. 58
○ *Ladies' Home Journal,* March 1931, p. 67
○ *McCall's,* March 1931, p. 65
◉ *Pictorial Review,* March 1931
○ *The Saturday Evening Post,* January 3, 1931, p. 76
○ *Woman's Home Companion,* March 1931, p. 58

The fourth version (D) appeared only in the more upscale magazines and has additional text modifications.

Version D (Vic 1d) [text difference]
◉ *Country Life,* February 1931, p. 78
● *Junior League Magazine,* February 1931, p. 4 (B&W)
◉ *The Sportsman,* February 1931, p. 58
◉ *Vanity Fair,* February 1931, p. 17
◉ *Vogue,* February 1, 1931, p. 80+

Some Model A Ford magazine ads have noticeable differences in the illustration, headline or other key elements that allow immediate identification of different ad versions. In other cases, only very minor differences in the text within the ad cause the classification of separate ad versions.

The Victoria *"Chauffeur at Club"* ad provides a good example of different ad versions based on somewhat minor text differences. With "Version A" as the base, "Version B" differs by the addition of the words *"carefully tailored and"* and *"colors"* and the substitution of *"car"* for *"automobile"* in the third paragraph. The text in "Version C" has several differences compared to "Version A" – including the removal of the *"four-passenger"* reference in the first paragraph and its addition in the second paragraph.

TREE HORN.
In keeping with the horse riding and hunting theme of this Victoria magazine ad, the young girl waiting on the stairs holds a riding crop in her hand. A brass fox hunter's horn hangs from the tree above her head.

VICTORIA

For Greater Safety on Every Highway

EVERY FORD CAR IS EQUIPPED WITH A SHATTER-PROOF GLASS WINDSHIELD

For greater safety in driving, every Ford car is equipped with a Triplex shatter-proof glass windshield. By reducing the dangers of flying glass it has saved many lives and prevented injuries in accidents.

The value of this important safety factor has been known for years, but its use has been limited by expense. It is brought to you on the Ford as standard equipment only because of the efficiency and economy of Ford methods. Much pioneering work has been done in finding ways to manufacture in large volume at low cost.

It is interesting to know how the Triplex shatter-proof glass windshield of the Ford is made and why it gives so much extra protection.

Two pieces of plate glass, carefully ground and polished, are covered on one side with a thin coating of gelatine. This coating is baked hard, sprayed with liquid celluloid and treated with a solvent.

Then, between the two pieces of glass, like the middle of a sandwich, is inserted a layer of special celluloid. This also has been treated with a solvent.

When heat and pressure are applied to the glass sandwich, this solvent helps to dissolve the surfaces in contact and they are actually fused together. The final operation is sealing the edges for protection against air and moisture.

This laminated windshield will withstand a 50% harder impact before breaking than plate glass of equal thickness, and is more flexible under impact. When struck an unusually hard blow it will crack, but the danger from flying glass is minimized because the pieces adhere to the layer of celluloid.

High speed and crowded traffic make Triplex shatter-proof glass one of the greatest contributions to safety since four-wheel brakes.

No Flying Glass Here

A woman and three children were in this Ford when a passing car upturned a horseshoe and sent it crashing into the windshield. No one was hurt because of the shatter-proof windshield. The glass did not fly.

Thirteen Million Square Feet of Glass

The Ford Motor Company was the pioneer in making glass by a continuous machine process. Its unusual manufacturing facilities make it possible to give you a Triplex shatter-proof glass windshield on the Ford without extra cost. The Rouge plant alone has a capacity of 13,000,000 square feet of glass annually. This calls for a consumption of 27,300,000 pounds of silica sand, 8,580,000 pounds of soda ash, 7,930,000 pounds of limestone, 1,820,000 pounds of salt cake, 6,136,000 pounds of cullet, 78,000 pounds of charcoal, and 156,000 pounds of arsenic.

The Ford Victoria—one of fourteen body types. You may purchase the Ford on convenient, economical terms through the Authorized Ford Finance Plans of the Universal Credit Company

The *"Woman's League"* meeting at the *"Community House"* has ended and the Ford Victoria awaits its passengers for the trip home. The entire text of this ad is devoted to the safety aspects of the Ford Triplex shatter-proof windshield.

Version A (Vic 2a)
○ *The American Magazine,* June 1931, p. 19
○ *Cosmopolitan,* June 1931, p. 115
○ *The Literary Digest,* May 2, 1931, p. 28
◉ *The Redbook Magazine,* June 1931, CII

COMMUNITY HOUSE

While two additional versions (B and C) of the 1931 Victoria *"Community House"* magazine ad contain only minor text variations, the headline and text for the fourth version (D) is completely different.

Version B (Vic 2b) [text difference]
◉ *Collier's,* May 9, 1931, CIII
○ *The Saturday Evening Post,* May 9, 1931, p. 88

Version C (Vic 2c) [text difference]
○ *McCall's,* June 1931, p. 62
◉ *Pictorial Review,* June 1931

The first three versions of this 1931 Victoria ad contain insert illustrations showing the Ford Triplex shatter-proof windshield. One of these inserts shows a horseshoe imbedded in the windshield – with the message that the woman and three children in the car were not hurt.

No Flying Glass Here

The last ad version of this Model A Victoria ad (D), appeared only in the more upscale magazines. This edition contains a larger illustration and has the ad text placed below the illustration. With this modified format, this ad version does not include the two insert illustrations about the Ford Triplex shatter-proof windshield.

◀ **Version D (Vic 2d)**
◉ *Country Life,* May 1931, p. 9
◉ *Harper's Bazaar,* May 1931, p. 137
◉ *Vanity Fair,* May 1931, p. 88
◉ *Vogue,* May 15, 1931, p. 127+

BEAUTY THAT APPEALS TO WOMEN'S EYES

MEN speak knowingly of ball and roller bearings, of valves and pistons, of the many points of mechanical excellence that make the Ford such a good car to own and drive.

But to a woman's appraising eye, trained to line and color, there are no features of greater importance than its distinctive beauty of appearance and the richness of its appointments.

The Ford Victoria, illustrated above, is a striking example of this high quality. The comfortable, roomy seats are deeply cushioned and upholstered in luxurious mohair or fashionable Bedford cord, according to your preference. Hardware reflects the quiet good taste and character that you

expect in a Ford car. In addition to full rich maroon, you may choose from a changing variety of body colors.

Most exposed bright metal parts are made of Rustless Steel that will maintain its gleaming luster throughout the life of the car.

Every detail of the Ford reflects care and craftsmanship in manufacture. The ensemble is in keeping with the latest mode.

MOM DRIVING FAMILY

◆

A splendid choice for those who wish

Something different in a closed car

HERE is something quite different in a Ford car—a beautiful body-type specially designed and built *for four people.*

There's a growing need for a car of this kind. In many, many families a two-passenger car is too small—a five-passenger sedan is too large. The Ford Victoria solves the problem by combining the compactness of a coupe with just the right amount of room for four people. It's easy to drive—economical to run—and so distinctive in line that it brings an admiring nod of approval on every highway.

In interior finish, the Ford Victoria reflects the rich quality of a custom-built car. The comfortable seats are deeply cushioned. You may choose fine broadcloth or deep-piled, luxurious mohair upholstery.

Quiet good taste characterizes the de luxe appointments. You have a feeling that everything has been carefully, expertly planned to be just right.

See this beautiful four-passenger Victoria at the nearest Ford dealer's and arrange for a demonstration. Here is a high degree of beauty, comfort, convenience and performance at low cost.

FORD MOTOR COMPANY

PRINTED IN U. S. A.   THE INLAND PRESS DETROIT

A mother is shown driving a new Ford Model A Victoria with her husband and kids in the car. This unique drawing shows the Victoria with no other illustrations or background details

Version A (Vic 3a)
● *The State Trooper,* December 1931, CIV

With a December 1931 date, this was the latest Model A passenger car magazine ad produced.

FORDOR SEDAN

	TOTAL	1928	1929
Ford Body Style		60-A	60-A 60-B 60-C 170-A
Weight (pounds)		2,467	2,286
Price (FOB Detroit)		$570	$625
Units Produced (U.S.)	228,446	82,349	146,097
Number of U.S. Ads			
Primary Formats	13	3	10
Ad Variations	33	8	25
Magazine Insertions	69	18	51

Following the initial five Model A body styles introduced in December 1927, the Fordor Sedan (60-A) became available in May 1928. This vehicle was a four-door, two-window sedan with a brown artificial leather-covered roof, manufactured by Briggs. Later, in 1929, the Briggs-manufactured black artificial leather top (60-B) and black steel top (60-C) Fordor Sedan models were added. In July 1929, Briggs also produced a new two-window Model A Fordor Sedan (170-A), using more steel in the structural body parts.

Ford promoted the Model A Fordor Sedan in 1928 and 1929 using 33 different magazine ad variations. All of the 1928 magazines ads featured Fordor Sedans with Seal Brown artificial leather top treatments (60-A). In 1929, most of the ads showed cars with black artificial leather covered roofs (60-B). However, the last two ads produced in 1929 featured Fordor Sedans with black painted steel roofs (60-C).

WHITE TRELLIS

◆

The Farmer's Wife, October, 1928

Strikingly beautiful are the lines and colors of the new Fordor Sedan

COLORFUL as the newest autumn shades, stylish as the latest mode, strikingly beautiful in line and contour is the new Fordor Sedan.

Seeing it drawn up before your home, its exquisite two-tone color harmonies set off by bright touches of gleaming metal, you half expect a liveried chauffeur to step out and bow you to your seat. For it is a car like that —with a bit of an air about it.

The rich beauty of its finish and appointments will charm you no less than its beauty of line and color. All hardware is full-nickeled, in distinctive scroll design. Lounge seats are wide and deeply cushioned. Upholstery is soft and luxurious,

The new Fordor Sedan has been built to seat five people in real comfort. Note the generous room between front and rear seats.

yet long wearing, with a brown hairline stripe in pleasing harmony with the light brown trimming.

Arm rests, oval bow light, flexible robe rail and embossed cloth paneling around the doors and front seat are other welcome and distinctive touches which help to give the new Fordor Sedan the appearance of a custom built car.

Above all, you will like the new Fordor Sedan because it is so roomy and so comfortable.

The new transverse springs and Houdaille hydraulic shock absorbers soften the force of road shocks and bumps and eliminate the side sway and the bouncing

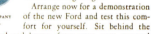

FORD MOTOR COMPANY
Detroit, Mich.

rebound which are the cause of most motoring fatigue.

Arrange now for a demonstration of the new Ford and test this comfort for yourself. Sit behind the wheel and know, from your own personal experience, the thrill of driving this great new car.

Then you will realize that here, at a low price, is everything you want or need in a modern automobile . . . beautiful low lines . . . choice of colors . . . 40-horse-power engine . . . speed of 55 to 65 miles an hour . . . quick acceleration . . . restful riding comfort . . . mechanical, internal expanding four-wheel brakes and separate emergency or parking brakes (all fully enclosed) . . . 20 to 30 miles per gallon of gasoline, depending on your speed . . . Triplex shatter-proof glass windshield . . . reliability . . . economy of operation and low cost of up-keep.

Two women, one with her dog in her arms, admire the leatherback Ford Fordor Sedan parked in front of the white trellis. The new Model A has also drawn the attention of two maids, who have interrupted their duties to stare at the car.

Version A (FdS 1a)
○ *The Farmer's Wife,* October 1928, p. 32
○ *Ladies' Home Journal,* October 1928, p. 99
○ *McCall's,* October 1928

WHITE TRELLIS

While the Ford Fordor Sedan was available in May 1928, this first magazine ad for this Model A body style did not appear until October 1928.

A second version (B) of the *"White Trellis"* Fordor Sedan magazine ad has fairly major text changes.

Version B (FdS 1b) [text difference]
○ *Good Housekeeping,* October 1928
◉ *Harper's Bazaar,* October 1928, p. 49
◉ *Vanity Fair,* October 1928, p. 17
◉ *Vogue,* October 27, 1928, CIV

VENTED.
This is the only Model A Ford magazine ad to show a cowl vent door positioned behind the hood of the car. Only the early 1928 Fordor Sedans were fitted with this cowl vent.

SEATS PARTY OF FIVE.
Both versions of this Fordor Sedan ad include an insert illustration dramatizing the roominess of the new Model A. This drawing shows the interior of the Fordor Sedan through the open front and rear doors.

The caption beneath the interior illustration indicates:

"The new Ford Sedan has been built to seat five people in real comfort. Note the generous room between the front and rear seats."

The ad text continues with additional commentary about the Fordor Sedan's interior appointments:

"Arm rests, oval bow light, flexible robe rail and embossed cloth paneling around the doors and front seats are other welcome and distinctive touches which help to give the new Fordor Sedan the appearance of a custom-built car."

DOWNTOWN STREETCAR

◆

THE NEW FORDOR SEDAN

You'll have a feeling of security and confidence when you drive the new Ford

THROUGH thickest traffic, down steepest hills, you have a feeling of security and confidence in driving the new Ford because of the quick, effective action of its six-brake system.

A feature that appeals particularly to women is the smooth, positive operation of these brakes. The four-wheel brakes take hold with a firm, commanding grip at a slight pressure

All of the new Ford cars come to you equipped with a Triplex shatter-proof glass windshield. This also is an important safety feature.

of the foot on the brake pedal. An effortless pull on the brake lever is sufficient to apply the emergency or parking brakes.

The six-brake system on the new Ford gives you the highest degree of safety and reliability because the four-wheel brakes and the separate emergency or parking brakes are all of the mechanical, internal expanding type, with braking surfaces fully enclosed for protection against mud, water, sand and grease.

The very definite advantages of this type of braking system have long been recognized. They are brought to you in the new Ford through a series of mechanical improvements embodying much that is new in design and construction.

The comforting assurance that your brakes are equal to every need and emergency means a great deal to your peace of mind and adds immeasurably to the pleasure of motoring.

FORD MOTOR COMPANY
Detroit, Michigan

Ease of steering and of shifting gears, the smooth-working clutch, and quick acceleration are other important control features that make the new Ford such a good car for a woman to drive.

It is also comforting to know that no matter where you live or where you go, in this country or abroad, every Ford dealer is your dealer —open until nine and ten o'clock at night to provide prompt, intelligent, forward-looking service that will lengthen the life of your car and give you many more miles of pleasant, enjoyable driving.

The whole idea back of the new Ford is to make the benefits of modern, economical transportation available to all the people and to help you get the greatest possible use from your car over the longest period of time at a minimum of trouble and expense. As long as you drive a Ford, you are entitled to 100 per cent service from every Ford dealer.

Two ladies negotiate downtown traffic near a streetcar in their new Ford Fordor Sedan. In the rear seat, two children are separated by their nanny. Behind the streetcar, a double-decker bus appears in the background.

Version A (FdS 2a)
- ○ *The Farmer's Wife,* November 1928, CIII
- ○ *Good Housekeeping,* November 1928
- ○ *Ladies' Home Journal,* November 1928, p. 105
- ○ *McCall's,* November 1928, p. 8

DOWNTOWN STREETCAR

In keeping with the *"security"* and *"confidence"* headline used in this Fordor Sedan magazine ad, the text indicates:

"Through thickest traffic, down steepest hills, you have a feeling of security in driving the new Ford because of the quick, effective actions of its six-brake system."

A second version (B) of this ad has only very minor text modifications.

Version B (FdS 2b) [text difference]
◉ *Vogue*, November 24, 1928, p. 121

The caption below this view through the windshield illustration indicates that:

"All of the new Ford cars come to you equipped with a Triplex shatter-proof windshield. This also is an important safety feature."

INSIDE OUT.
These Fordor Sedan ads include an interesting drawing showing the view through the windshield of the Model A Ford. (Note that the green body color of the Fordor Sedan in the primary illustration is carried through in the drawing of the car's interior.)

The text in this ad reviews the Ford six-brake system, the ease of steering and shifting gears and other Ford features – and concludes with a Ford Motor Company positioning statement:

"The whole idea back of the new Ford is to make the benefits of a modern, economical transportation vehicle available to all the people and to help you get the greatest possible use from your car over the longest period of time at a minimum of trouble and expense."

HIGH UP!
A closer look at the top of the double-decker bus reveals two men and a child in the open-air seating area. All are dressed in coats and hats as protection from the cold November air. Both men appear to be tending to the child – who is surely a little chilled by the breeze as they travel high up downtown.

183

DOWNTOWN CONSTRUCTION

◆

THE SPORTSMAN

Remarkable simplicity
of design is revealed in the new Ford

"MAKE it better—make it simpler" has always been the keynote of Ford engineering and manufacturing methods. This policy has been carried forward to its highest, fullest expression in the new Ford.

Take, for instance, the six-brake system, which works so smoothly and silently. This system is unusually reliable and effective because both the four-wheel brakes and the separate emergency or parking brakes are of the mechanical, internal expanding type, with all six brakes fully enclosed for protection against water, sand, dirt and grease.

For many years this has been recognized as the ideal combination. It is now brought to you on the new Ford because a simple, easy way has been found to accommodate two sets of full internal brakes in a two-in-one brake drum on the rear wheels.

Another exclusive Ford development is shown in the construction of the housing of the steering gear mechanism. This is made of three steel forgings, electrically welded together. The housing is then electrically welded to the steering column, making a one-piece steel unit.

Many other parts of the new Ford are also electrically welded, thus giving greater strength than if several parts were used and riveted or bolted together.

The ignition system of the new Ford also reflects much that is new in mechanical design. A unique feature is the elimination of high-tension cables from the distributor to the spark-plugs, these connections being made by means of thin bronze springs. There is but one high tension cable and this connects the coil with the distributor.

The distributor head is water-proof and has been specially designed to prevent short circuits from rain, snow, etc. The breaker-plate is a steel forging, cadmium-plated to prevent rusting. When the spark is advanced or retarded, only the plate moves.

The Ford engine is unusually simple in design and represents a new development in automobile engineering because it develops 40-brake-horse-power at only 2200 r. p. m. (revolutions per minute). This means you can do 55 to 65 miles an hour in the new Ford, yet you do not have a high-speed engine. This low revolution speed contributes to greater efficiency and longer life because it follows that the lower the speed of your engine, the less the wear on its parts.

The whole idea back of the new Ford is to bring the benefits of modern, economical transportation to all the people and to help every motorist get the greatest possible use from his car over the longest period of time at a minimum of trouble and expense.

Ford

FORD MOTOR COMPANY
Detroit, Michigan

The new Ford Sport Coupe. Low, fleet, smart. An especially good all-weather car for a woman to drive because it is so reliable and easy to handle. Rumble seat is standard equipment. Your choice of a variety of beautiful two-tone color harmonies.

As two couples drive through downtown traffic in their new leatherback Ford Fordor Sedan a passing businessman, briefcase in hand, admires the new Ford. A high-rise building is under construction in the background.

Version A (FdS 3a)

◉ *Country Life,* December 1928, p. 23
◉ *The Sportsman,* December 1928, p. 76

Version B (FdS 3b) [text difference]

◉ *Liberty,* December 8, 1928, p. 7

DOWNTOWN CONSTRUCTION

A third version (C) of this 1928 Fordor Sedan ad uses a larger car image and changes from a Sport Coupe insert illustration to one of the interior of the Model A.

Version C (FdS 3c) ➤
○ *Cosmopolitan,* November 1928, p. 117
◉ *The Redbook Magazine,* November 1928, p. 90

The two-page ad edition (D) returns to a wider view of the *"Downtown Construction"* scene and has a new headline and two different insert illustrations – one for a Sport Coupe and one a Tudor Sedan.

Version D (FdS 3d) ∨
◉ *The Saturday Evening Post,* October 27, 1928, pp. 90-91

The safety of the fully-enclosed six-brake-system is an outstanding feature of the new Ford

One of the first things you will notice when you drive the new Ford is the quick, effective action of its six-brake system.

This system gives you the highest degree of safety and reliability because the four-wheel brakes and the separate emergency or parking brakes are all of the mechanical, internal expanding type, with braking surfaces fully enclosed for protection against mud, water, sand and grease.

The many advantages of this type of braking system have long been recognized. They are brought to you in the new Ford through a series of mechanical improvements embodying much that is new in design and construction.

There is perhaps no single feature of the new Ford which represents such a decided step forward in automobile engineering as the unique yet simple way by which a special drum has been constructed to permit the use of two separate sets of internal brakes on the rear wheels.

The brake construction on the front wheels also is unusual. Here the brakes are fully enclosed without the necessity of a leather boot or sliding joint to protect the linkage between the brake rods and the mechanism on the brake plate. Such simplicity of design helps to insure reliability and long life.

A further improvement in braking performance is effected by the self-centering action of the four-wheel brakes—an exclusive Ford

feature. This construction brings the entire surface of the shoe in contact with the drum the instant you press your foot on the brake pedal.

There are definite reasons, therefore, for the safety and reliability of the new Ford brakes—for their quick ease of operation—for the smooth yet commanding way they take hold at a slight pressure on the brake pedal or hand lever.

Another feature of the brakes on the new Ford is the ease of adjustment. You can do it yourself quickly and without trouble.

The four-wheel brakes are adjusted by turning a regulating screw located on the outside of each brake plate. This screw is so notched that you can set all four brakes alike simply by listening to the "clicks."

The emergency or parking brakes require little attention. However, should they need adjustment, consult your Instruction Book for a clear explanation. If you do not care to do the work yourself, see a Ford dealer who will give you prompt, courteous and economical service.

FORD MOTOR COMPANY
Detroit, Michigan

The luxurious finish of the new Fordor Sedan is comparable to that of a custom built car. Note the lounge seat and convenient arm rests. Enclosed paneling around the doors is another pleasing feature.

---

90   91

The New Ford has a very Simple and Effective Lubrication System

If you could look into the engine of the new Ford, you would be surprised at the simplicity of the lubrication system. It is a combination of pump, splash and gravity feed—an exclusive Ford development and unusually effective.

The action is like this—

The oil pump draws the oil from the bottom of the oil pan through a fine mesh wire screen or filter and delivers it quickly to the valve chamber. Even

when you are traveling at only thirty miles an hour, the five quarts of oil in the pan pass through the pump *twice* in every mile.

From the valve chamber the oil flows by gravity to the main bearings of the crankshaft and front camshaft bearing. Reservoirs of oil are provided for each main bearing pipe opening through a series of ingenious dams at the bottom of the valve chamber.

After filling these reservoirs, the surplus oil flows down an overflow pipe to the front of the oil pan tray. In this tray are four troughs into which dip the scoops on the connecting rods. These scoops pick up the oil and throw it into the grooves of the swiftly moving crankpin bearings. They also send an oil spray over the cylinder walls, camshaft and timing gears. From the tray the oil flows back to the oil pan, from where it is again drawn through the oil strainer into the pump.

The only movable part in the entire Ford engine lubrication system is the oil pump. From valve chamber down, the entire flow of oil is an easy, natural flow—as simple in principle as water running down-hill. There is no need for pressure.

Because the new Ford is such a good car and is built to such close and exact measurements, it should be given the care that is given every fine piece of machinery.

When you consider that each piston

The new Fordor Sedan is a strikingly beautiful car because of its long, low, streamline body, attractive colors, and the many distinctive features of finish and appointment usually found only in custom built bodies. Designed to seat five people in real comfort.

moves up and down 1300 times a minute when your car is moving at only thirty miles an hour, you can see the need of complete and proper lubrication. And the piston is only one of many moving parts in the engine!

The oiling system of the new Ford is so simple in design and effective in action that it requires practically no service attention. Like every other Ford part, it has been built to give you many thousands of miles of use at a minimum of trouble and expense.

There is only one thing to do, but that is a very important thing — *watch the oil.* Keep enough oil in the oil pan so that the indicator rod always registers full (F) and change the oil every 500 miles.

If the oil level is allowed to fall below full, the supply becomes insufficient to oil all parts as they should be oiled. The oil also loses its lubricating properties more rapidly because it is used faster.

The lubrication of the chassis is also

FEATURES OF
THE NEW FORD CAR

Beautiful low lines
Choice of colors
55 to 65 miles an hour   40-horse-power engine
Remarkable acceleration
Fully-enclosed six-brake system
New transverse springs
Houdaille hydraulic shock absorbers
20 to 30 miles per gallon of gasoline
Triplex shatter-proof glass windshield
Reliability and low up-keep cost

important. It has been made simple and easy in the new Ford by the high pressure grease gun system. In order to insure best performance, the chassis should be lubricated every 500 miles.

Every 1000 miles the distributor cam should be cleaned and given a light film of vaseline. At 2000 miles, the lubricant in the differential and transmission should be drained, housings flushed with kerosene and new lubricant added.

The oiling and greasing of an automobile is so important and means so much to economical, satisfactory performance that it ought not to be neglected or carelessly done.

Ford dealers everywhere have been specially trained to oil and grease the new Ford. They know the best oil to use for each part during each season of the year and they have special equipment to do the job right.

No matter where you live or where you go, you will find Ford dealers prompt and reliable in their work, fair in their charges, and sincerely eager to help you get continuously good service from your car.

The new Ford is an especially good car for a woman to drive because of its comfort, safety, reliability and ease of control. Shown on the left is the new Ford Sport Coupe. Rumble seat is furnished as standard equipment with this car.

The car illustrated is the new Ford Tudor Sedan in the attractive Andalusite Sand color. Upholstery is rich in appearance and long wearing. All appointments are fully matched. Like all the new Ford cars, the Tudor Sedan is equipped with a Triplex shatter-proof glass windshield and four Houdaille shock absorbers.

FORD MOTOR COMPANY
Detroit, Michigan

COUPLES ARRIVING

◆

To help you get many thousands of miles of carefree, economical motoring

THE new Ford is a remarkably fine car for one that costs so little. It is simple in design, constructed of the finest materials and manufactured with unusual accuracy. These are the reasons it performs so wonderfully. These are

also the reasons its service requirements are so few and the up-keep costs so low.

When you receive your new Ford, the dealer will explain the simple little things that should be attended to at regular intervals to insure the best performance. He will also tell you about the Free Inspection Service to which every purchaser of the new Ford is entitled at 500, 1000 and 1500 miles.

This inspection service includes a check-up of the battery, generator charging rate, distributor, carburetor adjustment, lights, brakes, shock absorbers, tire inflation and steering gear. The engine oil is also changed and the chassis lubricated through the high-pressure grease gun system. A check-up of wheel alignment and spring shackles is included in the final inspection.

No charge whatever is made for labor or materials incidental to this service except where repairs are necessary because of misuse,

FORD MOTOR COMPANY
Detroit, Michigan

accident or neglect. The labor of changing the engine oil and lubricating the chassis is also free, although a charge is made for new oil.

The inspection described on the left is free for the first 1500 miles only, yet the completeness and watchfulness of Ford Service does not stop there.

Every time you take your car to the Ford dealer for oiling and greasing it will be a good plan to have him check over important points that have a bearing on continuously good performance and tell you exactly what the car needs. You will find him prompt in his work, fair in his charges, and sincerely eager to do a good and thorough job at all times.

His constant effort is to relieve you of every detail in the care of your car and to help you get thousands upon thousands of miles of low-cost motoring without a care—without even lifting the hood. That is the true purpose and the true meaning of Ford Service.

FEATURES OF
THE NEW FORD CAR

Beautiful low lines
Choice of colors
Remarkable acceleration
Smoothness at all speeds
55 to 65 miles an hour
40 horse-power
Fully enclosed, silent six-brake system
New transverse springs
Houdaille hydraulic shock absorbers
Triplex shatter-proof glass windshield
Economy of operation
Reliability and long life

Two couples have arrived in their new Ford Fordor Sedan. One of the women appears to be adjusting the large bow on her dress as they are greeted and prepare to enter the building. This ad includes a list of the *"Features of The New Ford Car."*

Version A (FdS 4a)
◉ *The American Boy,* February 1929, p. 31

This unique Fordor Sedan magazine ad appeared only once in the U.S., in February 1929.

COUPLES ARRIVING

This 1929 Ford Fordor Sedan ad is one of the many unique, black and white ads appearing in *The American Boy.*

A second version of this Fordor Sedan ad provides an example of how a Williamson Model A illustration was slightly modified when used outside of the United States.

When this illustration appeared in an oversized, brown-tone Italian magazine ad, a man standing at the doorway of the building is an added feature. This man's appearance – bow tie, long apron and menus under his arm – confirms the couples' visit is to a club or restaurant.

Example ad from Italy ➤
◉ *Il Secolo Illustrato,* 1928, p. 6

Ecco una vettura di lusso
al prezzo di una vettura economica

La nuova Ford è bella ed elegante, la sua linea è bassa e slanciata. La finitura è perfetta nei più minuti dettagli. Le carrozzerie sono comode ed equipaggiate con sobria ricchezza.

La costruzione meccanica è l'ultima parola in fatto di modernità, impiegando materiali di primissima classe, quali vengono usati solamente nelle vetture di più alto prezzo.

Tutto ciò dice chiaramente che la nuova Ford è in realtà una vettura di lusso, in tutto fuorché nel prezzo.

Infatti il basso prezzo d'acquisto e l'economia di esercizio fanno della nuova Ford la vettura economica e utilitaria per eccellenza. Inoltre la facilità e la sicurezza di funzionamento esimono i possessori della nuova Ford dall'impiego di un meccanico.

In questo appunto è la ragione per cui la nuova Ford, segna veramente l'inizio di un'era nuova nella storia dell'automobilismo.

Provatela e vi persuaderete che la nuova Ford è una vettura veramente ideale sia per il turismo e la montagna che per l'uso in città.

Sue particolari caratteristiche sono le seguenti:

Velocità fino ai 100 Km. orari - Frenatura dolce e potente sulle quattro ruote - Molleggio perfetto integrato da quattro ammortizzatori idraulici - Consumo inferiore ai 10 litri di benzina sui 100 Km. - Ripresa fulminea (da 10 a 60 Km. in 154 m.) - Eccezionale potenza in salita.

Il suo equipaggiamento in serie comprende:

5 ruote gommate pneus balloon - Ammortizzatori Houdaille - Paravento in cristallo infrangibile Triplex - Livello di benzina - Tergicristallo - Lampadina al

cruscotto - Specchio retrovisivo - Fanalino posteriore e stop - Dispositivo di bloccaggio all'accensione - Conta chilometro e tachimetro - Amperometro - Borsa completa di utensili.

PREZZI

(variabili senza preavviso) per vetture, senza paraurti, franco Trieste, adoganate, con 5 ruote gommate Pneus Balloon.

Spider	L. 18.000
Torpedo	» 18.600
Coupé	» 22.400
Guida interna a 2 porte	» 22.400
Coupé sport	» 25.800
Guida interna a 4 porte	» 25.800

FORD MOTOR
COMPANY D'ITALIA S. A.
TRIESTE

LIGHTING UP!
A closer look at the two men in this Model A ad reveals that one is lighting a cigarette for the other as they stand behind their Fordor Sedan. Since Henry Ford was known as an opponent of tobacco use, this ad element must have escaped notice during the ad approval process.

It is ironic that, in the U.S., this ad appeared only in *The American Boy,* a publication aimed at young boys.

CANOPY ENTRANCE

To help you get many thousands of miles of carefree, economical motoring

THE new Ford is a remarkably fine car for one that costs so little. It is simple in design, constructed of the finest materials and manufactured with unusual accuracy. These are the reasons it performs so wonderfully. These are also the reasons its service requirements are so few and the up-keep cost so low.

When you receive your new Ford, the dealer will explain the simple little things that should be attended to at

regular intervals to insure the best performance. He will also tell you about the Free Inspection Service to which every purchaser of the new Ford is entitled at 500, 1000 and 1500 miles.

This inspection service includes a check-up of the battery, generator charging rate, distributor, carburetor adjustment, lights, brakes, shock absorbers, tire inflation and steering gear. The engine oil is also changed and the chassis lubricated.

No charge whatever is made for labor or materials incidental to this service except where repairs are necessary because of accident, neglect, or misuse. The labor of changing the engine oil and lubricating the chassis is also free, although a charge is made for new oil.

The above inspection is free for the first 1500 miles only, yet the completeness and watchfulness of Ford Service does not stop there.

Every time you take your car to the Ford dealer for oiling and greasing it will be a good plan to have him check

Ford Motor Company
Detroit, Michigan

over important points that have a bearing on continuously good performance and tell you exactly what the car needs. You will find him prompt in his work, fair in his charges, and sincerely eager to do a good job at all times.

His constant effort is to relieve you of every detail in the care of your car and to help you get thousands upon thousands of miles of low-cost motoring without a care.

FEATURES OF
THE NEW FORD CAR

Beautiful low lines
Choice of colors
55 to 65 miles an hour
Remarkable acceleration
Smoothness at all speeds
Fully enclosed, silent six-brake system
New transverse springs
Houdaille hydraulic shock absorbers
Triplex shatter-proof glass windshield
Economy of operation
Reliability and long life

There's an air of sturdy strength in the low, trim, graceful lines of the new Ford Coupe. A splendid all-weather car because it is so snug and comfortable, so safe and easy to handle under all conditions.

It's a snowy night as two couples arrive for the party in their new Ford Fordor Sedan. At the canopy-covered entrance, the valet attendant, in his service cap and long coat, hurries to take care of their car.

Version A (TdS 5a)

◉ *Country Life,* February 1929, CII
◉ *The Sportsman,* February 1929, p. 78

Four different versions of this 1929 Fordor Sedan ad were produced.

CANOPY ENTRANCE

The second version (B) of this 1929 Fordor Sedan magazine ad has only a minor text change. The third and fourth versions (C and D) retain the modified ad text but drop the *"Features of the Ford Car"* insert.

While other ad elements vary, all four *"Canopy Entrance"* ad versions employ the *"To help you get many thousands of miles of carefree, economical motoring"* headline.

Version B (FdS 5b) [text difference]
⊙ *Collier's,* February 16, 1929, CIII

Version C (FdS 5c) ➤
⊙ *Liberty,* February 9, 1929, p. 16

To help you get many thousands of miles of carefree, economical motoring

To help you get many thousands of miles of carefree, economical motoring

The only difference in the final version (D) of this Fordor Sedan ad is in the color of the car in the illustration. All of the earlier *"Canopy Entrance"* ad versions (A, B and C) feature a brown car (Ford color: Rose Beige) with a black artificial leather-covered roof (60-B). However, the last ad version (D) presents a green car (Ford color: Vagabond Green) with a Seal Brown artificial leather-covered roof (60-A).

◀ **Version D** (FdS 5d)
○ *Cosmopolitan,* February 1929, p. 115
⊙ *The Redbook Magazine,* February 1929

This is the only Model A Ford magazine ad variation based solely on a change in the color of the car's body and roof.

BABY CARRIAGE PARK

◆

March, 1929   LADIES' HOME JOURNAL

You will find the new Ford a comfortable easy-riding car

IN DAYS gone by, it was Mother who seemed destined to get most of the bouncing on those Sunday afternoon rides. Bumps that seemed like innocent little bumps to Dad in the front seat were quite large and aggravating by the time they reached the riders in the rear.

Perhaps Mother mentioned it in clear, brisk tones. Perhaps, being long-suffering, she didn't. There seemed no way it could be helped in a low-priced car.

Then along came the new Ford and with it a new idea of riding ease. Now there is no dividing line for comfort. Everybody can lean back and relax because even rough stretches may be taken at a reasonably fast pace without the exaggerated bouncing rebound which is the cause of most motoring fatigue.

This comfort means so much to the joy of motoring that it should be one of the first things you think about in selecting a motor car. "Is it a comfortable car to drive?" is almost as important as "Is it an economical car to operate?"

The new Ford brings you truly remarkable riding ease not only because of its low unsprung weight and transverse springs but because it has four Houdaille shock absorbers. Formerly these were installed as standard equipment on only the most expensive automobiles. Their use on the new Ford is an example of the quality that is built into every part of the car.

FORD MOTOR COMPANY
Detroit, Michigan

Shown on the left is the interior of the new Fordor Sedan. Upholstery is soft and luxurious, yet long wearing. All appointments are fully nickeled. Note the wide door, the convenient arm rests, the air of restful riding comfort.

The illustration on the right shows the roominess of the front compartment of the new Fordor Sedan. Here, as in rear view, you can see the restful tilt of the wide, deeply cushioned seat, the richness of every detail of finish and appointment.

A new Ford Fordor Sedan speeds along the road at the edge of the city park. All of the attention of the five lady passengers is focused on the nearby mother and child tending to an infant in the baby carriage.

Version A (FdS 6a)
○ *The Farmer's Wife,* March 1929, p. 33
○ *Good Housekeeping,* March 1929, p. 112
○ *Ladies' Home Journal,* March 1929, p. 81
○ *McCall's,* March 1929

BABY CARRIAGE PARK

The Fordor Sedan in the *"Baby Carriage Park"* ad drawing does not have a windshield wiper blade – as was the case with many Model A Ford advertising drawings. However, the wiper blade is visible in the insert illustration showing a view of the front interior of the car.

A second version (B) of this 1929 Fordor Sedan magazine ad retains the *"You will find the new Ford a comfortable easy-riding car"* headline but contains a slight modification in the ad's text.

Version B (FdS 6b) [text difference]

◉ *Harper's Bazaar,* March 1929, p. 44
◉ *Vogue,* March 16, 1929, p . 16

This Fordor Sedan ad stresses the accomplishments of the new Ford in producing a comfortable and easy-riding car – and proclaims the bane of the *"long-suffering"* Mom riding in the family car:

"In days gone by, it was Mother who seemed destined to get most of the bouncing on those Sunday afternoon rides. Bumps that seemed like innocent little bumps to Dad in the front seat were quite large and aggravating by the time they reached the riders in the rear."

"Perhaps Mother mentioned it in clear, brisk tones. Perhaps, being long-suffering, she didn't. Then along came the new Ford and with it a new idea of riding ease."

Rear interior –
which provides *"restful riding comfort."*

Front interior –
with the *"restful tilt of the wide, deeply cushioned seat."*

MONDAY FARM

◆

Reliability and economy of new Ford are as important as its beauty, speed, safety and comfort

You are buying proved performance when you buy the new Ford. You know exactly what it will do. There is nothing of an experiment about it.

Letters from users show a delivered value far beyond expectations. Almost without exception they stress reliability. You sense a feeling of sincere pride in the oft-repeated phrase—"Let me tell you what my new Ford did."

A well-known tire company, solely to test tires, drove a new Ford more than 90,000 miles in six months. Throughout that time, the car was run day and night, an average of twenty-two hours out of every twenty-four. The entire cost of repair parts was only $38 for the entire 90,000 miles. Another tire company, making a similar test, drove the new Ford more than 80,000 miles in a short period, at a cost per mile that was fully 63% less than any figure it had previously known.

One of the first of the new Fords was driven from Dearborn, Michigan, to Los Angeles to San Francisco to New York and back to

Dearborn—a distance of 8328 miles —in twenty-one days. Through ice and sleet, up mountain peaks, through desert sands, over macadam and deeply rutted dirt roads, it traveled at an average speed of 40.9 miles an hour. Practically a year of average driving was done in three weeks, yet the entire trip was made without the need of a single major adjustment or repair.

Another new Ford, as a test of hill-climbing, was driven from San Bernardino, California, over the National Old Trails and Swartout Valley Highway, to the Big Pines Recreation Camp. The entire 36.2 miles were made in high gear—a particularly severe test because of the sharp turns and a stretch of 5.7 miles where the grade rises precipitously from 3000 to 6075 feet.

Other incidents are even more dramatic. A letter from the East tells how the Triplex shatter-proof glass windshield of the new Ford prevented injuries from flying glass when the car was forced off the road into a telegraph pole. A news-reel photographer tells how the

Ford

FORD MOTOR COMPANY
Detroit, Michigan

brakes on the new Ford saved his life when, speeding through a blizzard to film a shipwreck, he found himself suddenly on the very edge of a 50-foot cliff. From a far western state a husband and father writes gratefully to tell how the sturdiness of the new Ford "saved the lives of my family" when the car was struck by a hit-and-run driver.

The reason for such complete and well-rounded performance is found in the fundamental Ford policy of doing business. The new Ford was not designed primarily for sales and profits. It goes beyond men and materials. It is the expression of an ideal—an ideal that looks toward bringing the benefits of modern, economical transportation to all the people.

Back of the new Ford are manufacturing methods as unusual as the car itself. Without these, it would be impossible to give you the value that is in the new Ford. Because of these methods, the new Ford can be made at a low price without sacrificing quality anywhere along the line.

The family has just arrived at the *"Fred F. Monday"* farm in their new Ford Fordor Sedan. As they get out of the car, Fred walks over and extends his hand to his friend while the farm hand stares at the new Ford.

Version A (FdS 7a)

○ *The Country Gentleman,* March 1929, p. 151
○ *Farm & Fireside,* March 1929, p. 47
○ *Successful Farming,* March 1929, CIII

MONDAY FARM

A second version (B) of this 1929 Fordor Sedan magazine ad utilizes a slightly modified *"Reliability of new Ford is as important as its beauty, speed, safety and comfort"* headline. It retains the same ad text, but adds an insert list that presents the many *"Features of the New Ford Car."*

> **Version B (FdS 7b)** ➤
> ⊙ *Southern Agriculturist*, March 1, 1929

The third *"Monday Farm"* ad version (C) is unchanged, except for having a slightly shorter text.

> **Version C (FdS 7c) [text difference]**
> ⊙ *Capper's Farmer*, March 1929, p. 19

In line with the farm setting used in the drawing, the *"Monday Farm"* ad appeared only in farm-related magazines.

Reliability of new Ford is as important as its beauty, speed, safety and comfort

Most Williamson Model A ad drawings usually position individuals either behind or immediately to the front or rear of the Model A vehicle being featured. In this drawing, however, the two women are shown almost spotlighted in the foreground of the illustration.

FORGET ABOUT IT!
The woman who has just departed the Fordor Sedan appears more interested in chatting with her friend. However, the farmer's wife, still in her apron, momentarily ignores her to look back and admire the Model A.

TRAIN RACING

◆

Good performance with economy

THE new Ford is more than a new automobile. It is the expression of an ideal—an ideal that looks to bringing the benefits of modern transportation to all the people.

Because of this purpose, the price is low and great care has been taken to insure economy of operation and upkeep. Few features are of greater importance to millions of motorists.

FEATURES OF THE NEW FORD CAR

Fully enclosed, silent six-brake system

Four Houdaille hydraulic double-acting shock absorbers

Triplex shatter-proof glass windshield

Vibration-absorbing engine support

Alemite chassis lubrication

Ten body types

Choice of a number of colors in each body type

Quick acceleration

55 to 65 miles an hour

Reliability and economy

Conservative figures show that the new Ford averages 20 miles per gallon of gasoline, with many Ford owners reporting greater mileage on long trips. Oil consumption is also low per hundred miles. There is a considerable saving on tires due to the balance of the car, ease of steering and perfected wheel design.

All tires used on new Ford cars and recommended for replacement are specially built by leading tire manufacturers according to specifications laid down by the Ford Motor Company. Mechanical upkeep is low because of simplicity of design and the enduring quality that has been built into every part.

Definite evidence of the economy of the new Ford is shown in repeated and growing purchases by Federal and city governments, by police departments, and by large industrial companies which keep careful day-by-day cost records.

The new Ford has been chosen only after exhaustive tests covering every feature of automobile value and performance—from the time of purchase to the final trade-in. Here the Ford policy of not making yearly changes serves to protect and maintain the investment of every Ford owner. All improvements in the new Ford are made so that present owners may take advantage of them quickly and at low cost.

The low cost of replacement parts and labor, the availability of Ford dealers throughout the world and close factory supervision of all service are additional reasons for the economy of the new Ford.

It has always been our belief that a sale does not complete the transaction between us and the buyer but establishes a new obligation on us to see that his car gives him service. We are as much interested in his economical operation of the car as he is in our economical manufacture of it.

For that reason we have installed a system of controlled service to take care of all Ford car needs in an improved manner.

FORD MOTOR COMPANY
Detroit, Michigan

This service begins with proper instruction when you buy the car and includes a free inspection and checking-up of important parts at 500, at 1000 and at 1500 miles.

No matter where you live or where you go, you will never be very far from an authorized Ford dealer who has been specially trained and thoroughly equipped to help you get many thousands of miles of pleasant, enjoyable motoring at a minimum of trouble and expense.

"Good performance with economy" is the reason for the unusual value that is brought to you in the new Ford.

As they head down the country road, Father just can't resist giving the train a little run for its money. Junior seems quite fascinated by the undertaking while Mother, in the back seat with her face turned away, does not.

Version A (FdS 8a)
○ *The Country Gentleman,* March 1929, p. 124

Version B (FdS 8b) [text difference]
◉ *Capper's Farmer,* May 1929, p. 17

TRAIN RACING

The first four versions of the *"Train Racing"* magazine ad include an insert listing the various *"Features of the New Ford Car."*

As with the second ad version (B), the third and fourth versions (C and D) of this Fordor Sedan ad each have minor ad text differences.

Version C (FdS 8c) [text difference]
⊙ *Southern Agriculturist,* May 1, 1929, CIII (B&W)

Version D (FdS 8d) [text difference]
○ *Farm & Fireside,* May 1929, CIII
○ *Successful Farming,* May 1929, CIII

However, the fifth version (E) of the *"Train Racing"* ad employs a completely different headline and a text which lists and discusses eight different Ford features that will *"appeal to the woman motorist."*

Version E (FdS 8e) ▽
○ *The Farmer's Wife,* May 1929, p. 19

The Farmer's Wife, May, 1929

The new Ford has many features that appeal to the woman motorist

Triplex Shatter-Proof Glass Windshield—This glass is so made that it will not shatter or fly under the hardest impact. It is an important safety factor, and a point to remember in the purchase of an automobile.

Choice of Colors—All of the new Ford cars are finished in a variety of beautiful two-tone color harmonies. You have the privilege of selecting from among these the color you like best.

Ease of Control—The new Ford is a particularly good car for a woman to drive because of the ease of steering, shifting gears, parking, etc. This ease of control gives you more confidence in driving.

Safety—The Ford six-brake system is easy to operate and is unusually effective and reliable. The balance of the car, the sturdy frame, and the extensive use of steel in the bodies also contribute to the safety of the car.

Comfort—You ride in real comfort in the Ford because of its specially designed springs and the use of four Houdaille hydraulic double-acting shock absorbers—one on each wheel. This easy-riding comfort is especially welcome on rough roads.

Reliability—You are comfortable in mind too because of the mechanical reliability of the new Ford. No matter how long the trip —on good roads and bad—you know it will bring you safely, quickly to the journey's end.

Economy—The new Ford is a good car to own and drive because

of its low first cost and the low cost of operation and up-keep. It has been built to bring the benefits of modern, economical transportation within reach of all the people.

Service—It has always been our belief that the sale does not complete the transaction between us and the buyer, but establishes a new obligation on us to see that the car gives good service. For that reason we have installed a system of controlled service to take care of all the needs of the Ford car in an improved and economical manner. No matter where you live or where you go, you will never be very far from a Ford dealer who has been specially trained and equipped to give you prompt, courteous, intelligent attention.

Ford

Ford Motor Company
Detroit, Michigan

C'MON MOM!
While the headline of the fifth ad version (E) indicates *"The New Ford Has Many Features That Appeal to the Woman Motorist,"* this woman's apparent disinterest in its ability to outrun a train must not be one of them!

You can almost hear the son saying to his mother *"Look Mom … we're winning the race!"*

TRAIN RACING

The exciting scene of a car racing a train was a popular illustration theme used in U.S. automobile art and advertising during the 1920s and 1930s. Apparently, this was also the case in other parts of the world – as evidenced by the use of similar ads for the Model A Ford outside of the United States.

The Williamson drawing used in the U.S. Fordor Sedan *"Train Racing"* ad also appeared in a Swedish magazine ad in early 1929.

> **Example ad from Sweden** ➤
> ⊙ *Bonniers Veckotidning,* April 21, 1929, p. 5

Many Williamson drawings found their way into Model A advertising produced in other countries. However, this was not the case in France, where the French created their own Model A advertising illustrations.

While a "train race" magazine ad from France does not employ a Williamson illustration, it uses a very similar theme – with, of course, the Model A still winning the race!

> ◀ **Example ad from France**
> ⊙ *Le Vie Automobile,* May 25, 1930, p. 23

HORSE'S KNEE

134   THE SATURDAY EVENING POST   March 2, 1929

Simplicity of electrical and ignition systems a feature of the new Ford

FEATURES OF THE NEW FORD CAR

Beautiful low lines
Choice of colors
55 to 65 miles an hour
Remarkable acceleration   Smoothness at all speeds
Fully enclosed silent six-brake system
Houdaille hydraulic shock absorbers
Triplex shatter-proof glass windshield
Airmite chassis lubrication
Economy of operation
Reliability and long life

FORD MOTOR COMPANY
Detroit, Michigan

THE SATURDAY EVENING POST   135

In a two-page magazine ad for the 1929 Ford Fordor Sedan a group of men dressed in their bright red coats are assembling for a fox hunt. As a woman waits in the car and the riders rest, one of the riders checks the knee of his horse.

The *"Horse's Knee"* ad also includes two smaller insert illustrations and an insert listing the *"Features of The New Ford Car."*

The text of this Fordor Sedan ad concentrates on the electrical and ignition system of the new Ford and explains the roles of the ignition coil, distributor, generator, starter and the theft-proof ignition lock.

Version A (FdS 9a)
⊙ *The Saturday Evening Post,* March 2, 1929, pp. 134-135

This is a unique Model A ad. It was prepared only in a two–page edition and appeared in only one magazine, on only one date.

Of particular note is the fact that this Fordor Sedan ad also uses three unique Williamson drawings – the main Fordor Sedan illustration plus insert illustrations of a Ford Coupe at a hat shop and a Sport Coupe in a golf lesson setting. None of these three drawings were used as the primary illustration in any other U.S. Model A Ford magazine ad.

ARCHED WINDOWS

◆

The Farmer's Wife, April, 1929

Ease of control and mechanical reliability are especially important to the woman driver

ONE of the fine things about driving the new Ford is the way it takes you over the miles without fuss or fatigue.

Mentally you are at ease because you are sure of the mechanical performance of the car. No matter how long the trip or rough or devious the roadway, you know it will bring you safely, quickly to the journey's end.

Through thickest traffic, up steepest hills, along the open road, you will drive with security and confidence because the new Ford is so alert and capable and so easy to operate and control.

The steering wheel answers to the touch of a finger. Gears shift smoothly, silently. Brakes take hold quickly and firmly even on rain-swept highways. Unusual acceleration and abundant speed and power are especially appreciated in emergencies. A space little longer than the car itself is all you need for parking.

These features simplify the mechanics of driving and, together with reliability, add a great deal to the joy of motoring. The comforting assurance that everything is just right is especially important to the woman driver.

Physically, too, you will feel fresh and relaxed in the new Ford because it is such a roomy, comfortable car.

The restfully tilted seats are made generously wide and are deeply cushioned, with coil springs of both the straight and hour-glass type. The backs are carefully designed to conform to the curves of the body.

Perhaps the most outstanding feature of the new Ford is its riding

The new Ford is distinguished by the trim, graceful simplicity of its lines and the beauty of its colors. Without being extreme, it has struck a new note in automobile designing. Shown on the left is the Ford Coupe. Above is the Fordor Sedan.

comfort. The rough spots are there, just as they have always been, but you do not feel them. There are no hard bumps or jolts, nor any exaggerated bouncing up and down. Somehow, you seem to just glide along, as if every road were a good road.

The Houdaille hydraulic shock absorbers and transverse springs take up or absorb the force of every unevenness in the road before it reaches the body, frame and chassis of the car.

As someone has said, it is almost as if a giant hand had smoothed the way, so evenly and easily do you ride along in the new Ford.

FORD MOTOR COMPANY
Detroit, Michigan

This means relaxation and comfort in both front and rear seats and also contributes to better, more reliable and economical performance and longer life for every mechanical part.

Two women, holding hands, are leaving a building with large arched windows next to a palm tree-lined street. A woman passing by takes note of their beautiful new Ford Fordor Sedan parked along the curb.

Version A (FdS 10a)
○ *The Farmer's Wife,* April 1929, p. 57
○ *Good Housekeeping,* April 1929, p. 100
○ *Ladies' Home Journal,* April 1929, p. 93
○ *McCall's,* April 1929, p. 93

ARCHED WINDOWS

A second version (B) of the *"Arched Windows"* Fordor Sedan ad changes the text and uses a new headline – about the new Ford's *"fuel system."*

Version B (FdS 10b) ➤
- ⊙ *Collier's,* April 13, 1929, CIII
- ○ *Cosmopolitan,* April 1929, p. 6
- ⊙ *Liberty,* April 6, 1929, p. 9

The two-page ad edition (C) utilizes a third headline (about the Ford's *"electrical and ignition systems"*), keeps the insert illustrations of the Ford Coupe and adds a new insert illustration of a Ford Sport Coupe.

Version C (FdS 10c) ⋁
- ⊙ *The Literary Digest,* March 9, 1929, CF
- ⊙ *The Saturday Evening Post,* February 16, 1929, pp. 88-89

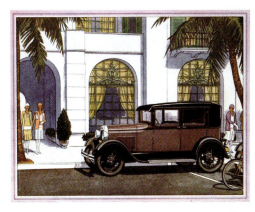

Fuel system of the new Ford has been designed for reliability and long service

DEPARTING INSTRUCTIONS

◆

June, 1929   LADIES' HOME JOURNAL

Spring brings beautiful colors for the new Ford car

MATCHING the fresh brilliance of Spring itself are the beautiful colors of the new Ford. They are rich in tone, yet carefully chosen, with a quiet good taste that endures.

There are eleven different Ford body types and all, with the single exception of the Station Wagon, are finished in a changing variety of colors.

You have the privilege of selecting from among these the color harmony that best suits your motoring needs and personal preference. Such choice is of course unusual in a low-price car and is one of the very special features of the new Ford.

Interior finish, upholstery and appointments are in keeping with this beauty of color and the trim, substantial lines which are so characteristically Ford. To the last least little detail, you can see evidence of the sincere quality that has been built into the car and the care that has been taken in its manufacture.

In all that goes to make a good automobile—in appearance—in safety—in comfort—in reliability—in economy—in alert, satisfying performance—the new Ford is an unusual value at a low price. Its ease-of-operation and control and its freedom from mechanical troubles make it a particularly good car for a woman to drive.

FORD MOTOR COMPANY
Detroit, Michigan

It's a bright summer day and a couple is preparing to leave home in their new Ford Fordor Sedan. As the husband impatiently reaches to check his pocket watch, his wife provides departing instructions to the (very patient looking) maid.

Version A (FdS 11a)
- ○ *Cosmopolitan,* June 1929, p. 115
- ○ *The Farmer's Wife,* June 1929, p. 23
- ○ *Good Housekeeping,* June 1929
- ○ *Ladies' Home Journal,* June 1929, p. 79
- ○ *McCall's,* June 1929
- ◉ *The Redbook Magazine,* June 1929, p. 102

DEPARTING INSTRUCTIONS

A new headline – *"The charm of beautiful colors, carefully chosen"* – but the same text appears in the second version (B) of this 1929 Fordor Sedan magazine ad. The third ad version (C) has just a minor text change.

> ### Version B (FdS 11b) ➤
> ⊙ *Collier's*, June 8, 1929, CIII

> ### Version C (FdS 11c)
> ⊙ *Liberty,* June 1, 1929, p. 17

The two-page edition (D) of the *"Departing Instructions"* ad provides a wider view in front of the house, utilizes a different headline and includes two insert illustrations.

> ### Version D (FdS 11d) ⌄
> ⊙ *The Literary Digest,* April 6, 1929, CF
> ⊙ *The Saturday Evening Post,* March 30, 1929, pp. 66-67

The charm of beautiful colors, carefully chosen

MATCHING the fresh brilliance of Spring and early Summer are the beautiful colors of the new Ford. They are rich in tone, yet carefully chosen, with a quiet good taste that endures.

There are eleven different Ford body types, and all, with the single exception of the Station Wagon, are finished in a changing variety of colors.

You have the privilege of selecting from among these the color harmony that best suits your motoring needs and personal preference. Such choice is of course unusual in a low-price car and is one of the very special features of the new Ford.

Interior finish, upholstery and appointments are in keeping with this beauty of color and the trim, substantial lines which are so characteristically Ford. To the last least little detail, you can see evidence of the sincere quality that has been built into the car and the care that has been taken in its manufacture.

In all that goes to make a good automobile—in appearance—in safety—in comfort—in reliability—in economy—in alert, satisfying performance—the new Ford is an unusual value at a low price. Its ease of operation and control and freedom from mechanical troubles make it a particularly good car for a woman to drive.

Fuel system of the new Ford has been designed for reliability and long service

THE practical value of Ford simplicity of design is especially apparent in the fuel system. The whole purpose is to give you many thousands of miles of use without trouble of any kind.

The very location of the gasoline tank is an example of this careful planning. It was one of the first things considered in designing the new Ford because of the importance of the fuel system in the performance of an automobile.

There was no manufacturing problem. Having started fresh in the building of the new Ford, the way was open to put the gasoline tank in any position that seemed best.

The result desired was a direct gravity feed without any intermediate step—the simplest and most effective way of feeding gasoline to the carburetor without variations in pressure.

So the gasoline tank was placed where that would be possible. Service to the public was placed above precedent. Because of the central location of the gasoline tank in the new Ford, there is no need of a long fuel line with its multiplied possibilities of trouble. The Ford fuel line, as a matter of fact, is only eighteen inches long and is easily accessible all the way.

The tank itself is made of heavy pressed steel, and is term plated to prevent rust or corrosion. An additional factor of strength is the fact that it is composed of only two pieces, instead of the usual three or four, and is electrically welded—not soldered.

The carburetor in the new Ford also has many interesting features. It is unusually reliable in action because there are no moving parts in any way affecting the mixture. All adjustments are fixed except the needle valve and idler, so there is practically nothing to get out of order. "Keep-it-clean" and "don't tinker" are the two things to remember in the care of the Ford carburetor.

The choke on the dash of the new Ford acts not only as a primer but likewise provides an easy and convenient way for you to regulate the gasoline mixture and thereby increase gasoline mileage.

For quick starting, the choke button should be turned out, full turn counter-clockwise and then pulled outward to be released the instant the engine starts.

As the engine warms up, the choke should be turned clockwise until it is approximately ¼ turn open. This is the best adjustment for average driving. For cross-country driving at sustained speeds, the choke adjustment may often be kept almost fully closed. The general rule should be to keep the mixture as lean as possible without sacrificing the power of the engine.

Throughout the fuel system of the new Ford is so simple in design and so carefully made, that it requires very little attention.

There are really only three things to do, at intervals of 1000 to 2000 miles. (1) Clean the sediment bulb. (2) Remove the carburetor screen and wash it in gasoline. (3) Take out the drain plug at the bottom of the carburetor and drain the carburetor for a few seconds.

Make it a point to have your Ford dealer look after these important little details for you when you take the car to him for periodic oiling and greasing.

A thorough checking-up costs little, but it has a great deal to do with long life and continuously good performance.

Ford

FEATURES OF
THE NEW FORD CAR

Ten body types

Choice of a number of colors in each body type

Quiet acceleration

55 to 65 miles an hour

Fully enclosed, silent six-brake system

Four Houdaille hydraulic double-acting shock absorbers

Triplex shatter-proof windshield

Minute chassis lubrication

Vibration-absorbing engine support

Reliability and economy

FORD MOTOR COMPANY
Detroit, Michigan

BALLOON VENDOR

◆

THE SATURDAY EVENING POST   139

›››››○‹‹‹‹‹

THE FORD IS AN UNUSUALLY STRONG AND STURDY CAR

THE FORDOR SEDAN

The Ford is an unusually strong and sturdy car because of the enduring quality that has been built into every part. Of special interest and importance to every motorist is the extensive use of fine steel.

The story of Ford steel dates back to 1905, when the Ford Motor Company developed the use of a new alloy which raised the tensile strength of steel threefold. That was the beginning of the Ford idea of using specific steels for specific parts—an idea which has perhaps its highest expression in the new car.

Today, more than forty different kinds of steel are used in the Ford—each particular kind being selected and perfected to fit the particular needs of each part. Seven kinds of steel are used in the transmission alone because research and experience have proved that seven kinds of steel will give greater efficiency and reliability than one or two.

There is no limit to selection—no thought that any certain steel must be made to do for many parts to save expense. The Ford policy has always been to use the best possible material for each part, and then, through large production, to give it to the public at low cost.

The Ford open-hearth furnaces have a yearly capacity of 600,000 tons. The quality and uniformity of this steel are held to even closer limits than those used in industry generally.

As important as the steel itself is the Ford method of heat-treating by automatic control so that

Ford
FORD MOTOR COMPANY
Detroit, Michigan

the same piece of steel, though in one unit, may have different degrees of hardness at different points.

A further development of this one-piece principle has been made possible by perfecting the art of electric welding. This permits the use of an unusual number of steel forgings instead of malleable castings or stampings, without increased weight, yet with a considerable gain in strength and simplicity.

Such high quality of material has a direct bearing on the performance of the Ford car. Throughout, it has been designed and built to give you many thousands of miles of faithful, uninterrupted service at a very low cost per mile.

›››››○‹‹‹‹‹

Having parked their new Ford Fordor Sedan at the stadium, two couples are on their way to the big football game. Before heading to their seats, they pause to consider the souvenirs displayed for sale by the balloon vendor.

Version A (FdS 12a)
◉ *The American Boy,* November 1929, p. 33 (B&W)
○ *The Literary Digest,* November 9, 1929, p. 13
○ *The Saturday Evening Post,* November 2, 1929, p. 139

BALLOON VENDOR

Given the two colors of the balloons in this 1929 Williamson drawing, it is quite possible that the setting for this illustration is a Harvard (crimson) versus Yale (blue) football game. (Williamson attended Yale and graduated in 1923.)

Befitting *"The Ford is an Unusually Strong and Sturdy Car"* headline, the text of this ad is devoted to reviewing the quality of the steel used in the new Ford. It indicates that:

"Today, more than forty different kinds of steel are used in the Ford – each particular kind being selected and perfected to fit the needs of each part."

And concludes with:

"Such high quality of materials has a direct bearing on the performance of the Ford car. Throughout, it has been designed and built to give you many thousands of miles of faithful, uninterrupted service at a very low cost per mile."

HOW 'BOUT THIS ONE?
It's obvious that the souvenir selection process is not an easy one – as evidenced by the undecided man as he ponders the choices offered by the vendor. The woman, with hands on her hips, also appears involved in this decision process.

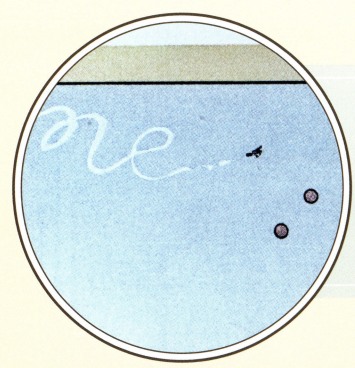

SKYWRITER.
High in the sky above the stadium is a message being scripted by the skywriting airplane. With only *"…ome"* visible, the plane may be providing a *"Welcome"* message to those who have ventured out to the football game on this cold November afternoon.

UP, UP AND AWAY!
There may be a child sobbing somewhere nearby. A closer look to the sky above also reveals two balloons that have recently escaped their owner.

CARD PARTY

◆

THE FORDOR SEDAN

The Ford is an unusually strong and sturdy car

THE FORD is an unusually strong and sturdy car because of the enduring quality that has been built into every part. Of special importance to the woman motorist is the extensive use of steel—not only in the chassis but also for the body. Beneath its beautiful finish is a substantial ruggedness and a carefully planned strength of construction that add a great deal to the safety of motoring.

Today, more than forty different kinds of steel are used in the Ford—each particular kind being selected and perfected to fit the particular needs of each part.

Seven kinds of steel are used in the transmission alone, because research and experience have proved that seven kinds of steel will give much greater efficiency and reliability than one or two.

There is no limit to selection —no thought that any certain steel must be made to do for several parts to save expense. The Ford policy has always been to use the best possible material for each part and then, through large production, to give it to the public at low cost.

Such high quality of material has a direct bearing on the performance of the Ford car. Throughout it has been designed to give you many thousands of miles of faithful service. In comfort, in safety, in economy, in reliability —in all that goes to make a good automobile—it represents a value far above the price you pay.

FORD MOTOR COMPANY
Detroit, Michigan

It's a card party and a group of players has parked their new Ford Fordor Sedan in front of the house. Behind the iron fence and through the large window, a group of women are seen seated at the table, cards in hand.

Version A (FdS 13a)

○ *The Farmer's Wife,* November 1929, CIII
○ *Good Housekeeping,* November 1929, p. 129
○ *Ladies' Home Journal,* November 1929, p. 80
○ *McCall's,* November 1929, p. 105

DE LUXE SEDAN

	TOTAL	1930	1931
Ford Body Style		170-B (Dlx.)	170-B (Dlx.) 160-C
Weight (pounds)		2,488	2,488
Price (FOB Detroit)		$650	$630
Units Produced (U.S.)	16,105	12,854	3,251
Number of U.S. Ads			
Primary Formats	3	2	1
Ad Variations	7	6	1
Magazine Insertions	38	17	21

Production of the 1929 Model A (standard) Fordor Sedan (170-A) continued into 1930 (as 170-B Standard) and, in May 1930, received an upgraded interior and cowl lights. With these changes, it was reclassified as the De Luxe Sedan (170-B De Luxe). This two-window Model A sedan, produced by Briggs, was available until June 1931. With Ford's change to the slant-windshield models in mid-1931, both Briggs and Murray began producing the two-window De Luxe Sedan in the slant-windshield design (160-C).

Ford did not produce magazine ads for the two-window Fordor Sedan body styles (170-A and 170-B Standard) in 1929 or 1930. However, several ads were created in 1930 and 1931 for the upgraded De Luxe Sedan (170-B De Luxe). The basic illustrations used in the three primary Model A Deluxe Sedan magazine ads ranged from women driving the car in downtown traffic, to a farmer admiring the car in the country, to a chauffeur waiting on the car's passenger to finish her shopping activities. No magazine ads were produced for the slant-windshield De Luxe Sedan (160-C).

DOWNTOWN STATUE

THE NEW FORD DE LUXE SEDAN

An easy car for a woman to drive

THE new Ford is a splendid choice for the woman motorist because it is so reliable and easy to handle. Particularly in heavy traffic you will appreciate its quick acceleration, alert speed, effective four-wheel brakes, and ease in steering, shifting gears, turning and parking. « « « « «

Another factor that contributes to your feeling of confidence and security in driving the new Ford is the Triplex shatter-proof windshield. This reduces the danger of flying glass, a frequent cause of injuries in automobile collisions. The Ford Motor Company has provided it for you on the new Ford as a contribution to greater safety on every highway. « « « « « »

Two women negotiate downtown traffic as they pass a large statue in their new Ford De Luxe Sedan.

⊙ *Delineator,* July 1930, CII
○ *The Farmer's Wife,* July 1930, p. 13
○ *Good Housekeeping,* July 1930, p. 117

Version A (DSn 1a)
● *Junior League Magazine,* June 1930, p. 3 (B&W)
○ *Ladies' Home Journal,* July 1930, p. 62
○ *McCall's,* July 1930 p. 100
⊙ *Pictorial Review,* July 1930, CIII
⊙ *True Story,* July 1930, p. 57
○ *Woman's Home Companion,* July 1930, p. 47

DOWNTOWN STATUE

Two different two-page editions were produced for this De Luxe Sedan ad. The second two-page version (C) contains an insert illustration of the new Ford Sport Coupe.

Version B (DSn 1b) ⋁
⊙ *The Literary Digest,* April 26, 1930, CF

The Literary Digest for April 26, 1930

The Literary Digest for April 26, 1930

Quality that endures

THE extra value built into the new Ford is reflected in its alert, capable performance, reliability and long life. . . . Beneath its flashing beauty of line and color there is a mechanical excellence unusual in a low-priced car. Many measurements are accurate to the thousandth of an inch — some to three ten-thousandths of an inch. Every part has been carefully designed and made to give you many months and years of faithful, uninterrupted service. In safety, comfort, speed, power, economy — in all that goes to make a good automobile — it is a value far above the price. The quality of the new Ford is a quality that endures.

Outstanding Features of the New Ford

New streamline bodies. • Choice of colors. • Adjustable front seats in closed bodies. • Triplex shatter-proof glass windshield. • Four Houdaille double-acting hydraulic shock absorbers. • Bright, enduring Rustless Steel for many exterior metal parts. • Fully enclosed four-wheel brakes. • Steel-spoke wheels. • Aluminum pistons. • Chrome silicon alloy valves. • Torque-tube drive. • Three-quarter floating rear axle. • Unusually large number of ball and roller bearings. • Extensive use of steel forgings instead of castings or stampings. • 55 to 65 miles an hour. • Quick acceleration. • Ease of control. • Low first cost. • Low cost of operation and up-keep. • Reliability and long life. • Good dealer service.

THE FORD DE LUXE SEDAN
One of the newest Ford cars. A truly de luxe sedan in line and color and in the richness of its appointments and upholstery. Generous room for five people. Front seat is adjustable. Rear seat has a disappearing center arm and arm rests at each side. An economical car because of the low first cost and the low cost of operation and up-keep.

Version C (DSn 1c) ⋁ ⊙ *The Saturday Evening Post,* June 14, 1930, pp. 76-77

76   THE SATURDAY EVENING POST   June 14, 1930   THE SATURDAY EVENING POST   77

QUALITY THAT ENDURES

THE extra value built into the new Ford is reflected in its alert, capable performance, reliability and long life. Beneath its flashing beauty of line and color there is a high quality of material and mechanical excellence. Many measurements are accurate to the thousandth of an inch — some to three ten-thousandths of an inch. Every part has been carefully designed and made to give you many months and years of faithful, uninterrupted service. In safety, comfort, speed, power, economy — in all that goes to make a good automobile — it is a value far above the price. The quality of the new Ford is a quality that endures.

Outstanding Features of the New Ford

New streamline bodies. • Choice of colors. • Adjustable front seats in closed bodies. • Triplex shatter-proof glass windshield. • Four Houdaille double-acting hydraulic shock absorbers. • Bright, enduring Rustless Steel for many exterior metal parts. • Fully enclosed four-wheel brakes. • Steel-spoke wheels. • Aluminum pistons. • Chrome silicon alloy valves. • Torque-tube drive. • Three-quarter floating rear axle. • More than twenty ball and roller bearings. • Extensive use of fine steel forgings. • 55 to 65 miles an hour. • Quick acceleration. • Ease of control. • Low first cost. • Low cost of operation and up-keep. • Reliability and long life. • Good dealer service.

THE NEW FORD SPORT COUPE
A particularly good car for the woman motorist because of its surprising ease of operation and control. Equipped with a wide substantial rumble seat. The Triplex shatter-proof glass windshield is an important safety feature.

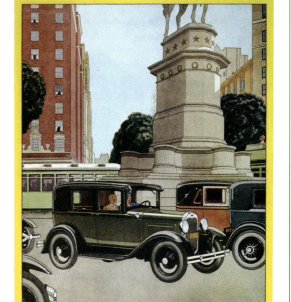

One of the newest Ford cars. A truly de luxe sedan in line and color and in the richness of its appointments and upholstery. Generous room for five people. Front seat is adjustable. Rear seat has a disappearing center arm and arm rests at each side. An economical car to own and drive because of the low first cost and the low cost of operation and up-keep.
THE NEW FORD DE LUXE SEDAN

DOWNTOWN STATUE

A fourth version (D) of this 1930 De Luxe Sedan ad is a single-page edition using the same headline as the two two-page ads, but with a different format and a changed ad text. This ad appeared in only one magazine, in June 1930.

Version D (DSn 1d) ➤

⊙ *Liberty,* June 28, 1930, p. 19

At least one of the other cars shown in this downtown traffic illustration appears to be drawn as a Ford automobile. However, the rather odd looking car with the triangular window and landau bar behind the Model A De Luxe Sedan was purposely drawn to be a non-Ford automobile.

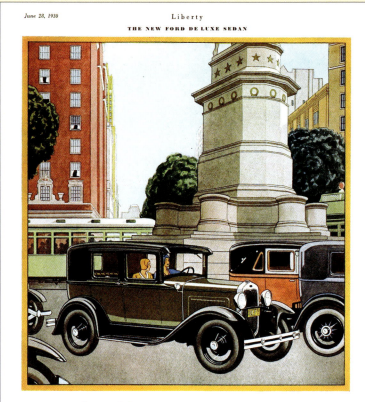

Note that in this magazine ad, as in all other Model A ads featuring deluxe body styles, Ford chooses to use the more uncommon *"De Luxe"* spelling of this term.

OBLIVIOUS DRIVER!

A close-up look at the two ladies in the Ford De Luxe Sedan shows a quite happy, talkative driver and an attentive companion passenger – despite the perils of negotiating downtown traffic. This setting matches the first (version A) *"Downtown Statue"* ad headline: *"An easy car for a woman to drive."*

TAKING A BREAK
DE LUXE SEDAN

THE NEW FORD DE LUXE SEDAN

Outstanding Features of the New Ford

NEW streamline bodies. • • Choice of colors. • • Adjustable front seats in closed bodies. • • Triplex shatter-proof glass windshield. • • Four Houdaille double-acting hydraulic shock absorbers. • • Bright, enduring Rustless Steel for many exterior metal parts. • • Fully enclosed four-wheel brakes. • • Steel-spoke wheels. • • Aluminum pistons. • • Chrome silicon alloy valves. • • Torque-tube drive. • • Three-quarter floating rear axle. • • More than twenty ball and roller bearings. • • Extensive use of fine steel forgings. • • 55 to 65 miles an hour. • • Quick acceleration. • • Ease of control. • • Low first cost. • • Low cost of operation and up-keep. • • Reliability and long life.

The farmer has stopped plowing and has climbed down from his tractor to take a break. He leans on the fence while chatting with his friend who has just pulled up in his new Model A Ford De Luxe Sedan.

Version A (DSn 2a)
⊙ *Capper's Farmer,* July 1930, CIII
○ *The Country Gentleman,* July 1930, p. 56
⊙ *Farm and Ranch,* July 5, 1930, p. 13

TAKING A BREAK

De Luxe Sedan and Tudor Sedan Ads

This 1930 De Luxe Sedan ad does not contain the usual Ford ad text in paragraph form. Instead it simply lists the many different *"outstanding features"* of the new Ford car.

A second version of the *"Taking a Break"* magazine ad (B) contains a modified list of these features.

Version B (DSn 2b) [text difference]
O *The Country Home,* July 1930, CII
O *Successful Farming,* July 1930, CII

Ford also used this Model A Ford De Luxe Sedan illustration in a magazine ad for the Ford Tudor Sedan.

The De Luxe Sedan illustration in this magazine ad was altered by removing the cowl lights and rear door handles and shifting the window positioning (and view through the windows) so the car appears as a Tudor Sedan body style.

It is not known which of the two advertising illustrations was prepared first and then modified to produce the second ad. Perhaps this modification was made to the basic Williamson drawing by another artist in order to meet the last-minute need to have a second illustration available for a magazine ad for the other Model A body style.

These De Luxe Sedan and Tudor Sedan ads use the same headline but have slightly different ad texts. Both ads appeared in July 1930.

"Taking a Break"
De Luxe Sedan
Ad Illustration
July 1930

"Taking a Break"
Tudor Sedan
Ad Illustration
July 1930

The *"Taking a Break"* drawing was used to promote both the De Luxe Sedan and the Tudor Sedan. This is the only example of the same (modified) drawing appearing in magazine ads for two different Model A body styles.

BROWN'S SHOP CHAUFFEUR

◆

JANUARY 1931

MᶜBrown's Domestic Service Bureau.

HATS ROBERTS GOWNS

NEW FORD DE LUXE SEDAN

The Beauty of Fine Upholstery

THE BEAUTY of fine upholstery gives charm and distinction to the interior of the new Ford De Luxe Sedan.

In this car, as in the Town Sedan and the De Luxe Coupe, you may choose tan Bedford cord, or brown mohair. The Bedford cord has an all-worsted face and heavy woolen yarns under each cord. The soft, luxurious mohair will not crush easily and is long-wearing because it is faced with genuine Angora mohair and fine wool worsted. In both types of upholstery, beauty and utility have been combined in unusual degree.

Great care is taken to maintain the quality of the fabrics used for the Ford cars. Laboratory tests for weight, the character of the cloth and the grade of the yarns are constantly being made. There are also daily tests of the dyes, the count in the warp and woof, the percentage of wool, the thickness of the mohair pile, and rubbing tests equivalent to years of actual wear.

In every detail of trim and finish, as in mechanical performance, you will note the substantial worth that has been built into the Ford car. It has been made to endure.

While her Ford Town Sedan and chauffeur wait at the curb, a lady has just hired two maids from *"Mrs. Brown's Domestic Services Bureau."* The maids, in white gloves, wait at the door while the paperwork is being finalized.

Version A (DSn 3a)

○ *The American Magazine,* January 1931, p. 68
○ *Cosmopolitan,* January 1931, p. 15
◉ *Country Life,* January 1931, p. 94
◉ *Delineator,* January 1931, CII

(continued)

BROWN'S SHOP CHAUFFEUR

◄ **Version A** (DSn 3a) [continued]
- ○ *The Farmer's Wife,* January 1931, CII
- ○ *Good Housekeeping,* January 1931, p. 9
- ◉ *Harper's Bazaar,* January 1931, p. 9
- ◉ *Holland's,* January 1931, p. 38
- ○ *Ladies' Home Journal,* January 1931, p. 43
- ◉ *Liberty,* March 7, 1931, p. 66
- ○ *The Literary Digest,* February 7, 1931, CII
- ○ *McCall's,* January 1931, p. 46
- ◉ *Pictorial Review,* January 1931, CIII
- ◉ *The Redbook Magazine,* January 1931, CII
- ○ *The Saturday Evening Post,* January 31, 1931, p. 37
- ◉ *The Sportsman,* January 1931, p. 71
- ◉ *True Story,* January 1931, p. 59
- ◉ *Vanity Fair,* January 1931, p. 17
- ◉ *Vogue,* January 1, 1931, p. 17
- ○ *Woman's Home Companion,* January 1931, p. 46
- ○ *Woman's World,* January 1931

With the open door on the Ford De Luxe Sedan allowing a full view of the rear seat, the text for this ad concentrates on the beauty, durability and quality of the upholstery and fabrics used in the new Ford car.

"Great care is taken to maintain the quality of the fabrics used for the Ford cars. Laboratory tests for weight, the character of the cloth and the grade of the yarns are consistently being made. There are also daily tests of the dyes, the count in the wrap and woof, the percantage of wool, the thickness of the hair pile, and rubbing tests equivalent to years of actual wear."

This Ford De Luxe Sedan magazine ad was published in 21 different magazines in early 1931. These magazines included virtually all of the non-farm-related publications used by Ford to advertise the Model A. However, unlike most other Model A ads that appeared in numerous magazines, only one version of the *"Brown's Shop Chauffeur"* ad was produced.

Across all four years of advertising specific Model A body styles, no other magazine ad appeared in this many publications without some variation in the ad illustration, headline or text.

AT YOUR SERVICE!
The chauffeur, his whisk brush still in hand, appears somewhat inquisitive (and maybe a little impatient) as he waits to meet these two newest members of madam's household staff.

TOWN SEDAN

	TOTAL	1929	1930	1931
Ford Body Style		155-A 155-B	155-C 155-D	155-C 155-D 160-B
Weight (pounds)		2,475	2,475	2,475
Price (FOB Detroit)		$695	$670	$630
Units Produced (U.S.)	245,374	84,970	104,935	55,469
Number of U.S. Ads				
Primary Formats	13	4	4	5
Ad Variations	37	5	14	18
Magazine Insertions	119	18	58	43

Beginning in 1929, the basic Model A Three-Window Fordor Sedan was also available in a deluxe model, known as the Model A Town Sedan. The Town Sedan differed from the (standard) Three-Window Fordor Sedan in having deluxe interior trim, cowl lights and a different paint stripe scheme. Two manufacturers produced Town Sedan bodies in 1929 – Murray (155-A) and Briggs (155-B). The same manufacturers also produced the 1930 and 1931 Town Sedan bodies – Murray (155-C) and Briggs (155-D). Beginning in mid-1931, the Model A Town Sedan was also available as a slant-windshield model (160-B).

The Town Sedan was a heavily advertised Model A body style. Ford produced 37 different magazine ad variations for this body type – with most of the ads produced for the 1930 and 1931 models. The majority of the Town Sedan magazine ad illustrations were for the Murray body style (slightly arched window top treatment), rather than the Briggs body style (straight window top treatment). Magazine ads for the Model A Town Sedan appeared in a wide variety of U.S. magazines – including general interest, woman's fashion, upscale, youth-oriented and farm-related publications.

CAR WASH

82 THE SATURDAY EVENING POST June 15, 1929

Economical Transportation *for* All The People

Twenty-one years ago, when the Model T was first made, and again in December, 1927, when the new Ford was introduced, the policy of the Ford Motor Company was announced in these words—

"We will build a motor car for the great multitude. It will be large enough for the family, but small enough for the individual to run and care for. It will be constructed of the best materials, by the best men to be hired, after the simplest designs that modern engineering can devise. But it will be so low in price that no man making a good salary will be unable to own one."

Nearly seventeen million Ford automobiles have been made since this announcement was first printed. The passing years have brought many changes—in appearance—in performance—in manner of manufacture. But there is one thing that has never changed—the fundamental idea behind the Ford car.

The Ford Motor Company was formed, and exists today, not merely to make automobiles—not primarily for sales or profits—but to provide economical transportation for all the people. Far more important than the car itself is the part it plays in the lives, the happiness, and the prosperity of millions of people.

Before the Ford was introduced the automobile was considered more or less as an expensive toy, for only the wealthy to drive. There was no conception of its uses and possibilities as we know them today. It was accepted in much the same manner that the airplane was accepted five years ago. Great emphasis was placed upon its racing speed and very little upon its practical utility.

The Ford Coupe, like all the new Ford cars, has a Triplex glass windshield. This is so made that it will not fly or shatter under the hardest impact. It is a particularly important safety feature in heavy traffic.

THE SATURDAY EVENING POST 83

The new Ford Town Sedan. Richly upholstered and appointed in the manner of a custom-built car. Driver's seat is adjustable. Rear compartment has bow light, silk curtains at rear and rear quarter windows and flexible robe rail. Deeply cushioned rear seat has the new center arm rest and arm rests at each side.

With the coming of the Ford, however, it became possible for men in all walks of life to enjoy the benefits of transportation that formerly had been limited to a fortunate few.

A great change came over the country and with it a new prosperity. By freeing the movements of men, the Ford also freed their thoughts and created new opportunities. The barriers of time and distance were broken down. Good roads followed close behind the automobile and the isolation of country districts disappeared. The nation grew as people learned to use this newly developed horse-power and fit it to their needs.

Into the hands of men of moderate means—to the workers in factories—to the toilers on the farm—was given a means to increase their income and enjoy the leisure which that increased income should bring. The working day became shorter because men could do in eight hours the tasks that previously had taken ten or twelve—and do them better. Always it should be remembered that we do not have automobiles because we are prosperous. We are prosperous because we have them.

FEATURES OF THE NEW FORD CAR

Silent, fully enclosed six-brake system
Four Houdaille hydraulic double-acting shock absorbers
Triplex shatter-proof glass windshield
Eleven body types and choice of a number of colors in every passenger body type
Quick acceleration
55 to 65 miles an hour
Vibration-absorbing engine support
Smoothness at all speeds
Alemite chassis lubrication
Tilting beam headlamps
Reliability and economy

Today, with all its improvements—with all its new beauty of line and color—with all the betterments and changes that have been made during the past twenty-one years—the Ford is still "a motor car for the great multitude."

It is not just a new automobile—not just so many mechanical parts carefully put together to run on wheels—but Progress—Achievement—a part of the very life and fabric of the nation.

Business of every kind moves forward at a faster pace because of it. To countless homes it brings the rewards of widening opportunity, happiness, and priceless hours of relaxation in the open air.

All of this not merely because of its safety, its comfort, its reliability, its speed, its acceleration, its ease of control, but because of a fundamental purpose that is greater than all of these. Because, in larger degree than ever, it provides economical transportation for all the people.

Ford Motor Company
Detroit, Michigan

The first magazine ad for the Model A Ford Town Sedan appeared as a two-page edition in June 1929. Unlike the pattern with virtually all other two-page Model A Ford ads, a one-page version of this ad was not produced.

This Town Sedan ad appeared in both magazines containing two-page Model A ads and is the only Model A magazine ad to utilize an octagon-shaped illustration.

In addition to the primary illustration of the man washing his new Ford Town Sedan, this ad includes a unique Williamson drawing of the Ford Coupe. The Coupe drawing does not appear in any other Model A Ford magazine ad.

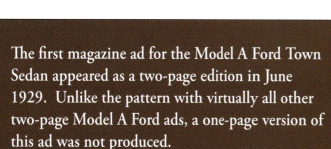

Version A (TnS 1a)

- *The Literary Digest,* June 1, 1929, CF
- *The Saturday Evening Post,* June 15, 1929, pp. 82-83

In line with the *"Economical Transportation for All The People"* headline, the ad text proclaims:

"Today, with all its improvements – with all its new beauty of line and color – with all the betterments and changes that have been made during the past twenty-one years – the Ford is still 'a motor car for the great multitude.'

It is not just a new automobile – not just so many mechanical parts carefully put together to run on wheels – but Progress – Achievement – a part of the very life and fabric of the nation."

CAR WASH

This 1929 Ford Town Sedan magazine ad also includes an element common to many Model A Ford ads – an insert listing the many *"Features of the New Ford Car."* The specific features listed vary somewhat across different Model A ads using this element. In this ad they include the promise of *"quick acceleration,"* speeds of *"55 to 65 miles an hour"* and *"smoothness at all speeds."*

As with many Williamson Model A Ford advertising illustrations, this drawing provides a story beyond the one seen at first glance about a man preparing to wash his Model A Ford.

The proud owner, about to give his new Town Sedan a wash, has been distracted by the sight of a man high in the branches of a nearby tree. This man, his saw dangling from a rope, has decided to interrupt his tree-trimming activities to take a nap.

The Town Sedan owner, bucket filled and running hose in hand, seems somewhat distracted as he gazes up at the man in the tree. The disgusted look on his face may mean the man sleeping in the tree is the guy he hired to do some landscaping work around his yard!

ZZZZZZZ!
This sure seems like an odd place to select to take a nap. But at least the man anticipated his weariness by first securely tethering his saw to a branch of the tree. With no evidence of any shortened limbs nearby, a nap must have been first on his agenda this summer afternoon.

A WET WAKEUP?
How likely is it that he is wondering if he could reach the snoozing man with a stream of water from that distance?

PEPPER CATERING

◆

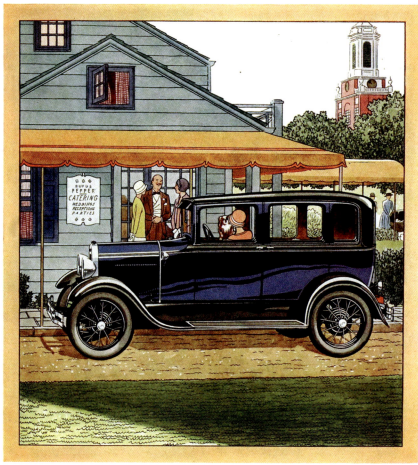

McCALL'S MAGAZINE AUGUST 1929

THE COMFORTING ASSURANCE
THAT EVERYTHING IS JUST RIGHT

The new Ford Town Sedan

OF ALL the many features of the new Ford, there is none that means so much to the woman motorist as the comforting assurance that everything is just right.

You have confidence in the mechanical performance of the car because it has, to a greater degree than ever, the reliability that has always been associated with the name Ford. Equally important is your confidence in the safety of the car.

Your first impression of the new Ford is one of sturdy strength. This is due not only to the substantial, well-built frame and the extensive use of steel in the body, but also to the carefully-planned balance of the car. The way it holds the road is particularly noticeable on curves and in traveling at more than average speed.

The six-brake system of the new Ford, is, of course, one of its outstanding features. It is unusually reliable and effective because the surfaces of all six brakes are fully enclosed. There is thus no possibility of water, dirt or oil entering the brake mechanism and interfering with brake action under ordinary driving conditions. Silent, easy operation is another feature you will appreciate.

A further factor in the safety of the new Ford is the Triplex glass windshield. This is so made that it will not shatter or fly under the hardest impact. Such protection becomes increasingly necessary as traffic increases and is an important point to remember in the purchase of an automobile.

Ease of steering and of shifting gears, quick acceleration, abundant speed and power for every emergency, and full vision front, side and rear also contribute to the safety of the new Ford and are among the reasons why it is such a good car for a woman to drive.

FORD MOTOR COMPANY
Detroit, Michigan

The mother and bride-to-be have parked their new Ford Town Sedan at the *"Rufus Pepper Catering"* shop and are discussing their catering needs with Rufus. A third woman waits in the car, entertaining a small dog.

Version A (TnS 2a)

○ *The Farmer's Wife,* August 1929, p. 19

○ *Good Housekeeping,* August 1929

○ *Ladies' Home Journal,* August 1929, p. 73

○ *McCall's,* August 1929, p. 9

PEPPER CATERING

A second version (B) of this 1929 Ford Town Sedan magazine ad changes to a new headline and utilizes a much shorter ad text. The text, in line with the *"Features of the Ford Car"* headline, simply lists the characteristics and attributes of the new Ford — including *"four Houdailie hydraulic double-action shock absorbers"* and *"vibration-absorbing engine support."*

This *"Pepper Catering"* Model A Town Sedan ad version appeared in only two magazines.

Version B (TnS 2b) ➤
○ *Cosmopolitan,* August 1929, p. 106
◉ *The Redbook Magazine,* August 1929, p. 98

The new Ford Town Sedan

Features of the Ford car

Sturdy body construction ⋄ Ease of control ⋄ Four Houdaille hydraulic double-acting shock absorbers ⋄ Triplex shatter-proof glass windshield ⋄ Fully enclosed, silent six-brake system ⋄ Quick acceleration ⋄ 55 to 65 miles an hour ⋄ Smoothness, balance and security at all speeds ⋄ Vibration-absorbing engine support ⋄ Choice of colors ⋄ Tilting beam headlamps ⋄ Theft-proof ignition lock ⋄ Reliability ⋄ Economy ⋄ Long life

LA CONFORTADORA SEGURIDAD DE QUE TODO ESTA BIEN

El nuevo TOWN SEDAN Ford

DE todas las características del nuevo Ford no hay ninguna que signifique tanto para la mujer que gusta de conducir su propio coche como la que constituye la seguridad de que todo está bien.

Ella—la mujer automovilista—tiene confianza en el funcionamiento mecánico del carro porque éste posee, hoy más que nunca, la estabilidad, la superioridad que ha distinguido en todo tiempo a los productos Ford. Asimismo la mujer automovilista pone toda su confianza en la seguridad de su coche.

La primera impresión que uno recibe al encontrarse por primera vez ante un nuevo Ford es de solidez, de fuerza, de potencia. Esto es así, no sólo por lo solidamente construido que está el bastidor, y por la profusión con que se ha empleado el acero en la fabricación de la carrocería, sino también por el equilibrio, tan cuidadosamente proyectado, del carro. El modo como se adhiere, por así decirlo, a la carretera

se echa de ver, principalmente, en las curvas y cuando se viaja a alta velocidad.

El sistema de seis frenos con que está equipado el nuevo Ford es, desde luego, uno de sus rasgos característicos más dignos de mención. Es excepcionalmente eficaz y seguro por razón de la superficie de enfrenamiento de todos los seis frenos está perfectamente resguardada, protegida. Se ha abolido la posibilidad de que el agua, la grasa o la suciedad en general, se introduzcan en el mecanismo de los frenos y entorpezcan su funcionamiento en condiciones normales. Otra de las características del carro que el automovilista consciente no podrá menos de apreciar es la manera tan silenciosa y suave con que funcionan los frenos.

Un elemento más de seguridad que ofrece el nuevo Ford es el cristal TRIPLEX de que está formado el parabrisas. Este cristal está fabricado de modo tal que

cuando por razón del golpe recibido llega a quebrarse, sus fragmentos no saltarán para ir a herir el rostro de los automovilistas, caso de que la rotura acaeciese en una colisión. Esta protección es digna de tomarse en cuenta al adquirir un automóvil, especialmente ahora cuando el tránsito es más intenso que nunca.

La facilidad con que se dirige el nuevo Ford y se hace el cambio de velocidad; la rápida aceleración; la superabundancia de velocidad y potencia, muy conveniente en casos de emergencia; la espléndida visibilidad por el frente, por los lados y por detrás, contribuyen en no pequeña medida a la seguridad que ofrece este magnífico autocar y constituyen algunas de las razones por que el nuevo Ford es el carro ideal para las mujeres que gustan del automovilismo. La mujer que guía un nuevo Ford puede tener la CONFORTADO RA SEGURIDAD DE QUE TODO LE IRA BIEN.

FORD MOTOR COMPANY
Sucursal de la Habana

With the substitution of a Spanish language text, this Williamson Town Sedan illustration was also used in advertising outside of the United States.

While the Town Sedan *"Pepper Catering"* ad ran in August 1929 in the United States, it did not appear in a Cuban magazine until early 1930.

◀ **Example ad from Cuba**
◉ *Social,* January 1930, p. 7

SAILBOAT LAKE

◆

THE FORD TOWN SEDAN

Gliding smoothly over the miles

BECAUSE of its eager flow of speed and unusual riding comfort, the miles that stretch ahead from *Here* to *There* are swift and pleasant miles in the Ford.

So pronounced is this riding ease that you will come to look on it as one of the outstanding features of the car. For no other single thing adds quite so much to the joy of driving.

On long trips particularly you will like the way the Ford carries you along, smoothly and evenly, without hard jolts or bumps or the exaggerated bouncing which is the cause of most motoring fatigue. The disturbing force of every road shock is cushioned and absorbed before it reaches the frame, chassis and body of the car.

The principal factors in this comfort are the special Ford transverse springs, low unsprung weight and four Houdaille hydraulic double-acting shock absorbers. These shock absorbers also have a considerable bearing on safety.

By keeping all four wheels firmly on the ground, they insure more positive traction, contribute to better brake action and help to eliminate sidesway.

Even at comparatively high speeds you have a feeling of substantial security in the Ford because of its carefully planned balance. No matter how far the goal, or rough or devious the highway, you know it will bring you safely, comfortably, quickly to the journey's end.

FORD MOTOR COMPANY
Detroit, Michigan

It's a bright fall day as the new Ford Town Sedan heads toward the sailboat docks. The driver, his captain's hat already in place, is in a hurry to get to his boat and out on the water. This Model A ad appeared only in upscale magazines.

Version A (TnS 3a)

◉ *Country Life,* September 1929, p. 97

◉ *Harper's Bazaar,* September 1929, p. 117

◉ *The Sportsman,* September 1929, p. 83

◉ *Vanity Fair,* September 1929, p. 17

◉ *Vogue,* September 28, 1929, p. 33

STOREFRONT TURKEY

◆

COUNTRY LIFE

THE FORD TOWN SEDAN

The Ford is an unusually strong and sturdy car

THE FORD is an unusually strong and sturdy car because of the enduring quality that has been built into every part.

Of special interest and importance is the extensive use of steel—not only in the chassis but also for the body. Beneath its beautiful finish is a substantial ruggedness and a carefully planned strength of construction that add a great deal to the safety of motoring.

Today, more than forty different kinds of steel are used in the Ford, each particular kind being selected and perfected to fit the particular needs of each part.

Seven kinds of steel are used in the transmission alone, because research and experience have proved that seven kinds of steel will give much greater efficiency and reliability than one or two.

There is no limit to selection— no thought that any certain steel must do for several parts to save expense. The Ford policy has always been to use the best possible material and then, through large production, to give it to the public at low cost.

Such high quality of material has a direct bearing on the performance of the Ford car. Throughout, it has been designed to give you many thousands of miles of faithful, uninterrupted service.

In comfort, in safety, in economy, in reliability—in all that goes to make it a good automobile—it represents a value far above the price you pay.

FORD MOTOR COMPANY
Detroit, Michigan

Two fur-clad women, having parked their new Ford Town Sedan at the door, shop in the downtown gift shop. It's almost Thanksgiving, as evidenced by the turkey in the store's window display.

Version A (TnS 4a)

◉ *Country Life,* November 1929, p. 93

◉ *Harper's Bazaar,* November 1929, p. 153

◉ *The Sportsman,* November 1929, p. 84

◉ *Vanity Fair,* November 1929, p. 41

◉ *Vogue,* November 23, 1929, p. 25

FLAGSTONE SHOWOFF

Pride of Possession

THE NEW FORD TOWN SEDAN

YOU will take a real pride in the smart style and fresh new beauty of the Ford just as you will find an ever-growing satisfaction in its alert, capable performance. From the new deep radiator to the tip of the curving rear fender, there is an unbroken sweep of line—a flowing grace of contour and harmony of color heretofore thought possible only in an expensive automobile. Craftsmanship has been put into mass production.

Two ladies have parked their new Ford Town Sedan on the flagstone driveway. As they show off the new Ford to their friend, the car has also drawn the attention of the butler, the family dog and the man at the upstairs window.

Version A (TnS 5a)
◉ *Country Life,* February 1930, p. 92
◉ *The Sportsman,* February 1930, p. 77
◉ *Vogue,* February 1, 1930, p. 120+

Four different versions of this 1930 Town Sedan ad were produced.

FLAGSTONE SHOWOFF

A second version (B) of this 1930 Town Sedan ad appeared in numerous magazines and employs a *"New Beauty for the New Ford"* script headline and a more abbreviated text, set in bold, capital letters.

⊙ *The American Boy,* March 1930, CII (B&W)

○ *The American Magazine,* March 1930, p. 94

⊙ *Collier's,* March 15, 1930, CIII

○ *Cosmopolitan,* March 1930, p. 115

⊙ *Delineator,* March 1930, p. 112

○ *Good Housekeeping,* March 1930, p. 111

◉ *Harper's Bazaar,* March 1930, p. 33

● *Junior League Magazine,* March 1930, p. 3 (B&W)

○ *Ladies' Home Journal,* March 1930, p. 91

⊙ *Liberty,* March 8, 1930, p. 19

○ *McCall's,* March 1930, p. 56

⊙ *The Redbook Magazine,* March 1930, CII

⊙ *True Story,* March 1930, p. 57

◉ *Vanity Fair,* March 1930, p. 88+

○ *Woman's Home Companion,* March 1930

◄ **Version B (TnS 5b)**

The third ad version (C) retains the same headline and text – but places the headline below the illustration of the Ford Town Sedan.

Version C (TnS 5c) ➤

○ *The Farmer's Wife,* March 1930, p. 14

FLAGSTONE SHOWOFF

The fourth *"Flagstone Showoff"* ad version (D) is a two-page edition. This ad uses the same basic Town Sedan illustration, but with a slightly expanded view of the flagstone drive in the foreground and the top of the house.

Version D (TnS 5d)

- *The Literary Digest,* February 15, 1930, pp. 42-43
- *The Saturday Evening Post,* February 22, 1930, pp. 72-73

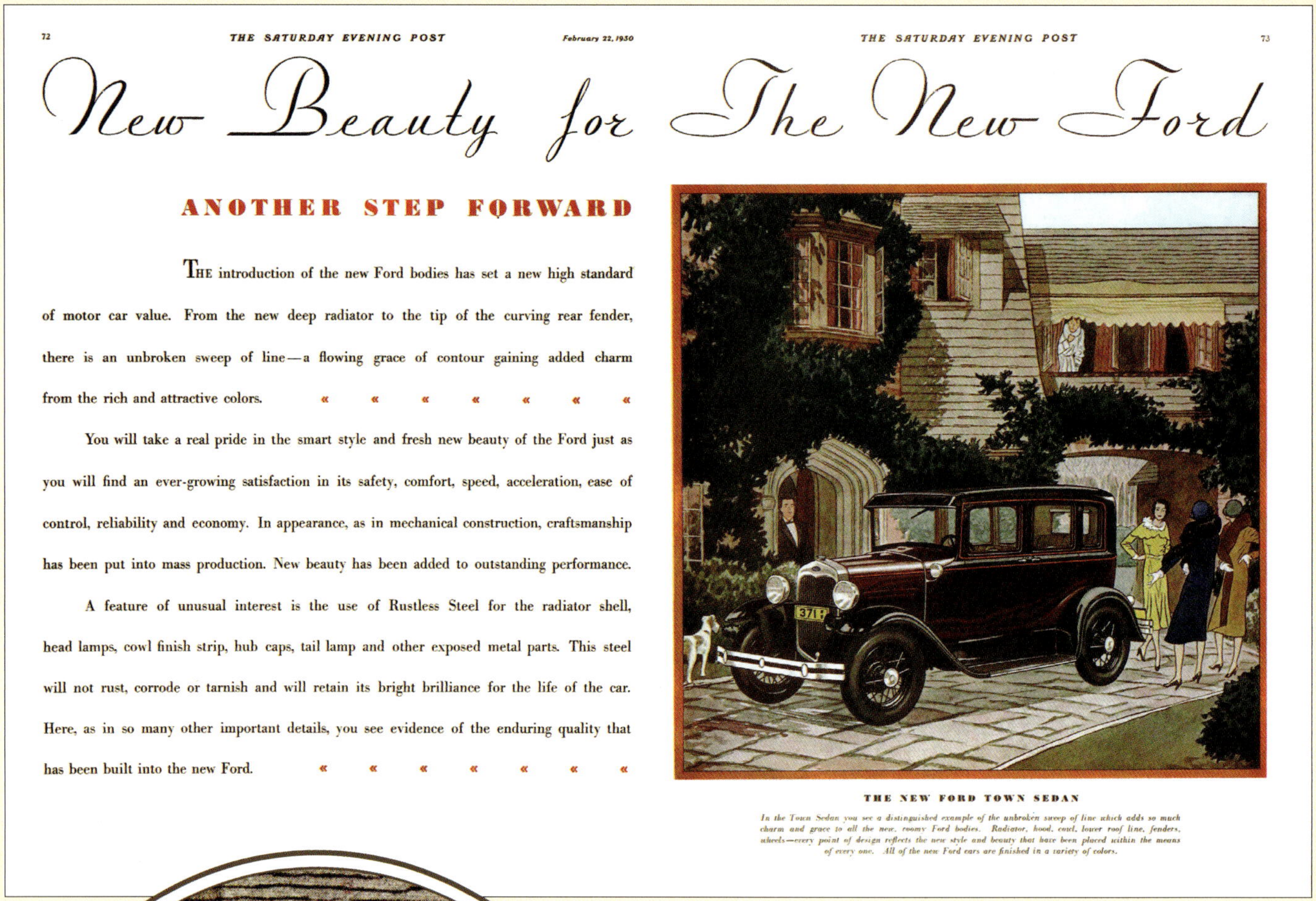
72
THE SATURDAY EVENING POST
February 22, 1930
THE SATURDAY EVENING POST
73
New Beauty for The New Ford
ANOTHER STEP FORWARD
THE introduction of the new Ford bodies has set a new high standard of motor car value. From the new deep radiator to the tip of the curving rear fender, there is an unbroken sweep of line—a flowing grace of contour gaining added charm from the rich and attractive colors.
You will take a real pride in the smart style and fresh new beauty of the Ford just as you will find an ever-growing satisfaction in its safety, comfort, speed, acceleration, ease of control, reliability and economy. In appearance, as in mechanical construction, craftsmanship has been put into mass production. New beauty has been added to outstanding performance.
A feature of unusual interest is the use of Rustless Steel for the radiator shell, head lamps, cowl finish strip, hub caps, tail lamp and other exposed metal parts. This steel will not rust, corrode or tarnish and will retain its bright brilliance for the life of the car. Here, as in so many other important details, you see evidence of the enduring quality that has been built into the new Ford.
THE NEW FORD TOWN SEDAN
In the Town Sedan you see a distinguished example of the unbroken sweep of line which adds so much charm and grace to all the new, roomy Ford bodies. Radiator, hood, cowl, lower roof line, fenders, wheels—every point of design reflects the new style and beauty that have been placed within the means of every one. All of the new Ford cars are finished in a variety of colors.

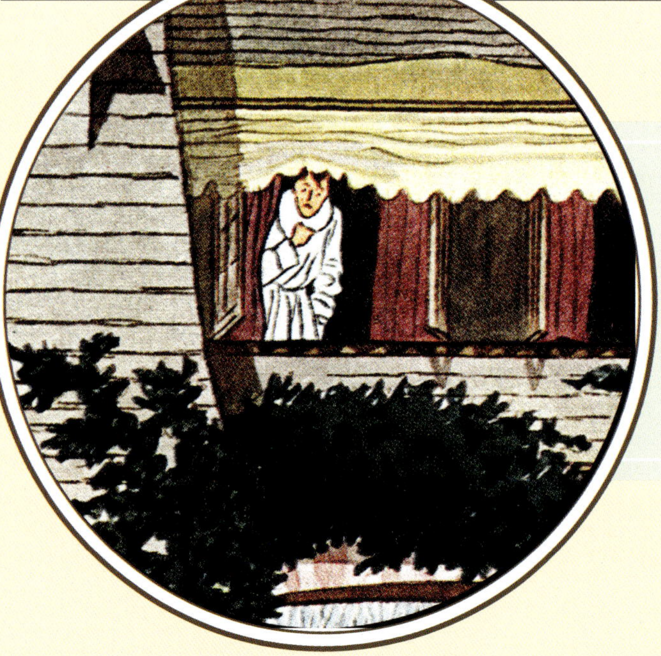

HARD HEAD!
Not all attention focused on the new Ford Town Sedan comes from ground level. This man must have just stepped out of the shower and thrown on his bathrobe. His eagerness to get a glimpse of the new Ford from the upstairs window doesn't seem to be diminished by the discomfort of having his head jammed up under the window awning.

FLAGSTONE SHOWOFF

This 1930 Town Sedan drawing is also found in magazine advertising produced outside of the United States.

A *"Flagstone Showoff"* Spanish-language ad edition for the *"El Neuvo Ford Town Sedan"* appeared in an Argentine magazine in May 1930.

Note that this Williamson Town Sedan drawing was slightly modified – by changing the position of the steering wheel. In this ad version, the steering wheel appears on the right-hand side of the Town Sedan in order to match other right-hand drive cars sold in Argentina.

Example ad from Argentina ➤
⊙ *El Suplemento,* May 1930

Nueva Belleza para el Nuevo Ford

EL NUEVO FORD
TOWN SEDAN

Nuevas y cómodas carrocerías...
Nuevas y armoniosas líneas...
Nuevos colores...
Nuevo radiador...
Nuevos paragolpes...
Nuevas ruedas...
Nuevo acero inoxidable...
Nueva tapicería...

Ahora, más que nunca, el Nuevo Ford representa un valor muy superior a su precio.

FORD MOTOR COMPANY

A somewhat modified version of this Williamson drawing also appeared in a magazine ad in Malaya a month later. This Dutch-language ad uses the same basic setting but adds a palm tree – along with changes in the building, the women admiring the car, and the butler standing in the doorway. The dog and the car's license plate have also been removed.

As with the Argentine *"Flagstone Showoff"* ad example, this ad edition also includes a right-hand drive steering wheel.

◀ **Example ad from Malaya**
● *unknown magazine,* June 20, 1930

SCHOONHEID
gepaard aan
WERKELIJKE WAARDE

DE STADS SEDAN
„Een Schoonheid"

Een heel gewone uitdrukking met een groote diepte van beteekenis.
De bewezen werkelijke waarde van het Model „A" wordt nog verhoogd door de prachtige nieuwe lijnen der carrosserieën en alle modellen.
De ondernemingsgeest van Ford heeft een automobiel geproduceerd, die de prima prestaties vereenigt met alle voorwaarden voor een gedistingeerd voorkomen, vroeger alleen maar mogelijk geacht in een automobiel van hoogen prijs.

Wanneer U de vlugge gratie ziet van deze nieuwe carrosserielijnen zult U beseffen dat een groote stap vooruit gedaan is in carrosserie ontwerpen, dat inderdaad opvallende schoonheid is toegevoegd aan werkelijke waarde.
Er is geen verandering gemaakt in de kwaliteit en de mechanische kenmerken, waardoor het Ford model „A" zich zulk een merkwaardigen naam heeft verven op het gebied van prestaties <eeo
Elke Fordhandelaar zal U gaarne een demonstratie geven.

510

FORD MOTOR COMPANY OF MALAYA, LIMITED, SINGAPORE, S.S.

BARNYARD ARRIVAL

◆

THE NEW FORD TOWN SEDAN

Quality that endures

THE extra value built into the new Ford car is reflected in its alert, capable performance, reliability and long life.

Beneath its flashing beauty of line and color, there is a mechanical excellence unusual in a low-priced car. Many measurements are accurate to the thousandth of an inch. Every part has been carefully designed and made to give you many thousands of miles of faithful, uninterrupted service.

In safety, comfort, speed, power, economy — in all that goes to make a good automobile — it is a value far above the price. The quality of the new Ford is a quality that endures.

A man, dressed in his Sunday best, presents his new Ford Town Sedan for his neighbors to see. He parks in their barnyard and heads to the barn. Two farm hands, wiping their hands and dropping their tools, advance to see the new car.

Version A (TnS 6a)

- ⊙ *Capper's Farmer,* April 1930, CII
- ○ *The Country Gentleman,* April 1930, p. 68
- ○ *Country Home,* April 1930, CII
- ⊙ *Southern Agriculturist,* April 5, 1930, CIV (B&W)
- ○ *Successful Farming,* April 1930, CIII

BARNYARD ARRIVAL

The second version (B) of this 1930 Town Sedan ad is identical to the first (A), except for the addition of the Ford logo. The text in both of these ad versions indicates that *"The extra value built into the new Ford is reflected in its alert, capable performance, reliability and long life."*

Version B (TnS 6b) ➤

⊙ *Farm and Ranch,* April 5, 1930, p. 13

○ *The Farmer's Wife,* June 1930, p. 14

The third *"Barnyard Arrival"* ad version (C) presents an *"Extra Value Without Extra Cost"* headline and a different text.

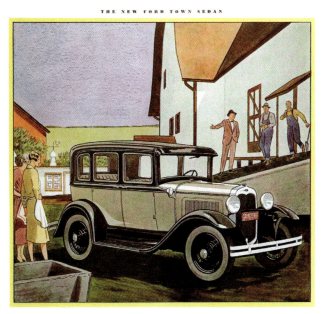

Delivering against the *"Extra Value Without Extra Cost"* headline, the text in the third version (C) of this Town Sedan ad proclaims that *"Because the Ford is made economically, distributed economically, serviced economically – and because it runs economically – it is a value far above the price you pay."*

◄ **Version C (TnS 6c)**

⊙ *Capper's Farmer,* May 1930, p. 53

In line with the farm setting illustration used in the *"Barnyard Arrival"* ad, all versions of this Town Sedan ad appeared only in farm-related magazines.

TUXEDO ADMIRERS

◆

Beauty of line and mechanical excellence

THE NEW FORD TOWN SEDAN

BEAUTY has been built into the graceful flowing lines of the new Ford and there is an appealing charm in its fresh and varied harmony of color. Yet more distinctive even than this beauty of line and color is its alert and sprightly performance. « « « « « « « « « « « « «

As days go by, you will find that it becomes more and more your favorite car to drive—so responsive, so easy to handle, so safe and comfortable that it puts a new joy in motoring. « « « « «

The city dweller—the farmer—the industrial worker—the owner of the spacious two-car garage in the suburbs—to all of these it brings a new measure of reliable, economical service. « « « «

Craftsmanship has been put into mass production. Today, more than ever, the new Ford is "a value far above the price." « « « « « « « « « « « « « «

A father and his son, dressed in tuxedos, leave the dinner party to stand on the veranda and admire a new Ford Town Sedan. Inside, beneath the chandelier, the waiter lights candles on the banquet tables. This Town Sedan ad appeared in all of the upscale magazines of the day.

Version A (TnS 7a)
⊙ *The American Boy,* May 1930, p. 29 (B&W)
⊙ *Collier's,* May 10 1930, CIII
◉ *Country Life,* May 1930, p. 110
◉ *Harper's Bazaar,* May 1930, p. 152
◉ *The Sportsman,* May 1930, p. 81
⊙ *Vanity Fair,* May 1930, p. 88+
◉ *Vogue,* May 10, 1930, p. 129

TUXEDO ADMIRERS

The only change in the second version (B) of the *"Tuxedo Admirers"* Town Sedan ad is a change in the text format and the addition of the Ford logo. Note that this identical ad appeared in *The State Trooper* in four separate, sequential issues in mid-1930.

Version B (TnS 7b) ➤

○ *The American Magazine,* June 1930, p. 109

○ *Cosmopolitan,* June 1930, p. 115

● *Junior League Magazine,* May 1930, p. 3 (B&W)

◉ *Liberty,* May 3, 1930, p. 15

◉ *The Redbook Magazine,* June 1930, p. 104

● *The State Trooper,* May, June, July and August, 1930, all p. 4 (B&W)

The two-page ad edition (C) features a secondary insert illustration of the new Ford Roadster.

Version C (TnS 7c) ⋁

◉ *The Literary Digest,* March 29, 1930, CF

◉ *The Saturday Evening Post,* April 19, 1930, pp. 96-97

GETTING DIRECTIONS

THE NEW FORD TOWN SEDAN

Blazing New Trails in a Ford

THE STURDINESS and reliability of the new Ford, so evident in the customary, every-day uses of a motor car, are revealed also in many unusual tests of stamina and endurance.

A little while ago a new Ford was driven to the top of the Dieng Plateau, one of the highest mountains in Java. Previously the ascent to the old Hindu statues at the summit had been made only by horseback to the rest-house, thence on foot.

Equally significant was the choice of the new Ford by the expedition organized to chart the route for a new continental road from California to Argentine. This was described by engineers familiar with the rough country and the almost impassable mountain trails as one of the most arduous trips ever undertaken by an automobile.

In England, Germany, France, Italy, Switzerland and Denmark —in Russia, South America and South Africa—the new Ford has won many contests for reliability and all-round good performance. Through desert sands and snow, over deeply rutted trails, it has gone forward to new conquests of time and distance.

The quality that has been built into every part of the car is the reason for its good performance under all conditions. Its reliability and economy mean a considerable saving each year in the cost of operation and up-keep.

Ford

The family is out for a drive in their new Ford Town Sedan and has stopped at the filling station so the husband can get directions – surely at the wife's insistence. Meanwhile, the wife and child wait in the car, which is loaded with luggage.

Version A (TnS 8a)

⊙ *The American Boy,* November 1930, p. 31 (B&W)
◯ *The Country Gentleman,* November 1930, p. 46
⊙ *Southern Agriculturist,* November 1, 1930, CIII (B&W)
⊙ *Farm and Ranch,* November 1, 1930, p, 13

GETTING DIRECTIONS

The second version (B) of this 1930 Town Sedan ad appeared only in smaller page size magazines and, in turn, uses a slightly shorter text. The third version (C) has a completely different text and a new *"You Save in Many Ways When You Buy a Ford"* headline.

Version B (TnS 8b) [text difference]
○ *The Country Home,* November 1930, CII
○ *Successful Farming,* November 1930, CII
● *The State Trooper,* November 1930, p. 2 (B&W)

The two-page ad edition (D) allows for a slightly larger illustration, showing more of the roof of the filling station.

Version D (TnS 8d) ▽
⊙ *The Literary Digest,* November 15, 1930, CF
⊙ *The Saturday Evening Post,* November 29, 1930, pp. 46-47

Version C (TnS 8c) ▽
⊙ *Collier's,* November 22, 1930, CIII
⊙ *Liberty,* November 15, 1930, p. 15

THE NEW FORD TOWN SEDAN

You save in many ways when you buy a Ford

SKI CHALET

◆

CRAFTSMANSHIP

in volume production

ONE of the outstanding features of the new Ford is the precise care with which each part is made and assembled. Many measurements are accurate to within one one-thousandth of an inch. Some to three ten-thousandths of an inch.

This craftsmanship in volume production is particularly apparent in the pistons, valves and crankshaft—the most important moving parts of an automobile engine.

To insure perfect fit in the cylinders, the aluminum pistons of the new Ford are held true to within one one-thousandth of an inch of the specified diameter of $3\frac{7}{8}$ inches. In weight they are not permitted to vary more than two grams (1/14 of an ounce). The wrist-pin holes are diamond bored within a variation of three ten-thousandths of an inch.

The Ford valves are made of chrome silicon alloy, selected because of its durability and resistance to the oxidizing effect of hot gases. The valve stems are held exact in diameter to one one-thousandth of an inch along their entire length. There is never a variation of more than two one-thousandths of an inch from the seat to the mushroom end.

Each half of the hole in the guide through which the valve

stem passes is made to limits of five ten-thousandths of an inch. This insures accurate centering of the valve and minimizes gas leakage and loss of compression. It also reduces carbon deposits which cause sticking.

The Ford crankshaft is made of carbon manganese steel and is machined to measurements as fine as five ten-thousandths of an inch. Ford crankshafts receive more than 150 gage tests for accuracy.

Great care is taken to insure the proper static and dynamic balance

of the crankshafts. The machines for the dynamic balance tests are set on rubber foundations and are so delicately adjusted that the very air which surrounds them is first cleansed and then held at 68° by thermostatic control.

This accuracy in manufacturing, combined with simplicity of design and high quality of materials, has a definite bearing on the good performance of the new Ford. It has been made for many months and years of satisfactory motoring.

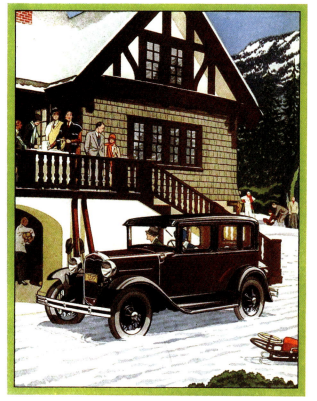

NEW FORD TOWN SEDAN

A beautiful family car, distinguished by the beauty of its appointments and upholstery. You may choose either Bedford cord or luxurious mohair. A choice of body colors is offered also. Other features of the new Ford Town Sedan are its fully enclosed four-wheel brakes, Triplex shatter-proof glass windshield, four Houdaille double-acting hydraulic shock absorbers, more than twenty ball and roller bearings, and the Rustless Steel used for the head lamps, radiator shell, cowl finish strip, hub caps, and other bright exterior metal parts. The first cost is low and the economy of operation and up-keep will save you many dollars each year.

Skiing activities are interrupted as lunch is served on the balcony of the ski chalet. However, many of those on the balcony seem to prefer to gaze at the new Ford Town Sedan passing below instead of enjoying their meal.

Version A (TnS 9a)
- ○ *The American Magazine,* February 1931, p. 117
- ○ *Cosmopolitan,* February 1931, p. 116
- ○ *The Country Home,* January 1931, p. 27
- ○ *The Farm Journal,* January 1931, p. 17
- ◉ *The Redbook Magazine,* February 1931, CIII
- ○ *Successful Farming,* January 1931, CII

SKI CHALET

The second version (B) of this 1931 Ford Town Sedan ad includes an expanded text and an insert illustration of the Johansson Gage Blocks used for precision in manufacturing.

Version B (TnS 9b) ➤

- ◉ *The American Boy,* January 1931, CII
- ◉ *Capper's Farmer,* January 1931, CII
- ○ *The Country Gentleman,* January 1931, p. 39

The third version (C) is a two-page edition using the same insert illustration and ad text.

Version C (TnS 9c) ▽

- ◉ *The Saturday Evening Post,* December 27, 1930, pp. 54-55

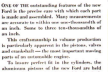

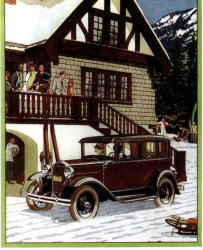

DOCTOR'S HOUSE CALL

When winter sweeps down from the North

THROUGHOUT this country — in Canada and in Europe — the new Ford has made an unusual record for endurance and reliability. Cold weather emphasizes the value of its simplicity of design and dependable performance under all conditions.

The 1930 Automobile Winter Race, arranged by the Royal Automobile Club of Sweden, resulted in a sweeping victory for the Ford cars. This run was made over slippery mountainous roads. At times, the cars were half hidden by snow. During the night the temperature was twenty degrees below zero.

At Fernan Lake, Idaho, a Ford car went through the ice and was submerged in fifteen feet of water. It was finally raised after twelve days and found to be in good condition. After a new battery and carburetor bowl were installed it was driven away under its own power. Even the exterior finish showed no serious harm.

There have been countless other examples of the way the new Ford stands up under the added stress and strain of winter driving.

Through swirling sleet and drifting snow it has fought its way on missions of business and of urgent need. Lives have been saved by its ability to "get through." Men, mails and materials have been moved with greater speed and with less interruption for a longer period each year. Thousands upon thousands of Ford owners have found that it is no longer necessary to lay up the car in idleness when winter sweeps down from the north.

The beautiful new Ford Town Sedan is richly finished and upholstered. You may purchase it on convenient terms through the Authorized Ford Finance Plans of the Universal Credit Company

It's a cold winter's night and a Ford Town Sedan has fought through the snow so the doctor can make a house call. The man answering the door in his robe looks a little "under the weather" as he shudders against the cold wind.

Version A (TnS 10a)

⊙ *Collier's,* January 17, 1931, CIII

⊙ *Liberty,* February 21, 1931, p. 15

This 1930 Town Sedan ad appears in both a one-page and two-page format.

DOCTOR'S HOUSE CALL

The two-page edition (B) of this Model A ad retains the same headline and Town Sedan illustration but adds a smaller insert illustration of a Ford Coupe, also drawn in a snow setting.

Version B (TnS 10b) ∨
⊙ *The Literary Digest,* January 24, 1931, pp. 22-23
⊙ *The Saturday Evening Post,* January 17, 1931, pp. 56-57

When winter sweeps down from the North

It's assumed that the individual half-way up the telephone pole in the smaller Ford Coupe insert illustration is not also a physician, but a (rather cold) telephone line repairman.

DOC I.D.
The Ford Town Sedan drawn in this *"Doctor's House Call"* magazine ad displays a radiator badge identifying its driver as a physician. (Also note that the doctor carries his physician's case as he goes to the patient's aid.)

LADIES' SOCIAL

◆

For Greater Safety on Every Highway

EVERY FORD CAR IS EQUIPPED WITH A SHATTER-PROOF GLASS WINDSHIELD

FOR greater safety in driving, every Ford car is equipped with a Triplex shatter-proof glass windshield. By reducing the dangers of flying glass it has saved many lives and prevented injuries in accidents.

The value of this important safety factor has been known for years, but its use has been limited by expense. It is brought to you on the Ford as standard equipment only because of the efficiency and economy of Ford methods. Much pioneering work has been done in finding ways to manufacture in large volume at low cost.

It is interesting to know how the Triplex shatter-proof glass wind-shield of the Ford is made and why it gives so much extra protection.

Two pieces of plate glass, carefully ground and polished, are covered on one side with a thin coating of gelatine. This coating is baked hard, sprayed with liquid celluloid and treated with a solvent.

Then, between the two pieces of glass, like the middle of a sandwich, is inserted a layer of special celluloid. This also has been treated with a solvent.

When heat and pressure are applied to the glass sandwich, this solvent helps to dissolve the surfaces in contact and they are actually fused together. The final operation is sealing the edges for protection against air and moisture.

This laminated windshield will withstand a 50% harder impact before breaking than plate glass of equal thickness, and is more flexible under impact. When struck an unusually hard blow it will crack, but the danger from flying glass is minimized because the pieces adhere to the layer of celluloid.

High speed and crowded traffic make Triplex shatter-proof glass one of the greatest contributions to safety since four-wheel brakes.

No Flying Glass Here

A woman and three children were in this Ford when a passing car upturned a horse-shoe and sent it crashing into the windshield. No one was hurt because of the shatter-proof windshield. The glass did not fly.

Thirteen Million Square Feet of Glass

The Ford Motor Company was the pioneer in making glass by a continuous machine process. Its unusual manufacturing facilities make it possible to give you a Triplex shatter-proof glass windshield on the Ford without extra cost. The Rouge plant alone has a capacity of 13,000,000 square feet of glass annually. This calls for a consumption of 27,300,000 pounds of silica sand, 8,580,000 pounds of soda ash, 7,930,000 pounds of limestone, 1,820,000 pounds of salt cake, 6,136,000 pounds of cullet, 78,000 pounds of charcoal, and 156,000 pounds of arsenic.

The beautiful new Ford Town Sedan is a striking example of value far above the price. The first cost is low and you can purchase for a small down payment on convenient, economical terms, through the Authorized Ford Finance Plans of the Universal Credit Company.

A woman, assisting with the *"Ladies' Auxiliary Social and Sale,"* has arrived in her new Ford slant-windshield Town Sedan. With supplies in hand and a prominent parking space, she must be on the committee responsible for the event.

Version A (TnS 11a)

○ *The Country Home,* June 1931, CIII

○ *Successful Farming,* June 1931, CII

○ *The Farm Journal,* June 1931, p. 19

LADIES' SOCIAL

Two additional versions (B and C) of the 1931 *"Ladies' Social"* magazine ad for the Town Sedan were produced.

Each of these ad versions retains the same Town Sedan illustration, insert illustrations and headline. However, minor text differences exist in both of these ad versions.

Versions B (TnS 11b) [text difference]
⊙ *Capper's Farmer,* June 1931, p. 14
○ *The Country Gentleman,* June 1931, p. 51

Version C (TnS 11c) [text difference]
○ *The Farmer's Wife,* June 1931, CII

This Town Sedan ad appeared only in June 1931 in farm-related magazines.

Along with several other Model A magazine ads, the three *"Ladies' Social"* ads for the Town Sedan each contain a small brown-tone insert illustration of a horseshoe embedded in the windshield of a Model A.

Using somewhat of a "scare tactic" approach, the text below the obviously alarming photograph of the horseshoe sticking out of the windshield indicates:

"A woman and three children were in this Ford when a passing car upturned a horse shoe in the road and sent it crashing into the windshield. No one was hurt because of the shatter-proof windshield. This glass did not fly."

The entire text of the *"Ladies' Social"* ads deals with the Ford Triplex shatter-proof windshield and begins with:

"For greater safety in driving, every Ford car is equipped with a Triplex shatter-proof glass windshield. By reducing the dangers of flying glass, it has saved many lives and prevented injuries in automobile accidents."

"The value of this important safety factor has been known for years, but its use has been limited by expense. It is brought to you on the Ford as standard equipment only because of the efficiency and economy of Ford methods."

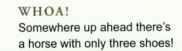

WHOA!
Somewhere up ahead there's
a horse with only three shoes!

No Flying Glass Here

YACHT DOCK

◆

JUNE 1931

For Greater Safety on Every Highway

THE NEW FORD TOWN SEDAN

EVERY FORD CAR IS EQUIPPED WITH A SHATTER-PROOF GLASS WINDSHIELD

FOR greater safety in driving, every Ford car is equipped with a Triplex shatter-proof glass windshield. By reducing the dangers of flying glass, it has saved many lives and prevented injuries in automobile accidents.

The value of this important safety factor has been known for years, but its use has been limited by expense. It is brought to you on the Ford as standard equipment only because of the efficiency and economy of Ford methods. Much pioneering work has been done to find ways to manufacture in large volume at low cost.

It is interesting to know how the Triplex shatter-proof glass windshield of the Ford

is made and why it gives so much extra protection.

Two pieces of plate glass, carefully ground and polished, are covered on one side with a thin coating of gelatine. This coating is baked hard, sprayed with liquid celluloid and treated with a solvent.

Then, between the two pieces of glass, like the middle of a sandwich, is inserted a layer of special celluloid. This also has been treated with a solvent.

When heat and pressure are applied to the glass sandwich, this solvent helps to dissolve the surfaces in contact and they are actually fused together. The final operation is sealing the

edges as protection against air and moisture. This laminated windshield will withstand a 50% harder impact before breaking than plate glass of equal thickness, and is more flexible under impact.

When struck an unusually hard blow it will crack, but the danger from flying glass is minimized because the pieces adhere to the layer of celluloid. Many improvements in methods and material have been made in the past three years.

Today, the Triplex shatter-proof plate glass windshield of the Ford is recognized as one of the greatest contributions to safety since the introduction of four-wheel brakes.

Ford

Two ladies are parking their new Ford slant-windshield Town Sedan at the boat dock as the boat captain barks orders to his crew. Both women seem quite engrossed with the three well-tanned sailors as they work with the sails on the yacht.

Version A (TnS 12a)

◉ *Country Life,* June 1931, p. 94

◉ *Harper's Bazaar,* June 1931, p. 137

◉ *The Sportsman,* June 1931, p. 71

◉ *Vanity Fair,* June 1931

◉ *Vogue,* June 15, 1931

YACHT DOCK

Eight additional versions of the Town Sedan *"Yacht Dock"* ad were produced.

While the second version (B) of this 1931 Town Sedan ad adds two smaller insert illustrations, the third edition (C) has only a minor ad text change.

Version B (TnS 12b) ➤

○ *Good Housekeeping,* June 1931, p. 165
◉ *Holland's,* June 1931, p. 28
○ *Woman's World,* June 1931, CIII

Version C (TnS 12c) [text difference]

◉ *Life,* May 1931, CII

For Greater Safety on Every Highway

EVERY FORD CAR IS EQUIPPED WITH A SHATTER-PROOF GLASS WINDSHIELD

EVERY WOMAN who drives a car will be interested in knowing that the windshield of the Ford is made of Triplex shatter-proof glass. By reducing the dangers of flying glass it has saved many lives and prevented countless injuries in automobile accidents.

The value of this important safety factor has been known for years, but its use on automobiles has been limited by expense. It is brought to you on the Ford as standard equipment only because of the efficiency and economy of Ford methods. Much pioneering work has been done in finding ways to manufacture in large volume at low cost. The Triplex shatter-proof windshield of the Ford is beautifully clear and looks like one piece of glass. Yet it is really two. Between the two pieces of fine plate glass, like the middle of a sandwich, is inserted a layer of special celluloid.

You can't see it, but it means a great deal to your security in driving. The Ford windshield will withstand a 50% harder impact before breaking than plate glass of equal thickness. When struck an unusually heavy blow it will crack, but the danger of flying glass is minimized because the pieces adhere to the layer of celluloid.

Because of the extra protection it affords, the Triplex shatter-proof glass windshield of the Ford is recognized as one of the greatest contributions to safety since the introduction of four-wheel brakes. High speed and crowded traffic emphasize its need and value — particularly where there are women and children.

No Flying Glass Here

A woman and three children were in this Ford when a passing car ruptured a horse-shoe in the road and sent it crashing into the windshield. No one was hurt because there was no flying glass.

13,000,000 Square Feet of Glass

The Ford Motor Company was the pioneer in making glass in a continuous machine process. Its manufacturing economies and unusual facilities make it possible to give you a Triplex shatter-proof glass windshield on the Ford without increasing the price of the car. The Rouge plant alone has a capacity of 13,000,000 square feet of glass annually. This calls for 22,100,000 pounds of silica sand, 8,580,000 pounds of soda ash, 7,950,000 pounds of limestone, 1,820,000 pounds of salt cake, 6,136,000 pounds of cullet, 70,000 pounds of charcoal, and 156,000 pounds of arsenic. For grinding and polishing, the machines use 118,190,000 pounds of sand, 2,274,000 pounds of rouge, 2,715,000 pounds of garnet, and 223,000 pounds of rouge.

The beautiful new Ford Town Sedan is distinguished by the richness of its upholstery and appointments. The first cost is low and you can purchase it for a small down payment, on convenient, economical terms, through the Authorized Ford Finance Plans of the Universal Credit Company.

The fourth version (D) employs a new headline and completely different ad text.

With a *"The Beautiful Finish of the Ford is Made to Last"* headline, the fourth version (D) of this 1931 Town Sedan ad does not contain the two smaller insert illustrations present in the earlier editions.

◄ Version D (TnS 12d)

◉ *Collier's,* June 6, 1931, CIII
◉ *Delineator,* July 1931, p. 58
○ *McCall's,* July 1931, p. 44
◉ *The Redbook Magazine,* July 1931, CII
○ *Successful Farming,* July 1931, CIII

THE Beautiful Finish of the Ford IS Made to Last

Many coats are used to give a mirror-like sheen to Ford bodies. Rustless Steel is another reason for enduring beauty

WHEN you buy the Ford you buy enduring beauty.

As you drive it from the showrooms for the first time you will have a feeling of pride in the glistening sheen of its body finish and the bright silvery luster of its exposed metal parts. With reasonable care you can maintain that good appearance for a long period.

Months of constant service will put many thousands of miles on the speedometer, yet you will not think of it as an old car, nor will your friends. And when the time comes to trade it in, you will find that the lasting beauty of its finish is a factor in re-sale value.

There are definite reasons why time and weather are kind to the Ford car. First is the body finish, with its primer coat, two surfacer coats, two double coats of pyroxylin lacquer, finish solvent coat, polishing and buffing. Through long experience, the Ford Motor Company has found the way to make a body finish that will stand up under varying weather conditions in every part of the world—through the heat of summer and the cold of winter.

Another important reason for the enduring beauty of the Ford is the use of Rustless Steel for the radiator shell, head lamps, hub caps, cowl finish strip, gasoline tank cap, radiator cap, door handles and rear lamp.

This remarkable metal will not rust, corrode or tarnish under the severest weather conditions. It never needs polishing. All it requires is wiping with a damp cloth as you wipe the windshield. Its gleaming luster is never lost. There is no plate to scale or chip off because it is the same bright metal all the way through. And it is exceptionally difficult to dent because it has twice the strength of ordinary steel.

A Beautiful New Ford Body

From all over the country come enthusiastic comments about the new Ford Town Sedan introduced but a few weeks ago. Motorists everywhere have been quick to note and appreciate the richness of its appointments and new features of comfort and convenience.

The body of the new Ford Town Sedan is longer and wider. Seats are newly designed, more luxurious and restful. Front or rear—wherever you ride—you travel in real comfort in this beautiful, roomy car.

Ease of entering and riding is another outstanding example of high quality at low cost. A choice of upholstery and body colors is offered.

Before Rustless Steel was adopted by the Ford Motor Company it was put through many severe tests. In one test, samples were subjected to a salt spray for four hundred hours, or the equivalent of forty years' service. There was not the slightest suggestion of tarnish, rust or corrosion. Seventy-six acids, alkalis, etc., likewise failed to dim its brilliance.

In a further effort to prevent rust, the Ford Motor Company is now treating the wheels, fenders, running boards, running board shields and front splash pans with Bonderite before they are enameled. If the enamel is scratched this new treatment will help to stop rust from spreading and causing the enamel to peel.

The careful finish of the Ford, the Rustless Steel, and the Bonderizing process add a considerable amount to the cost of manufacturing, yet the cost of the car itself remains low. These outstanding features, like so many others, are made possible by the Ford low-profit policy. Every purchaser shares the benefits of large production and the efficiency and economy of Ford methods. The first cost of the Ford is low and you can purchase on convenient, economical terms through the Authorized Ford Finance Plans of the Universal Credit Company.

YACHT DOCK

The fifth version (E) of this 1931 Town Sedan ad introduces a drawing of a Model A car front end as an insert illustration and retains *"The Beautiful Finish of the Ford is Made to Last"* headline. The ad text explains the benefits of using *"Rustless Steel"* and *"Bonderite."*

> ### Version E (TnS 12e) ➤
> ⊙ *Capper's Farmer,* July 1931, CIII

The sixth ad version (F, not shown) retains the Model A front end insert illustration, but changes to a *"The Beauty of the Ford is an Enduring Beauty"* headline and has minor text changes.

> ### Version F (TnS 12f)
> **[headline and text differences]**
> ○ *Ladies' Home Journal,* July 1931, p. 44
> ○ *The Literary Digest,* May 16, 1931, CII

The seventh version (G) of this 1930 Town Sedan magazine ad uses the same *"The Beauty of the Ford is an Enduring Beauty"* headline (but printed in a different format) and drops the Model A front end insert illustration.

> ### ◄ Version G (TnS 12g)
> ○ *The American Magazine,* June 1931, p. 83
> ○ *The Country Gentleman,* July 1931, CIV
> ○ *The Saturday Evening Post,* June 20, 1931, p. 41

YACHT DOCK

The eighth version (H) of this 1930 Town Sedan ad is a black and white edition that retains the same headline and, at first glance, uses the same drawing of the *"Yacht Dock"* scene.

However, a closer look reveals many minor differences in the illustration: the three sailors (and the sail itself) have disappeared, the signage on the building has changed, fewer houses now appear on the hill and a different license plate is on the Town Sedan.

Version H (TnS 12h) ➤
◉ *Southern Agriculturist,* June 1, 1931, p. 17

THE **Beauty of the Ford is an Enduring Beauty**

Good appearance of the Ford over a long period increases your pride of ownership and is a factor in re-sale value

A Beautiful New Ford Body

The last *"Yacht Dock"* ad version (I) employs a unique *"Interesting Things for You to Know"* headline and includes several smaller insert illustrations. This Town Sedan ad, which appeared only in *The American Boy*, attempts to educate its youthful readers on a wide variety of topics. These include: how cement is made from slag, what a distributor does, accuracy in manufacturing and where the first Ford was made.

This ad also includes a signed statement by Henry Ford indicating *"This is a great time to be young."*

◀ **Version I (TnS 12i)**
◉ *The American Boy,* July 1931, CII

239

TOWN SEDAN

FRAMED TOWN SEDAN

"More *genuine satisfaction* than any car I ever owned"

THE FORD TOWN SEDAN

THE FORD is good-looking. It is safe. Comfortable. Speedy. Reliable. Long lived. Economical. Everything a good car should be.

There is, too, an added something about it that brings enthusiastic comments from every one who has ever driven a Ford . . . the joy it puts in motoring.

"I have been a car owner continuously for nearly 20 years," writes a motorist connected with a leading university. "During this period I have bought eleven new automobiles. Eight of the eleven were in the middle-price field, one cost three thousand dollars, and the last is a Ford that I purchased thirteen months ago.

"In the light of this experience I can say in all sincerity that I have derived more genuine satisfaction from the Ford than any car I ever owned. In saying this, I am thinking in terms of comfort, safety, driving pleasure, ease of control and economy. My next car will also be a Ford because it will give me what I want at a price I can afford to pay."

When you get behind the wheel of the Ford and drive it yourself you will know it is a truly remarkable car at a low price. You will like it when you first buy it. You will become more and more enthusiastic the longer you drive it. See the nearest dealer for a demonstration.

FORD MOTOR COMPANY

PRINTED IN U. S. A.
THE INLAND PRESS, DETROIT

This straightforward Model A Ford Town Sedan ad shows the car in a frame with no background illustration. The text provides a testimonial from a satisfied Ford owner, indicating that *"my next car will also be a Ford."*

240

Version A (TnS 13a)
● *The State Trooper,* November, 1931, CIV

With a date of November 1931, this is one of the latest magazine ads for a Model A passenger car.

THREE-WINDOW FORDOR SEDAN

	TOTAL	1929	1930	1931
Ford Body Style		165-A 165-B	165-C 165-D	165-C 165-D
Weight (pounds)		2,462	2,500	2,462
Price (FOB Detroit)		$650	$625	$590
Units Produced (U.S.)	113,201	53,941	41,133	18,127
Number of U.S. Ads				
Primary Formats	3	–	2	1
Ad Variations	10	–	8	2
Magazine Insertions	53	–	48	5

While sometimes referred to simply as the Model A Ford "Standard Sedan," this body style was called the "Three-Window Fordor Sedan" in Ford advertising. The Three-Window Fordor Sedan was, basically, the Town Sedan body style without cowl lights and the upgraded interior. Two manufacturers supplied bodies for the Model A Three-Window Fordor Sedan – Murray (165-A and 165-C) and Briggs (165-B and 165-D). There were some minor appearance differences between these two manufactures' bodies – with the most noticeable being the side window treatments. The Briggs bodies had a square window shape, while the Murray bodies had a slightly arched window appearance.

The Model A Three-Window Fordor Sedan was first available in 1929. However, magazine ads did not appear for this body style until mid-1930. Only three primary ads were created for the Three-Window Fordor Sedan – although different versions of the two 1930 ads appeared in almost all magazines used by Ford to advertise the Model A.

MOUNTAIN LODGE

◆

THE NEW THREE-WINDOW FORDOR SEDAN

Wherever the long trail leads

THROUGH heavy city traffic — across fertile valleys and desert sands — to the top of snow-capped mountains — wherever the long trail leads — you will find the Ford car and cheery words about it. . . . Its flashing beauty gives it distinction at the Country Club, yet it is no stranger to deeply rutted roads and hard daily usage in the far-off places. Its sturdy strength, reliability and capable performance, at all times and under all conditions, reflect the care and enduring quality that have been built into it. . . . By its constant, faithful service through many months and years you will know that it is a "value far above the price."

September 1930 Good Housekeeping

Having arrived in their new Ford Three-Window Fordor Sedan, two women welcome their friends on the stairs of the mountain lodge.

○ *The American Magazine,* July 1930, p. 109
○ *Cosmopolitan,* July 1930, p. 131
○ *The Country Home,* August 1930, CII

Version A (TWS 1a)
○ *Good Housekeeping,* September 1930, p. 112
◉ *Liberty,* July 26, 1930, CIII
◉ *The Redbook Magazine,* July 1930, CII
○ *Successful Farming,* August 1930, CIII
◉ *True Story,* September 1930

MOUNTIAN LODGE

The second version (B) of this Three-Window Fordor Sedan
magazine ad displays the text in the corner of the illustration.

Version B (TWS 1b) ➤

◉ *The American Boy,* July 1930, p. 27 (B&W)

◉ *Capper's Farmer,* August 1930, CIII

◉ *Collier's,* July 5, 1930, CIII

○ *The Country Gentleman,* August 1930, p. 58

◉ *Country Life,* July 1930, CII

◉ *Delineator,* September 1930, p. 61

◉ *Farm and Ranch,* August 2, 1930, p. 13

○ *The Farmers Wife,* September 1930, p. 17

◉ *Harper's Bazaar,* July 1930, p. 120+

○ *Ladies' Home Journal,* September 1930, p. 73

○ *McCall's,* September 1930, p. 85

◉ *Pictorial Review,* September 1930, CIII

◉ *Southern Agriculturist,* August 15, 1930 CIII (B&W)

◉ *The Sportsman,* July 1930, p. 75

◉ *Vogue,* July 5, 1930, p. 17

○ *Woman's Home Companion,* September 1930, p. 56

The third version (C) is a two-page edition and includes
a small drawing of the new Ford Coupe.

Version C (TWS 1c) ⋁

◉ *The Literary Digest,* July 26, 1930, CF

◉ *The Saturday Evening Post,* July 12, 1930, pp. 58-59

HALLOWEEN PARTY

◆

Colors That Match the Season's Mode

The New Three-Window Fordor Sedan

AMONG the features of the Ford car is the privilege of selecting from a variety of beautiful colors. These colors are rich in tone and are changed at frequent intervals, in keeping with the season's mode. Frequently you will find that one of Fashion's newest shades, or a harmonious blending of it, is available also in the Ford car. With reasonable care, the smooth, gleaming finish of the Ford car as it comes fresh from the showrooms may be maintained for a long period. The pyroxylin lacquer is not affected by heat or cold and is easily polished to a shimmering luster. The Rustless Steel used for the radiator shell, hub caps, cowl finish strip and other exterior metal parts is an additional assurance of permanent beauty. Throughout the life of the car it will not scale, tarnish or corrode.

The neighborhood Halloween party is in full swing. One group of party-goers has parked their new Three-Window Fordor Sedan between two jack-o-lanterns. The costumed merrymakers can be seen through the windows of the house.

Version A (TWS 2a)

⊙ *Delineator,* November 1930, p. 71

○ *The Farmer's Wife,* November 1930, CIII

○ *Ladies' Home Journal,* November 1930, p. 64

○ *McCall's,* November 1930, p. 74

⊙ *Pictorial Review,* November 1930, pg. 74

○ *Woman's Home Companion,* November 1930, p. 53

HALLOWEEN PARTY

Four additional versions of the 1930 *"Halloween Party"* ad were produced.

While using the same headline and text, the second version (B) of this Three-Window Fordor Sedan ad has the text appearing above the illustration.

> **Version B** (TWS 2b) ➤
> ○ *Good Housekeeping,* November 1930, p. 98
> ◉ *True Story,* November 1930, p. 57

The third version (C) utilizes a different text and a new headline – *"The Same Good Car Through Many Seasons."*

Colors That Match the Season's Mode

AMONG the features of the Ford car is the privilege of selecting from a variety of beautiful colors. These colors are rich in tone and are changed at frequent intervals, in keeping with the season's mode. Frequently you will find that one of Fashion's newest shades, or a harmonious blending of it, is available also in the Ford car.

With reasonable care, the smooth, gleaming finish of the Ford car as it comes fresh from the showrooms may be maintained for a long period. The pyroxylin lacquer is not affected by heat or cold and is easily polished to a shimmering luster. The Rustless Steel used for the radiator shell, hub caps, cowl finish strip and other exterior metal parts is an additional assurance of enduring worth and permanent beauty. Throughout the life of the car it will not scale, tarnish or corrode.

November 1930 Good Housekeeping   THE NEW THREE-WINDOW FORDOR SEDAN

The Same Good Car Through Many Seasons

AT THIS SEASON of the year, as autumn prepares to bid adieu, it is good to know that the new Ford is fully prepared to meet the sterner needs of winter driving.

Cold weather emphasizes the value of its simplicity of design and its trustworthy performance under all conditions. There is an enduring quality, too, in its exterior finish. The pyroxylin lacquer is not affected by cold, or the usual hazards of snow or water. The Rustless Steel used for the radiator shell, hub caps, cowl finish strip, and other exterior metal parts is an additional assurance of permanent beauty. It will not scale, tarnish, or corrode.

With reasonable care the new Ford will maintain its original sheen and brilliance for a long period. Mechanically it has been so excellently made that it will give you many thousands of miles of comfortable, satisfactory motoring at a very low cost per mile.

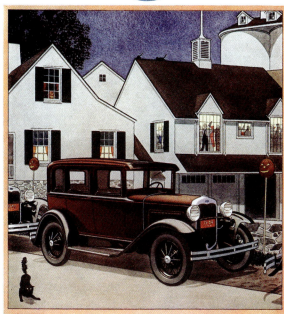

THE NEW THREE-WINDOW FORDOR SEDAN

In line with the ad's headline, the text within the third *"Halloween Party"* ad version (C) indicates that *"the new Ford is fully prepared to meet the sterner needs of winter driving."*

> ◄ **Version C** (TWS 2c)
> ○ *The American Magazine,* November 1930, p. 105
> ○ *Cosmopolitan,* November 1930, p. 117
> ○ *The Country Home,* October 1930, p. 28
> ◉ *Liberty,* October 18, 1930, p. 19
> ◉ *The Redbook Magazine,* November 1930, p. 91
> ○ *Successful Farming,* October 1930, CII

HALLOWEEN PARTY

The fourth *"Halloween Party"* ad version (D), which appeared only in larger format magazines, has the same ad text and headline — but with the text appearing below the illustration.

Version D (TWS 2d) ➤
- ⊙ *The American Boy,* October 1930, p. 31 (B&W)
- ⊙ *Capper's Farmer,* October 1930, p. 29
- ⊙ *Collier's,* October 25, 1930, CIII
- ○ *The Country Gentleman,* October 1930, p. 131
- ⊙ *Farm and Ranch,* October 4, 1930, p. 13
- ⊙ *Southern Agriculturist,* October 1, 1930, p. 4 (B&W)

The two-page ad edition (E) has text changes but retains the same headline. This ad version includes smaller insert illustrations of four additional new Ford body styles.

Version E (TWS 2e) ⋁
- ⊙ *The Literary Digest,* October 18, 1930, CF
- ⊙ *The Saturday Evening Post,* November 1, 1930, pp. 56-57

The Same Good Car Through Many Seasons

THE NEW THREE-WINDOW FORDOR SEDAN

AT THIS SEASON of the year, as autumn prepares to bid adieu, it is good to know that the new Ford is fully prepared to meet the sterner needs of winter driving. . . . Cold weather emphasizes the value of its simplicity of design and its trustworthy performance under all conditions. There is an enduring quality, too, in its exterior finish.

The pyroxylin lacquer is not affected by cold, or the usual hazards of snow or water. The Rustless Steel used for the radiator shell, hub caps, cowl finish strip, and other exterior metal parts is an additional assurance of permanent beauty. . . . With reasonable care the new Ford will maintain its original sheen and brilliance for a long period. Mechanically it has been made to give you many thousands of miles of comfortable, satisfactory motoring at a very low cost per mile.

56   THE SATURDAY EVENING POST   November 1, 1930   THE SATURDAY EVENING POST   57

The Same Good Car Through Many Seasons

AT THIS SEASON of the year, as autumn prepares to bid adieu, it is good to know that the new Ford is fully prepared to meet the sterner needs of winter driving.

Cold weather emphasizes the value of its simplicity of design and its dependable performance under all conditions. There is an enduring quality, too, in its exterior finish.

The pyroxylin lacquer is not affected by cold, or the usual hazards of snow or water. The Rustless Steel used for the radiator shell, hub caps, cowl finish strip, and other exterior metal parts is an additional assurance of permanent beauty.

The fabrics used for trimming the interior of the new Ford are selected both for appearance and durability. Unusual care is taken to maintain their high quality.

Laboratory tests are constantly being made for weight, the character of the cloth, and the grade of the yarns used in these fabrics and trims. There are also numerous daily tests of the dyes, the count in the warp and woof,

the percentage of wool, and a rubbing test equivalent to years of actual wear.

The interiors of the Town Sedan, De Luxe Sedan and De Luxe Coupe are examples of this craftsmanship in manufacture. In these body types you may choose either tan Bedford cord, made of fine wool worsted, or brown mohair. Though soft and luxurious, this mohair will not crush easily and is long wearing because it is faced with genuine Angora mohair and wool worsted.

The Ford Motor Company purchases millions of yards of upholstery material yearly and is therefore enabled to give you exceptionally high quality without increasing the price of the car.

With reasonable care the new Ford will maintain its original sheen and brilliance for a long period of time. Mechanically it has been made to give you many thousands of miles of comfortable, satisfactory motoring at a very low cost per mile.

FORD MOTOR COMPANY

THE NEW THREE-WINDOW FORDOR SEDAN

THE NEW FORD ROADSTER   THE NEW FORD COUPE   THE NEW FORD TUDOR SEDAN   THE NEW FORD DE LUXE SEDAN

CHURCH CARPORT

THE NEW THREE-WINDOW FORDOR SEDAN

The Ford is the Universal Car

IN CITY, town and country, the new Ford is helping to shorten the miles and extend the limits of opportunity for millions of people.

It brings the open fields closer to the city and removes the isolation of rural districts. Daily it carries great numbers of men to work and home again, takes children safely to school and lightens the duties of women everywhere. Thousands of salesmen use it to cover larger territories and render better service to their customers and the companies for which they work.

Where heavy storms break down the wires, the Ford fights its way through mud and snow and enables linemen to make quick repairs, so that the business of the nation may go on. While you sleep, the new Ford delivers the necessities of life to countless homes, and speeds a physician on a hurried call.

Policemen use it for greater protection to widening areas.

Wherever there is movement of men and materials, you will find the Ford is an accepted part of the program of the day because of its low first cost, good performance and economy of operation and up-keep. You may purchase it on convenient, economical terms through the Authorized Ford Finance Plans of the Universal Credit Company.

Everyone is gathering at the church for the hay ride and the new Three-Window Fordor Sedan has been parked next to a Ford Sport Coupe. A woman, with her thermos bottle and picnic basket in hand, is preparing to join the fun.

Version A (TWS 3a)
O *The Country Home,* February 1931, CII
O *The Farm Journal,* February 1931, p. 17
O *Successful Farming,* February 1931, CIII

CHURCH CARPORT

A thin crescent moon peeks through the bare trees above the sleigh in this Ford Three-Window Fordor Sedan magazine ad.

A second version (B) of this Model A ad retains the same illustration and headline – but includes a minor text variation and adds the Ford oval logo.

> **Version B** **(TWS 3b)** ➤
> ⊙ *Capper's Farmer,* February 1931, CII
> ○ *The Country Gentleman,* February 1931, p. 44

In keeping with *The Ford is the "Universal Car"* headline, the text in this magazine ad proclaims:

"In city, town and country, the new Ford is helping to shorten the miles and extend the limits of opportunity for millions of people."

44   THE COUNTRY GENTLEMAN   February, 1931

THE NEW THREE-WINDOW FORDOR SEDAN

**The Ford is
The Universal Car**

In city, town and country, the new Ford is helping to shorten the miles and extend the limits of opportunity for millions of people.

It brings the open fields closer to the city and removes the isolation of rural districts. Daily it carries great numbers of men to work and home again, takes children safely to school and lightens the duties of women everywhere. Thousands of salesmen use it to cover larger territories and thereby render better service to their customers and the companies for which they work. Where heavy storms break down the wires, the Ford fights its way through mud and snow and enables linemen to make quick repairs, so that the business of the nation may go on. While you sleep, the Ford delivers the necessities of life to countless homes, and speeds a physician on a hurried call. Along darkened highways, policemen use its alert speed and reliability for greater protection to widening areas.

Wherever there is movement of men and materials, you will find the new Ford is an accepted part of the program of the day because of its low first cost, good performance and economy of operation. You may purchase it on convenient, economical terms through the Authorized Ford Finance Plans of the Universal Credit Company.

The *"Universal Car"* headline used in these 1931 Ford magazine ads is an advertising theme used frequently in earlier Model T Ford advertising efforts.

DEEP HAY!
At the front door of the church, the pastor in his black hat observes as some of the children are already boarding the sleigh. The hay is so deep on the sleigh that only the hats of several of the children can be seen.

STANDARD SEDAN

◆

	TOTAL (1931)
Ford Body Style	160-A
Weight (pounds)	2,462
Price (FOB Detroit)	$590
Units Produced (U.S.)	NA
Number of U.S. Ads	
Primary Formats	3
Ad Variations	3
Magazine Insertions	10

The word "standard" is often used in describing Model A Ford body styles – especially in differentiating standard versus deluxe models. However, the "standard" designation was not used by The Ford Motor Company in advertising specific Model A body styles. The single exception was in referencing a low-production, late 1931 Model A body type – the Standard Sedan (160-A).

The Model A Ford Standard Sedan, first available in July 1931, was the slant-windshield edition of the Three-Window Fordor Sedan. A more deluxe version of this basic Model A body style was also produced in 1931 – as the slant-windshield Town Sedan (160-B).

Magazine ads for the Model A Standard Sedan first appeared in late June 1931. Only three primary magazine ads were created to promote the slant-windshield Standard Sedan. Two of these ads are unique – each appearing in a single magazine on only one date. The third Standard Sedan ad, however, appeared in a wide variety of U.S. magazines.

STANDARD ANNOUNCEMENT

◆

JUNE, 1931   3

Announcing

THE NEW FORD
STANDARD SEDAN

A beautiful five-passenger car, with longer, wider body, slanting windshield, and attractive, comfortable interior. On display by Ford dealers throughout the country. The price is five hundred and ninety dollars, f. o. b. Detroit.

F. O. B. Detroit, plus freight and delivery. Bumpers and spare tire extra at low cost

Please mention the Junior League Magazine when answering advertisements.

The introduction ad for the new Ford Standard Sedan is a simple line drawing. The ad lists the features and the price of the car (*"five hndred and ninety dollars, f.o.b. Detroit"*) – with a footnote indicating that *"Bumpers and spare tire extra at low cost."*

Version A (StS 1a)
● *Junior Legue Magazine,* June 1931, p. 3

This unique magazine ad for the Standard Sedan appeared only once, in June 1931.

SWIM CLUB

THE LITERARY DIGEST   JUNE 20, 1931

The Beautiful Ford Standard Sedan

A beautiful five-passenger car, with longer, wider body, and attractive, comfortable interior. The slanting windshield is made of polished plate safety glass. You can now have the new Ford delivered with this glass in all windows and doors at slight additional cost.

Mother has arrived at the swim club in her new Ford Standard Sedan to pick up her children. As the boy climbing the sliding board watches, the nanny escorts her two kids beneath the awning to the waiting car.

Version A (StS 2a)

⊙ *The Literary Digest,* June 20, 1931, p. 26

This is a unique Model A ad. It appeared only once, but in a fairly common magazine.

PASSING CIRCUS

◆

EDITOR SAYS

73,000 *Miles is only a Start*

SOME weeks ago we published an account of a Ford that had been driven 73,000 miles in less than a year by three mail carriers in Iowa.

The article created much comment and brought many letters telling of the unusual reliability, economy and long life of the Ford. Here is an interesting letter from the editor of a newspaper in Kansas:

"In one of your recent advertisements in weekly newspapers you tell of a Ford that has been driven 73,000 miles in less than a year.

"That's no mileage at all for a Ford. There is a Ford in this community that was driven 120,000 miles before it was traded in.

"The car was bought in August, 1928, and driven until November, 1930, by its owner. He is a carrier of the *Wichita Daily Eagle*,

making a route of 150 miles daily with a morning and evening paper. On Sunday, only one trip of 75 miles is made. About 50 miles of the route is over paved streets — the rest is on rough dirt and gravel streets through three small towns.

"Operating and up-keep costs were exceptionally low. After the car was traded in for a new Ford I am informed that it was overhauled and is now giving good service to its new owner."

Letters like this are indicative of the substantial worth of the Ford and the high quality built into every part. In every detail of construction it is made to endure — to serve you faithfully and well for many thousands of miles. The price is low because of large production and unusual Ford manufacturing facilities.

THE NEW FORD STANDARD SEDAN. *Longer, wider, more luxurious. Low first cost. Economical terms through Authorized Ford Finance Plans of Universal Credit Company*

It's circus time and two children strain to look out the window of their father's new Ford Standard Sedan as they pass the elephants and the Big Top.

⊙ *Collier's,* July 4, 1931, CIII

○ *The Country Home,* July 1931, CII

Version A (StS 3a)

○ *The Farm Journal,* July 1931, p. 19

⊙ *Holland's,* July 1931, p. 45

⊙ *Life,* June 26, 1931, CII

○ *The Literary Digest,* July 18, 1931, p. 21

○ *The Saturday Evening Post,* July 18, 1931, p. 34

⊙ *Southern Agriculturist,* July 1, 1931, CIII (B&W)

TOWN CAR

	TOTAL	1928	1929	1930
Ford Body Style		140-A	140-A	140-B
Weight (pounds)		2,500	2,500	2,525
Price (FOB Detroit)		NA	$1400	$1200
Units Produced (U.S.)	1,065	89	913	63
Number of U.S. Ads				
Primary Formats	2	–	2	–
Ad Variations	3	–	3	–
Magazine Insertions	10	–	10	–

The Model A Ford Town Car was first available in early 1929. The production run for this unique Model A body style was quite low – with only slightly over 1,000 units built. This was the most luxurious Model A body style and commanded an introduction price of $1,400 – almost twice that charged for any other Ford Model A body type.

The Town Car, with only a snap-on fabric cover for the open chauffer's compartment, provided plenty of "snob appeal" for the otherwise fairly common Model A Ford automobile line. With a body inspired by LaBaron, the Town Car was the first chauffeur-driven car offered by an American manufacturer in the medium- or low-priced fields. A Model A Town Car Delivery vehicle (295-A) was also produced in 1931.

Only two basic magazine ads (one with a headline and text variation) were produced for the Model A Ford Town Car. There were no individual magazine ads for the Town Car Delivery vehicle. However, this body style did appear as small vignette illustrations in several magazine ads featuring multiple Model A Ford light commercial vehicles and Model AA trucks.

VOLTAIRE PAU

◆

The New Ford Town Car

THE new Ford Town Car is formal in appearance, with extremely precise lines. It is a personal car of intimate size, delightful convenience and unquestioned taste.

The body is custom-designed and finished in a choice of colors—new, in the modern mode, yet quietly restrained in tone. The back is square-cornered, in the Continental manner, with French landau leather rear quarters and rear panel.

Interior trimming is of English Bedford cords or French broadcloths—optional with the purchaser. The seat in

the rear compartment is upholstered in the fashionable plain panel style, deeply cushioned and comfortable. Hardware is of distinctive scroll design, enameled to match the lining cloth. Accoutrements of the rear compartment include a vanity case mirror and notebook, clock, electric cigarette lighter and ash tray, center bow light and silk robe rail. Arm rests and individual hassocks are other pleasing features.

The chauffeur's compartment

is upholstered in black leather and is separated from the passenger compartment by a glass partition, with sliding center window.

Triplex shatter-proof glass is used throughout the new Ford Town Car—for the windows and front glass partition, as well as the windshield. The transverse springs and four Houdaille hydraulic double-acting shock absorbers give unusual riding comfort. The price is $1400, f.o.b. Detroit, Michigan.

FORD MOTOR COMPANY
Detroit, Michigan

The lady's Town Car has just arrived at the exclusive *"Voltaire Pau"* building with the "7" street address. As the woman enters, the chauffeur stands by the door and gazes up at the ladies in the upstairs windows.

Version A (TnC 1a)
● *Country Life,* May 1929, p. 112
● *Harper's Bazaar,* May 1929, p. 33
● *The Sportsman,* May 1929, p. 89
● *Vanity Fair,* May 1929, p. 20
● *Vogue,* May 11, 1929, p. 19

VOLTAIRE PAU

Model A Ford magazine ads were also produced in other countries – and sometimes with borrowed Williamson illustrations that were initially used in U.S. ads.

The Ford Town Car, as the most luxurious Model A body style, was no exception to this practice – as evidenced by two examples of non-U.S. versions of the *"Voltaire Pau"* Town Car magazine ad.

> **Example ad from China** ➤
> ● *The China Weekly Review,* July 20, 1929

中華郵政特准掛號認為新聞紙類   Registered at the Chinese Post Office as a newspaper for transmission with special marks privileges in China.

New Ford Town Car

Now on display
Telephone our dealer For a demonstration ride

Nothing could be smarter than the new Ford Town Car. Formal in appearance, with extremely precise lines, it is designed after the French mode. Its square corner back, as found in the petite cars so fashionable on the European boulevards, gives it Continental distinction, as do its French landau leather quarters and back panel and its belted moulding that runs severely back from the radiator shell.

For men and women who are quick to appreciate personal conveyance of such intimate size, delightful convenience and unquestioned taste, the Town Car is the most luxurious car.

Ford Motor Company Exports Inc.
SHANGHAI

El nuevo "TOWN CAR" Ford

Es este un carro diferente de todos los demás tipos que integran el ramo de productos Ford. Su aspecto es el de un automóvil de etiqueta, hecho para las grandes ocasiones. Es de elegancia sobria, severa, y sus líneas son sencillas, precisas, esbeltas. El ambiente todo que rodea a este coche es del gusto más depurado.

La carrocería está construida expresamente, acabada en una gran variedad de colores, todos atractivos sin ser estridentes. La parte posterior de la carrocería forma esquinas a la manera de los coches europeos, con el compartimiento trasero estilo Landau, de cuero legítimo.

Las guarniciones interiores son de un material acordonado, de fabricación inglesa de la más alta calidad, o de *broadcloth* francesa, a opción del comprador. El asiento posterior está tapizado con suntuosidad y buen gusto, de los más finos materiales. Sus cojines, extraordinariamente mullidos, ofrecen el máximo de comodidad. Los ornamentos y aditamentos, tanto exteriores como interiores, son de un diseño especial, muy atractivos por su originalidad; esmaltados en un color que harmoniza con el de la tapicería. Los accesorios del compartimiento posterior comprenden una *vanity case* con su espejo y libreta de notas, un reloj, un encendedor eléctrico para cigarros con su correspondiente cenicero, una lámpara muy elegante en el centro y un porta-manta flexible de seda. Otros detalles de interés son los descansabrazos del asiento y los escabeles que tan cómodos resultan.

El compartimiento para el chófer está tapizado de cuero negro legítimo y queda separado del compartimiento para pasajeros mediante una división de cristal cuya parte central es corrediza, lo que permite establecer comunicación fácil y expedita con el driver.

Tanto la división a que acabamos de referirnos como las ventanas y el parabrisas son de cristal "TRIPLEX" que tiene la propiedad de no saltar en fragmentos aunque se quiebre, lo que es una garantía de seguridad en caso de accidente. Como resultado de los muelles transversales semielípticos y los cuatro amortiguadores hidráulicos Houdaille con que está equipado, este carro posee un andar que es sobremanera cómodo y suave. Su precio en la Habana es de $1,390.00.

FORD MOTOR COMPANY
Sucursal de la Habana

The conversion of an original full-color Model A ad illustration to a black and white drawing was also a frequent practice – both in the U.S. and in other countries.

While the black and white *"Voltaire Pau"* ad version that appeared in *The China Review Weekly* followed the May 1929 U.S. ad issue date by two months, the full-color edition from Cuba was not published until the end of 1929.

> ◀ **Example ad from Cuba**
> ● *Social,* December 1929, p. 87

EQUESTRIAN ONLY

The favorite personal car of many women of wide interests

WOMEN of wide interests who use an automobile constantly for shopping, the theater, for varied business and social activities, have found the Ford Town Car ideally suited to their needs. Rarely is there to be had such a combination of charm and utility.

By its correct, formal lines and simple dignity, the Ford Town Car appeals particularly to those of assured position who have no need of ostentatious display and to whom the matter of price, large or small, is invariably a secondary consideration.

Similarly, the alert performance and relatively small size of the Ford Town Car commend it to those who realize

that congested traffic conditions have made necessary a new type of car for city driving. With it, you can weave in and out of traffic with greater ease and safety, and have your chauffeur stop and park in spaces that would deny entrance to a larger car.

What woman has not wished, on inclement days particularly, that she might be delivered to the very point of call, promptly and without confusion!

The body of the Ford Town Car is after a design by Le Baron, and is finished in a choice of rich colors. Interior trimming is of English Bedford cord or French broadcloth—optional with the

purchaser. Accoutrements of the rear compartment include a vanity case, mirror and notebook, clock, electric lighter and ash tray, center bow light and individual hassocks.

Especially worthy of note is the easy-riding comfort of the car and the use of Triplex shatter-proof glass. This is used throughout—not only for the windshield, but for the side windows and the partition dividing the chauffeur's seat from the rear compartment.

The protection and safety afforded by this glass are of course apparent. The price of the Ford Town Car is $1400 f. o. b. Detroit, Michigan.

FORD MOTOR COMPANY
Detroit, Michigan

The Ford Town Car has just dropped off two lady riders at the *"Equestrian Only"* riding path at the city park. As the chauffeur returns a coat to the car, a gentleman assists the ladies as they prepare for their ride.

Version A (TnC 2a)
● *Harper's Bazaar,* October 1929, p. 24
● *Vanity Fair,* October 1929, p. 104+
● *Vogue,* October 26, 1929, p. 112+

EQUESTRIAN ONLY

A second version (B) of this 1929 Ford Town Car magazine ad features a modified headline and a completely different text. The ad points out that the Town Car has a body *"after a design by Le Baron"* and a square-cornered back that gives it a *"Continental distinction."*

Version B (TnC 2b) ➤

● *Country Life,* October 1929, p. 25
● *The Sportsman,* October 1929, p. 88

The *"Equestrian Only"* ad text lists the price of the new Ford Town Car as *"$1400 f.o.b. Detroit"* (As the most expensive Model A, the Town Car commanded a price almost twice that of any other Model A Ford body type.)

A new vogue in town driving

The two 1929 Model A Ford Town Car ads appeared only in the five most upscale magazines of the era. The first ad (*"Voltaire Pau"*) was published in May and the second ad (*"Equestrian Only"*) in October 1929.

A LITTLE LONGER, PLEASE.
A closer look at the drawing of the two ladies and their horses reveals that the gentleman is making a last minute stirrup adjustment for one of the ladies before they enter the park for their ride.

TOWN CAR ADVERTISING

Individual Ford dealers sometimes produced their own magazine ads to supplement the advertising efforts provided by the Ford Motor Company.

An example of this practice is evident in a 1930 quarter-page Ford Town Car ad created by Theodore Luce, Inc., a New York City Ford dealer.

> **Example Ford Dealer ad** ➤
> ◉ *The New Yorker,* March 22, 1930, p. 42

Promotional activities for the Model A Ford in magazines were not limited to paid advertising efforts. With the popularity of "The New Ford," automobile, industry publications appeared eager to publish news they thought would interest their readers about the Model A. As an example, the recent addition of the Taxicab and Town Car models to the Ford Model A line were announced in this "unpaid ad" published in early 1929.

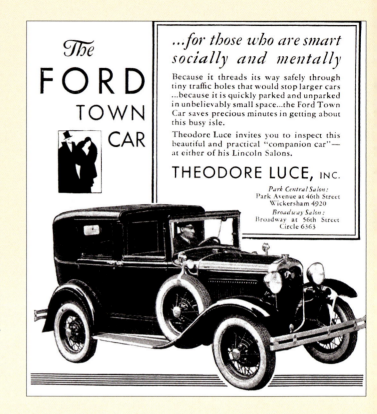

> **Example Ford publicity announcement** ▽
> ◉ *Automotive Industries,* February 2, 1929, p. 163

*T*WO *new models recently added to the Ford Model A line are shown here. The taxicab (left) was placed in production several weeks ago and sells for $800. It seats four passengers. The other model, the town car, is a chauffeur-driven job and lists at $1,400*

STATION WAGON

	TOTAL	1928	1929*	1930	1931
Ford Body Style		150-A	150-A	150-B	150-B
Weight (pounds)		2,482	2,482	2,505	2,505
Price (FOB Detroit)		NA	$695	$650	$625
Units Produced (U.S.)	11,317	5	4,954	3,510	2,848
Number of U.S. Ads					
Primary Formats	1	–	1	–	–
Ad Variations	1	–	1	–	–
Magazine Insertions	5	–	5	–	–
* Produced through May 1930					

With the introduction of the Model A Station Wagon in January 1929, Ford was the first automobile company to provide a production station wagon vehicle. Very few Station Wagons were actually factory-built by Ford. Initially, the Murray Body Company built and shipped the wood Station Wagon bodies to Ford assembly plants for installation on the chassis. In 1930 and 1931, the Baker Raulang Company also produced Station Wagon bodies.

The Station Wagon was seen by some as a Ford light commercial vehicle and by others as a passenger car. While it could serve as an efficient delivery unit, it could also accommodate eight passengers – with additional space for luggage on the lowered tailgate.

While this Model A body style was available for sale across three years, Ford produced only one magazine ad for the Station Wagon. There were no variations produced in this Station Wagon ad and it appeared only once, in June 1929.

JUNIPER YACHT

◆

The New Ford Station Wagon

THE new Ford Station Wagon has been designed to meet the needs of large estates, country clubs and families having summer homes in the country or by the seashore. It is particularly well suited to such use because it combines the sturdiness of a light truck with the flexibility and comfort of a passenger car.

Seating accommodations are provided for eight people, including the driver. Baggage is carried on the large tail-gate.

The seats in the rear compartment, though securely anchored when in use, can be removed quickly and easily when the car is used for hauling.

In appearance, the new Ford Station Wagon reflects its sturdy construction. The body has uprights of hard maple, with ply-wood sides finished in natural grain. The sill is unusually rugged. Fenders are full-crown, heavy and capable. Seats are wide, deeply-cushioned and finished in blue-gray artificial Spanish leather. Doors are wide, carefully fitted and substantial, with full-nickeled handles in conservative scroll design. The side curtains, which can be put up easily and quickly in bad weather, are made in tan-gray to harmonize with the body finish.

The new Ford Station Wagon brings you the same alert performance, ease of control, safety, speed, power, reliability and economy that are characteristic of all the new Ford cars. Its easy-riding comfort is particularly appreciated on rough roads.

FORD MOTOR COMPANY
Detroit, Michigan

A family departs their Ford Station Wagon at the dock of the *"Juniper"* yacht. While the chauffeur holds the family dog, the boat captain checks the paperwork. (Note the absence of a left-side mounted spare wheel on the Station Wagon.)

Version A (StW 1a)
- *Country Life,* June 1929, p. 27
- *Harper's Bazaar,* June 1929, p. 180
- *The Sportsman,* June 1929, p. 84
- *Vanity Fair,* June 1929, p. 121
- *Vogue,* June 8, 1929, p. 120+

JUNIPER YACHT

Only one magazine ad for the Model A Ford Station Wagon was produced. This striking ad appeared once – in the June 1929 editions of the same five upscale magazines used to advertise the Model A Ford Town Car.

The Model A Ford also appeared in Ford dealer-produced magazine ads. As an example, the Theodore Luce, Inc. Ford dealership in New York City prepared a half-page ad featuring the Model A Ford Station Wagon. (Note that, while the ad was published in May 1930, the Station Wagon shown is a 1929 model.)

IS THIS JAMES WILLIAMSON?

The man in the straw hat standing at the rear of the Station Wagon in the *"Juniper Yacht"* ad has a striking resemblance to James Williamson, the artist who drew the Model A Ford ads.

Could it be that Williamson, who once indicated that Ford did not permit artists to sign their Ford advertising drawings, was able to slip a "face signature" into at least one of his illustrations?

While several Model A Ford ads were autographed by Williamson sometime after their appearance in magazines, no Williamson signatures or initials have been found within original Model A advertising drawings.

Every Country Estate
Needs a

FORD
STATION WAGON

THERE are literally dozens of uses for the new Ford Station Wagon in connection with country life.

Used as a passenger-carrying car, it accommodates eight persons with ample space for luggage on the lowered tailgate. With the rear seats removed it is converted into an effective haulage unit.

The body, built with hard maple and finished in natural wood, combines attractiveness with rugged construction.

It is for these reasons that in America's most exclusive suburbs and country resorts more and more Ford Station Wagons are in evidence.

Examine this smart, practical addition to country-life transportation, at

THEODORE LUCE, INC.

AUTHORIZED LINCOLN DEALER

533 West 57th Street
Columbus 7731

Broadway Salon
1760 BROADWAY
Circle 6363

Park Avenue Salon
247 PARK AVENUE
Wickersham 4920

Example Ford Dealer ad ⌃
◉ *The Winged Foot,* May 1930, p. 47

LIGHT COMMERCIAL VEHICLES

	1928	1929	1930*	1931
Ford Body Style				
Open-cab Pick-up	76-A	76-A	76-B	76-B
Closed-cab Pick-up	82-A	82-A	82-B	82-B
Panel Delivery	79-A	79-A	79-B	79-B
Drop Floor Panel Delivery	–	–	–	225-A
De Luxe Delivery	130-A	130-A	130-B	130-B
Drop Floor De Luxe Delivery	–	–	130-B	130-B
Special Delivery	–	–	–	255-A
Town Car Delivery	–	–	–	295-A

*While the 1929 to1930 model change-over date for Model A passenger cars was January 1930, the commercial vehicle change-over date was not until June 1930.

Using the standard Model A 103-1/2 inch chassis, Ford produced a wide variety of light commercial vehicles. Ford prepared at least one magazine ad for most of these specialized delivery vehicles. (The Station Wagon is covered as a separate body style in this book.)

Ads featuring Model A light commercial vehicles often included several different models and, sometimes, delivery vehicles built on the larger 131-1/2 or 157 inch chassis and Model AA trucks. (Note that ads containing light commercial vehicles but featuring, primarily, large commercial vehicles or Model AA trucks are not included in this book.)

With the exception of the Station Wagon, magazines ads for Model A light commercial vehicles did not appear prior to 1931 and some of these ads carried over into March 1932. Many of the Model A light commercial vehicle ads were placed in very specialized industry magazines – e.g., publications for dry cleaners, bakeries, dairies, builders, etc.

MARTELL CLEANERS

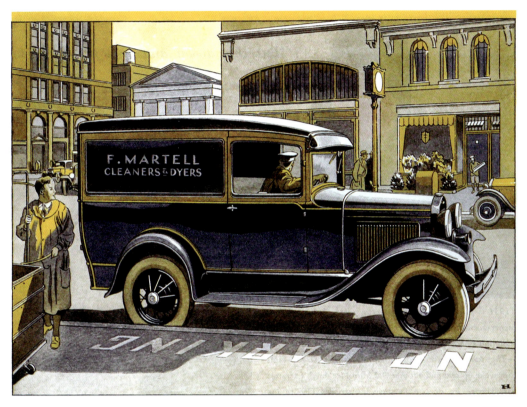

A drop-floor panel body now brings Ford economy to new commercial fields

DAILY, throughout the country, Ford commercial units are doing new jobs. A steadily increasing range of body-types, a choice of two different chassis, and a variety of especially designed equipment, all help to adapt the Ford for service in many businesses.

It is possible to select a Ford truck, or a Ford delivery-car, which is exactly suited to almost any work required. Thus, the reliability, excellent performance, and definite economy of Ford units become directly available to a larger number of industries.

For example, a new body is offered on the light-delivery chassis. It is of the drop-floor panel type, a body of special convenience to cleaners and dyers, florists, radio dealers and others whose deliveries require unusual height from floor to roof. It is also used by specialty-salesmen, as it permits easy loading and removal of bulky samples.

In addition to a wide selection of commercial bodies on the Model A chassis, there is a range of types on the 1½-ton truck chassis, with either 131½- or 157-inch wheelbase. With the truck, there is a choice of open or closed cabs, of single or dual rear wheels, and of high or low rear-axle gear-ratios.

Your Ford dealer can show you a commercial unit, and equipment, suited to the requirements of your particular business.

Complete Commercial Exhibits at New York, Philadelphia, Boston, Detroit, Dallas, and Los Angeles

FEATURES
of Ford Commercial Units

Four-cylinder, 40-horse-power engine. Torque-tube drive. Internal-expanding mechanical brakes, all fully enclosed. Sturdy frames, cross-members, axles, and springs. Forty different kinds of specific steels for special purposes. Extensive use of fine steel forgings. Precision built. Three different wheelbases. Two different chassis. Triplex shatter-proof windshields for safety. Low first cost. Low cost of operation and maintenance. Reliability and long life.

A man, with a clothes cart and a coat hanger in his hand, waits while the driver for *"F. Martell Cleaner's & Dyers"* parks his drop-floor panel body Model A Ford *"commercial unit"* in a *"No Parking"* area.

Version A (PnD 1a)
◉ *The Saturday Evening Post,* January 24, 1931, p. 60

The small *"H"* in the lower right corner is the initial of Peter Helck, the artist for this ad.

FRAIM TESTIMONIAL

◆

"40 miles a day, 150 stops, and 7 days a week . . . the Fords stand up without faltering"

IN THE day-in, day-out service which a milk dealer expects of a truck, the value of Ford reliability and strength is well displayed. These features are built into the Ford by the use of forty different kinds of steel in the chassis, more than twenty ball and roller bearings, precision workmanship, and simplicity of construction.

Bodies for every kind of service are available. On the light commercial chassis, there are express or pick-up, and panel bodies. On the 1½-ton truck chassis, there are panel, stake, and open and canopy-top express bodies. In addition, there are other types, for many special purposes. Open or closed cabs, single or dual rear wheels, high or low rear-axle gear-ratios, and 131½-inch or 157-inch wheelbase are available.

Your Ford dealer can supply a truck that is specifically adapted to your hauling needs.

BRAESIDE BABY MILK
A. A. GUERNSEY MILK
GRADE A NURSERY MILK
PASTEURIZED MILK
TABLE CREAM
WHIPPING CREAM

RAW GUERNSEY MILK
SWEET BUTTER
SALT BUTTER
BUTTER MILK
COTTAGE CHEESE
SOUR CREAM

FRAIM'S DAIRIES
VANDEVER AVE. & LAMOTTE ST.   WILMINGTON, DELAWARE.
THE MILK FOR HEALTH

December 19, 1930.

Ford Motor Company,
Dearborn, Michigan.

Gentlemen:-

      We have been operating Ford trucks for some years and have found them satisfactory in every way, particularly our present units. These are giving us greater satisfaction than any previous ones we have had.

      Our business is hard on trucks. We expect them to stand up under a 7-day-week delivery system with minimum time out for repairs. A daily grind means up to 40 miles and up to 150 stops. We believe this is about as severe a test for durability and dependability as can be devised in the course of ordinary business. And the Fords stand up under it without faltering and in such a way as to win the praise of our mechanics.

           Very truly yours,

           Clarence Fraim

When writing to FORD MOTOR COMPANY please mention The Milk Dealer.

The Model A Ford vehicles parked in front of *"Fraim's Dairy"* include two Ford Panel Delivery Cars and the company's Ford Roadster. The ad text features a testimonial letter from *"Clarence Fraim."*

Version A (PnD 2a)
◉ *The Milk Dealer,* February 1931, p. 17

This Model A Ford ad is unique to a specialized dairy industry magazine.

PANEL DELIVERY CAR — Specialized Ads

Many Model A Ford light commercial magazine ads appeared in specialized publications aimed at specific businesses requiring delivery vehicles.

Four Ford Panel Delivery Cars are parked at the *"Rex Cole Company"* in New York City. The testimonial letter from Cole featured in the ad proclaims the *"excellent service given by the 18 Ford de luxe delivery cars we operate."*

Cole Testimonial – Version A (PnD 3a) ➤
◉ *The Commercial Car Journal,* March 1931, p. 99

"The Ford is uniformly reliable in performance and highly economical in service," says Rex Cole, Inc., of New York City

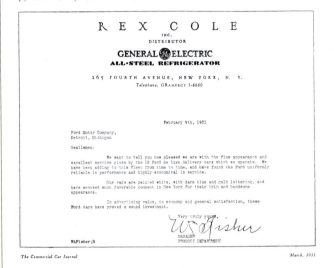

THE low first cost of Ford commercial units makes them especially desirable for the operators of large fleets. Cost figures show that this small initial investment is only the beginning of Ford economy. Often, the saving in operation and maintenance is far greater than the saving in first cost alone.

Many features of Ford units contribute to economical service. Special steels and other fine materials are used in their construction, to increase strength, reliability and endurance. Simplicity of design adds further to reliable performance and lowers the cost of all maintenance work.

More than forty standard bodies are available for the Ford commercial units. Any Ford dealer can supply these units, complete, for use in every business.

REX COLE
INC.
DISTRIBUTOR
GENERAL ⒼⒺ ELECTRIC
ALL-STEEL REFRIGERATOR
265 FOURTH AVENUE, NEW YORK, N. Y.
Telephone, GRAmercy 5-6660

February 9th, 1931

Ford Motor Company,
Detroit, Michigan

Gentlemen:

We want to tell you how pleased we are with the fine appearance and excellent service given by the 18 Ford de luxe delivery cars which we operate. We have been adding to this fleet from time to time, and have found the Ford uniformly reliable in performance and highly economical in service.

Our cars are painted white, with dark blue and gold lettering, and have aroused much favorable comment in New York for their trim and handsome appearance.

In advertising value, in economy and general satisfaction, these Ford cars have proved a sound investment.

Very truly yours,

W. A. Fisher
MANAGER
PRODUCT DEPARTMENT

WAFisher:B

The Commercial Car Journal   *March, 1931*

June 15, 1931   THE STARCHROOM LAUNDRY JOURNAL   109

For quick delivery service at low cost...

THE FORD MODEL "A" PANEL DELIVERY CAR

IN ORDER to give especially prompt service, many laundries are making more frequent delivery trips. By using the Ford panel delivery car, which is low in first cost and highly economical to operate, they are able to give this extra service at minimum expense.

Because of its reliability and long life, this car is well adapted to constant, hard usage. Its medium size and weight, its sturdy, 40-horsepower engine, its alert performance and ease of handling enable it to get around quickly.

Other Ford types giving service to laundries in all parts of the country are the Ford 1½-ton panel truck with 131½-inch wheelbase, and the large panel truck with 157-inch wheelbase. They are available from all Ford dealers, at low cost, and can be obtained in many different color combinations. In principal cities there are centralized exhibits of Ford commercial units.

Ford Panel Delivery Car

The panel delivery body affords full protection to driver and load. It has steel panels outside and is of wood construction inside. Steel plates eleven inches high rise from the floor on either side. Above these are wooden slats. Provision is made for the installation of any type of shelving at small additional cost. Double doors at the rear give a wide opening for loading. Loading space: length, 59½ inches; width, 46⅜ inches; height, 51 7/16 inches. Wheelbase, 103½ inches.

The *"Quick Service Laundry"* Ford Panel Delivery Car is being unloaded for a delivery at an apartment building. The ad text describes the merits of the Ford Panel Delivery Car and points out its *"alert performance and ease of handling."*

This Model A ad appeared only once, in an mid-1931 laundry services magazine.

◀ **Quick Service Laundry – Version A (PnD 4a)**
● *The Starchroom Laundry Journal,* June 15, 1931, p. 109

PANEL DELIVERY CAR – Specialized Ads

Additional Ford Panel Delivery Car magazine ads were produced later in 1931. Each ad appeared only once in a single (specialized) magazine.

A man makes an upstairs delivery from the *"Marchl's Bakery"* Panel Delivery Car. The ad text indicates the Ford Panel Delivery Car is *"meeting the needs of bakers everywhere."*

Marchl's Bakery – Version A (PnD 5a) ➤

● *Bakers Weekly,* June 27, 1931, p. 31

The Ford Panel Delivery Car
covers a route
at minimum cost

Retail delivery-service, from door to door, makes heavy demands on hauling equipment. Constant stopping and starting, fast speeds for short distances, gears shifted, doors opened and slammed a hundred times a day . . . these conditions require a delivery unit with good brakes, a lively engine, a sturdy transmission and clutch, and a body that is ruggedly built for service.

That is why the Ford Model A panel delivery car is successfully meeting the needs of bakers everywhere. It is attractive in appearance, chassis and body alike are built to stand the strain of door-to-door delivery-service, and it is highly economical to operate and maintain.

One of the reasons why this car offers such great reliability is because of the high quality built into it. For instance, it has a large number of ball and roller bearings—more than twenty. These reduce friction and wear, lessen strains on hard-used parts, greatly prolong the life of the chassis.

Other Ford types which are serving bakers in all parts of the country are the de luxe panel delivery car, also on the passenger-car chassis, and the Ford 1½-ton panel truck, which is widely used for wholesale deliveries. In principal cities there are centralized exhibits of Ford commercial units.

The panel delivery body affords full protection to driver and load. It has steel panels outside and is of wood construction inside. Steel plates eleven inches high rise from the floor on either side. Above these are wooden slats. Provision is made for the installation of any type of shelving and insulation at small additional cost. Double doors

at the rear give a wide opening for loading. There is a small window in each door. Seats are of the folding type, giving the driver easy access to the interior of the body from the driver's compartment. Loading space: length, 59⅛ inches; width, 46⅜ inches; height, 51 inches. Wheelbase, 103½ inches.

Ford Panel Delivery Car

"NOW USING FIVE FORD UNITS
2½ years' experience with them
SHOWS MINIMUM COST"

Every laundry is interested in keeping down costs. Prompt delivery-service is a big factor in customer good-will, but delivery-expense must be held to a minimum if profits are to be realized.

That is the main reason why so many successful laundries are using Ford trucks and delivery cars. These Ford units are handsome in appearance, with excellent advertising value, and they give well-rounded, speedy performance.

Even more important is their marked economy. They are low in first cost. Operating costs are also low, for they are easy on gas, oil and tires. Because they are strong and sturdy, simple in mechanical design, and built of fine materials, they give long and faithful service at small up-keep cost.

Whatever your needs in a truck, there is a standard Ford unit to meet them. It is no longer necessary to order a special body to suit your business. There are Ford panel trucks with two different wheelbases, and Ford light delivery cars with panel, de luxe panel, and drop-floor panel bodies—all available, in many different color-combinations, from any Ford dealer. In most principal cities, there are centralized exhibits of Ford commercial units.

Ford de luxe panel delivery car

The body is all-steel, and is highly attractive in appearance and finish. Rustless Steel is used for radiator-shell, head lamps, and other exterior metal parts. The interior is finished in heavy, durable, wood-fiber composition. The driver's compartment has two

folding seats. There is easy access to the loading compartment both from the driver's seat and through a large door at the rear. Panel window in door gives the driver rear vision. All doors provided with locks. Wheelbase 103½ inches.

Large Ford panel truck; wheelbase, 157 inches

Ford 1½-ton panel truck; wheelbase 131½ inches

The Ford De Luxe Panel Delivery Car owned by the *"American Cleaners & Launderers, Inc."* is about to receive some dirty wash. The ad text proclaims that *"these Ford units are handsome in appearance, with excellent advertising value."*

As is often the case with Ford light commercial vehicle magazine ads, this ad also includes Model AA Ford trucks.

◄ **American Cleaners – Version A (PnD 6a)**

● *The Starchroom Laundry Journal,* September 15, 1931, p. 95

TRI-MOTOR DELIVERY

◆

Are you in need of a
SPECIAL-PURPOSE HAULING-UNIT?
Investigate the standard Ford line

The U. S. Department of Commerce, Airways Division, needed a light haulage-unit for use as a radio test car. In the Ford special delivery car (natural wood) they found precisely what they needed . . . at low cost. You are almost certain to find available a Ford car or truck for any specific hauling job.

THE essential requirement in this radio test car was that the body contain no metal other than door-handles, screws, and similar small parts. Unusual as such a requirement is, it is significant that in the extensive Ford line there was a haulage-unit exactly suited. It is literally true that there is a Ford truck or light commercial car for every hauling-need.

In the standard Ford line, there are more than forty different types, with a choice of thirty-eight color-combinations. The Ford 1½-ton truck is available with 131½-inch or 157-inch wheelbase, with open or closed cabs, high or low rear-axle gear-ratios, and single or dual rear wheels. The light commercial chassis is the same as that of the Model A Ford car.

Among the Ford types of widest interest for municipal purposes are the 2 and 3 cubic yard garbage trucks, the standard and de luxe police patrols, the ambulance, and stake and platform trucks. In addition, there are many other types, on both chassis, one or more of which may be perfectly adapted to your special needs. All are low in cost, strong, reliable, powerful, and economical over extended periods of usage. They are available from any Ford dealer. In most principal cities, there are centralized exhibits of Ford commercial units. Investigate them for low-cost hauling.

Ford

Do you mention THE AMERICAN CITY? Please do.

A Ford Special Delivery Car has arrived at the airport, bringing cargo to a Ford Tri-Motor airplane. The ad indicates the Airways Division of the U.S. Department of Commerce found what they needed in this Ford *"light haulage-unit."*

Version A (SpD 1a)
⊙ *The American City,* July 1931, p. 51

This unique 1931 magazine ad features a rare Model A body style – the Ford Special Delivery Car.

TENNIS PLAYER DELIVERY

66 THE SATURDAY EVENING POST July 25, 1931

★

Added convenience, more loading-space . . . New Ford Pick-up

THE pick-up light-delivery car, one of the more than forty standard Ford commercial types, is widely used by retail merchants, jobbers, distributors and others because of its sturdy and durable construction, alert performance, reliability and proved economy. It is a car that can be used for quick deliveries of many kinds of merchandise, as a service-car, and for all kinds of rough work with medium-size loads.

New features have been incorporated into the Ford pick-up which add greatly to its convenience, usefulness, and value. Most important is a loading-compartment of improved design, which has a flat bottom with straight sides and with square corners. This provides full-width loading-space at the floor. The floor is of sheet steel with pressed skid-strips. The body is larger, with a capacity of 22¼ cubic feet.

The Ford pick-up is available either with or without a canopy-top. The top, which is provided with curtains, is supplied at small additional cost.

Another new Ford type is the de luxe pick-up, in which body and cab have the appearance of a single unit. Exterior metal parts are of Rustless Steel, there are chromium-plated brass side-rails, and the spare wheel is carried in a fender-well.

Any Ford dealer can supply a Ford unit, complete, specifically adapted to your needs. You can find the name and address of the nearest dealer in your "Where to Buy It" Classified Telephone Directory, under the name "Ford." In principal cities, there are centralized exhibits of Ford trucks and light-delivery cars.

Ford

As the workers unload the large wood crate from the Ford Pick-up they are interrupted by a young man on his way to the tennis courts. This Model A ad uses a second illustration showing the Model A Pick-up with a canopy top.

Version A (PkU 1a)

⊙ *The Saturday Evening Post,* July 25, 1931, p. 66

This magazine contained two-color ads for both Ford trucks and commercial vehicles in 1931 and early 1932.

TENNIS PLAYER DELIVERY

A second version (B) of this Model A Ford Pick-up ad is a black and white edition. Although it uses the same headline, illustrations and a similar ad text, the ad format is slightly different.

While the first version (A) of this ad appeared in a high-circulation, consumer magazine, the second version (B) appeared in a very specialized industry publication.

Version B (PkU 1b) ➤
◉ *The Commercial Car Journal*, August 1931, p. 51

New Ford Pick-up

Added convenience, more loading space . . .

THE pick-up light-delivery car, one of the more than forty standard Ford commercial types, is widely used by retail merchants, jobbers, distributors and others because of its sturdy and durable construction, alert performance, reliability and proved economy. It is a car that can be used for quick deliveries of many kinds of merchandise, as a service-car, and for all kinds of rough work with medium-size loads.

New features have been incorporated into the Ford pick-up which add greatly to its convenience, usefulness, and value. The loading-compartment is of improved design. It has a flat bottom with straight sides and with square corners, providing full-width loading-space at the floor. The floor is of sheet steel with pressed skid-strips. The body is larger, with a capacity of 22¼ cubic feet.

The Ford pick-up is available either with or without a canopy-top. The top, which is provided with curtains, is supplied at small additional cost.

Another new Ford type is the deluxe pick-up, in which body and cab have the appearance of a single unit. Exterior metal parts are of Rustless Steel, there are chromium-plated brass side-rails, and the spare wheel is carried in a fender-well.

Any Ford dealer can supply a Ford unit, specifically adapted to your needs. In most principal cities, there are centralized exhibits of Ford commercial units.

The Commercial Car Journal — *August, 1931*

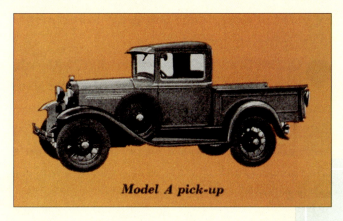

Model A pick-up

SCARCE PICK-UPS.
Beyond the 1931 *"Tennis Player Delivery"* ad, the Model A Ford Pick-up did not appear as the primary vehicle featured in any other Model A Ford magazine ads.

The Ford Pick-up image did, however, appear as smaller, secondary illustrations in several Model A ads featuring other vehicles. Shown here are two examples of these smaller insert illustrations – both from **The Saturday Evening Post**.

There were no magazine ads for the open-cab Model A Pick-up.

GOLDEN PARK PHARMACY

◆

51

THE FORD DE LUXE DELIVERY CAR

is sturdy, reliable,
and pleasing in appearance

Ford de luxe delivery car

THE FORD de luxe delivery car is designed for the operator who requires a unit of distinctive appearance. This car is suitable for retail deliveries, for salesmen's use, and for a wide variety of light-haulage purposes. Its performance is alert and capable, whether in city traffic or on open highways. It offers reliability, safety, long life and economy.

To meet the light hauling requirements of every business, in addition to the de luxe delivery car, there is a number of other standard Ford types, on the light commercial chassis with 103½-inch wheelbase.

For operators requiring heavier units, there is the Ford 1½-ton truck, with 131½-inch or 157-inch wheelbase, high or low rear-axle gear-ratios, single or dual rear wheels, and a comprehensive range of bodies, which offers economical hauling for every business. All are low in cost, and are available, complete, from Ford dealers everywhere.

The body is all-steel, and is highly attractive in appearance and finish. Rustless Steel is used for radiator shell, head lamps, and other exterior metal parts. The interior is finished in heavy, durable, waterproof wood-fiber composition. There are two folding seats in the driver's compartment. There is easy access to the loading compartment, both from the driver's compartment and through a large door at the rear. All doors are provided with locks. Loading space: length 57 9/16 inches, width 43⅝ inches, height 45 27/32 inches.

The chassis is similar to that of the Model A Ford car. It is strong and sturdy, built to strictest standards of excellence, in design, materials and workmanship. Forty different kinds of steel, for specific purposes, are used in its construction. There are more than twenty anti-friction ball and roller bearings at important chassis points. These, and other features, such as the torque-tube drive, three-quarter floating rear axle, and the fully-enclosed mechanical brakes, contribute to reliability, good performance, long life, and low cost of up-keep.

The Commercial Car Journal   *May, 1931*

The *"Golden Park Pharmacy"* makes a delivery at a high-rise building from their Ford De Luxe Delivery Car. The ad text reviews the features and dimensions of the Ford De Luxe Delivery Car and larger Model AA Ford trucks.

Version A (DDy 1a)
◉ *The Commercial Car Journal*, May 1931, p. 51

This unique ad appeared only once, in a 1931 commercial vehicle magazine.

DE LUXE DELIVERY CAR – Specialized Ads

As with the Ford Panel Delivery Car, magazine ads for the Ford De Luxe Delivery Car appeared in specialized publications aimed at businesses requiring delivery vehicles.

The *"Morey La Rue Laundry"* De Luxe Delivery Car is being loaded while a passenger looks on. This ad also shows two larger Ford Panel Trucks. The text indicates that Ford vehicles are built for *"individual delivery needs."*

> **LaRue Laundry – Version A** (DDy 2a) ➤
> ● *The Starchroom Laundry Journal*, July 15, 1931, p. 105

July 15, 1931   THE STARCHROOM LAUNDRY JOURNAL   105

THERE IS A STANDARD
Ford Unit
FOR EVERY TYPE OF LAUNDRY SERVICE

EVERY laundry, whether operating a single delivery-unit or an entire fleet of trucks, can benefit from the reliability, excellent performance, long life and marked economy that are characteristic of the Ford. For there is a variety of Ford types, especially built for the individual delivery needs of every operator.

For speedy, economical deliveries of medium-size loads, there are the Ford panel delivery car, and the de luxe panel delivery car, which is the type illustrated and used by the Morey-La Rue Laundry, both mounted on the Ford passenger-car chassis with 103½-inch wheelbase.

For the operator with longer routes and larger loads, there are the Ford 1½-ton panel truck with 131½-inch wheelbase, and the large panel truck with 157-inch wheelbase.

These Ford units are built to strictest standards of excellence, in design, materials and workmanship. They are built to give long service under the hardest kind of usage, are highly economical in operation and up-keep. All are low in cost, and are available from Ford dealers everywhere, in a wide variety of color combinations. In most principal cities, there are centralized exhibits of Ford commercial units.

De Luxe Delivery Car

This is a car of distinctive appearance, having excellent advertising value. The body follows closely the lines of the Ford Tudor Sedan. It is all-steel, and has a wide belt running around it. The interior is finished in heavy, durable, water-proof wood-fiber composition. The roof is covered with bright, black, heavy-coated rubber material. Easy access to the loading compartment is afforded both from the driver's compartment and through the large door at the rear. All doors are provided with locks. Exterior bright metal parts are of Rustless Steel.

De Luxe Panel Truck. Wheelbase, 131½ inches

Large Panel Truck. Wheelbase, 157 inches

21   THE NATIONAL PROVISIONER   October 24, 1931

What type hauling-unit do you need?
YOU WILL FIND IT IN THE STANDARD FORD LINE

The DeLuxe Delivery is only one of several Ford body types which exactly fit the Packer's delivery needs. In addition to its economy of operation and alert performance this unit has exceptionally fine appearance—an important advertising consideration. It offers deluxe equipment at no extra cost—four houdaille shock absorbers, steel spoke wheels and spare wheel carried in a fender-well.

NO longer is it necessary to go to the extra trouble and expense to have special bodies built to meet your hauling needs. No matter what your particular problems may be, there is a standard Ford unit built to solve them. There are delivery types large and small, panel cars and trucks, and a town-car delivery which is the final note in smart equipment. In all there are 10 different body types available, mounted on four different chassis lengths — 103½-inch or light commercial chassis; the 131½ and 157-inch truck chassis; also the new 112-inch Standrive for house to house delivery service. All are available, in many beautiful color-combinations, at low cost. Your Ford dealer will gladly help you in your delivery problems. In most principal cities, there are centralized exhibits of Ford trucks and light commercial cars.

A Ford De Luxe Delivery Car, used by *"Swift's Premium Hams and Bacon,"* is parked on a downtown street. The ad text explains that *"no longer is it necessary to go the extra trouble and expense to have special bodies built."*

This Model A ad appeared only once, in an October 1931 specialized industry magazine.

> ◄ **Swift's Premium – Version A** (DDy 3a)
> ⊙ *The National Provisioner*, October 24, 1931, p. 34

DE LUXE DELIVERY CAR - Specialized Ads

This De Luxe Delivery Car is used by the *"Ira Wilson & Sons Dairy Co."* Unlike most other Model A Ford light commercial vehicle ads, this ad appeared in multiple magazines.

Wilson Testimonial – Version A (DDy 4a) ➤

◉ *American Builder & Building Age,* December 1931, p. 61

◉ *The American City,* December 1931, p. 118

● *Baker's Weekly,* December 19, 1931, p. 75

◉ *The Black Diamond,* December 12, 1931, p. 51

● *Highway Engineer & Contractor,* December 1, 1931, p. 13

◉ *The Ice Cream Review,* December 1931, p. 9

◉ *The Milk Dealer,* December 1931, p. 18

● *The Starchroom Laundry Journal,* November 15, 1931, p. 37

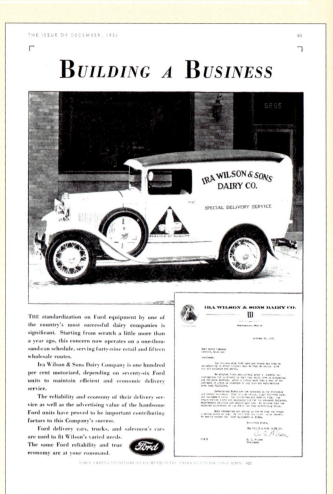

BUILDING A BUSINESS

THE standardization on Ford equipment by one of the country's most successful dairy companies is significant. Starting from scratch a little more than a year ago, this concern now operates on a one-thousand-can schedule, serving forty-nine retail and fifteen wholesale routes.

Ira Wilson & Sons Dairy Company is one hundred per cent motorized, depending on seventy-six Ford units to maintain efficient and economic delivery service.

The reliability and economy of their delivery service as well as the advertising value of the handsome Ford units have proved to be important contributing factors to this Company's success.

Ford delivery cars, trucks, and salesmen's cars are used to fit Wilson's varied needs. The same Ford reliability and true economy are at your command.

AT A *faster* PACE

Ford De Luxe Delivery

MANY a business moves at a faster pace today because of the Ford truck. And this accelerated pace means extra profits, greater turnover, better service to the customer. • Fast-moving business chooses the Ford truck because of its thoroughly proved economy—in low first cost, in operation, in reliability and long life—in speed—in its carefully determined load capacity—in Ford service universally available at typical low prices. Many Ford dealers operate 24-hour-a-day service.

• Extra strength built into every vital part protects your investment, enabling the Ford truck to run for many thousands of miles, and setting depreciation at a remarkably low figure. A list of Ford truck users would show the names of the largest companies in the country, firms whose equipment is bought on definite proof of performance. • Any street and any road will reveal the Ford serving the most diverse uses, carrying merchandise and materials economically, reliably, swiftly.

There are many different types of Ford commercial units, meeting the needs of diversified industries. Ask your Ford dealer to show you how the Ford truck can contribute to the profits of your business.

When writing to FORD MOTOR COMPANY please mention The Ice Cream Review.

This early-1932 magazine ad features a Ford De Luxe Delivery Car used by *"Fosselman's Delicious Ice Cream."* The ad text reviews the reliability, low cost and long life of the Ford *"commercial units."*

This unique black and white ad is one of the latest Model A magazine ads produced. It appeared only once, in February 1932.

◀ **Fosselman's Ice Cream – Version A (DDy 5a)**

◉ *The Ice Cream Review,* February 1932, p. 7

FOUR UNITS IN USE

◆

You can choose a Ford body designed for your particular business

Natural Wood Delivery. *Combining smartness and sturdy construction, this body appeals to many merchants for their suburban or rural deliveries. Built of hard maple and birch, finished in the natural grain. Exterior bright metal parts are of Rustless Steel. Loading space: length, 58 inches; width, 50 inches; height, 43 inches.*

Town Car Delivery. *A body of special interest to exclusive retail shops for city or town deliveries. The body is of metal. Veneer panels, in natural color, cover the strong wooden frame of the interior. The driver's seat is upholstered in black genuine leather. Loading space: length, 46 inches; width, 43½ inches; height, 42 inches.*

De Luxe Panel Delivery. *This car is especially useful for retail deliveries of fragile merchandise, by florists, jewelers and others. The body is all-steel, with interior finish of durable, water-proof composition. Driver's compartment has two folding seats. Loading space: length, 57 9/16 inches; width, 43½, height, 45 27/32 inches.*

Panel Delivery. *A sturdy body widely used for general delivery purposes. Made of steel panels outside, and of wood construction inside, with slats to protect the body from the load. There are wide, double doors at the rear. Loading space: length, 59½ inches; width, 46¾ inches; height, 51 7/16 inches.*

IT IS now possible for any operator to obtain a complete Ford commercial unit that is exactly suited to his requirements.

Illustrating, in some measure, the wide variety of bodies available on Ford chassis, are the four delivery-types shown above. They are standard Ford units, and can be furnished in any color-combination desired. Each serves a definite field, emphasizing the wide range of choice that is offered by the Ford.

Other types on the light-delivery chassis include a drop-floor delivery and a pick-up body. The drop-floor body is used by cleaners and dyers, florists, radio dealers and others to whom the extra height of 12½ inches from floor to roof at the rear is of advantage.

Ford bodies are built to strictest standards of excellence. They are designed to meet the requirements of the work they are to do. Fine materials are used in the construction of these bodies, to make them strong and sturdy — able to give long service at low cost.

For heavy hauling there is a wide choice of standard bodies for the Ford 1½-ton truck. It is available with 131½-inch and 157-inch wheelbase, single and dual rear wheels, and with high and low rear-axle gear-ratios.

Your Ford dealer can supply a standard Ford unit especially designed to meet your requirements. In New York, Philadelphia, Boston, Detroit, Dallas and Los Angeles, there are special Ford commercial exhibits.

★ FEATURES ★
of Ford Commercial Units

Four-cylinder, 40-horse-power engine. Torque-tube drive. Internal-expanding mechanical brakes, all fully enclosed. Forty different kinds of steel for specific purposes. Extensive use of fine steel forgings. More than 20 ball and roller bearings. Three different wheelbases. Two different chassis. Triplex shatter-proof windshields. Low first cost. Low cost of operation. Reliability and long life. You may purchase a Ford truck or light commercial car on convenient, economical terms through the Authorized Ford Finance Plans of the Universal Credit Company.

This ad shows four Ford Model A *"commercial units"* in use. Included are the Natural Wood Delivery, Town Car Delivery, De Luxe Panel Delivery and Panel Delivery.

Version A (Mpl 1a)
⊙ *The Saturday Evening Post,* March 21, 1931, p. 87

This is the first of several two-color, multiple-vehicle Ford light delivery ads to appear in this magazine.

TEN UNITS

What type hauling-unit do you need?

YOU WILL FIND IT IN A STANDARD FORD BODY...AT LOW COST

Drop-floor panel delivery

Natural wood panel delivery

Open express truck with 131½-inch wheelbase

Stake truck with 157-inch wheelbase

WHETHER it is a police patrol needed in Tulsa, a coal truck in Butte, or a smart town car delivery in Manhattan, the Ford Motor Company, through its nation-wide dealer organization, can supply standard Ford bodies to meet your needs.

The same principles of volume production which govern the manufacture of Ford chassis are applied to these specialized truck bodies. The result is low production cost — a saving which is passed on to the public in terms of low price and high value. In addition, the purchaser of any Ford type, in any vicinity, is assured of quick delivery and of convenient service.

No longer is it necessary to sacrifice time and money in having special truck bodies built to suit your particular needs. In the Ford line there is a standard commercial body ready to start working for you. Here in the utility, performance, and low cost of the Ford truck you will find the solution to your transportation problems — assured low cost per ton-mile.

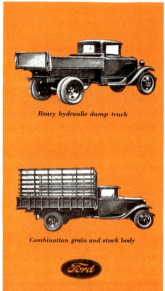

Heavy hydraulic dump truck

Combination grain and stock body

Ford

Town car delivery

Model A pick-up

Service-car

De Luxe panel truck

Ten different Model A Ford light commercial vehicles and Model AA trucks are shown in this multi–vehicle, two-color ad. The ad text reviews the overall value and low price of the *"standard Ford bodies."*

Version A (Mpl 2a)

⊙ *The Saturday Evening Post,* September 19, 1931, p. 92

The rare Natural Wood Panel Delivery and Town Car Delivery vehicles are included in this 1931 magazine ad.

FOUR UNITS

◆

De Luxe Delivery Units at Ford low cost

Now, every merchant, every store, and every business which offers a delivery-service can enjoy the added prestige that comes of operating smart and handsome delivery-units. There are several such de luxe types in the standard Ford line, completely appointed and equipped . . . but priced well within reach of any operator.

The *town-car delivery* is a final step in distinctive appearance. This is a car for the boulevard and avenue, one perfectly at home in any assemblage of smart motor cars. The front seat is upholstered in black genuine leather. The spacious loading compartment, of ample proportions, is finished with veneer panels in natural color. Six steel-spoke wheels, two fender-wells, an ornamental light on each side, two dome-lights and an extension-mirror are standard equipment.

Other handsome units take care of a wide variety of delivery require-ments. The *de luxe delivery* is used by many druggists, specialty grocers, caterers, jewelers, silversmiths, stationers, florists, and others who need a fully enclosed unit of good capacity.

The *de luxe panel truck* is designed for the larger load. The *de luxe pickup* is a favorite choice with those who need an open delivery unit for carrying high-grade merchandise.

Because the de luxe appointments are standard equipment, these Ford units are unusually low in cost. Durable materials and rugged construction throughout, and low gasoline and oil consumption make them economical to maintain and operate.

Your Ford dealer will be glad to help you in your delivery problems. In most principal cities, there are cen-tralized exhibits of Ford trucks and light commercial cars.

Four different *"De Luxe Delivery Units"* are pictured in this two-color Ford ad. Each vehicle is shown against an aqua background. The ad text explains the features and benefits of each of the four Ford body styles.

Version A (Mpl 3a)
⊙ *The Saturday Evening Post*, October 31, 1931, p. 82

This ad contains drawings of two rare Model A Ford body styles – the Town Car Delivery and the De Luxe Pick-up.

October 15, 1931   THE STARCHROOM LAUNDRY JOURNAL   83

What type hauling-unit do you need?

YOU WILL FIND IT IN THE STANDARD FORD LINE

PANEL DELIVERY uses the Ford chassis with 103½-inch wheelbase. This is a sturdy unit that will give long service in general delivery work. Its performance is speedy and alert, and it is highly economical.

PANEL TRUCK with 131½-inch wheelbase. This may almost be termed the standard delivery unit for laundry use, because it is serving laundries everywhere. It combines good appearance, large capacity, rugged strength and economy.

DE LUXE DELIVERY, also on the 103½-inch wheelbase, has the same lines as the Ford Tudor Sedan, making it truly distinctive in appearance. It is widely used, for light delivery purposes, by large and small laundries.

LARGE PANEL TRUCK with 157-inch wheelbase. This is a fully enclosed unit for carrying unusually bulky loads. There is also a de luxe panel truck with 131½-inch wheelbase, which has excellent advertising value, due to its fine appearance.

NO LONGER is it necessary to have special bodies built to suit your particular delivery needs. Now, in the standard Ford line, you will find bodies especially adapted to your purpose. There are Ford trucks and light delivery cars in more than forty different types. They are available, in forty color-combinations, through any Ford dealer. In most principal cities, there are centralized exhibits of Ford commercial units.

This ad features four different Ford *"hauling-unit"* vehicles. In addition to the Panel Delivery and the De Luxe Delivery, two larger-wheelbase Ford AA Panel Trucks are included.

Version A (Mpl 4a)
● *The Starchroom Laundry Journal,* October 15, 1931, p. 83

This unique ad appeared only once, in a late-1931 laundry industry magazine.

276

CORPORATE TEXT ADS

	TOTAL	1929	1930	1931	1932
Number of Ads					
Primary Formats	5	1	2	-	2
Ad Variations	7	2	3	-	2
Magazine Insertions	60	20	38	-	2

While most automobile magazine ads include at least one car illustration in addition to the ad text, some Model A Ford ads contained no illustrations of a car. These black and white, text-only, ads appeared, primarily, in December 1929 and January and February 1930.

This time period coincided with the model change-over between the 1929 and 1930 Model A passenger body types. During this time, magazine advertising efforts for specific Model A body styles were virtually non-existent. Further, some magazines that didn't begin to advertise the Model A until 1930 did not contain a Model A ad in their publication until March of that year.

These "corporate text" ads did not reference specific features of the Model A. Instead, they reviewed the contributions that Ford has made in *"extending the limits of man's opportunities,"* how *"service is the cornerstone of the Ford business,"* and the *"pride of ownership"* associated with the Ford car. These very plain looking ads were quite numerous and appeared in a wide variety of publication types – including the major upscale magazines of the day.

While no Model A "corporate text" ads appeared during 1931, two of these text-only ads were published in early 1932, after production of the Model A Ford had ended.

Extending the Limits of Man's Opportunity

● *Only a few generations ago the life of man was circumscribed by his own physical limitations . . . the dexterity of his fingers, the strength of his back, the speed of his limbs, and the labor of domestic animals. . . . The interchange of commodities was slow, difficult. There were no good roads, as we know them today, nor any way to travel swiftly, surely, over these roads. The deeply rutted wagon trail was a long, hard trail. . . . Though boundless acres were all about, it was only the adventurous few who traveled far. Many a man lived and died without ever having been more than fifty miles from home. . . . Then was born an idea that was destined to reshape the frontiers and the future of the entire country—the idea of making a small, strong, simple automobile so low in price that it might be placed within the means of all the people.*

● THE coming of this new means of transportation not only changed the industrial life of the nation, but helped to change the private lives of every one for all the generations to come.

It leveled hills, extended horizons, created new opportunities, furnished the means to earn more money and to enjoy the leisure which that increased income should bring.

In creating and building a small, strong, simple automobile at a low price, and in using it, man became accustomed to thinking of machinery as a servant. He made power work for him.

More and more as time went on, in industrial plants and on the farm, heavy labor was taken off the back of man and placed upon the shoulders of the machine.

The Ford moved everywhere, blazing the way over miry roads and rocky mountain trails, through gumbo and sand, creating a rising demand for swifter, smoother travel that resulted in the construction of hundreds of thousands of miles of cement and macadam highways reaching to all parts of the country.

The benefits resulting from the introduction of the low-priced automobile have done more than perhaps any other single thing to increase the standards of living and to make this a truly united country.

All the people are blended together by the flexibility and swiftness of automobile transportation. The prairie farmer, the industrial worker, and the city business man are governed by similar impulses, similar tastes, similar demands upon highly specialized machinery to serve them.

● This civilization can show no greater example of disciplined machinery than in the operation of the Ford Industries. The great miracle is not the car, but the machines that make the machine—the methods that make it possible to build such a fine car, in large numbers, at a low price. Craftsmanship has been put into mass production. Millions and millions of parts are made —each one so accurate and so exactly like the other that they fit perfectly to the thousandth of an inch when brought together for assembly into complete units.

Men by the thousands and the hundred thousand are employed at the Rouge plant alone and there are hundreds of acres of plant equipment. Yet the purpose today is wholly the same as when the equipment of the Ford organization was housed in a single small building.

Everything that has been done has been done to give further scope and expression to the Ford Idea.

● That idea is not merely to make automobiles—not merely to create so much additional machinery and so many millions of additional horse-power—but to make this a better world in which to live through providing economical transportation for all the people.

For that purpose the first Model T was made twenty-one years ago. For that purpose the new Ford is made today. In 1929, as in 1908, it is again helping to reshape the frontiers and the future of the country and to further extend the limits of man's opportunity.

FORD MOTOR COMPANY
Detroit, Michigan

This late-1929 all-text Ford ad does not reference a specific Ford body style. Instead, it elaborates on Ford's progress in automobile transportation and with the idea of *"making a small, strong, simple automobile."*

Version A (CTx 1a)

O *The American Boy,* December 1929, p. 33
O *Capper's Farmer,* December 1929, p. 13
O *Collier's,* December 14, 1929, p. 5

(continued)

"EXTENDING" TEXT

◀ **Version A** (CTx 1a) [continued]

○ *The Country Gentleman,* December 1929, p. 41

◉ *Country Life,* December 1929, p. 29

○ *Farm & Fireside,* December 1929, p. 4

○ *The Farmer's Wife,* December 1929, p. 17

○ *Good Housekeeping,* December 1929, p. 134

◉ *Harper's Bazaar,* December 1929, p. 31

○ *Ladies' Home Journal,* December 1929, p. 83

○ *Liberty,* December 14, 1929, p. 29

○ *McCall's,* December 1929, p. 3

○ *The Redbook Magazine,* December 1929, p. 5

○ *Southern Agriculturist,* December 1, 1929, p. 5

◉ *The Sportsman,* December 1929, p. 81

○ *Successful Farming,* December 1929, p. 4

◉ *Vanity Fair,* December 1929, p. 115

◉ *Vogue,* December 21, 1929, p. 87

This Ford corporate text ad appeared in a wide variety of magazines at the end of 1929.

Among the publications containing the *"Extending Text"* corporate text ads were general interest, women's fashion, upscale, youth-oriented and farm-related magazines.

In addition, a two-page edition (B) of this all-text ad appeared in two magazines. While this ad covers two pages in these magazines, the text is identical to that contained in the one-page ad version. The two-page ad does not contain the Ford logo present in the one-page version.

Version B (CTx 1b) ▾

○ *The Literary Digest,* December 7, 1929, pp. 54-55

○ *The Saturday Evening Post,* December 14, 1929, pp. 68-69

---

54 *The Literary Digest for December 7, 1929*   *The Literary Digest for December 7, 1929* 55

EXTENDING
the Limits of   Man's Opportunity

Only a few generations ago the life of man was circumscribed by his own physical limitations . . . the dexterity of his fingers, the strength of his back, the speed of his limbs, and the labor of domestic animals. . . . The interchange of commodities was slow, difficult. There were no good roads, as we know them today, nor any way to travel swiftly, surely, over these roads. The deeply rutted wagon trail was a long, hard trail. . . . Though boundless acres were all about, it was only the adventurous few who traveled far. Many a man lived and died without ever having been more than fifty miles from home. . . . Then was born an idea that was destined to reshape the frontiers and the future of the entire country—the idea of making a small, strong, simple automobile so low in price that it might be placed within the means of all the people.

THE coming of this new means of transportation not only changed the industrial life of the nation, but helped to change the private lives of every one for all the generations to come.

It leveled hills, extended horizons, created new opportunities, furnished the means to earn more money and to enjoy the leisure which that increased income should bring.

In creating and building a small, strong, simple automobile at a low price, and in using it, man became accustomed to thinking of machinery as a servant. He made power work for him.

More and more as time went on, in industrial plants and on the farm, heavy labor was taken off the back of man and placed upon the broader shoulders of the machine.

THE Ford moved everywhere, blazing the way over miry roads and rocky mountain trails, through gumbo and sand, creating a rising demand for swifter, smoother travel that resulted in the construction of hundreds of thousands of miles of cement and macadam highways reaching to all parts of the country.

The benefits resulting from the introduction of the low-priced automobile have done more than perhaps any other single thing to increase the standards of living and to make this a truly united country.

ALL the people are blended together by the flexibility and swiftness of automotive transportation. The prairie farmer, the industrial worker, and the city business man are governed by similar impulses, similar tastes, similar demands upon highly specialized machinery to serve them.

This civilization can show no greater example of disciplined machinery than in the operation of the Ford Industries.

The great miracle is not the car, but the machines that make the machine—the methods that make it possible to build such a fine car, in large numbers, at a low price.

Craftsmanship has been put into mass production. Millions and millions of parts are made—each one so accurate and so exactly like the other that they fit perfectly to the thousandth of an inch

when brought together for assembly into complete units.

Men by the thousands and the hundred thousand are employed at the Rouge plant alone and there are hundreds of acres of plant equipment. Yet the purpose today is wholly the same as when the equipment of the Ford organization was housed in a single small building.

Everything that has been done has been done to give further scope and expression to the Ford Idea.

THAT idea is not merely to build automobiles—not merely to create so much additional machinery and so many millions of additional horse-power—but to make this a better world in which to live through providing economical transportation for all the people.

For that purpose the first Model T was made twenty-one years ago. For that purpose the new Ford is made today. In 1929, as in 1908, it is again helping to reshape the frontiers and the future of the country and to further extend the limits of man's opportunity.

FORD MOTOR COMPANY
Detroit, Michigan

◆

JANUARY, 1930 79

SERVICE

In the *Ford Motor Company* we emphasize service equally with sales ⅄ It has always been our belief that a sale does not complete the transaction between us and the buyer, but establishes a new obligation on us to see that his car gives him service ⅄ We are as much interested in your economical operation of the car as you are in our economical manufacture of it ⅄ This is only good business on our part ⅄ If our car gives service, sales will take care of themselves ⅄ For that reason we have installed a system of controlled service to take care of all Ford car needs in an economical and approved manner ⅄ We wish all users of Ford cars to know what they are entitled to in this respect, so that they may readily avail themselves of this service.

FROM the very earliest beginning, SERVICE has been the cornerstone of the Ford business.

Far back in 1908, when the first Model T Fords were made, there were few people who understood the operation of an automobile and fewer places to which the purchaser might turn for help when repairs were needed.

Frequently in those days, Mr. Ford would deliver the car personally to the new owner and see to it that some arrangements were made to keep it in good running order.

Usually he would find the best mechanic and explain the construction of the car to him. Sometimes, when no such mechanic was available, the town blacksmith would be pressed into service.

Then, as the business grew, capable men were appointed, in a widening circle of towns, to devote their entire time to the care of Ford cars. These men, wherever located, worked under close factory supervision and according to certain set standards.

For just as the Ford Motor Company was the pioneer in the making of "a strong, simple, satisfactory automobile at a low price," so it was also the pioneer in establishing complete and satisfactory service facilities.

For the first time in the automobile business it became possible for the purchaser of a car to buy parts quickly and readily and to have repairs made at a reasonable cost. Where formerly it had been the accepted practice to charge the highest possible prices for these repairs, a new policy was instituted for the protection of the owner. The unusual character of Ford Service was soon recognized as one of the outstanding features of the car.

Today there are more than 8000 Ford dealers in the United States alone, with thousands of others located throughout the world. Their mechanics have been trained in special schools conducted by the Ford Motor Company and they have been equipped with all the latest service machinery. The well-ordered cleanliness of the shops and salesrooms and the uniform courtesy of all dealer employees are particularly appreciated by the woman motorist.

Wherever you live, or wherever you go, you will find the Ford dealer prompt and businesslike in his work, fair in his charges, and sincerely eager to do a good and thorough job at all times.

His constant effort is to relieve you of every detail in the care of your car and to help you get thousands upon thousands of miles of satisfactory, enjoyable motoring at a very low cost per mile.

That is the purpose for which the Ford car was designed and built. That is the true meaning of *Ford Service*.

FORD MOTOR COMPANY
Detroit, Michigan

A second text-only Ford ad followed in January 1930. This ad, which also has extensive text, emphasizes how service has been the *"cornerstone of the Ford business."*

Version A (CTx 2a)

O *The American Boy,* January 1930, CII

O *Capper's Farmer,* January 1930, p. 15

O *Collier's,* January 18, 1930. p. 49

(continued)

"SERVICE" TEXT

This all-text ad appeared in many different 1930 publications – with a second, slightly shorter, text version (B) appearing in early 1932.

◀ **Version A (CTx 2a) [continued]**
○ *Cosmopolitan,* January 1930, p. 113
○ *The Country Gentleman,* January 1930, p. 44
◉ *Country Life,* January 1930, p. 89
◉ *Farm and Ranch,* January 4, 1930, p. 7
○ *The Farmer's Wife,* January 1930, CIII
○ *Good Housekeeping,* January 1930, p. 135
◉ *Harper's Bazaar,* January 1930, p. 133
○ *Ladies' Home Journal,* January 1930, p. 93
○ *Liberty,* January 11, 1930, p. 19
○ *McCall's,* January 1930
○ *Southern Agriculturist,* January 15, 1930, CIII
◉ *The Sportsman,* January 1930, p. 81
○ *Successful Farming,* January 1930, p. 6
◉ *Vanity Fair,* January 1930, p. 79
◉ *Vogue,* January 18, 1930, p. 95

The *"Service Text"* ad was also formatted as a two-page ad edition (C).

Version B (CTx 2b) ∨
◉ *The State Trooper,* February 1932, CIV

Version C (CTx 2c) ∨
○ *The Literary Digest,* January 11, 1930, pp. 50-51
○ *The Saturday Evening Post,* January 25, 1930, pp. 58-59

"PRIDE" TEXT

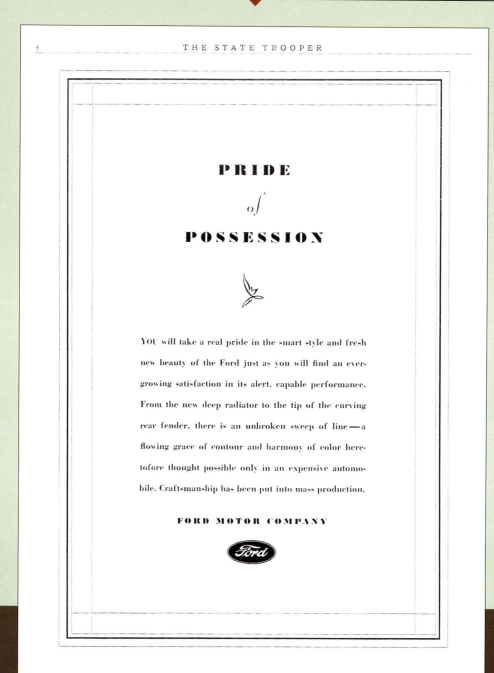

PRIDE

of

POSSESSION

YOU will take a real pride in the smart style and fresh new beauty of the Ford just as you will find an ever-growing satisfaction in its alert, capable performance. From the new deep radiator to the tip of the curving rear fender, there is an unbroken sweep of line—a flowing grace of contour and harmony of color heretofore thought possible only in an expensive automobile. Craftsmanship has been put into mass production.

FORD MOTOR COMPANY

The third Ford all-text corporate ad uses a relatively short text.

- ○ *The American Boy,* February 1930, p. 31
- ○ *Capper's Farmer,* February 1930, p. 17
- ○ *Cosmopolitan,* February 1930, p. 131
- ○ *The Country Gentleman,* February 1930, p. 62
- ○ *The Country Home,* February 1930, p. 3
- ○ *The Farmer's Wife,* February 1930, p. 17
- ○ *Good Housekeeping,* February 1930, p. 9

Version A (CTx 3a)

- ◉ *Harper's Bazaar,* February 1930, p. 137
- ○ *Ladies' Home Journal,* February 1930, p. 122
- ○ *McCall's,* February 1930, p. 3
- ○ *The Redbook Magazine,* February 1930, p. 2
- ○ *Southern Agriculturist,* February 15, 1930, CIII
- ◉ *The State Trooper,* February, March and April, 1930, all p. 4
- ○ *Successful Farming,* February 1930, p. 35
- ◉ *Vanity Fair,* February 1930, p. 81

"POSITIVE PROOF" TEXT

◆

Positive Proof
of FORD ECONOMY

City of Detroit purchases 137 Ford cars

Hundreds now in use prove low cost of operation

THESE 137 Ford cars represent one of the largest deliveries ever made to a municipality at one time.

21 radio-equipped Ford scout cars were traded in on this purchase. They had been operated day and night for two years in heavy traffic and all kinds of weather.

Their individual records ranged from 78,434 miles to 143,723 miles with a grand total of 2,283,097 miles. The operating cost of the 21 cars was 2.284 cents a mile — less than 2 1/3 cents. This cost included all fuel, oil, tires, repairs and every other item except depreciation and insurance.

Of 577 Ford cars in Detroit City service, the 300 in the Police Department traveled a total of 6,591,937 miles during the past fiscal year, at an average cost of 2.9 cents a mile.

Many claims have been made on operating costs, but here in the carefully kept motor car records of the City of Detroit is positive proof of Ford economy.

In the preceding paragraphs, it is seen that 21 Ford scout cars averaged less than 2 1/3 cents a mile and 300 Ford cars in all branches of Detroit police work averaged 2.9 cents a mile!

Day and night, twenty-four hours a day, these Ford cars are in operation. Few branches of transportation demand such grueling service. The records show that low fuel and oil consumption is but one of the Ford's many economies. Ford materials, simplicity of design and accuracy in manufacturing provide unusual strength, stamina and freedom from replacements and repairs.

The individual car buyer as well as the purchasing department of a city or a business cannot afford to ignore the proved economy of the Ford car.

FORD MOTOR COMPANY

PRINTED IN U. S. A.   THE INLAND PRESS, DETROIT

This early-1932 Ford corporate all-text ad explains how the 137 Ford cars used in the city of Detroit have driven a total of 2,283,723 miles at a very economical average operating cost of only 2.9 cents a mile.

Version A (CTx 4a)
◉ *The State Trooper,* January 1932, CIV

This unique ad appeared only once – in the January 1932 issue of a specialized magazine.

YOUR FORD
IS SERVICED PROPERLY

when you take it to an
Authorized Ford Dealer

YOUR Ford was built for many thousands of miles of dependable, fault-free service. But no matter how good a car may be—how fine the parts or great the skill with which they are made and fitted — certain attention is necessary from time to time. Then, it is essential that men who know the Ford car in every part, men who work with *precision* machinery and *accustomed* fingers, should do the servicing or make the repairs.

Your neighborhood Ford dealer therefore is the man to see when you need service, parts, or accessories of any kind. His clean, well-ordered shops are equipped with factory-endorsed service machinery. The parts used are genuine Ford parts—high in quality, low in cost.

Ford service is always most economical — always dependable and safe — but at this particular time, when many cars require extra attention, special prices are in effect. Drive into the nearby Ford Service Department and ask about them. A free inspection will be made of your car. You will know the cost of the work you order before it's started—and will find it agreeably low.

FORD MOTOR COMPANY

PRINTED IN U. S. A.   THE INLAND PRESS DETROIT

This early-1932 Ford text-only ad indicates the importance of having the Model A serviced properly and stresses the need to take your Ford to your authorized neighborhood Ford dealer.

Version A (CTX 5a)
◉ *The State Trooper,* March 1932, CIV

This was the latest Model A Ford magazine ad produced. It appeared only once – after the production of the Model A ended.

ADVERTISING PROOF ADS

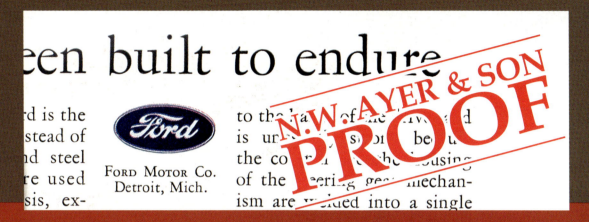

Advertising proof ads were produced as by-products in the process of developing and placing Model A Ford ads in magazines. These ads were created, in very limited quantities, by N.W. Ayer & Son, the advertising agency for the Ford Motor Company during the Model A era.

A proof ad was prepared (usually with extra wide margins and on heavy stock paper) and provided to Ford for final approval of the Model A ad illustration, format and text prior to committing the ad to appear in specific magazines. Accordingly, the reverse sides of these ads were always blank because proof ads never actually appeared in a magazine. Instead, they were prepared for the internal use at N.W. Ayer & Son, the Ford Motor Company, or its dealers. Proof ads usually had evidence of a horizontal center fold mark because, being over-sized, they were often folded when handled or filed during the internal ad development, approval and documentation process. Several types of proof ads exist:

Poster Ads. The most common type of proof ad was printed on heavy stock paper, blank on the back, and contained no additional ad agency or ad production information in the margins. While quite rare, multiple copies of "poster" proof ads for a specific Model A magazine ad have been found. These proof ads were produced in limited quantities and probably provided only to Ford personnel. Ford dealers may also have received copies in order to keep them informed of upcoming Ford Motor Company national advertising efforts or for use in their local dealership promotional activities.

Media Record Ads. These proof ads were similar to "poster" proof ads except that they contained internal ad agency notations (often added by typewriter) within the top or bottom margins to document the ad code number, intended magazines and issue dates. Therefore, these ads provide a behind-the-scenes look at the development and placement of a specific Model A Ford magazine ad and are rare examples of Ford advertising history.

Copy Edit Ads. As part of the magazine ad development process, draft Model A ads would be subject to approval of the specific format and text to be partnered with the selected Model A illustration. The final ad sign-off approval would then occur at Ford prior to the commitment of the ad to the magazine. Accordingly, a Model A ad still in the development stages may have had notes and text change suggestions hand-written directly on the draft ad. These "copy edit" proof ads were never seen by the public or even the Ford dealer in their less-than-final form. The "copy edit" proof ad is, therefore, a one-of a-kind document and the rarest form of a Model A advertising proof ad.

MEDIA RECORD PROOF AD
FORDOR SEDAN - "TRAIN RACING"

FILE PROOFS
One page   Four colors

Successful Farming   May, 1929
Farm & Fireside   May, 1929

Good performance with economy

THE new Ford is more than a new automobile. It is the expression of an ideal—an ideal that looks to bringing the benefits of modern transportation to all the people.

Because of this purpose, the price is low and great care has been taken to insure economy of operation and up-keep.

Conservative figures show that the new Ford averages 20 miles per gallon of gasoline, with many Ford owners reporting greater mileage on long trips. Oil consumption is also low. There is a considerable saving on tires due to the balance of the car, ease of steering and perfected wheel design. Mechanical up-keep is low because of simplicity of design and the enduring quality built into every part.

Definite evidence of the economy of the new Ford is shown in repeated purchases by Federal and city governments, by police departments, and by large industrial companies which keep day-by-day cost records.

The new Ford has been chosen only after exhaustive tests covering every feature of automobile value and performance—from the time of purchase to the final trade-in. Here the Ford policy of not making yearly changes serves to protect the investment of every Ford owner. All improvements in the new Ford are made so that present owners may take advantage of them at low cost.

The availability of Ford dealers throughout the world and close factory supervision of all service are additional reasons for the economy of the new Ford.

It has always been our belief that a sale does not complete the transaction between us and the buyer, but establishes a new obligation on us to see that his car gives him service. We are as much interested in his economical operation of the car as he is in our economical manufacture of it. For that reason we have installed a system of controlled service to take care of all Ford car needs in an economical and improved manner.

This service begins with proper instruction when you buy the car and includes a free inspection and checking-up of important parts at 500, 1000 and 1500 miles.

The purpose of Ford Service is identical with that for which the car was built—to help you get thousands of miles of enjoyable motoring at a minimum of trouble and expense.

FEATURES OF THE NEW FORD CAR

Fully enclosed, silent six-brake system
Four Houdaille hydraulic double-acting shock absorbers
Triplex shatter-proof glass windshield
Vibration-absorbing engine support
Alemite chassis lubrication
Ten body types
Choice of a number of colors in each body type
Quick acceleration
55 to 65 miles an hour
Reliability and economy

Ford

FORD MOTOR COMPANY
Detroit, Michigan

5227—6 5-6x10 3-4

This is an example of a typical "media record" Ford Model A advertising proof ad. This proof ad contains Ford ad agency identification information related to the type and size of the ad, as well as the publications that will contain it.

MEDIA RECORD PROOF AD
FORDOR SEDAN - "TRAIN RACING"

This advertising proof ad for the 1929 Fordor Sedan *"Train Racing"* ad includes internal N.W. Ayer & Son information placed within the top and bottom margins.

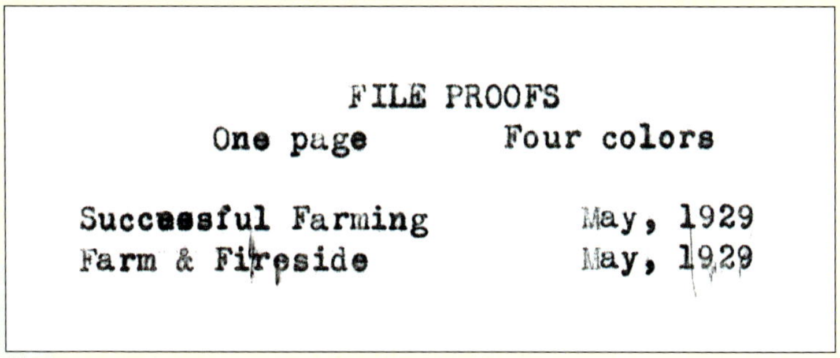

```
             FILE PROOFS
      One page          Four colors

  Successful Farming        May, 1929
  Farm & Fireside           May, 1929
```

TOP MARGIN INFORMATION

At the top of the proof ad is a typed documentation of the ad size (*"one-page"*), the type (*"four colors"*), the magazines to carry the ad (**"Successful Farming"** and **"Farm & Fireside"**) and the issue date for both publications ("May, 1929").

While the page sizes of the two magazines to carry this ad are relatively small (approximately 8 x 12 inches), the overall page size of the proof ad is much larger (approximately 11 x 15 inches). The extra wide margins on proof ads allowed space for adding supplemental classification information that would not appear when the ad was printed in the magazine.

As with most Model A advertising proof ads, this proof ad retains evidence of a distinct horizontal fold mark at the middle of the ad, indicating the (oversized) ad had been folded to allow for easier handling and filing.

All Model A "media record" proof ads also contained additional information printed in the bottom left margin of the ad.

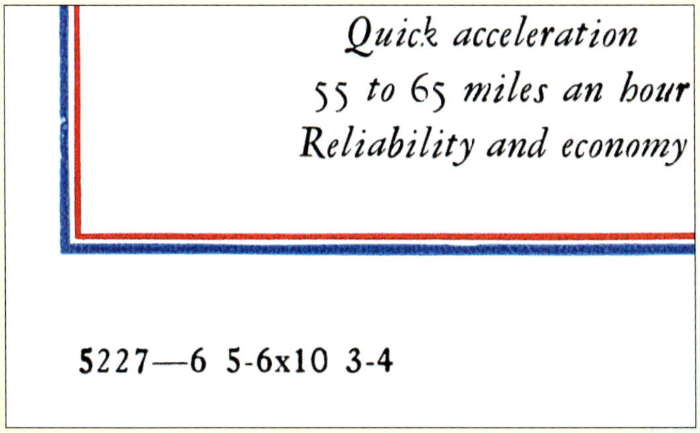

*Quick acceleration
55 to 65 miles an hour
Reliability and economy*

5227—6 5-6x10 3-4

BOTTOM MARGIN INFORMATION

For this advertising proof ad, the N.W. Ayer & Son information includes a code number (*"5227"*) and the size of the ad image (*"6 5-6 x 10 3-4"*). While advertising proof ad code numbers appeared in increasing numerical order as ads were produced, there is no information available regarding what specific meanings may be associated with these code numbers.

COPY EDIT PROOF AD
TOWN SEDAN – "GETTING DIRECTIONS"

For File
#5-2m-1930
1-page   4-colors
Country Home   - November 1930
Successful Farming   November 1930

THE NEW FORD TOWN SEDAN

Blazing New Trails in a Ford

THE STURDINESS and reliability of the new Ford, so evident in the customary, every-day uses of a motor car, are revealed also in many unusual tests of stamina and endurance.

A little while ago a new Ford was driven to the top of the Dieng Plateau, one of the highest mountains in Java. Previously the ascent to the old Hindu statues at the summit had been made only by horseback to the rest-house, and from there on foot.

Equally significant was the choice of the new Ford by the expedition traveling from Washington (D. C.) to Buenos Aires (Argentina) in the interest of a new Pan-American highway. This trip was charted through vast stretches of tropical jungle and equatorial swamp. The car was provided with paddle wheels, so that it might travel on sea as well as land.

The quality that has been built into every part of the car is the reason for its good performance under all conditions. Its reliability and economy mean a considerable saving each year in the cost of operation and up-keep.

new text

Ford

24059—7x10 3-16

This Model A advertising proof ad confirms the use of these internal ad documents in making last-minute changes in advertising content. In this example, major revisions in the text of the magazine ad were made.

COPY EDIT PROOF AD
TOWN SEDAN – "GETTING DIRECTIONS"

This advertising proof ad shows evidence of a decision to make a major change in the text of the ad following the preparation of the initial ad but before producing the final ad as it actually appeared in print.

This ad was scheduled to appear in *Country Home* and *Successful Farming*, with an issue date of November 1930.

TEXT CHANGE NOTE
A hand written *"new text"* notation appears in the margin to the right of the third paragraph in the original proof ad. A comparison between this draft ad and the ad as actually published in the magazine confirms that this paragraph was re-written. In addition, the Ford oval logo was changed from black to blue.

Argentina)
n highway.
tretches of
The car was
t it might

every part
erformance

ails in a Ford

Washington (D. C.) to Buenos Aires (Argentina) in the interest of a new Pan-American highway. This trip was charted through vast stretches of tropical jungle and equatorial swamp. The car was provided with paddle wheels, so that it might travel on sea as well as land.

The quality that has been built into every part of the car is the reason for its good performance under all conditions. Its reliability and economy mean a considerable saving each year in the cost of operation and up-keep.

INITIAL AD TEXT
The original ad wording referred to Ford's participation in an expedition into the *"equatorial swamps"* of South America in the interest of a *"new Pan-American highway."* Further, that in doing so, *"the car was provided with paddle wheels, so it might travel on the sea as well as land."*

rails in a Ford

chart the route for a new continental road from California to Argentina. This was described by engineers familiar with the rough country and the almost impassable mountain trails as one of the most arduous trips ever undertaken by an automobile.

The quality that has been built into every part of the car is the reason for its good performance under all conditions. Its reliability and economy mean a considerable saving each year in the cost of operation and up-keep.

FINAL AD TEXT
The revised ad changed the Pan-American highway reference to *"a new continental road"* and, perhaps fearing that readers may have difficulties believing that a Model A Ford could traverse both water and land, removed the reference to adding *"paddle wheels"* to the Model A.

COPY EDIT PROOF AD
SPORT COUPE – "TENNIS CLUB"

For File
#5-GB-1930
Onepage   Full-color
Country Life   June 1930
Sportsman   "
Vanity Fair   "
Vogue   June 7, 1930
Harper's Bazaar   June 1930

A charming companion for a busy day

THE NEW FORD SPORT COUPE

THE new Ford offers many advantages to the woman who uses an automobile constantly for quick trips to the Country Club, for shopping, the theater, for the many social and business activities of a busy day. Rarely is there to be found such an ideal combination of charm and utility. « « « « « « « «

In addition to the beauty of line and color, the new Ford brings you an unusual degree of mechanical excellence and good performance. You will drive with a new feeling of confidence because of its safety and ease of control. « « «

In providing the opportunity for a final check on the content of the intended Model A Ford magazine ad, it is obvious that production of the final ad could be held up for very minor changes. In this "copy edit" advertising proof ad example, the change involved a single word.

COPY EDIT PROOF AD
SPORT COUPE – "TENNIS CLUB"

This Sport Coupe *"Tennis Club"* ad was scheduled to appear in five different upscale magazines in June 1930. It carries the ad agency identification code *"#5-GB-1930,"* which has not been deciphered.

This "copy edit" advertising proof ad example provides evidence of the editor's proofreading attention in reviewing Model A magazine ads prior to their publishing. Here, a one word change was suggested in the ad text.

```
                For File
               #5-GB-1930
    Onepage                 Four-colors
  Country Life              June 1930
  Sportsman                     "
  Vanity Fair                   "
  Vogue                     June 7, 1930
  Harper's Bazaar           June 1930
```

THE new Ford offers many advan
for quick trips to the Country Cl
business activities of a busy day.
of charm and utility.   «   «

In addition to ~~the~~ *its* beauty of
degree of mechanical excellenc
feeling of confidence because of

17544—8 1-4x11 1-4

PROOF AD TEXT
The second paragraph of the original ad begins with a reference to the new Ford's appearance by indicating *"In addition to the beauty of line and color…"*. However, a pencil notation added in the left hand margin indicates that *"the"* should be changed to *"its."*

THE new Ford offers many advar
for quick trips to the Country C
business activities of a busy day.
of charm and utility.   «   «

In addition to *its* beauty of
degree of mechanical excellenc
feeling of confidence because o

FINAL AD TEXT
The finalized ad was printed with the word *"its"* substituted for *"the."* No other text changes were made. This Model A Sport Coupe ad was produced using three slightly different ad text variations. The text area common to each of these three ad versions contains *"its"* instead of the original *"the."*

COPY EDIT PROOF AD
CABRIOLET – "DOCK NO. 2"

GOOD PERFORMANCE WITH ECONOMY

THE NEW FORD CONVERTIBLE CABRIOLET

"IT has always been our belief that a sale does not complete the transaction between us and the buyer, but establishes a new obligation on us to see that his car gives him service. We are as much interested in his economical operation of the car as he is in our economical manufacture of it.

"For that reason we have installed a system of controlled service to take care of all Ford car needs in an economical and improved manner. We wish all users of Ford cars to know what they are entitled to in this respect, so that they may readily avail themselves of this service."

Henry Ford

THE new Ford is more than a new automobile. It is the expression of an ideal—an ideal that looks to bringing the benefits of modern transportation to all the people.

Because of this purpose, the price is low and great care has been taken to insure economy of operation and up-keep. Few features are of greater importance to millions of motorists.

Figures from many sources show that the new Ford averages 20 miles per gallon of gasoline, with thousands of Ford owners reporting greater mileage on long trips. Oil consumption is also low. There is a considerable saving on tires due to special Ford design, the balance of the car, ease of steering and perfected wheel design.

Mechanical up-keep is low because of simplicity of design and the enduring quality that has been built into every part.

Definite evidence of the economy of the new Ford is shown in repeated and growing purchases by Federal and city governments, by police departments, and by large industrial companies which keep day-by-day cost records.

The new Ford has been chosen only after exhaustive tests covering every feature of automobile value and performance—from the time of purchase throughout the life of the car. Here the Ford policy of not making yearly changes serves to protect and maintain the investment of every Ford owner. Wherever possible, improvements in the new Ford are made so that present owners may take advantage of them quickly and at low cost.

The availability of Ford dealers throughout the world and close factory supervision of all service are additional reasons for the economy of the new Ford. This service begins with proper instruction when you buy the car and includes a free inspection and checking-up of important parts at 500, at 1000 and at 1500 miles.

No matter where you live or where you go, you will never be very far from a Ford dealer who has been specially trained and equipped to help you get many thousands of miles of pleasant, enjoyable motoring at a minimum of trouble and expense.

FORD MOTOR COMPANY
Detroit, Michigan

The newest Ford car—the Town Sedan. Distinguished by its roomy comfort, beautiful colors and rich finish. Rear and rear quarter window chintz silk curtains. Driver's seat is adjustable. Folding center arm and side arm rests add to comfort of rear seat. Three side windows, large rear window and narrow pillars give unusual vision.

Advertising proof ad reviews also provided the advertising agency or Ford the opportunity to confirm the specific colors to appear in the finalized Model A Ford magazine ad. This "copy edit" proof ad example documents the decision to change the ink colors to be used in parts of the final Model A ad.

COPY EDIT PROOF AD
CABRIOLET – "DOCK NO. 2"

This Cabriolet *"Dock No. 2"* magazine ad was scheduled to appear in only one magazine – *Liberty,* with an issue date of July 27, 1929.

Advertising proof ads also served to provide a final check on the colors to be used in the finalized magazine ad. In this example, several areas originally printed in black in the initial ad were designated to change to blue for the final ad.

```
#4-FW-1929
FILE PROOFS

One page        four colors

Liberty         July 27, 1929
```

INITIAL AD TEXT
The original proof ad contains five separate hand written notations in red pen. Each of these identifies a specific part of the ad that the editor felt should be changed from the original black ink to blue ink. These suggested changes included the Ford oval logo and Henry Ford's signature.

FINAL AD TEXT
The finalized ad, as it appeared in the magazine, included all of the designated areas printed in blue. Some Model A ads did have the Ford oval logo printed in black. Therefore, the desire to have the Henry Ford signature appear as if signed in blue ink was, perhaps, the initial impetus for these color changes.

MAGAZINES CONTAINING MODEL A FORD ADS

Magazine advertising for Model A Ford passenger cars and light commercial vehicles appeared in over 40 different commercially-available magazines in the United States beginning in early 1928 and ending in early 1932. Ford utilized a wide variety of publications in advertising "The New Ford" and included general interest magazines, youth-oriented magazines, upscale magazines, weekly news magazines, woman's fashion magazines, and farm-related publications. For Model A light commercial vehicles, Ford often chose very specialized publications intended for targeted audiences in businesses requiring delivery vehicles – e.g., bakeries, dairies, dry cleaners, etc.

Model A Ford passenger car and light commercial vehicle ads appeared in a total of 44 different magazines.

Magazines Containing Model A Ford Advertising

- *The American Boy*
- *American Builder and Building Age*
- *The American City*
- *The American Magazine*
- *Bakers Weekly*
- *Capper's Farmer*
- *Collier's*
- *The Commercial Car Journal*
- *Cosmopolitan*
- *The Black Diamond*
- *The Country Gentleman*
- *The Country Home*
- *Country Life*
- *Delineator*
- *Farm & Fireside*
- *Farm and Ranch*
- *The Farmer's Wife*
- *The Farm Journal*
- *Good Housekeeping*
- *Harper's Bazaar*
- *Highway Engineer and Contractor*
- *Holland's*
- *The Ice Cream Review*
- *Junior League Magazine*
- *Ladies' Home Journal*
- *Liberty*
- *Life*
- *The Literary Digest*
- *McCall's*
- *The Milk Dealer*
- *The National Provisioner*
- *Pictorial Review*
- *The Redbook Magazine*
- *The Saturday Evening Post*
- *Southern Agriculturist*
- *The Sportsman*
- *The Starchroom Laundry Journal*
- *The State Trooper*
- *Successful Farming*
- *True Story*
- *Vanity Fair*
- *Vogue*
- *Woman's Home Companion*
- *Woman's World*

In most cases, a specific Model A Ford ad appeared in multiple magazines at about the same time – either in a single ad format or with one or more different ad variations. In much more limited cases, a unique Model A ad appeared only once in a single magazine on a single date.

With some magazines, it is obvious that the Model A Ford ad was developed specifically for that publication and the ad appeared only in that magazine. Examples here would include the special series of youth-oriented Model A ads appearing in *The American Boy* and the custom light commercial vehicle ads created for specialized business and service industry magazines.

MAGAZINES CONTAINING MODEL A FORD ADS

While the beginning and ending publication dates for Model A Ford ads varied widely across individual host magazines, Ford advertising plans appear to have had the general pattern of placing a Model A Ford ad in all issues of monthly magazines during the selected advertising period. In weekly publications, it appears that Ford generally aimed at having a Model A ad appear about once each month. Therefore, not every issue of a weekly publication that carried Model A ads during the advertising run period will contain an ad.

In virtually all cases, only one Model A Ford ad appeared per magazine, per issue – and, once the ad appeared, it never appeared again in that publication. However, there were a few exceptions to this pattern. In a few cases, the magazine may have contained a mixture of Ford ads, issue to issue. For example, a given issue of *The Saturday Evening Post* could have contained a Model A passenger car ad, or a Model A or AA commercial vehicle ad, or a Model AA truck ad. The *Farm and Ranch* and *Southern Agriculturist* magazines sometines contained both Model A and Model AA ads – and sometimes in the same issue. In an extreme variation from the pattern, *The State Trooper* magazine sometimes contained the identical Model A ad repeat-printed in several sequential issues.

The Saturday Evening Post and *The Literary Digest* were the only U.S. magazines containing two-page Model A Ford ads. The two-page ads in *The Saturday Evening Post* were always on two separate, but facing, pages. However, *The Literary Digest* two-page Model A ads appeared both on separate pages and as centerfold ads. (Particular care should be taken in collecting ads from these magazines because in locating an ad you may have unknowingly selected only one page of a two-page ad.)

The information contained on the following pages review the magazines containing Model A Ford passenger car and light commercial vehicle ads. Included are the beginning and ending ad publish dates and (where known) the Model A Ford ad publishing patterns for each magazine. (Note that the listed ad dates cover all Ford vehicle advertising efforts in the magazine – including Model A passenger cars, Model A and AA commercial vehicles and Model AA trucks.)

This interesting drawing showing the view through the windshield of the Model A Ford appeared as an secondary illustration in the first magazine ad for the Model A Coupe in July 1928.

MAGAZINES CONTAINING MODEL A FORD ADS

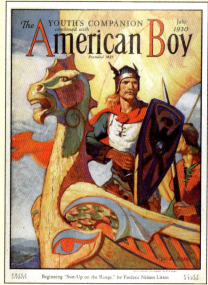

The American Boy
(Monthly)
Ad every issue 6/28 – 7/31
[color and black & white ads]

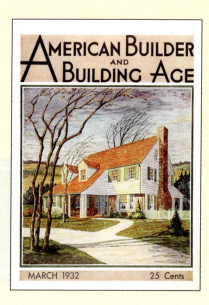

American Builder and Building Age
(Monthly)
Ad every issue 6/31 – 3/32
[commercial and truck ads]

The American City
(Monthly)
Ad every issue 3/31 – 2/32
[commercial and truck ads]

The American Magazine
(Monthly)
Ad every issue 3/30 – 7/31

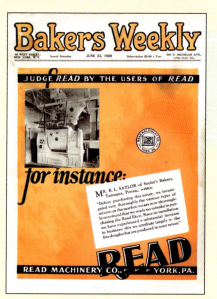

Bakers Weekly
(Weekly)
Ad some issues 6/31 – 1/32 (assumed)
[commercial and truck ads]

The Black Diamond
(Monthly)
Ads most issues 2/31 – 2/32
[commercial and truck ads]

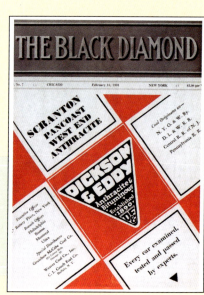

MAGAZINES CONTAINING MODEL A FORD ADS

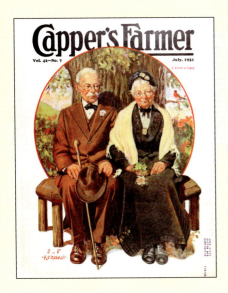

Capper's Farmer
(Monthly)
Ad every issue 1/29 – 7/31

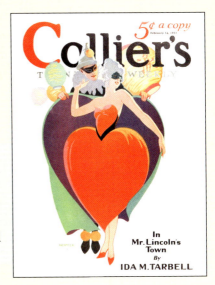

Collier's
The News Weekly
(Weekly)
One or more ads each month 1/29 – 7/31

The Commercial Car Journal
(Monthly)
Ad every issue 2/31 – 3/32
[commercial and truck ads]

Hearst's International
Cosmopolitan
(Monthly)
Ad every issue 6/28 – 6/31

The Country Gentleman
(Monthly)
Ad every issue 1/29 – 7/31

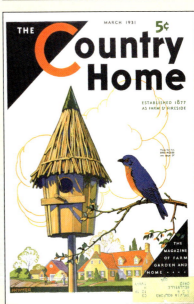

The Country Home
(Monthly)
Ad every issue 2/30 – 7/31

MAGAZINES CONTAINING MODEL A FORD ADS

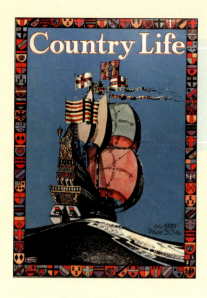

Country Life
(Monthly)
Ad every issue 6/28 – 7/31

Delineator
(Monthly)
Ad every issue 3/30 – 7/31

Farm & Fireside
The National Farm Magazine
(Monthly)
Ad every issue 1/29 – 12/29

The Farmer's Wife
The Magazine for Farm Women
(Monthly)
Ad every issue 6/28 – 6/31

National
The Farm Journal
(Monthly)
Ad every issue 1/31 – 7/31

Good Housekeeping
(Monthly)
Ad every issue 6/28 – 5/31

No cover photo: *Farm and Ranch* (Weekly),
One, sometimes two ads each month, 1/30 – 3/32 [car and truck ads]

MAGAZINES CONTAINING MODEL A FORD ADS

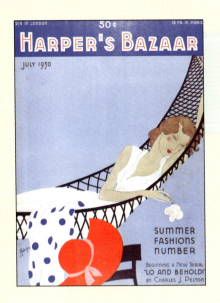

Harper's Bazaar
(Monthly)
Ad every issue 6/28 – 6/31

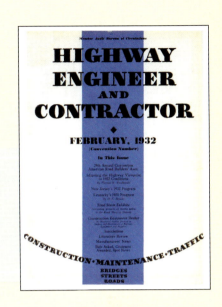

Highway Engineer and Contractor
(Monthly)
Ads some issues 4/31 – 2/32
(assumed)
[commercial and truck ads]

Holland's
The Magazine of the South
(Monthly)
Ad every issue 1/31 – 7/31

The Ice Cream Review
(Monthly)
Ad every issue 6/31 – 2/32
[commercial and truck ads]

Junior League Magazine
(Monthly)
Ad every issue 3/30 – 7/31

Ladies' Home Journal
(Monthly)
Ad every issue 6/28 – 7/31

MAGAZINES CONTAINING MODEL A FORD ADS

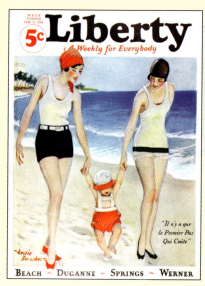

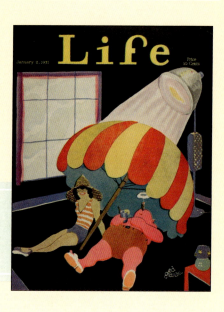

Liberty
A Weekly for Everybody
(Weekly)
One, sometimes two, ads each month
6/28 – 6/31

Life
(Monthly)
Ad every issue 1/31 – 7/31

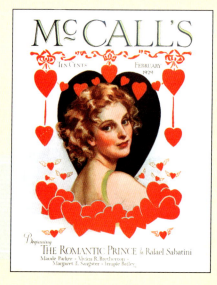

The Literary Digest
(Weekly)
One, sometimes two, ads each month
6/28 – 7/31

McCall's
(Monthly)
Ad every issue 6/28 – 7/31

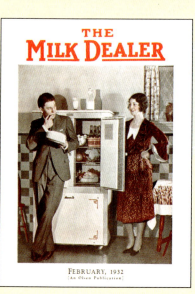

The Milk Dealer
(Monthly)
Ad each issue 2/31 – 2/32
[commercial and truck ads]

Pictorial Review
(Monthly)
Ad every issue 4/30 – 6/31

No cover photo: *The National Provisioner,* (Monthly),
Ad most issues 6/31 - 3/32 (assumed)

MAGAZINES CONTAINING MODEL A FORD ADS

The Redbook Magazine
(Monthly)
Ad every issue 6/28 – 6/31

The Saturday Evening Post
(Weekly)
One to four ads each month 6/28 – 3/32
[car, commercial and truck ads]

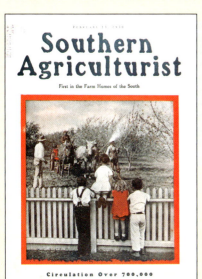

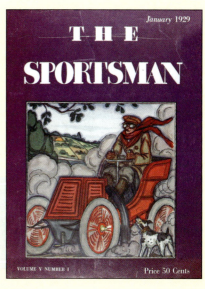

Southern Agriculturist
First in the Farm Homes of the South
(Bi-Weekly)
One, sometimes two, ads each month
1/29 – 3/32
[some issues contained both car and truck ads]

The Sportsman
(Monthly)
Ad every issue 6/28 – 6/31

The Starchroom Laundry Journal
Ad every issue 6/31 – 3/32 (assumed)
[commercial and truck ads]

The State Trooper
(Monthly)
Ad every issue 2/30 – 3/32
[sometimes, same ad appeared
in sequential issues]

MAGAZINES CONTAINING MODEL A FORD ADS

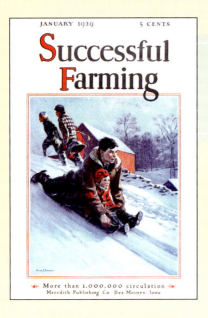

Successful Farming
(Monthly)
Ad every issue 1/29 – 7/31

True Story
Truth is Stranger Than Fiction
(Monthly)
Ad every issue 4/30 – 6/31

Vanity Fair
(Monthly)
Ad every issue 6/28 – 7/31

Vogue
(Bi-Weekly)
One, sometimes two, ads each month
6/28 – 7/31

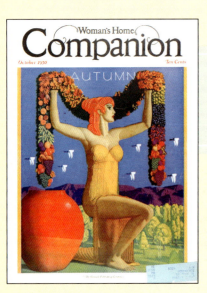

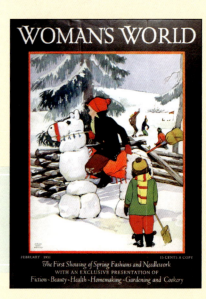

Woman's Home Companion
(Monthly)
Ad every issue 3/30 – 6/31

Woman's World
(Monthly)
Ad every issue 1/31 – 6/31

About The Author

Jim Thomas has collected Model A Ford advertising and memorabilia for over 25 years. Like most collectors, his initial interest in this hobby sprung from owning a Model A and discovering that there were very interesting advertisements for "The New Ford" in several old magazines he found at an antique show.

As predecessors to his interest in Model A Ford advertising were general interests in antiques and memorabilia, art and advertising coursework in college and his first job out of graduate school in a Detroit area advertising agency, working on an automotive advertising account.

Jim is a member of the Model A Ford Club of America (MAFCA) and The Model A Restorers Club (MARC). He has served on the MARC Board of Directors and on the Model A Ford Foundation, Inc. (MAFFI) Board of Trustees. Jim has contributed numerous articles on Model A advertising to MARC, MAFFI and The Model A Ad Collectors Club and has presented several Model A advertising seminars at MARC national conventions.

Along with his interests in Model A Ford advertising, he currently owns two Model A's and is active in the Ohio Valley Region Model A Ford Club. He has restored a Model A for MARC national judging and has participated in numerous Model A driving tours and touring adventures in the United States, Canada, Europe and Australia.

Jim, who recently retired from a career in marketing research, lives with his wife Pam in Cincinnati, Ohio.

◆

Jim Thomas in his 1930 Model A Ford Cabriolet

Selected Bibliography

De Angeles, George and Francis, Edward P. and Henry, Leslie R. *The Ford Model "A" – "As Henry Built It,"* Fifth Edition. G. DeA Publishing Co., South Lyon, Michigan, 2001.

The Ford Motor Company. *The Ford News*. Volume VIII, Number 19. Dearborn, Michigan, December 22, 1927.

Graduate School of Business Administration. *First Five Years, Harvard Advertising Awards, 1924-1928*. McGraw-Hill Book Company, Inc., New York, New York, 1930.

Griffiths, Gwilym G. "The Man Who Drew the Model A Ads." *The Restorer*. January/February 1986. The Model A Ford Club of America, Inc., La Habra, California.

Henry, Leslie R. *Henry's Fabulous Model A*. Clymer Publications, Los Angeles, California, 1959.

Minners, Howard A. "Early Advertising for The New Ford." *The Restorer*. January/February 1989. The Model A Ford Club of America, Inc., La Habra, California.

Minners, Howard A., *Model A Ad Collectors Newsletter* (selected issues). Model A Ad Collectors Association. Bethesda, Maryland.

Shield, James J. *Selling The New Ford - 1927-1931*, Second Edition. The Auto Review. Florissant, Missouri, 1996.

Winnewisser, Peter. *The Legendary Model A Ford*. Krause Publications, Iola, Wisconsin, 1999.